The Last Crusade

A Negotiator's Middle East Handbook

The Last Crusade

A Negotiator's Middle East Handbook

William R. Brown

Nelson-Hall **nh** Chicago

To my mother

and the memory of my father

Library of Congress Cataloging in Publication Data

Brown, William R
   The last crusade.

   Includes index.
   1. Near East—Foreign relations—United States.
2. United States—Foreign relations—Near East.
3. Kissinger, Henry Alfred. 4. Jewish-Arab
relations—1973–   5. Near East—Politics
and government—1945–   6. Statesmen—United
States—Biography. 7. United States—Foreign
relations—1969–1974. I. Title.
DS63.2U5B76   327.56'073   79–18462
ISBN 0-88229-554-3 (cloth)
ISBN 0-88229-738-4 (paper)
Copyright © 1980 by William R. Brown

Manufactured in the United States of America

10 9 8 7 6 5 4 3 2 1

Contents

Preface

As the reader will see, much of this book is the record of the odyssey of Henry Kissinger in his quest for peace in the Middle East. In a certain sense, it has been a search for the author as well. But my purpose has simply been for a better understanding of Middle East politics. In this respect, it is accurate to say that work on the manuscript began a long time ago and that great numbers of people have contributed to it. Perhaps it was Elie Salem who first introduced me to Arab politics while I was still at the University of Cincinnati. Among the earliest to have an influence on my thinking in Cairo was Dick Mitchell, who always comes up with good insights. Thereafter, long conversations and thousands of pumpkin seeds and pistachios with Charles Widney, Phebe Marr and Ralph Phillips had a place in shaping my ideas. Talking to Wilton Wynn or Les Burgess about Arabs and oil is always useful and enjoyable. Among my friends in the Middle East, Mahmoud Ghanem and Ibrahim Ezzat made a difference, along with two who are no longer with us, Issa El Korashi and Zuhair Kuzbari. Many acquaintances have also left their mark. It is not that these friends will agree with all my interpretations of the Arab political scene. At times, debates with them over one point or another have been intense, and we have made one another quite uncomfortable. Nevertheless, they have all been important to what I have to say.

In the production of the manuscript itself, others have had a hand: Janice Shockley, Gail Gregson, and Helen Schlemp from Stockton and Judy Filipek and Maureen Duly at Central. Throughout the writing of this piece, I have benefited from the advice of the severest of editorial critics, Loje. In addition, there have been her eight thousand tiny bird fingers. To all these people I am indebted. I also wish to thank the Earhart Foundation for supporting my research.

Introduction

For those of us who have devoted our careers to the Middle East, Henry Kissinger's stewardship of American foreign policy marked a period of innovation in dealing with Arabs and Israelis. New approaches to negotiation were introduced and new results were achieved. For the first time Arabs and Israelis went beyond a mere truce to sign agreements having political stipulations. Although difficult problems were still to be confronted, important segments of the Arab world tacitly accepted Israel's existence and began to regard an eventual settlement as being within the realm of possibility. Significantly, some Arab leaders seemed to be trying to reshape their internal and regional politics to allow for peace with the Jewish state.

Active American diplomacy in the Arab world began more or less in October 1952 with negotiations between Egypt's Gamal Abdal Nasser and a variety of State Department officials and White House representatives over the possibility of the United States' providing Nasser's army with weapons. These exchanges were directed toward establishing a network of Middle East defenses for the Western alliance. Even though the negotiations failed, the Western powers still attempted to maintain a military presence in the area. In addition, the United States insisted on assuming responsibility for the integrity of Israel. The situation engendered a bitterness that left those who worked on U.S.-Arab affairs with little latitude for developing major themes of cooperation. Yet bargaining, haggling, threatening, and cajoling continued between the West and the Arabs, initially over regional defense and then over Palestine. On economic matters there was muted interplay over the exploration for and marketing of oil. Before Kissinger appeared on the scene with his personal style and new ideas, the world had seldom witnessed a less productive set of negotiating relationships. But the dialogue continued, principally because neither side was in a position either to dominate the relationship or to extricate itself from the necessity of dealing with the other. The tie between the Arabs and the West has indeed been compelling.

The position of the United States in the Middle East reached its nadir in 1967, when in the wake of the Six Day War most Arab governments broke diplomatic relations with us while asserting that we had assumed a direct combat role in the rout of Egyptian and Syrian armies by Israel. Despite the hostility of the Arabs, the United States was not free to ignore them. Gradually, we managed to work our way back into acceptable relationships through the commercial dealings of multinational companies with oil-producing countries and by means of foreign assistance to Egyptian, Yemeni, Sudanese, and Syrian development schemes. With the sudden increase in income resulting from a fourfold rise in oil prices in 1973, the Arabs have been in a position to finance much of their own economic and social growth. In doing so they have looked largely to private American companies to supply the modern technology that they regard as synonymous with well-being. Simultaneously, American dependence on Arab oil has become a permanent feature of political and economic life, at least for the remainder of this century. Over the years, therefore, our links with the Arabs have become virtually inextricable.

The amazing thing about our continuing relationship with the Arabs is that despite its great importance to us, we actually know very little about how it operates. From the standpoint of an outsider who deals with Arabs, for example, what features of Arab society impinge on relations with others? Even for those of us who have worked in the Middle East for long periods, the response to this question is usually implicit. We all know something about Arab society and culture, but seldom do we specify directly and explicitly the factors that are involved when we approach Arabs. Rather, we rely on intuition, long-ingested information, and past experiences to guide our actions in ways that we often cannot describe to others.

In my case, Henry Kissinger provided the stimulus to state specifically how a negotiator in the Middle East might advantageously proceed. While he was operating from the White House as Nixon's security advisor, Kissinger avoided the Arab-Israeli problem. But when he became secretary of state in September 1973, his first act was to contact the Arabs. On September 25, he invited to lunch at the Waldorf-Astoria thirteen of the Arab foreign ministers who had come to New York for the meeting of the United Nations General Assembly. Kissinger had just finished the negotiations on Viet Nam. He had already identified the next area to receive his attention by asserting that 1973 was to have been "The Year of Europe." Thus far Watergate had precluded any real initiative in this area; yet his boundless energy, and perhaps his ego, would not permit him to allow the Arab-Israeli issue to go unattended when it offered such a fine opportunity for a virtuoso performance in diplomacy. I recall reading the paper the morning after his first exposure to the Arab dignitaries and commenting to myself, "Well, well, here he goes again." For me, at least, Kissinger's luncheon raised the question, How does an outsider negotiate with Arabs? The outbreak of hostilities between Arabs and Israelis a scant two weeks after the luncheon provided the imperative Kissinger needed to pursue an active role in the Middle East.

Since the Yom Kippur War of 1973 various books have provided detailed accounts of Kissinger's shuttle diplomacy, and my intention is not simply to add a few variations to what others have already said. An interesting observation about two of the more popular books on Kissinger's Middle East venture is that both attribute their significance to *revelations*.[1] One refers in its title to Kissinger's secret conversations. The other purports in its subtitle to be a secret history. I am not sure the authors so intended, but this approach reflects an essentially Middle East point of view—things are never quite as they seem. I shall devote attention to the origins of this outlook and its influence on diplomatic behavior, particularly in my consideration of the phenomenon of the "hidden hand." For now, let me say that I have no secrets to reveal. But, in common with the authors to whom I have referred, I must acknowledge that I too have written an "inside account" of Kissinger's diplomacy. It is, however, *inside* in a different way. I do not claim to divulge incidents that were critical to the Middle East situation but undisclosed to the public eye at the time of their occurrence. Rather, I attempt to explain events through something that is seldom approached directly—the state of mind, or preferably the national consciousness, in countries that participated in Kissinger's step-by-step diplomacy.

Long ago I discovered that the most frustrating predicament an outsider can create for himself while working on Middle East politics is to premise action or analysis on his own or someone else's notion of the *facts*. Such an approach leads only to turmoil, confusion, and unending debate because seldom do the parties agree on what the facts might be. Of greater importance is identifying the range of *perceptions* with which you may be confronted and establishing how these influence the response of various individuals and groups engaged in a common endeavor—whether it be war, negotiation, or the more casual give-and-take of less intensive diplomacy. Only in this way can an element of predictability be brought to our relations with this important part of the international community. Consequently, this book examines perceptions—those of the Arabs and those of the Israelis. Perceptions were the main concern of Kissinger as he faced first one group and then the other on the daily rounds of his shuttles. His efforts were devoted to changing the perceptions of the combatants in order to lead them step by step into increasingly comprehensive agreements. I attempt to build my explanations around this pervasive aspect of Kissinger's endeavors in the Middle East. Somewhat at variance with others who have written on this subject, I approach shuttle diplomacy from the standpoint of the meaning Kissinger's style and technique had for Arabs and Israelis.

The question that must immediately come to the mind of the

reader is: What sort of material is important in an explanation that utilizes Arab and Israeli perceptions? First of all, we must consider Arab society and culture, particularly the features that explain the antecedents of Arab political behavior and Arab nationalism. I provide such an explanation and set it into a brief account of the Arabs' efforts in the twentieth century to achieve national unity. I also attempt to determine why these efforts have failed. This material provides an interpretation of how culture and events have shaped the Arab's political outlook, how nationalism operates in the dynamics of Middle East politics, and in particular how it influences the conduct of the Arabs' diplomacy. For example, our newspapers report almost daily that one Arab leader or another either is being isolated or is attempting to avoid isolation. I offer an interpretation of the meaning of such reports within the context of the Arab political culture and of how they fitted into Kissinger's step-by-step diplomacy.

Also pertinent to an understanding of *how* diplomacy can be conducted in the Middle East—as opposed to the ends toward which it might be directed—are the limitations within which Arab leaders negotiate with outsiders. I see these as mental rather than material constraints, and at their core are the Arab perception of weakness and the alien aura (to Arabs) of the processes associated with international politics. In a quite unexpected way the Arabs' outlook influences their response to the traditional use of threats in diplomacy and gives them an unusual view of our assumption of equality at the negotiating table. Not unexpectedly, the Arab state of mind influenced Kissinger's diplomacy. In negotiating Israeli withdrawals, first with a truce and then with two disengagement agreements, he was unusually deft in avoiding the pitfalls that spring from the Arabs' sense of weakness. In his parallel efforts to ameliorate conditions created by the oil embargo and petroleum price increases, however, he constantly ran afoul of Arab sensitivities, largely because he used more traditional techniques in conceptualizing and implementing his diplomacy. Despite his best efforts, Kissinger could not separate oil from Arab thoughts of a settlement with Israel. Oil diplomacy weighed heavily upon his peace efforts.

A substantial portion of any study of Middle East diplomacy

must concern Israel. Critical to the negotiating environment within which Kissinger worked was the almost total absence of mutualities between the Jewish state and its Arab neighbors because of conflicting, and perhaps irreconcilable, national legitimacies. On this level the conflict has been fraught with symbolism that has been difficult for either combatant to relinquish. On one side is the biblical Land of Israel with all it means to every Jew. On the other side stand the Palestinians as the symbol of Arab sacrifice. Again, I maintain that in order to understand peoples' politics we must consider what is on their minds.

One outward manifestation of the symbolic standoff in the Middle East is the Israelis' compulsive drive for security which carries all the overtones of a quest for regional dominance. Considering the web in which Arabs and Israelis have been caught by their perceptions, it is not altogether surprising that the Israelis have followed this course or that the Arabs have reacted negatively to it. But even here in the tangibles of defense policies, we find creations of the mind influencing events. Israeli defense is dictated partially by the symbolism found in the boundaries of Old Testament Israel and by the passion to maintain the armed settlements wherever they may be. The prospect of the first withdrawal from the kibbutzim in the occupied Golan Heights or Sinai, for example, holds the horrible image for many Israelis of Zionism in decline. Moreover, the matter of self-image and the necessity to overcome what many Jews consider the shame of the past have led to an aggressiveness that confounds any effort by an outsider to bring Arabs and Israelis into agreement. All these factors influenced Kissinger's diplomacy.

What I have described here in a few statements, I develop in detail in the text. These were the conditions under which Kissinger's Middle East diplomacy was conducted. They were more important in Kissinger's case than for precursors because he personally interjected himself into efforts to achieve a Middle East settlement. Arab mental reservations and Israeli anxieties were brought to the fore by his intercession. Neither side could imagine that the concessions its opponent was being asked to make were comparable to those requested of itself. Both constantly complained of an American bias favoring the opposite side. These were the states of mind with which Kissinger had to contend. Quite often he was acted upon rather than being the initiator of action himself. The conventional wisdom that some observers saw in a solution imposed by the United States and buttressed by great-power guarantees was put to the test. I attempt to demonstrate that both concepts proved wanting.

Kissinger's diplomacy also operated within the confines of our own domestic politics. A matter that most writers handle with some circumspection for fear of being labeled anti-Semitic is the influence the American Jewish community employs in support of Israel. I attempt to deal with this subject openly and honestly and to balance it against the growing influence of Arab oil and wealth. Again, I utilize the vehicle of perceptions and develop my arguments in terms of the efforts of the two sides in the Middle East struggle to weigh on the American mind. I hope my explanation will not be considered offensive by the preponderance of Jews, Israelis, and Arabs.

Despite the serious limitation these conditions place on an outside mediator, I must conclude from my own experience that an American negotiator in the Middle East has certain assets that we often overlook. Kissinger understood these assets and used them well. The Arabs seem to like us and certainly they favor our technology. But why? The simple assertion of American superiority in cultural traits, business acumen, and mechanical ingenuity cannot be substantiated. There is something more, and I attempt to identify it.

In any study of diplomacy from the standpoint of perception, the participants become paramount. This is particularly true of Kissinger, whose role is viewed from the perspective of a trustee of peace, a characterization he adopted for himself. Essentially, his function was that of a mediator; but because the United States had a stake in the outcome of Kissinger's efforts, he was also a player in what at any moment could become a deadly game for all concerned. What distinguished Kissinger's diplomacy was its style and the interplay of that style with Arab perceptions and personality. He conveyed in his public actions and statements a particular philosophy of negotiation. It hinged on using a variety of psychological factors to change perceptions and thereby to build a momentum that would carry the negotiating parties toward agreement. As startling as it may seem for some readers, I have concluded that Kissinger was perhaps our first experiential negotiator. He emphasized process over content, and never has a statesman relied quite so heavily on the persuasive aspects of personal discussion to achieve his ends. As for these ends, Kissinger seemed to see them as any change in the outlook of Arabs and Israelis that would accommodate peace. He was not overly concerned with the specifics of the agreements. If he could induce new perceptions, the specifics would take care of themselves.

Kissinger's view of negotiations determined the method of his diplomacy. He planned carefully, positioned the negotiants with precision, structured discourse, and gave lavish attention to the act of communicating. In sessions with Arab and Israeli leaders he relied on a variety of techniques, particularly ambiguity and the factoring of issues into what he claimed were their component parts. Often this approach obfuscated the outcome that was to be expected from an understanding, but it was his way of rendering difficult problems soluble. Through the use of indirect assurances and the structuring of inducements that worked on the minds of his counterparts, Kissinger raised the process of acquiring commitments almost to an art. He even went so far as to share in the commitments himself. I examine all these facets of his diplomatic style.

Kissinger does, of course, have his critics, and they have had a great deal to say. They questioned his assumption that there was sufficient time to work through the tortuous process he devised before tensions would again bring the Arabs and Israelis into open conflict. They doubted that each step he induced would always make the next step easier to achieve. For some it appeared that Kissinger was doing little more than buying time—the strategy of the Israelis. Others have pointed out that any discernible movement toward peace probably resulted solely from changes in Arab outlook that *preceded* Kissinger's diplomacy. It has also been asserted that he was mistaken in not aiming for an overall settlement after the initial disengagement agreements. Several of Kissinger's critics have assumed commanding positions in the Carter administration's foreign policy establishment. By continuing to observe American mediation efforts under President Carter, or even subsequent presidents, and then comparing them with those of Henry Kissinger, we are provided with contrasts in style and purpose between Kissinger and those who would do things differently.

Admittedly, I have devoted more attention to the activities of Kissinger than to the criticisms of his detractors. For some, my work may seem to lack balance in this regard. But I also express criticism of Kissinger's diplomacy insofar as I believe that in the Sinai Accord he bargained away many of his own negotiating tools. Nevertheless, if we center our attention on what he seemed to be attempting to do—namely, change perceptions to allow for a cumulative (albeit lengthy) process of working gradually toward a settlement—we must acknowledge that he quickly grasped the mentality of the moderate Arabs and developed an atmosphere that permitted them to talk openly about peace with Israel. Certainly we can point to specific failures, but even the suggestion that the Sinai Accord had shortcomings provides recognition of Kissinger's achievements. Never before had an outside mediator been able to get Arabs and Israelis together long enough in negotiations for critics to be justified in saying that he had erred in not being bolder. It will remain a moot point whether the Arabs and the Israelis were ready for a settlement in 1975. In the final analysis we can only say that Kissinger's influence should be considered positive, because under his urging Arabs and Israelis adopted new attitudes that moved them closer to peace. If, in fact, a comprehensive settlement is reached within the next few years, we must concede in all fairness that Kissinger had a part in it.

Explanations of the kind I present rely heavily on personal insights. From more than sixteen years of experience in American embassies and AID missions in the Middle East, as well as from subsequent assignments as a consultant, I have concluded that working successfully with Arabs depends largely on acquiring a sense of what being Arab means. Such insight, which is critical to an understanding of our relations with them, can be obtained only by mastering what I call the lore of Arab society—taking enough time to become conversant with their history and not hesitating to use it in dealing with them, knowing their scandals, sharing their humor, being sympathetic to their hopes, and participating with them in the favorite and almost endless Arab pastime of pursuing ideas. It is necessary to accept the Arabs as being optimistic and speculative.

Insights obtained from experience in the Middle East provide the structure for this book. The material necessary for applying my interpretations to the events of Kissinger's diplomacy was obtained, largely for convenience, from the daily press and from numerous translations of Arabic and Israeli periodicals and newspapers that are available in this country. Finally, in order to verify and for-malize my interpretations of the influence Kissinger had on the Arab participants themselves, I traveled to the Middle East during the summer of 1976 to discuss the manuscript with individuals who had taken part directly in the negotiations and with those who were close observers of the negotiating process and had access to the Arab leaders and to Kissinger.

In a book using perceptions as a point of reference, I believe it is acceptable for the writer to consider what he hopes to do with the perceptions of the reader. My work goes beyond analysis. With it I would like to make the reader a private player in the continuing game of Middle East politics. In the broadest sense, I have looked to Kissinger's diplomacy for guiding principles in diplomatic ex-change. Admittedly, those I have specified apply mainly to the Middle East. With them the reader should be able to identify the major factors that determine the outcome of negotiations when the United States becomes involved in the affairs of the Arabs and Israelis. Thus the subtitle, which suggests that from this study any self-designated trustee of peace—whether as a personal observer or an official representative—can devise patterns and styles that are more likely than others to lead to the desired results.

No single approach is ideal, but distinctions among negotiating techniques can be made and the risks associated with each assessed. As events transpire, this work can be used to interpret situations in which present and future American negotiators, rather than

Henry Kissinger, are mediating between Arabs and Israelis. I hope the reader will thereby become sensitized to more than just the outcome of American diplomacy. A further matter is how statesmen go about their business. A small but good example was the practice of Secretary Vance during his first visit to the Middle East in February 1977 of sitting with a pad on his knee taking notes throughout discussions with Presidents Assad of Syria and Sadat of Egypt. Chapter 9 in particular tells what this scene projected with regard to the type of relationship Vance was likely to develop with Arab leaders had he continued this posture. The question it raises is whether the lawyer's brief and the formality Cyrus Vance exuded on his early Middle East ventures is as effective as the professor's seminar and the free-and-easy ways of Henry Kissinger. Or does this difference in style matter? This book should give readers the material for considering such a question.

It is also my intention to lessen the remoteness with which Arab perceptions and political practice are often viewed in our society. I have attempted to do so by explaining them within the context of the experience of Henry Kissinger as an American statesman—someone with whom the reader at the outset of this journey may be able to identify with more readily than with the Arabs themselves. I hope, in the process, to stimulate an intellectual interest in the Middle East on the part of those who use this book. Let me also emphasize that mine is only one explanation of the maze of Middle East politics. I am only one of numerous tour guides who would attempt to lead you through this labyrinth. Because of my purpose, I have made this work highly interpretive. What is important to me may seem insignificant to others who have equal or perhaps richer experience in the Middle East. Nevertheless, I believe this book will provide you with insight whether you have no experience in diplomacy and the Middle East or whether you are conversant in these topics and only wish to sharpen your faculties or recall your own past.

Finally, let's consider the title and the point of view it reflects. Early in my experience in the Middle East, I became acquainted with a professor of Arab ancestry but American citizenship who had taught at both Princeton and the American University of Beirut.

On one occasion as we were talking about the Arabs' relations with the West he commented, "Since the crusades it's just been one damned thing after another." At the time we had reason to be pessimistic over the future of the West's relations with the Arabs. Gamal Abdal Nasser and all he represented to us at that point in terms of virulent anti-Western Arab nationalism was dominant in the Middle East. Yet, even for the long run, the assertion by my acquaintance can be substantiated by a cursory review of the history of the Western powers in Arab lands. Throughout the modern era we have felt a constant need to intercede in the affairs of the Arab people, and our initiative has created a situation of great frustration for them. They have always been the weaker side in encounters with us, and as a result, they have only been able to react against our intentions. We have been viewed as an outside and antagonistic force. Because of us, the Arabs have seldom been able to initiate anything of political consequence.

But conditions are changing, and Kissinger's diplomacy can be viewed—perhaps with a touch of the dramatic—as the last act in a set of relationships that has existed for a long time. It is not enough to say that the Arabs through their oil and income now have power to counter the Western presence. Nor am I suggesting that we have at last made our peace with the Arabs. Surely tension over Israel will continue, and the Israelis, with their military strength, will for some time retain the capability for thwarting any antagonistic Arab national design or aspiration.

But there is a new factor—the Arabs themselves. On visits to the Middle East in recent years, I have been received in three distinct capacities—as a World Bank consultant assessing manpower, education, and social policy of aid recipients; as a member of a U.S. government mission that made the initial review of assistance possibilities after Kissinger extended $250 million to Sadat in 1974; and as a writer on Middle East politics. In each case I came away with the feeling that Arabs are not as parochial as they once were. While the Israeli question is still important, it no longer looms as the only political issue of consequence for them. The Arabs have other things on their minds. They see a new position for themselves in the international community. They have a point of view about their countries' development, and they are less defensive when confronted by outsiders. They can raise questions about themselves without feeling inferior. The Arabs can indeed get along without the great powers making all the decisions, and they now believe that they have something to contribute to the general human endeavor. This new outlook can be a force for peace, and all who approach the Arabs in either an official or a private capacity should be aware of the modification it calls for in our demeanor. Many factors have contributed to this change in Arab self-perception, and the influence of Kissinger's mediation is one of them. Thus in shuttle diplomacy we just might have witnessed the beginning of the Last Crusade.

Introduction

1. Matti Golan, *The Secret Conversations of Henry Kissinger*, (New York: Quadrangle/New York Times Book Co., 1976); Edward R. F. Sheehan, *The Arabs, Israelis, and Kissinger: A Secret History of American Diplomacy in the Middle East* (New York: Reader's Digest Press, 1976).

1

The Arab Condition

When representatives of the great powers negotiate in the Middle East, they commonly view their activity as relations with Syrians, Egyptians, Saudis, and the like. But they are also dealing with Arabs. Being Arab is more than an association through a language. Furthermore, being Arab has connotations that go beyond regional identification. Arabism has a national quality, but it is indistinct because it does not coincide with the political boundaries of any state. Thus the conventional vehicle for contemporary national expression—the nation-state—is not a feature of the political landscape.

We have all been exposed to manifestations of Arabism in the news of Middle East wars, plane hijackings, and denunciation of Israel by its neighbors. Arabs have also become linked in our minds to oil, a resource that makes it necessary for much of the world to pay considerable attention to the politics of these people. Despite a ready acknowledgment that Arab national consciousness is a compelling force, its nature is poorly understood. It is impossible to grasp the fundamentals of the negotiating process in the Middle East, however, without some idea of how Arabs conceptualize their nation.

Arab Nationalism

First of all, Arabs root their nationalism in faith. Within the Arab context it is difficult to distinguish nationalism from Islam.

The national character of the Arabs is seen as having been established by God.[1] Similarly, the inner core of Islam is considered
Arab.[2] Some Arabs have described Islam as their national culture.
Non-Arab Muslims are shrugged off as something apart. For
Arabs Islam is not just a religion. It has many of the characteristics
of "Americanism" and can be used just about as badly by politicians. It relates to the popular emotions of the initiates, but it
translates poorly into policy.

When Muhammad led his followers from Mecca in 622 A.D. and
established them at Medina, he was preoccupied with forging a
community of God in which belief would replace blood or clan
relationships—the organizing principle that heretofore had prevailed
in the Arabian Peninsula. His problems were those of political and
social control within this new community. As the revelations from
God embodied in the Quran took shape, they proved to be quite
legalistic, being dictates on questions of belief and conduct that
ordered the lives of those entering Muhammad's new society of
God. To this day Islam is set in a legal cast as opposed to the theo-
logical emphasis found in much of Christianity. It is the duty of
the Muslim through individual wisdom to discern the principles of
God and to apply them as guidance along the correct path in life.
Somewhat at variance with Christian perceptions, this mission is
not only of concern to the individual; it is the purpose of the society
as well. Temporal and spiritual matters cannot be neatly separated.
Because law is God-given it has few relative features, and its absolute nature gives an authoritative character to Islamic society. But
because this law applies to all, it also provides the concept of
equality that is so strong in Muslim countries. Nowhere in the
Islamic world are these attributes more evident than among the
Arabs. To a large extent, they describe the political culture an outside observer encounters in Egypt, Saudi Arabia, Syria, and other
Arab lands.

Not even the puritanical Wahhabi regime in Saudi Arabia can
control society today through Islamic law alone. As the influence
of technology has permeated the social fabric, life has become
more complex, and norms have changed. Civil law, particularly on
commercial matters, has been borrowed from Britain and France.

The more severe punishment prescribed by the Quran for failure to observe God's commands is seldom practiced except in a few Arab countries. Outwardly, juridical affairs in Egypt, for example, appear to be much like those in Europe. Nevertheless, a legalistic and sometimes rigid element is still to be found in the Arabs' approach to social order. The important factor from a political standpoint is that compromise with outsiders is difficult on matters that relate to the Arab nation because that nation and its social foundations stand on the principles of God. By way of contrast, we only impute the principles of God to our nation. For an Arab, any concession to a foreign entity immediately raises the question of whether the Arab leader involved is thereby undermining God's own social creation. Even in a secular age, if the compromise of political negotiations impinges on issues that relate to the nation, Arab nationalists find it unacceptable.

Arab nationalism acquires another feature from Islam. Muhammad's message was the revealed word of God. Power was in the language as well as the content of the message. The formal Arabic of today's newspapers does not vary appreciably from the language of the Quran. Consequently, Arabs acquire a sense of unity and intensity from their language which is associated with their faith. Few Arabs fail to cite language as an important characteristic of their nation.

A second element of Arabism is the consciousness of a "proud history." Although Arabs do have a common culture and a common language, questions can be raised about their common history. Observers often note that in an institutional sense Arabs have found it necessary to look back a thousand years to the Abbasid Empire in order to find anything even remotely resembling a common political experience. Truly, Arabs bridge the gap to the Abbasids with ease. Even though the glory of the Arab past is removed from the present by a millennium, it has power for Arab nationalists. In January 1975, when the shah of Iran declared his support for the Arab cause, Yasir Arafat, leader of the Palestine Liberation Organization, was moved to declare, ". . . thus we will take part in a renewal of the Abbasid caliphate, when Persians and Arabs united [to] spread their common culture across the world."[3]

Despite the image of a single purpose expressed in such rhetoric, the recent political experience of the various Arab peoples has been distinct. Even under the Abbasids, local dynasties—often in association with an inspirational religious leader—prevailed in the various parts of the empire. Acknowledgment of the religious authority of the caliph had little influence over matters of immediate political concern, but the bonds among the various parts of the empire were sufficient to assure orderly trade and financial patterns from the Atlantic to the Persian Gulf. By the time of the Crusades, however, the mercantile organizational principles of the Abbasids had given way in Arab society to feudal concepts. Individual Arab communities became isolated from one another as barriers to interregional communications brought an end to the empire. A degree of administrative unity was established throughout the Middle East again after 1500 by the Ottoman Turks, but it was never part of the Arab identity. In a historical sense, therefore, the concept of the Arab nation is tenuous.

Arab leaders usually explain the inconsistency between their history and their claims of a single tradition as the unnatural result of antagonistic outside forces. When confronted with national failure they attribute deficiencies to the national fragmentation that was fostered by European imperialists. They assert that Arab strength was destroyed by the machinations of the colonial powers and contend that Arab goals can be achieved only after the vile and divisive forces of imperialism are expunged from the nation's bosom and unity is reestablished.[4] The fragmentation, evident in the existing pattern of Arab states, did, in fact, come about as the result of the activities of the European powers. The Arabs themselves had little to do with it. Many advocates of Arabism consider the existing political order, therefore, as being alien to the Arab nation.

It is within this context that any champion of the nationalist cause can arouse Arab peoples against a particular leader of an Arab state simply by contending that as long as the individual in question works to preserve his government, he is blocking the Arab people's impulse for unity and is serving selfish interests from which only the imperialists can ultimately benefit. Bearing the charge of treason to the Arab nation is an implicit danger of being president of Egypt, Syria, or Iraq as well as king of Saudi Arabia or Jordan.

The final aspect of Arabism we will discuss here is perhaps the least understood in the United States and Europe. Both Arabs themselves and outsiders who are conversant with the Middle East generally agree that Arabism includes a strong element of individualism—combined with narrow allegiance.[5] Even socialists in the Middle East acknowledge a drive among Arabs for personal freedom, and they accept private property as the basis for individual initiative.[6] It would be a mistake, however, to view this individualism in contemporary Western terms. Arab theorists stoutly deny that Arabism is the harmonizing of group interests as in Western pluralism. Nor do they see it as Hegelian liberty to perform a role within the national spirit.[7] Rather, it seems to be the notion of a fully identifiable individual participating directly in his society. Belief in the individual gives the Arab an unbridled sense of personal optimism.

It is this attachment to the idea of the individual that deters practical moves toward national unity. One publicist went so far as to see Anwar Sadat's predecessor, the late Gamal Abdal Nasser, representing Arab individualism through "heroic selectivity." Nasser's strength, he said, was in his ability to liberate others, revolutionize them, and inspire their creativity. Supposedly, Nasser had unleashed this expression in all Arabs. For him to succeed, the sense of individualism must inspire independent leadership throughout the entire Arab world.[8] As long as such views are popular, it will be more than the legacy of an imperialized past that keeps the Arabs fragmented.

Although a responsiveness to personal freedom prevails, Arabism draws from Islam a strong sense of egalitarianism. Whenever a social construct is attempted, therefore, it usually has the Rousseau-like essence of authority dedicated to realizing a general will. Arab theorists never tire of exalting an unspecified social justice as the guiding principle of their community. Much of what Nasser attempted in Egypt could be more accurately interpreted in this light than according to any set of Marxist concepts.

Within Arab society itself, tension quite naturally exists between egalitarianism and the rather romantic notions about individual initiative. This quality is noted by outsiders as a certain built-in friction that can be observed in the transactions of daily life. But to understand fully the nature of social relationships, it is necessary to consider the Arabs' view of social reality. The Arab lives in a real, intimate, and immediate context that is uncharacteristic of modern Western society with its plethora of highly impersonal mass institutions in which the individual senses that his performance consists of marginal functions conducted in anonymity. Within the vivid social setting of the Arab, personal activities are not fragmented in a way that permits the individual to be depicted unidimensionally as in the West. He cannot be characterized, for example, as a "voter," a "consumer," or a "worker." His identity is whole and personal.

These three factors—individual initiative, egalitarianism, and a firm social context—constitute much of the fabric of Arab society. Social institutions reflect them. In a tradition that is not so different from that of the West, Arab social institutions are organized to provide a security system. In most Western countries, society has evolved beyond this point to a condition in which facilitating production is the major theme of social institutions. Throughout much of the European Mediterranean, however, it is still possible to see the older concept flourishing. The basic unit of this older system is the extended family, which in many places throughout the Middle East is stable in its composition and locale and serves the purposes of group and individual preservation. Because the family protects its members in what is seen as a generally hostile world, its purposes are paramount. Admittedly, social forces shaped by the family are under severe pressure from the Western influences that prevail in Cairo, Damascus, and Baghdad and that recently have made headway in Kuwait, Riyadh, and even Abu Dhabi. Nevertheless, the family is still an important feature of life even among the Western-educated elites of Egypt, Syria, and Iraq.

Sometimes we fail to grasp the importance of the individual in Arab society because we do not recognize that the expression of individualism has been fashioned largely as personal responsibility for upholding the integrity of the family. The outsider often sees this responsibility as an excessive concern for honor. It is an aspect of Arab society about which many observers comment.

The system does bring a clear definition to the role of the individual and reconciles individualism with the egalitarianism of corporate existence within the family. A related factor is that because an Arab's identity is so firmly imbedded in an immediate and real institution, he is ever mindful of the authority of the past. Tradition, therefore, has an important place in the life of an Arab, and social structure reinforces an Islamic law that over thirteen hundred years has slowly evolved to assume many of the characteristics of custom.

Social structure has important ramifications for public life in Arab countries. Because of the predominance of family loyalties, individuals sometimes have a difficult time identifying with their government or contributing to the common but impersonal objectives for which that government may stand. Moreover, being a community of faith and language, Arab society has not produced a strong sense of civic responsibility, and it sometimes appears to lack the cohesiveness or the urge for integration that is found in Western society. One good example of how these relationships are expressed in public life can be found in the Arabic word *mahsubiyya*. The dictionary offers as a definition "patronage" or "favored position," but it means much more than that. *Mahsubiyya* is the social institution by which members of an extended family (itself a protective instrument) serve their common purpose. With this device there is no compunction against using official position to favor a family member. Actions that otherwise seem irrational sometimes make sense when family ties can be discerned among participants in a set of political events.

For our purposes the important factor is that individualism is an integral feature of social structure. Along with faith and history, Arabs weave it into their view of the nation. While the concept serves inspirational purposes just as it does in highly individualistic American society, individualism also reaffirms tradition within the Arab construct. Moreover, individualism has negative connotations from the standpoint of national cohesiveness. Arab society still suffers a great deal of confusion over allegiance which, in turn, influences how Arabs perceive relations with other peoples.

Patterns in Arab Politics

Perhaps the best way to explain the political significance of this type of social organization is through the leadership that results from it. The traditional Arab approach to leadership is obedience voluntarily given to an individual. It has little to do with the Western principle of allegiance to an office that endows the incumbent with authority. Under Islam's God-given law, leadership is established by community acquiescence. Power rests with the community, but that entity is not seen as enacting law or certifying leadership by a vote. Leaders are maintained through a consensus derived from a process of revelation. All events are carefully followed for clues as to what the future might hold. It is one of the aspects of the Arab outlook that outsiders sometimes mistakenly identify as fatalism.

Within this tradition the quality of leadership is that of enunciating God's law. There is one God, one sovereign (truth), one spokesman, and popular acquiescence is proof of that spokesman's correctness. A leader who does not follow the correct path is eventually rejected by the faithful. He becomes isolated from the consensual community and is thereupon succeeded by a new bearer of truth, who raises the standard of revolt against him. Today, of course, the expression of leadership is highly secular, but the pattern persists. Three important elements emerge from this image of a leader. First, as the bearer of God's truth, the leader is an authoritative figure. Second, because there can be only one truth, politics cannot rest on a pluralism of beliefs. It should be expected, therefore, that the Western liberal tradition would have difficulty surviving—an expectation that has, in fact, been borne out in modern Arab history. Finally, a leader's effectiveness ends when he becomes isolated from the popular consensus. Thereupon, cries for his overthrow can be heard.

The differences that sometimes occur between Western and Arab statesmen can be understood by visualizing these attributes of Arab society as determinants of political action and then contrasting them with our own perceptions. For the Arab, action is grounded in faith; for an American the idealized basis for action is reason, often derived from self-interest. The actor in an Islamic society is some corporate body, traditionally the extended family, with each individual assuming a generalized responsibility for carrying out the actions of the group. In a Western polity, the individual undertakes action in his own name for the benefit of himself and perhaps a few close associates who may be linked to him through a contract. The sanction that legitimizes action in an Arab society is God-given law. In Western politics, secularity embodied in man-made law provides authority. Finally, the reference point that serves the Arab's need for consistency is tradition. Action must conform to a familiar and accepted social pattern. In Western formulations of action, we hold to some concept of scientism by which alternatives are assessed in a presumably value-free examination of evidence.

For readers who prefer static imagery, the difference between Arab and Western politics can be conveyed in an institutional sense. The key is the recognition of a feature of Western political tradition that we acknowledge only implicitly. Our politics depend on a network of abstractions that we seldom encounter in the real world. The concept of the state is such an abstraction, as are pluralism and its various embellishments—the weighting and intensity by which an individual supposedly sorts through his priorities and our society accommodates specific wishes of determined minorities. Even the idea of political action originating with the individual is highly abstract insofar as it ignores the social environment in which the individual acts. In our system, in fact, escape from social reality is the means for allowing individual freedom, even to the point of sanctioning inequality. The organizing principles of the Arab, on the other hand, are firmly imbedded in a concrete social context.

Another approach to the understanding of political institutions is through the values they embody. Here we encounter another difference between the Arab world and the West. Again, in the Arabs' Islamic setting values are absolute. From our normative perspective in Europe and the United States, values are generally relative. Even in the manner of viewing the structure of political institutions we also find divergence between the Arab and Western approaches. The Arab perceives a single community of faith and language that contrasts sharply with our emphasis on competing but mutually adjusting political factions. In the West, politics has a flavor of controlled conflict that the Arab regards as destructive to community. This difference leads to a divergence of views over political process between the two societies. In the Middle East the purpose of political institutions is to facilitate the constant unfolding or revelation of a popular consensus. According to the liberal democratic norms of the West, political institutions are dedicated to enacting the wishes of a tolerant majority.

These concepts are, of course, theoretical, and they admittedly constitute an overly simplified approach to politics. Nevertheless, they highlight our differences with Arab society and in this sense may help us understand seemingly confusing events in Arab politics. They will be used repeatedly in subsequent chapters to explain Arab political perceptions. They also offer a means for acquiring insight into the Arabs' approach to modernization. During the last seventy-five years reformers have attempted to strengthen Arab society by reconciling these differences between Arab and Western politics. This outlook on the part of Arabs is important to an understanding of their relations with the West.

Certainly, social perceptions in the Middle East are changing. In the lives of many Arabs, faith and tradition are not as important as they once were. Large numbers of Arabs are as fully imbued with the attributes of contemporary life in an industrial society as any American. Faith, however, is not necessarily synonymous with religious feeling. In the sense of nationalism, faith has been secularized. Its importance is not just in terms of Islam, but in the feeling that the Arab national condition, which originated with Islam, has somehow been sanctified by that origin. Thus strong emotions can arise from issues that touch the Arab national consciousness.

We should note that perhaps 6 million Arabs are Christians. Quite naturally their religious life occurs outside the context of Islam. At the same time, many Arab Christians acknowledge that their national life occurs within an Islamic setting. Those who do not accept this premise usually do not accept the Arab nation. The civil war in Lebanon in 1975 and 1976 developed to a large extent from certain Christians' rejection of Arabism in favor of a Lebanese identity. While such facts should be noted, they are not an integral part of this explanation. The purpose of this section is not to convey a social description of Arab countries but to provide benchmarks for an assessment of Arab nationalism as part of the circumstances of Arab-Israeli negotiations. The matters that have been discussed here are those features of an Arab's consciousness that make him feel distinct—that is, those things that make him an Arab.

The Historical Context of Nationalism

The features of nationalism that have been explained here were forged in a historical context. The nationalistic fervor that an outsider encounters among Arabs is tied to the assertive role assumed by European countries in the Middle East following World War I. Through the League of Nations mandate system, Great Britain and France established control over the Arab provinces of the old Ottoman Empire. At the time, many Arabs thought they had reached an understanding with the British that would allow for the formation of a unified and independent Sherifian Hashemite Kingdom ruled by Faisal ibn Hussein from Damascus and embracing virtually all Arab lands east of Suez. Instead, this territory was fashioned into Lebanon, Palestine, Syria, Transjordan, and Iraq and placed under British and French tutelage. Only the interior and Red Sea coast of the Arabian Peninsula were left free to govern themselves. The mandates were managed through Western administrative practices with British or French power only thinly disguised behind indigenous regimes of the Europeans' making. In each case liberal political institutions were created to give a formal expression of representative government. In essence, the Arabs' experience with parliaments amounted to constitutionalism, but certainly not democracy. The powers of imperialism would not have permitted the latter.

In Egypt the process had begun somewhat earlier, following the establishment in 1882 of British, and temporarily French, financial controls in the wake of the economic disaster stemming from the grandiose plans and extravagant international borrowing of the Khedive Ismail. At the outset of this relationship the British and French were in the position of creditors managing the affairs of a debtor in receivership. The Egyptians had originally encountered Western practices and thought during the invasion of Napoleon, who brought a large contingent of scholars and technicians along with the French expeditionary force that occupied Egypt between 1798 and 1801. Napoleon saw his mission as furthering the spirit of the French Revolution by remodeling Egypt into a progressive country. The Albanian captain Muhammad Ali, who finally established an Egyptian dynasty in 1806 under the suzerainty of the Ottoman Turks, picked up the strands left by Napoleon and proved to be one of the East's early developers. He adopted all varieties of Western technology in agriculture, health, transportation, manufacturing, and hydraulic engineering.

Many Egyptians concluded from the development of their cotton economy, the construction of the Suez Canal, and the Westernization of Cairo that theirs was a European country. Western liberal democratic thought was readily accepted by the salaried elite that was educated to manage the new technology. At the same time, this group was quick to see the anomaly of the West's espousal of representative councils while it insisted on having the final voice in determining the course of events throughout the Middle East. Considerable sentiment for classic liberal political and social formulations existed, but in the Arab mind they were always secondary to national independence. The important point is that the Arab elites became accustomed to thinking about their politics in Western terms, even though they did not always act according to the corresponding prescriptions. Until just a few years ago, it was still possible to generate a lively discussion among educated Arabs, for example, over Woodrow Wilson's Fourteen Points, a corpus of liberal self-determination that had been interred and forgotten perhaps forty years earlier in Western centers of power and learning.

By the early 1930s parliamentarianism had failed in most Arab countries. In Egypt elections were falsified to the point of farce. Between 1930 and 1934 Egypt's liberal constitution was arbitrarily set aside and replaced with an authoritarian regime. The Palace and the British manipulated the system at will. The concept of a loyal opposition was lost in partisan bickering and recalcitrance. No one was looking for common ground on which orderly government could proceed.

Conditions were no better for other Arabs. In Iraq, Arab officers of the defunct Ottoman Army dominated politics from the beginning of the constitutional monarchy proclaimed under British auspices in 1921. In 1936 even the pretense of representative government was brushed aside when the military commander assumed control following a coup de'etat. Thereafter, military intervention into the affairs of the government occurred periodically until 1941, when British officials claimed overriding authority in order to achieve the stability necessary for their wartime objectives. In Syria the French had intervened in the constitutional process from the outset of the mandate by suspending successive national assemblies whenever developments were not to their liking. Representative government was even more of an empty formality in Syria than in Iraq. As for Jordan, here government was a synthetic product of British pragmatic politics established without any thought of popular expression. Maintaining the monarchy and the army were the purposes of the state—a mission that could be achieved only with British subsidies. The parliament was affixed to the body politic almost as an afterthought. Even in the constitution the king was given powers that far exceeded those of the legislature with its so-called popular representatives.

Before castigating the Arab for his failures in democratic government, the nature of his introduction to representative institutions should be considered. It is also well to remember that during the 1930s the liberal system fared no better in Europe. Western economies had collapsed in the late twenties and only authoritarian regimes appeared to have answers to society's problems. Just as Arab intellectuals had earlier overreacted in a positive direction to the stimulus of European liberal thought, they now perhaps went too far in rejecting it. Frustration was heightened because, even though Europe was in disarray, Arab nationalists of all political inclinations could see no deliverance from foreign domination. To the contrary, it appeared that in the face of the world crisis, Britain and France sat even more heavily on their Middle East domains.

In response to this situation, nationalists engaged in what might be called an Islamic political revival. In their writings and commentary of the period, Arabs trotted out all the symbols of Islamic strength, from an omnipotent prophet to an authoritarian Muslim state and the justification of violence or *jihad* in its support. Considering the ideological interpretation the Europeans had given the tensions that were developing among Britain, France, Italy, and Germany, this aggressive Islamic stance is not surprising. It was consistent with the spirit of the time. It was also a defensive outburst of impotence.

One subtle twist of the neo-Islamic reaction of the 1930s should not be overlooked: from liberalism it borrowed concepts dedicated to man's social welfare. The values propagated in the name of Islam did not differ significantly from those of liberal secularists. Even though Arab intellectual expression in the 1930s was a rejection of Western political forms, the prevalence of humanitarianism assured that social thought of the immediate postwar period would continue to reflect Western sensitivities.

To a large extent, intellectual concerns during the 1940s and early 1950s were dominated by an introspective examination of Arab institutions. The purpose of the intellectuals in this essentially humanistic exercise of social reform was to detect and obliterate sources of national weakness. The League of Nation's mandates had formally been terminated, but political dependence, including the stationing of British troops in Egypt, Jordan, and Iraq, continued. In implying that their plight was the difference between the achievement of the Christian West and the ineffectiveness of the Muslim East, Arab publicists had assumed an essentially passive stance toward European domination. Their attention centered on social rather than political correctives.

Progressive liberal forces sought deliverance in land reform, women's rights, tax equity, and crude forms of socialism. The formulas for societal improvement popularized during this period were vague and often impossible to express in any operational sense. From one Arab thinker came the concepts of "generality of right," "the duty of consultation," and "solidarity of citizens despite class structure";[9] another advocated an "uprooting of luxury," a "self-sufficient economy" (meaning high consumption), and "full employment";[10] while a third advanced such ideas as the destruction of class lines and the eradication of economic barriers through public control of the means of production.[11] Both equality and individual freedom were somehow to be achieved. Arab history and Islam provided the framework within which progress was envisioned. Invariably, feelings of inferiority in the presence of Europe revealed themselves. The principal point of debate, in fact, was whether the precepts of Islam were adequate for a contemporary social and political system.

These features of Arab thinking culminated in the Egyptian Revolutionary Regime of Gamal Abdal Nasser and were embodied in the revolution's charter of 1962.[12] The charter's ideal of the people as a homogeneous force without class consciousness, its overly generalized normative premises of a good life, the rejection of pluralism, the support of social justice, public consultation for consensus but not for representation, and strong leadership are all characteristic of the propositions set forth in the 1930s and 1940s. They are also recognizable within Islam.

This approach to national development coincided with the moribund condition of the liberal Arab governments that staggered on from scandal to scandal and crisis to crisis. Only marginal concern was devoted to possibilities for marshaling the power necessary to alter the balance in relations between Arab countries and the imperialist West. Popular revolts had occurred in Egypt in 1919, in Iraq in 1920, and in Syria in 1925, but all such efforts were crushed by the military forces of the Mandatory Powers. Thereafter, periodic outbreaks of civil violence against European domination occurred on a smaller scale, principally in the form of street demonstrations in Cairo and Baghdad where frustrated mobs would vent their wrath on whatever symbols of Western culture were to be found in their midst. The exception to this pattern was, of course, Palestine, where a bloody revolt marked by fighting between Arabs and Jews broke out in 1936. Here the issue was not the rule of the Mandatory Powers themselves; rather, it was the status of the territory and whether it would be slowly alienated from the Arab homeland by Jewish settlers who held a national perception that was distinct from that of the Palestinians.

The Appeal of Arab Unity

The regime of Gamal Abdal Nasser reflected the tradition of Arab political developments of the preceding thirty years. It witnessed the failure of liberal democracy; it embodied a strong sense of Islam; and it was dedicated to social reform. But Nasser's ideas also represented something new. Even in their most crude and embryonic form, they constituted a thesis based on power rather than reform. They were expressed in terms of a "united struggle" against the West.[13] An examination of those periods in which Nasser had the greatest appeal for Arabs indicates that his defiance of the West was the critical factor in each case. Various Western observers have commented on this phenomenon. Tom Little considered the Soviet arms deal as the move that gave Nasser his influence in the Arab world.[14] Charles Cremeans saw Nasser's opposition to the Baghdad Pact and his survival of the 1956 Suez attack as the incidents that struck the responsive chord in the Middle East.[15] The Lacoutures also centered their attention on Suez, interpreting it not so much as Nasser's success, but as the British and French failure that provided the basis for the emotional trend in Nasser's favor.[16] Here was the development of a consensus determined by events. Had Nasser pulled off some fantastic feat that was not associated with a loss for the West, he would not have had the same appeal, for Nasser's strength was in the popular Arab reaction to the challenge he constituted to the West rather than in the intrinsic features of his programs and policies. Arabs saw the possibility of ridding themselves of Western interference within their own lifetime, and Nasser assured them they would succeed if they were unified in their struggle.

Arab politics, distinct from considerations that influenced Arab peoples under the Ottoman Empire, began after World War I with the supposition that a unified Arab state was about to be created east of Suez. The Arabs, of course, were to be disappointed, but in a modified form the idea of union continued to be nurtured as the dream of the Fertile Crescent, which was to include Trans-jordan, Syria, Iraq, and even Lebanon and Palestine. As late as 1958 it served as the inspirational device of the Hashemite family ruling in Jordan and Iraq. Nonmonarchists, many of whom were Christians, advanced a similar proposition in their advocacy of a Greater Syria. Even the House of Saud with its puritanical Wah-habi rebellion worked implicitly toward a Greater Arabia when, after unifying the Nejd, the Hedjaz, and Al Hassa (heretofore distinct regions of the peninsula), it made incursions into Jordan, Iraq, and Yemen during the late 1920s and early 1930s before being turned back by British intercession.

Unity was to remain a nationalist's dream. In the presence of the overriding foreign influence constituted by the Mandatory Powers, the Arabs were compelled to develop their mutual relations not as a nation but as a number of states that entered into treaties pledg-ing cooperation on such matters as trade, defense, and cultural exchange. With the conclusion of World War II these relationships were formalized through the machinery of the League of Arab States and after the 1948 defeat in Palestine, by an Arab Collec-tive Security Pact. Outwardly, therefore, the Middle East had the conventional appearance of states engaged in regional cooperation.

The underlying current of Arab politics, however, involved considerations that went far deeper than relations among states. Essentially, politics became an expression of the tension between the state system and the drive for national unity. It was to be seen in the intense rivalry among the leaders of the various states. Each figure either harbored a desire to be leader of all the Arabs him-self or suspected that his neighboring sovereign was plotting to seize his country and incorporate it into a larger political entity—all in the name of Arab unity.

Perhaps the earliest antagonism of the modern period was that of the Saudis for the Hashemite regimes of Jordan and Iraq. Having driven the Hashemite family from its position as protector of the holy places in Mecca and Medina, the Saudi king, Abdal Aziz, thereafter viewed with suspicion the intentions of the Hashemite rulers, King Abdullah of Jordan and King Faisal of Iraq, whom he suspected of working on his northern borders to bring the Saudi domain into a unified Arab state. Only the advent of aggressive and radical regimes in Egypt, Syria, and ultimately Iraq convinced Abdal Aziz's successors in the 1950s that they had a common interest with other Arab kings, even if they were Hashemites. Saudi-Jordanian hostility faded, therefore, before the threat to Saudi interests constituted by Egypt's Nasser. Particularly between 1962 and 1967, when Nasser threatened the Saudi position within the peninsula by supporting the republican regime in Yemen with up to seventy thousand troops, did Egyptian-Saudi rivalry influence Arab politics.

Curiously enough, for almost forty years following the establishment of the existing Arab states, Egyptian leaders had not shaped their politics to accommodate the ultimate objective of a unified Arab state. During the decade after World War I, Egypt attempted to develop a pharaonic identity independent of the Arabs, and themes of Arab unity were not popular. Admittedly, King Fuad temporarily saw himself as the rightful successor to the caliph (and to the leadership of all Muslims) when the Turks abolished the caliphate following the destruction of the Ottoman Empire. At one point Faruk followed his father's predilection and toyed with the idea of having himself declared caliph. This pretention could have drawn Egypt into some plan for unifying the Arabs that would no doubt have evolved into interdynastic rivalries.

Before Nasser, however, the principal Egyptian purpose was simply leadership among Arab governments within the context of the Arab League. This policy did place the Egyptians in opposition to Hashemite efforts at capturing Arab leadership and achieving unity through the appeal of their vehicle, the Fertile Crescent. But it did not bring Egypt's rulers into vitriolic rivalry with any other leaders over competing schemes for unifying the Arabs.

The situation changed when Nasser began to think of himself as the leader of the Arab people rather than just a leader among independent and equal chiefs of state. A bitter hostility developed between Nasser and the Iraqi Premier, Nuri Said, in 1955 when Nuri defied Nasser's budding claim to Arab national leadership by taking Iraq outside the confines of Arab politics and into the Western-sponsored Baghdad Pact with non-Arab states—Pakistan,

Turkey, and Iran. Egyptian-Iraqi differences continued after the downfall of the Hashemite Kingdom when first the erratic radical Abdal Karim Qassem and then the successive socialist governments of the Baath Party refused to follow Nasser's prescription for unity. Briefly, so-called 'Nasserist' regimes controlled Iraq, but even they were not prepared to accept Nasser's embrace in the name of unity. Only with Nasser's death in 1970 did the tension between Egypt and Iraq lessen. Even between Syria and Iraq, tensions appeared and reappeared as the two wings of the socialist Baath Party, which came to power in those countries in 1963, jockeyed over a formula for unity that would leave one or the other dominant in Arab politics.

The modern history of the Arabs has been more a record of interstate rivalries than of solidarity and agreement. In only three cases have Arab countries functioned under instruments that formalized unity. The union of Egypt and Syria in the United Arab Republic occurred in March 1958. Concurrent with the formation of the UAR, Yemen joined the Syrians and Egyptians in a loose federation, the United Arab States. Following Syria's withdrawal from the UAR in 1961, Nasser terminated the federation. There was also the short-lived Hashemite Arab Federation, which was established by Iraq and Jordan in April 1958 in response to the UAR and dissolved after the Iraqi revolution in July 1958. The only remaining union is the United Arab Emirates that was established in 1971 by the sheikhdoms of the British-protected trucial coast.

Despite these failures, the pull of unity persevered. In 1963 the Syrians and Egyptians were again talking of unity, this time under a three-way scheme with Iraq. Throughout the late 1960s the possibility of a union between Syria and Iraq was repeatedly reviewed by the governments of these two countries. Following Nasser's death Mu'ammar Qaddafi of Libya became the major proponent of Arab unity and reached agreement with Anwar Sadat and Hafez al Assad in April 1971 over the formation of a single federal state comprised of three regions—Egypt, Libya, and Syria. For a while the Sudanese contemplated taking part in the union but ultimately thought better of it. Despite almost unanimous approval of the scheme in a plebiscite, the Egyptians hesitated, much to the exasperation of the unrestrainable Qaddafi who in July 1973 amassed a mob of fifty thousand Libyans on his border for a march into Egypt and on to Cairo where public exuberance would supposedly have pressured Sadat into implementing the scheme.

Even after the 1973 war, schemes for unity continued to surface. During a period of apprehension and uncertainty prior to accepting a disengagement arrangement with Israel, Syrian leaders sought security by engaging the Iraqis in talks that could have led to a military alliance and eventual union between the two countries. The Syrians were prompted to consider this course because of their fear that Egypt, Saudi Arabia, and Jordan would move toward an accommodation with Israel that did not consider Syria's concern over the Golan Heights. An association with Iraq would have been the only means for Syria to avoid the isolation that would have left it facing Israel alone. Again after Sadat concluded the agreement with the Israelis at Camp David in September 1978, the Syrians and Iraqis turned their thoughts to union.

Perhaps the most unusual unity effort occurred in January 1974 when Mu'ammar Qaddafi of Libya literally telephoned President Bourgiba of Tunis and after a brief discussion flew off to meet him on the island of Djerba—fittingly the alleged home of Ulysses's lotus eaters. After a few hours together in a hotel room, the seventy-one-year-old patrician and the thirty-one-year-old colonel emerged displaying a piece of paper that declared unity and announced a referendum that would have allowed the voters only one day in which to absorb what was taking place before casting their ballots. The incident so enraged the governments of Morocco and Algeria that the Tunisians quickly retreated, announcing through their new foreign minister—who incidentally had just replaced the only senior official to accompany Bourgiba to Djerba—that Tunis did not wish to create unity in a spirit of disunity. The idea for a referendum was shelved. Thereafter, of course, Qaddafi was incensed, and ambiguous threats emanated from Libya to the effect that popular disturbances might soon occur against officials of neighboring countries who were obviously traitors to the struggle for the unity of the Arab nation.

Why Failure?

The questions that must be asked about this bewildering set of circumstances are: Why have the Arabs failed to achieve unity? Can we accept the assertion of Arab nationalists that success has eluded the proponents of union only because the evil leaders of some Arab states continue to give primacy to selfish interests (that is, to their personal positions of leadership) that would have to be sacrificed in any consolidation of the Arab nation?

Setting aside for the moment the purpose of unity and looking instead at its manifestations, we see that three characteristics stand out, and all point to failure. First, fervent advocates of unity have a naive belief in their ability to achieve their goal through national acclamation—as if some great force will sweep over the people, who will then emotionally embrace the concepts of Arabism, and thereafter a unified Arab nation will exist. Unity is viewed almost as an act of religious conversion. Organization, policy, and some purpose other than the erasure of political boundaries are seldom considered as part of the equation.

In any catalog of the weaknesses of the Arab national ideal, a second factor soon emerges. Nasser once characterized Arab unity as a mission in search of a leader. This remark has been interpreted in a number of ways, but it indicates that Nasser, far from being an ideologue, was steeped in the concrete and personal aspects of the Arab political tradition. He saw leadership in terms of Arab individualism and community consensus. Nasser himself reached the pinnacle of leadership in the hearts of the Arab people. But in the process of translating this force into operations, it was necessary for him to rely on a vast army of officials working within bureaucratic or political structures. Wherever Nasser's subordinates worked for unity, whether in Syria, Yemen, Libya, or the Sudan, they were viewed as Egyptians. Because of the way leadership is approached in the Arab world, it was never possible for Nasser to transmit his status to his lieutenants—a step that would have been necessary in the implementation of the normal functions of a unified Arab government.

Arab unity, therefore, has always been limited to rhetoric and to a symbolic quest for a largely undefined ideal that has something to do with the Arabs' desire for power. Given the emotional manner in which Arabs have approached union—that is, without any concern for the policy implications of such in act—the tradition of unity has not been sufficiently strong to permit national leadership to be transformed into national organization.

Perhaps the most ubiquitous element of Arab unity, and also an important reason for its failure, is Syria. Whether it be the Fertile Crescent, Greater Syria, the United Arab Republic, or Gaddafi's federation, Syria always is a part of the scheme. We can fairly say that Arab unity is a quest for power. What, then, does this formulation tell us about the way power has been conceptualized by the Arabs? Syriocentric schemes appear to be emotional projections of union based on Arab history. But is this area really the material from which a powerful state can be fashioned? Reaching into the Middle East heritage, union with Syria has proved to be a classic statement of the struggle between the civilizations of the Nile Valley and Mesopotamia over the areas located between them. In this respect Syria has attracted power but has never created it. Syria, in fact, has been cast in a position of weakness.

In its recent history Syria has literally defied political definition. The country includes a number of minority religious communities that identify with narrow geographic domains from which they can occasionally assert an influence over the whole of Syria that is greater than their numbers warrant. The principal groups are Druze in the southern mountains, Alawites in the central coastal area, and Kurds in the north and west. Of lesser significance are the Assyrians, Circassians, and Turkomans. President Assad, for example, is an Alawite. So were his immediate predecessors, Salah al Jadid and Muhammad Umran. Husni Zaim, the first postindependence military strong man, and Adib Shishakli, the second, were Kurds. Of the military leaders who have dominated Syria over the past twenty-five years, only Abdal Hamid Sarraj and Amin al Hafiz were from the Sunni Muslim majority. Even the Sunni have been divided. Those of the Homs region are suspicious of and set apart from the Damascene.

Lack of a clear vision of what Syria is and where it might be headed has produced chronic inconsistency in Syrian politics. In such a fragmented country the traditional wisdom was to avoid any permanent political coloration. No civilian politician could establish a generalized appeal. Political followings depended on regional, ethnic, or religious loyalties. Consequently, political dominance was transitory. For long periods the government would assert little authority over the strong Syrian sense of individualism. The country was literally run by organized mercantile forces. Under these circumstances, just about anyone could play at Syrian politics. Being the leader of Syria was not totally serious business. This attribute, for example, permitted the Syrians to slip into and out of the United Arab Republic with considerable ease.

Over the past fifteen years an ideological element has been added to the political equation in Syria. During this period the traditional politicians have become less and less effective. Conversely, the military has developed into a more important political force. In the Syrian context, the army must be grouped with intellectuals—journalists, lawyers, students, and teachers—as an advocate of rational authority. The officers' corps constitutes one of the few hierarchically organized groups that (theoretically at least) depends on efficient interdependent functioning and the use of modern technology to achieve its mission. The officers have both the wherewithal to control social institutions and an obsession with developing within their society the strength that permits Syria to rebuff the West. In short, they are a modernizing force. Ideology has appeal for any such group, possibly because it is the preferred vehicle for those who would use the state to realize what they consider to be popular ends. Because the officers had become alienated from the old-line conservative forces who did not think in progressive terms, they naturally gravitated at one time or another toward the ideologically oriented parties—the Syrian Social Nationalist Party, the Socialist Baath, and the Communists. The game of Syrian politics from the viewpoint of the civilian politicians who founded and ran these parties was to acquire the support of officers for their respective movements.

Most officers have acknowledged the ideological manifestation of military organization, but they have not been unduly influenced by it. The ideologues have had little popular following within the army even though ideology has a certain appeal for the officers. Loyalty to the abstractions of ideology has been weak because generally an ideology conveys only impersonal and functional roles within a political structure. The officers as a group may take pride in their adherence to such concepts, but for the individual, these same concepts are the antithesis of Arab political culture.

In the end, therefore, it was army officers, acting in accordance with traditional concepts disguised only with a thin veil of modernism, who gained control of the ideologically oriented parties. Within this rather confusing collage, much of Syria's political energy has been devoted to preserving the positions of the minorities—the motivation that brought the officers into public life in the first place. In the postwar era, therefore, Syria has been in a state of transition. In form, the political structure has been modern, but in the hearts of those who guide it, traditional ideas remain. It can reasonably be concluded that as long as Syria is subject to such conditions, it cannot be a unifying force for the Arab nation. This does not mean that Syria can be ignored in any movement toward national unity; it is too important to Arabism in historical terms, in both a millennial and a contemporary sense. Until Palestine wanes as an issue of Arab national concern, Syria as a confrontation state bordering on Israel will have a major role in Arab politics.

The curious thing about the major ethnic and religious minorities of Syria is that, whatever the divisions among them, they seem to have an Arab character. This factor alone keeps them attuned to Arab politics and places them in a much different position, for example, from that of most of the Lebanese Christian minority. Herein we can perhaps see the future of a more powerful Syrian entity. It is to be found in the reaffirmation of Greater Syria as an Arab state. President Hafez al Assad gave some evidence of appreciating this possibility when conditions in 1975 and 1976 forced him into closer association with King Hussein of Jordan and into taking a direct hand in the civil war then raging in Lebanon between Christians on the one side and Palestinians supported by Muslims on the other. What was involved was neither the emotional lunge that Arab leaders in the past have made toward unity nor the competitive game of inter-Arab alliances that have always been the outgrowth of tensions over unity. Assad's objectives seemed to be extraneous to the purposes that heretofore had inspired national leaders.

First, unity was not Assad's theme. His actions implied not an accentuation but rather a diminution of symbolic Arabism. Assad's was a clear vision of rationalized power in the areas to the north and east of Israel without regard for the political configurations of the remainder of the Arab world. Events led many observers to suspect that his moves were directed toward some sort of Greater Syrian confederation that would allow for peace with Israel and the reestablishment of Arab authority on the occupied West Bank. For our purposes, it is enough to say that Assad had a strategy—something nationalist leaders seldom have in the Middle East. In a calculated and unpretentious manner, he set out to achieve his objectives with an unassuming political association with Hussein, contacts with the United States and Israel to assure that his intentions were not misunderstood, and the use of military force to give Syria influence in Lebanon and to bring the Palestinians to heel.

In a series of steps that were less bombastic than those taken by Nasser or Qaddafi in their coveting of national leadership, Assad was attempting to give political continuity to Syria. As part of a larger whole, and perhaps with attention centering on something other than the claustrophobic concerns of the Damascene, Syria might make more sense than when it served the purposes of the minority-oriented and nationalistically inclined officers, the civilian politicians, or the great landowning and mercantile families of the French Mandate. It all pointed to one supposition—Syria of the future need not be Syria of the past. In 1975 and 1976 Assad did not fulfill his Greater Syrian strategy. But implemented forcefully, it could eventually give Syria political coherence and permit it to assume an important place in some new interpretation of Arab unity.

Thus we have identified the features of Arab national politics that make unity so illusive. Arabs expect union to be achieved by acclamation; they have approached leadership in such a way that a leader has no capability for implementing his ideas and plans, however popular these may be with the masses; and they have persistently looked to Syria as an integral part of all unity schemes even though it has been poor material for a unified state.

But all has not been said about Arab unity. Thus far in identifying its defects we have considered only the way in which the concept is structured. In addition we should also ask the meaning of unity for the Arab nationalist. In his mind, what is its purpose? Almost habitually Arabs respond to this question with the assertion that "unity is a revolution."[17] It will bring radical change insofar as it will end the undue influence of outside forces working to prevent the achievement of various national goals that would permit the Arabs to develop internally and to assume their rightful position in the international community. It seems, therefore, that unity is about *power*. Certainly, editorials during the past thirty years in virtually any Arab newspaper, as well as political discussions with Arab nationalists, support this conclusion. But the Arabs' national ideal also places value on something more than Arabs' being together politically. It sees them working together economically and socially. When unity is given economic and social attributes it acquires other features—it becomes *popular* and *progressive* —two important themes that have been present among Arab political aspirations since the 1930s. Actually, a union between two governments, as in the case of the United Arab Republic, need not be any of these things. In the sense of societal change, it may not even be revolutionary. The question, therefore, is whether unity is necessary for the fulfillment of the Arab national purpose as defined in terms of power, popular expression, and progressiveness.

The Arabs' own spokesmen seem to suggest that whenever the Arab people can jointly engage in progressive and popular activities that also display evidence of power, unity may no longer hold the imperative that it has in the past. Other formulations of these objectives are possible. Since the 1973 war we have witnessed changes in political outlook in the Arab countries that may permit the Arab people to realize national goals without structural unity. These changes have been directed toward developing new relationships within the Arab nation. They have also been the source of many contradictions that have tended to confound observers of the Arab political scene. If we are to understand the effect of Arab nationalism on the Arabs' international affairs, particularly as nationalism influenced Kissinger's diplomacy, we must examine with care the Arabs' evolving national perceptions. In the next chapter, therefore, we will explore how Arabism has functioned in the past, how it continues to function, and how it is changing. Thus some insight will be provided into the Arabs' quest for a new definition of national purpose that goes beyond unity and might someday lead to peace in the Middle East.

2

Political Dynamics of Arabism

Over the past twenty years, the Arab condition has led to a succession of attempts to establish a unified, stable, and powerful framework for political expression in the Middle East. But the result, alas, has been a long string of abortive plans for union and consequent worldwide scoffing at the Arabs' talk of national purpose. The clumsiness of the effort has permitted outsiders to ignore the sincerity and depth of national feeling that have kept the Arab world in turmoil. National untiy is a serious matter for Arabs. Their modern experience, including domination by the West, interstate rivalries, and headlong plunges into unity schemes has literally dictated the behavior of Arab leaders. A fruitful course for us to follow, therefore, is to consider the question, How does Arab nationalism operate in a dynamic political setting?

A good place to begin is with the attitude of the individual Arab. We have seen that national unity has been a matter of public concern for Arabs since World War I. Whereas an individual Arab may fashion his political conduct to conform to norms established by the state—and even experience a certain sense of duty to that state—chances are that his political identification transcends the state's boundaries. For the Arab, nationality and nationalism are not features of a state; they are the attributes of a people—the Arab people with their common language and culture realizing a destiny within the Islamic context.

Because the nation does not correspond to the state (which in conventional politics serves as the instrument of power for a nation), the purpose of Arab nationalism is ambiguous. Even in 1958 at the height of the fervor over the formation of the United Arab Republic, Gamal Abdal Nasser admitted that the concept of Arab unity covered principles ranging from solidarity among the people to constitutional union. Perhaps it would evolve, he mused, from solidarity to alliance, to union, and on to total constitutional unity.[1] In the main, however, Nasser himself was equivocal. From Arabism he simply saw the possibility of "exploding a terrific latent energy . . . capable of lifting this region up and making it play its positive role in the construction of the future of humanity.[2]

In its early formulation Nasser's statement anticipated similar interactions for Egypt with Africa and throughout the Islamic world as well. Much has been made of this position. Some contend that Nasser wished to dominate Africa and influence all Muslims. The African and Islamic addenda to Nasser's Middle East politics can be more accurately interpreted as a desire to break through the isolation imposed by imperialistic control and to associate with neighbors in a common cause. Such sentiment has been typical of most populous former colonies in Asia and Africa since independence. It was not peculiar to Nasser or to the Arabs. Virtually all new states have had strong inclinations for international association.

Perhaps the most persistent aspect of Middle East politics during the past sixty years has been the influence of Western Europe and the United States on the political development of the Arab people. Arab governments generally have been the losers in encounters with the West or with its surrogate, Israel. Arabs have long had feelings of humiliation and inferiority, therefore, in their official relations with the West. The crux of the problem for the individual Arab, in fact, has been that he is very much at home with a European or an American and can discern very little difference between his experience and that of someone of similar education and background from a Western country. Yet, within any institutional setting—whether it be in politics, economics, the military, or technology—Arab deficiencies when measured against Western capabilities for implementing policy have been painfully apparent.

Because the Arabs have placed the frustration arising from these circumstances into a national rather than a state context, their reaction to the West has involved raw feelings that have been largely beyond the political control of any government. Whatever his military strength, no Arab leader has ever had sufficient reach to use the force constituted by national feeling for precise policy purposes. While national fervor can provide an Arab leader with an awesome influence, it is also an enigma. With no generally accepted Arab national policy, and with the intense feelings Arabism can generate, Arab leadership has become transitory, depending on the conditions that permit a head of state or a popular figure to identify with the Arab cause.

Arab leadership is ephemeral insofar as it extends across state boundaries, gives the possessor no sanction to command through legitimate force, and depends on communications within a cultural milieu. In one instance it may not reach beyond those connected by word of mouth in a single city. With the use of radio it may affect all Arabs. Leadership becomes a prize to be seized by the individual in public life who happens to have sufficient charisma and good luck to fashion a popular consensus. Appeal has always depended on how well such a person expresses Arab frustrations. Because the popular force generated by Arabism is beyond the control apparatus of any state, and because it has a reactive quality arising from the Arabs' experience with the West, it has become an unstructured, negative attribute of politics that can deny but cannot achieve.

This implicit aspect of Arabism produces unending debate over the shape and content of the national ideal. A relative and tolerant perspective is not possible within the Arabs' world of absolute and God-given truth applied to a community that traditionally has had the purpose of guiding its members along a spiritually ordained path. The mode of community and political expression is such that in the competition for political leadership, each contender vilifies others as misguided, deceptive, and self-serving, or even as blasphemous proponents of some vile creed. The gem for which all vie and which transforms a state leader into a national leader is, in fact, the power to define things Arab.

Since World War II no Arab leader has succeeded for any appreciable period in openly advancing the interests of his state while expressly depreciating Arabism. If state interests require primary attention, a leader will usually ignore any perceptible contradictions between state and Arab goals to proclaim that his actions support Arabism. In fact he may be following a course that ignores the Arab dimension of policy altogether. Simultaneously, he may charge his detractors with the treasonous acts of false prophets. It seems, in fact, that Arab leaders are constantly being torn between their devotion to the nation and their obligation to a government.

Generally when an Arab chief of state who aspires to national leadership cannot achieve his purpose through rhetoric and finds himself slipping into an uncertain position, he will identify with the state. Even in the Arab world, the state operating through the mechanism of a government becomes the arbiter of policy. It also provides protection for those who are not riding the crest of national sentiment. But no matter what his intent, an Arab leader working through the state will attempt to camouflage his actions and attitudes with national trappings.

Although we usually think of Nasser as the most successful of nationalist leaders, quite often he was bettered in his skirmishes with competitors. In such instances he was required to opt for a policy that identified him much more closely with the Egyptian state than with the Arab nation. In 1959, when it became apparent that the rhetoric of Arab unity did not have sufficient power to compel the Iraqi leader, Abdal Karim Qassem, to bring his country into the United Arab Republic, Nasser improved relations with Jordan and Saudi Arabia and moved toward closer ties with the United States. He was clearly playing regional politics within the setting of sovereign states. Again in 1961, when Qassem's forces were about to march into Kuwait, Nasser forged a common cause with Jordan and Saudi Arabia and even coordinated his military movements with the British, who were also concerned with Kuwait's integrity. The logic of Arab nationalism would have been to permit Kuwait to be absorbed by Iraq in the knowledge that the imperialists' design of fragmentation had suffered a defeat and the Arab peoples were a step closer to union. Instead Nasser, who was on the defensive, was compelled to behave as an Egyptian by acknowledging the sovereignty of King Hussein and King Saud,

with whom he sought cooperation. In these cases he was even prepared to work with the imperialist powers that had been the source
of so much misery for the Arabs.[3]

Finally, later in 1961, Nasser's qualities as an Arab leader were
tested when Syria seceded from the United Arab Republic. At
this point he boldly maintained that Egypt was the conscience of
the Arab nation, if not the Arab nation itself. From Cairo came
the dualistic thesis of Egypt the State that would deal with other
governments, and Egypt the Revolution that would address itself
only to the Arab people. "Unity of ranks" with other Arab leaders
was replaced with "unity of purpose," that is, dedication to the
one truth—Arab nationalism—of which Nasser was the spokesman. As further protection Nasser also adopted "Arab socialism"
as a symbol of his national purity. Nevertheless, it was a doctrine
of socialism in one country; he had been compelled to recognize
the efficacy of the state. In facing the most critical challenge to
his national leadership, Nasser tried to have it both ways, and his
stance vividly portrayed the dilemma of an Arab leader caught
between the nation and the state.

By 1963 Nasser's position had changed. This time he had the
upper hand in talks with the Baath socialist leaders of Syria and
Iraq, whose ideology had again drawn them into discussing union
with the man whom they liked to consider "politically unscientific."
In planning the structure of the unified state, the Syrian and Iraqi
politicians obviously sensed Nasser's advantage when they insisted
on making the Federal Assembly, in which the three regions would
have equal representation, dominant in the bicameral legislature.
Nasser, with his tremendous popular appeal throughout the Arab
world and with his huge Egyptian population, opted for a more
powerful lower house, the National Assembly, in which representation would be popular rather than regional in nature. Here we
have a clear expression of one party attempting to use the instrument of the state, in the form of proposed regional governments in
Iraq and Syria, as a device for protecting itself against the power of
a competing leader who commands the emotions of the nation.[4]

The Meaning of Isolation

Whatever their politics, Arab leaders are loath to lose their
identification with Arabism. Despite major concerns with domestic

and international problems within the framework of their respective states, all seem to attach a sense of reality to the Arab nation. Quite naturally, the most serious punishment that can be inflicted on an Arab leader is to isolate him from the Arab identity. Within the political struggles among Arab leaders—which are usually over some version of a military or foreign policy identified with the Arab cause—attempts have been made repeatedly to deny the Arabness of the antagonist. If the label sticks, the alleged offender at a minimum will lose contact with and influence in neighboring Arab countries. At worst, he may face turmoil at home and conceivably be overthrown. Nasser utilized this technique repeatedly whenever Nuri Said and Abdal Karim Qassem of Iraq, King Hussein of Jordan, or King Faisal of Saudi Arabia refused to follow some aspect of Egypt's version of Arab policy.

In all such political interplay the charge that the culprit works against Arab purposes is phrased in terms of his serving the interests of the West, the Zionists, or the imperialists. Conversely, the forces of Arab goodness are identified as resting with the leader leveling the charges. In contrast to the enemy, he depicts himself as working to defy the outsider who is attempting to divide the Arabs and who is responsible for whatever terrible circumstance is at issue.

But Arabism is forgiving. If the offending leader recants and is willing to meet with the leader who happens to hold the imagination of the nation at the time, he is immediately restored to good grace. Following the 1967 war, the antagonisms between Faisal and Nasser were overcome in this manner at the Khartoum Conference. Just months before, as the two struggled over the outcome of the civil war in Yemen, Faisal had been castigated by Nasser as an enemy of the Arab people. In their reconciliation Faisal offered monumental foreign exchange support for the defeated Jordanians and Egyptians. In Arab eyes it appeared that Nasser was forgiving Faisal. Westerners might assume that this interpretation is faulty—that, in fact, it was Faisal who forgave Nasser. But, for the Arab nationalist, the happy event represented Nasser's and not Faisal's largesse. Within Arabism, the power of national symbols has habitually been regarded as being more potent than the voice of material resources.

Following the 1973 Arab-Israeli hostilities, the practices that have been attributed here to Arab politics were particularly evident. Egypt's acceptance of a cease-fire on October 22 did not take the Syrians altogether by surprise, but it did catch them unprepared. Many Syrians could not lay aside their rhetoric of "uncompromising struggle," even as Israeli armies approached Cairo and Damascus with little standing in their way if they chose to move to the very suburbs of these major Arab cities. At first no one raised the question of whether Sadat had betrayed the Arab nation in accepting a cease-fire. The Syrians did "note" Egypt's action, while Sadat hastened to justify his move by explaining that it was taken at the urging of the Soviets. King Hussein of Jordan supported Sadat but qualified his position by pointing out that the Jordanian troops in Syria were still under Syrian command and were free to fight on if the Syrian generals so directed. Although Iraq had limited forces committed in Syria, its territory and population were not suffering destruction at the hands of Israel, and Iraqi leaders rejected the cease-fire. In Libya, Colonel Qaddafi urged that the Arabs continue the struggle until the Zionist entity was dismantled. Specifically he called for the Palestinians to strike inside Israel. However unrealistic, the positions of Qaddafi and the Iraqis, as well as the equivocation of Hussein, corresponded to the dictates of Arab nationalism.

In accepting the cease-fire, Sadat was proceeding against the current of national honor as determined by the radical Arabs. It was a serious situation, even for Sadat. Three years later, the Egyptians were still so sensitive about the issue that they were attempting to obfuscate matters by claiming that just twenty-four hours after the fighting began, and two weeks before Sadat accepted a cease-fire, the Syrians were pressing Egypt to agree to an end to the fighting. The realities of the military situation supported Sadat's decision, and so did King Faisal of Saudia Arabia. With Faisal's backing, the fighting could at least be terminated without Sadat's risking the isolation imposed on one who appears to abandon the Arab cause. Instead, it was the Syrians who felt isolated. With Sadat out of the fighting and with the Jordanian-Israeli border peaceful, Syria would bear the full brunt of Israeli arms if hostilities continued. On October 24, therefore, the Syrians followed Sadat into a standstill arrangement with Israel.

Egypt and Saudi Arabia thereupon expressed an interest in

Secretary of State Kissinger's efforts to work toward some long-range accommodation between the Arabs and Israel. For the first time, no wave of revulsion swept over the Arab nation at this suggestion. The radical leaders' control of popular sentiment had been brought into question. The trend was accentuated by President Houari Boumediene of Algeria. Although generally counted among the ranks of the radicals, Boumediene decided at this juncture to support an Arab policy of discussing peace with Israel. In Syria, pressures were enormous. The leadership was divided between those who favored the traditional uncompromising stand toward Israel and others who saw some value in an exploration of peace. When Assad had joined Sadat in the attack on Israel, he personally was thinking in terms of the limited goals associated with a political solution. It was now a matter of persuading some of those who shared power with him to do likewise. The Syrians finally announced on November 19 their willingness to engage in talks with Kissinger. Thereupon the balance in Arab sentiment shifted toward a negotiated settlement. Perhaps for the first time since Arab politics had been formalized with the establishment of the Arab League in 1944, moderate forces appeared to be guiding the destinies of Arabism.

The future, however, was quite uncertain, and all players avidly sought the cover of Arabism to shield themselves from the charge of serving narrow state interests. No one wanted to be isolated. Since 1964, participation in summit conferences of Arab chiefs of state had afforded individual leaders a claim to Arab identity. Once again such a meeting was proposed. Iraq, Libya, and the Palestinian Liberation Organization refused to participate. They felt that under the circumstances such a gathering would not serve the "aims of the Arab masses in their quest for liberation through continuation of the struggle against Israel."[5]

The conference itself, which took place in Algiers in late November 1973, was classic in its expression of Arab nationalism. While the final communiqué gave credence to the positions of governments by speaking about the coordination of the policies of kings and chiefs of state, it also held forth the concept of a single people when it declared that the "Arab nation has never abandoned its national goals, nor has it backed down before the imperatives of its struggle." The demand in the communiqué for Israel's evacuation from its military gains of 1967 and 1973 referred to the withdrawal from "Arab territories" rather than from the lands of Egypt, Syrian, and Jordan. Finally, the Islamic character of the Arab nation was affirmed with the assertion that evacuation applied first of all to Jerusalem.

The heart of Arabism was expressed in the conference's demand for the "reestablishment of the full national rights for the Palestinian people." The Arab view was stated as a simple expectation that the "united struggle" would continue until Arab grievances were redressed. "So long as these conditions have not been met," the communique concluded, "it will be illusory to expect in the Middle East anything but a continuation of unstable and explosive situations and new confrontations."[6] The conferees did give guarded approval to a negotiated settlement with Israel, but their decision was couched in terms of traditional Arab nationalism that could only make it unacceptable to the Israelis. Even in the absence of the radical elements constituted by Iraq, Qaddafi, and the Palestinians, moderate Arab leaders had taken their stand as spokesmen of the Arab nation and not as heads of sovereign states united in a common purpose. Quite often, it has been these same moderate leaders who have not been able to measure up to the manifestations of the national purpose to which they have subscribed. Thus the charge of treason is leveled against a king or a president whenever the business of his state or government seems to overshadow the brave but impractical themes proclaimed at a summit conference.

Following Kissinger's second trip through the Middle East in mid-December 1973, the scene was set for the first direct meeting between Arabs and Israelis. But when faced with the test, the Syrians could not bring themselves to meet their enemy. Syrian foreign minister Khaddam later revealed that he had threatened to resign rather than represent Syria at a peace conference. The influence of family honor on Arab politics was certainly present in Khaddam's statement, "I do not want my son to be told that his father sat at the same table with Zionists to negotiate peace with them."[7] Egypt, therefore, proceeded alone, and with Faisal's blessing Sadat sent his foreign minister to the first session of the Geneva Conference.*

The response of the radicals to these developments was authentic Arab national rhetoric. An Iraqi spokesman accused Sadat and his supporters of "adopting an imperialist plan aimed at isolating Iraq."[8] Qaddafi called for a popular revolution by the Arab people to prevent their governments from reaching a peace agreement with Israel. The specter of isolation and appeals to the nation over the heads of chiefs of state were as much a part of the political scene as in Nasser's heyday.

Once the cease-fire was in effect and major Arab governments had indicated their support for a negotiated settlement, the next step was the disengagement of Arab and Israeli forces in Sinai and along the Golan Heights. As Kissinger's famous "shuttle diplomacy" got underway, the Syrians publicly warned Sadat not to proceed on Sinai without some Israeli assurances on both Golan and the national rights of the Palestinian people. Somewhat contrary to Western political perceptions, Sadat was free to negotiate for his Arab neighbors, but if he limited his concerns to Egyptian territories alone, he would clearly, in the eyes of other Arabs, be acting as the parochial leader of a single state. Any achievement would be contrary to the interests of the Arab nation. When Sadat finally concluded an agreement that extricated the Egyptian army trapped in Sinai by the Israelis, a Syrian spokesman said his government was so angry over Sadat's disregard for a united Arab front that it might break relations with Egypt.

The feelings of radical Arabs were more intense than Sadat

---

*Kissinger's mediation consisted of six phases. Partially through his efforts, Israel and Egypt arranged a cease-fire on October 22, 1973. Two days later Syria agreed to a cessation of hostilities. The Geneva Conference attended by Israel, Egypt, Jordan, the United States, and the Soviet Union was held on December 21-22, 1973. An agreement between Israel and Egypt to disengage their forces in Sinai was concluded on January 18, 1974. A similar agreement between Israel and Syria pertaining to military forces in Golan was reached on May 29, 1974. Negotiations between Egypt and Israel in March 1975 for the purpose of expanding the arrangement on Sinai failed. Finally, on September 1, 1975, Egypt and Israel signed the Sinai Accord by which Israel relinquished additional occupied territory in Sinai and Egypt agreed to certain limitations on the actions it might take in relation to Israel.

had anticipated. Explicit approval of key Arab governments was essential if he was to avoid isolation. Immediately Sadat undertook visits to eight Arab countries and sent envoys to others. He was well received in Morocco, Algeria, and the Persian Gulf states. In Syria, he was only partially successful in placating his partner in arms, President Assad. In Iraq President Hassan al Bakr refused to receive Sadat's representative. For the time being Qaddafi of Libya was ignored. Sadat was careful, however, to explain his position to Yasir Arafat of the Palestine Liberation Organization, and temporarily at least the Palestinians withheld criticism.

At best the situation was a stalemate. Sadat did not face immediate isolation, but the Egyptians made no secret of their belief that unless the Syrians could be persuaded to conclude a disengagement agreement with Israel, Sadat's position would eventually erode, with all the dangers this would signal for him. Arab nationalism was at work. There were indeed popular factors beyond Egypt's borders that Sadat was compelled to heed. Finally, in late January, Egypt's foreign minister, Ismail Fahmy, went to Moscow to elicit Soviet support in moving the Syrians toward disengagement. The Syrians' only response was to label Egypt's agreement with the Israelis as a betrayal. Yet, because popular sentiment had not swung against Sadat, the Syrians too felt the anxiety of being isolated from the Arab nation. As he was to do repeatedly, Syrian president Assad called for a summit meeting as a means of gaining national sanction for any move he might take as head of the Syrian state.

A meeting with Faisal, Sadat, and Boumediene in mid-February 1974 gave Assad more confidence. Thereafter he was prepared to explore the disengagement of military forces and adjustments in territory along the Golan front. Nevertheless, the Syrians still harbored resentment against Sadat's unilateral moves, and at the Arab League meeting in Tunis in late March the Syrian representative attacked Egypt for leaving his country isolated. The Egyptian foreign minister, who had not planned to attend the session, immediately flew to the meeting to inform Syria and the nineteen other sister states that "Egypt will never abandon Syria." Arab solidarity was to be preserved.

On May 29, after thirty-two days of traveling between Damascus and Jerusalem, Kissinger managed to arrange the disengagement of Israeli and Syrian forces. The significance of this development was that it took place almost totally within an Arab rather than just a Syrian context. Sadat, Faisal, and Boumediene all had a role in placing Assad on the course of disengagement. The Saudi and Egyptian foreign ministers, speaking on behalf of Syria, had held preliminary discussions with Kissinger in Washington toward this end. The Arab League meeting in Tunis had indicated a general Arab accord with disengagement. As pressures mounted during the Syrian-Israeli exchange taking place through Kissinger, Assad again became uneasy and returned to the idea of yet another meeting of heads of Arab states where disengagement could be legitimized. Throughout the negotiations, Assad was subject to constant urging from Sadat and more benign pressure from Faisal.

Even in signing the disengagement agreement with Israel and in arriving at arrangements for implementing the accord, the Syrians avoided a bilateral commitment. The agreement was signed under the guise of the original Egyptian-Israeli-Jordanian structure of the Geneva Conference with U.S. and Soviet representatives serving as chairmen. Military details were discussed by the "Egyptian-Israeli Working Group." It was almost as if Syria had no part in the disengagement of forces in Golan. This fiction was possible insofar as the Egyptian commander was technically in charge of troops in Syria by virtue of the joint military arrangement between Egypt and Syria.[9] Assad had so structured formalities that disengagement was an Arab rather than a Syrian matter. Sadat was content with this approach because it permitted him to avoid the stigma of being the only Arab leader to conclude an agreement with Israel. In Arab capitals there was full realization of what had taken place. The Egyptian leader was credited with having won his gamble by carrying Assad with him.

The events that transpired between the time Sadat accepted the cease-fire on October 22, 1973, and the point at which Syria accepted the disengagement agreement on May 31, 1974, provide us with the norms of Arab politics. At each step, proponents of traditional nationalism (here seen as the radicals) shouted betrayal because first Sadat and then Assad was negotiating with

Israel through channels provided by the United States. The extreme nationalists accepted only one course—continuation of the uncompromising struggle. No matter how senseless was this proposition from the standpoint of the military situation, it was compelling within the limits of Arab politics. As a result, the leaders who were working their way toward an accommodation with Israel sought to cover their bilateral negotiations with the Arabism of which uncompromising struggle was a part. As we have seen, Assad did so through two Arab summit conferences that gave legitimacy in Arab terms to the cease-fire he had accepted and the disengagement agreement he had signed. Sadat felt that he had retained the appearance of remaining true to the principles of the nation by establishing a new Arab consensus with Saudi support.

Yet each leader was insecure. It was necessary to take steps that ensured against isolation. To this end, Assad refused to send representatives to the Geneva Conference. Sadat, after signing the Sinai disengagement, either visited or sent representatives to virtually every Arab capital at almost a frenetic pace. He thereby verified that his own new consensus on negotiation rather than the traditional approach of confrontation with Israel would be sustained. Even then, the Egyptians acknowledged that they could hold their course only if Syria entered into a disengagement agreement as well. No one could go it alone. In 1974 no one could yet risk the dangers of national isolation.

During 1975 and 1976, the interplay that has been described here was repeated numerous times. Each leader cited the liturgy of Arab nationalism even when his actions contradicted it. Antagonists of one day became comrades of the next—all to avoid isolation. These events, in fact, provide the key to comprehending the maneuvers of Arab national politics. The principles involved are first, that the nation and the state are not contiguous, and second, that only professed allegiance to the nation assures final protection for an Arab leader. The game built from these rules may be called isolation: if a leader can be separated from his nation he can be bettered by other players—that is, by competing Arab leaders. Arab politics are always confusing, but they need not be mystifying if these principles are kept in mind.

To suggest the existence of patterns in Arab politics that provide us with understanding, and perhaps limited powers of prediction, is not to say that the Middle East is without change. On
the contrary, the cease-fire, the Geneva Conference, and the disengagement agreements made it clear that something new was
afoot in the Arab world. Sadat had demonstrated that the mere
exposure of a leader to radical rhetoric was insufficient to bring
him running back to the orthodoxy of castigating the imperialists
and their lackey, Israel. In his treaty with Israel concluded on
March 26, 1979, he was to test whether an Arab leader could
sign an accord with Israel without alienating himself from the
Arab nation.

Qaddafi: A Case Study

The change in Arab perceptions was signaled by the plight of
Libya's President Mu'ammar Qaddafi, a leading proponent of radical politics after the 1973 hostilities. As Arab sentiment discern-
ibly shifted toward a negotiated settlement with Israel, Qaddafi
sensed that his refusal to attend summit conferences and his call
for popular uprisings against leaders who favored negotiation had
left him isolated from the mainstream of Arab politics. In mid-
February 1974, therefore, he traveled to Cairo, and in a widely
publicized speech apologized to Sadat for having criticized Egypt's
acceptance of the cease-fire. Profuse in his praise of the Egyptian
leader, Qaddafi applauded Sadat for carrying the burden of the
entire Arab world. The Libyan was once again within the fold, and
although Radio Tripoli only a few days before had referred to
Faisal as the "Traitor King," Sadat hustled Qaddafi aboard a plane
and flew off to Riyadh to heal the breach between the Libyan
strongman and the Saudi monarch.

The Arabs accepted this little affair as a sign of a sturdier unity
forged by the October War. From the standpoint of Sadat and
Faisal, their display of forgiveness was worthwhile. It had silenced
one more critic of their policy, leaving only the Iraqis, and sometimes the Palestinians, to challenge their cause. Qaddafi was a
principal supporter of Palestinian organizations, and his shift apparently influenced their outlook. While he was in Cairo apologiz-
ing to Sadat, in fact, three major groups within the Palestine

Liberation Organization—al-Fatah, as as-Saiqa, and the Popular Democratic Front for the Liberation of Palestine—modified their stand on "uncompromising struggle" sufficiently to agree on the establishment of a Palestinian authority in any territory evacuated by Israel. The implication was that the Palestinians might some-day be prepared to enter into negotiations with their enemy.

Still, Qaddafi harbored fears that Sadat's efforts to negotiate a withdrawal of Israeli forces from the Sinai Peninsula would leave the Jewish state sufficiently intact to constitute a betrayal of the full national rights of the Palestinian people. Before long the Lib-yan was again plotting—meeting with and giving encouragement to a group of ultra-conservative Muslim Egyptians who were pre-paring to overthrow Sadat and establish a state derived wholly from the Quran. Qaddafi's inspiration led the group to attack the arsenal of a branch of the Cairo Military Academy in an effort to acquire arms with which they could seize Sadat, occupy the Egyptian National Assembly, and declare an Islamic state. Eleven persons were killed and twenty-seven wounded in the attack. The culprits were captured by Egyptian authorities, and in confessions they revealed their rationale. Qaddafi and the plotters saw Sadat's efforts to negotiate improvements in his position in Sinai not only as an affront to the Arab nation but also as a transgression against Islam. Little doubt existed in their minds regarding the Islamic nature of Arab nationalism. The episode visibly demonstrated that within the limits of Arab politics a leader does, in fact, risk over-throw if he goes beyond some indistinct boundary that violates national honor.

While denying complicity in the plot, Libya's collective leader-ship apparently attempted to restrain Qaddafi, a move that was attributed to the counterproductive nature of his activities and the isolation these created for all Libyans. Nevertheless, Qaddafi con-tinued his struggle through radio attacks and diplomatic notes, leveling against Sadat charges shaped largely in terms of Islamic concepts. Sadat was not accused of errors in policy that worked against the interests of one Arab state or another; rather, he was charged with subjecting the Arab people to a crisis of morality by sacrificing devotion to Islam. The Libyan had reached this con-clusion because in his eyes Sadat had committed the "crime of dismembering the Arab nation and relaxing under the American umbrella." Unmistakably, Islam and the Arab nation were inseparable.

Radio Tripoli assured its listeners that Sadat's government would be as short-lived as a soap bubble. This prediction was not simply propaganda. It was based on the same firm conviction that motivated the preposterous attack on the military academy— as long as Qaddafi was armed with Islamic truth, he would prevail. An imprisoned Sadat would repent; a nation confronted with the Islamic message pronounced from the speaker's podium of the National Assembly would accept the righteousness of God's new agent; by acclamation the people would accept the new regime. All the elements of Arab nationalism, the customary view of political dynamics, and the tradition of Islamic leadership were present.

Egypt thereupon terminated all plans to participate in Qaddafi's Federation of Arab States, and Sadat publicly dismissed the Libyan as a "loud-mouthed political adolescent."[10] In effect, Sadat had imposed isolation upon Qaddafi. An Arab leader—or any leader— separated from his nation suffers great uncertainty. Ultimately Qaddafi was once more drawn to Cairo, where he sought Sadat's forgiveness after the Sheikh of Abu Dhabi interceded to arrange a meeting between the two leaders. By standing again among the spokesmen of the Arab people, Qaddafi could demonstrate that he was attuned to the Arab nation. His isolation had ended.

But that was not the last to be heard from Qaddafi. He again reversed his position, and continued to castigate Sadat's moderation and to support those who opposed a settlement with Israel. Several acts of sabotage in Egypt as well as a bloody revolt in the Sudan could be traced to his machinations. He habitually refused to participate in meetings sponsored by more moderate Arab leaders to discuss the future of the Arab nation. He was intent on forming alliances with one Arab leader or another in attempts to isolate Sadat and hasten his downfall.

But not even Qaddafi could resist the pull of Arab togetherness. When King Khalid of Saudi Arabia brought the warring Arab leaders—Assad, Arafat, and Sadat—to Riyadh in October 1976 in an effort to resolve the civil war in Lebanon and to end the friction between Egypt and Syria over the Sinai Accord, Qaddafi was not invited. In fact, he remained uncharacteristically silent during this interlude. It was assumed that Libya would boycott a meeting of Arab foreign ministers called by Khalid and that Qaddafi would shun the subsequent gathering of the Arab chiefs of state that was to be held in Cairo the following week in order to sanctify the Riyadh agreements. Much to everyone's surprise, a spokesman for Qaddafi turned up just as the foreign ministers' meetings were concluding. In the aura of national unity inspired by the assemblage, this emissary announced that the Libyan leader was prepared to resume friendly relations with Sadat and as evidence of his good faith would cancel Egypt's sizable debt to Libya.

Actually neither Sadat nor Qaddafi had changed his position on the Israeli issue, and an outsider might puzzle over the meaning of this event. Surely the incident itself was to be taken no more seriously than Qaddafi's earlier professions of friendship. It did, however, demonstrate the attraction of Arab national politics for someone who can only claim leadership of a single Arab state. Here was the tradition of Arab nationalism. Just as in the case of Faisal and Nasser at Khartoum in 1967, it was Qaddafi, the possessor of wealth, who was seen in Arab eyes as seeking forgiveness from Sadat, the holder of the national consensus. Moreover, the substance of policy differences between the two was not as important as the common expression of an amorphously defined Arabism.

The Impact of Arabism on Foreign Relations

For non-Arab countries attempting to further their interests in the Middle East, Arabism is a complicating factor as well as a mysterious force. Usually outsiders do not recognize that sentiment for Arab unity inhibits the diplomatic initiatives of Arab leaders. While proceeding on the basis of conventional standards of bilateral diplomacy, a representative of the United States or a European country may fail to grasp that the position of his government is being assessed according to some overarching standard of Arab purpose as well as by the more conventional criteria of Egyptian, Syrian, or Saudi interests. If a Western proposal points too selectively to the interests of one Arab state, the issue of isolation looms for the leader of that government. The Arab chief of state involved in the negotiations may hesitate as other Arab leaders begin to speak darkly of outside attempts to disrupt Arab unity. Negotiations can founder in this morass while the Arab leader in contact with the West intermittently responds to two levels of consideration —that of his state and government and that of Arabism.

Henry Kissinger put Sadat in this position on four occasions during the two years of negotiations that followed the October War. At the very outset of his relationship with Kissinger, Sadat patently risked isolation in accepting first the cease-fire and then a disengagement agreement. Immediately thereafter Kissinger again compelled Sadat to run the gauntlet of Arab national perceptions by insisting that before the United States could proceed with its mediation between Israel and Syria, the Arabs must lift the oil embargo that had been imposed on the United States and other Western countries following the outbreak of hostilities. One by one the European countries and Japan had been exempted from the embargo by reciting the magic formula that affirmed support for the Palestinian cause and called on Israel to withdraw from occupied territories. But American representatives were loath to utter these incantations. Instead, Kissinger acted to exploit a weakness in the Arab position. If the United States suspended its mediation efforts, Sadat would be exposed as the only Arab to have signed an agreement with Israel. Without some movement, the Arab public could develop a sense of frustration, and sentiment could swing in favor of those who rejected a negotiated settlement. Sadat would be isolated and the Saudis, who were the controlling factor in the embargo, would be threatened for having supported Egypt's moderate position.

Kissinger's threat was fraught with inconsistencies, but it was adequate to frighten Sadat. In negotiating the Sinai disengagement agreement, Sadat formally accepted the obligation to persuade his fellow Arabs to end the embargo. Immediately thereafter, when he toured eight Arab countries to explain the agreement with Israel, he urged the Arab leaders to accept Kissinger's mediation as sufficient evidence of American good intentions to warrant lifting the embargo on the shipment of oil to the United States. Sadat's strong position on abandoning the most effective instrument of policy the Arabs had thus far devised set him apart from other

Arab leaders. Suspicions arose that perhaps the Egyptian had gone too far in his dealings with the American secretary of state. An Arab oil conference planned for February 14, 1974, was postponed for one month at the Saudis' suggestion in order to permit Sadat to avoid a confrontation with his antagonists, thereby saving him considerable embarrassment on the issue. When the meeting was finally held, Sadat had his way and the embargo was lifted, but only with Saudi support and because Boumediene, who had heretofore favored continuation of the embargo, saw that Arab effectiveness would diminish if Sadat were isolated at this point.

The unified Arab effort was by this time tenuous. Libya refused to agree to the termination of the embargo; Syria demurred, contending that an agreement on the Golan disengagement should have precedence. Iraq's stand remained ambiguous insofar as the Iraqis attacked the decision even though they had never subscribed to the embargo. By pressing too hard on the embargo issue, Kissinger had exposed Sadat to charges of abandoning the Arab cause. The opinion was widely expressed among officials in Arab capitals that the United States was not really helping the Arabs but only wanted to weaken them by destroying Arab unity.

The difficulties over the embargo had the unfortunate consequence of sharpening Arab consciousness regarding differences between the nation and the state. Sadat's independence in seeking a disengagement in Sinai, coupled with his attitude on the embargo, cast Israeli withdrawal from Arab territory in a questionable light. Was withdrawal the major issue confronting the Arab nation or was it a matter to be identified more closely with the interests of the individual Arab states? Particularly as Kissinger followed his stey-by-step plan of dealing first with Egypt and then with Syria, the problem of the occupied territories became associated more with the state and less with the aspirations of the nation.

In effect, the tensions among the Arab leaders over the embargo led to a stiffening of the Arab position. The upshot of Kissinger's maneuvers was to cause Sadat to hesitate before entering into further negotiations with Israel. Nine months were to elapse between the Golan agreement and Sadat's decision to accept another set of negotiations on Sinai. A firm Arab context had been established by the Syrians' approach to disengagement, and in any second round of talks, Sadat would have to behave accordingly. When the negotiations finally occurred, Sadat did not feel free to offer the Israelis what they wanted—long-range nonbelligerency in exchange for the evacuation of more Egyptian territory. Nonbelligerency would have removed Egypt from the contest without a resolution of the Palestinian issue or a final disposition of the occupied territories in the Golan Heights and the West Bank of the Jordan River. It would have amounted to an abandonment of the Arab position, an issue about which Sadat was sensitive.

When the second set of negotiations on Sinai began in mid-March 1975, we were to see the third occasion on which Kissinger's efforts threatened Sadat. On the eve of the negotiations, Assad warned Sadat against proceeding on Sinai without achieving simultaneously some assurance from Israel regarding the surrender of occupied Syrian territory and the acknowledgment of Palestinian rights. Egypt's president attempted to protect himself from the charge of working against the Arab cause by maintaining that any agreement with Israel was simply a military matter that had no political connotations. The implication of this argument was that a separate agreement on Sinai would have no influence on the fortunes of other Arabs. In order to strengthen this subterfuge, Sadat even considered having military officers negotitae certain features of the agreement in Sinai itself. When Sadat ultimately agreed to a new Kissinger initiative, it was in a joint statement with Faisal, who continued to give Arab legitimacy to the actions of the Egyptian leader.

In an effort to assure a more congenial atmosphere for negotiations, Kissinger traveled to the Middle East in February 1975 for discussions with various Arab leaders, including Hafez al Assad. But as he worked his way toward the renewal of American mediation, Kissinger was compelled to admit to Assad that the Israelis could not be persuaded to conclude a second interim agreement on Golan that would parallel the second accord he was about to begin negotiating on Sinai. The Israelis were firm that only in a general peace agreement would they consider surrendering more occupied Syrian territory. In effect, Kissinger's admission removed the protection of Arab national purpose from his approach of negotiating partial agreements with individual Arab countries. In proceeding with a second agreement on Sinai, Sadat could no longer claim that his policy served the nation. By making the distinction in how Israel viewed future negotiations with Egypt and Syria, Kissinger placed Sadat in the position of appearing to follow state interests. Syrian opposition to negotiations on Sinai thereby became pronounced. In official announcements from Damascus, Kissinger was accused of attempting to split the Arabs, and an active diplomatic campaign was launched against Sadat's intended move. Syrian representatives carried Assad's message to Faisal, Boumediene, Bourgiba, and the Persian Gulf sheikhs. Even King Hussein was included when an invitation was extended for his prime minister to visit Damascus.

As Egyptian-Israeli talks got underway in March 1975, Assad made a number of public statements in which he asserted his Arabness. Palestinians were set forth as the symbol of the nation when he declared, "Today as we witness feverish attempts to liquidate the rights of the Palestinian people, we feel more committed than ever to their cause." In response to the rhetorical question of who would determine the fate of peace in the area he said, "Only the Palestinians can because their rights constitute the foundation of peace." If Sadat was to insist on further negotiations, Assad, as a leader of the Arab nation, wanted veto power over any agreement the Egyptian reached with the Israelis. "Arab solidarity," he said, "is a very important matter and we will continue to work for its preservation. We will spare no effort to foil attempts to undermine this solidarity."[11]

Sadat's position was placed in bold relief by Assad's utterances. As an Egyptian, Sadat might have proceeded independently toward a settlement with Israel. But in so doing he would have been denying all association with Arabism. Egypt had tried an Egyptian/pharaonic identity in the 1920s and found it lacking. As "sons of the pharaohs" Egyptians related to nothing in the contemporary world. Egypt was clearly inseparable from its Arab image. In a more practical sense, Arabism was necessary to assure links with the Oil Arabs from whom Egypt received so much financial support. Even in terms of relations with the West, the rush of American and European businessmen to Cairo in 1974, all talking of investment and joint ventures, was largely the result of Western economies' attempts to establish their bona fides with the Arabs and not just with the Egyptians. The attraction of Cairo was that many companies found Egypt the only sizable Arab country in which a sensible investment could yet be made. The March 1975 negotiations between Egypt and Israel for a second agreement on Sinai failed. Failure may have been the result of Israeli intransigence as Secretary of State Kissinger was to claim, but there can be little doubt that the necessity for Anwar Sadat to negotiate within the context of Arabism was also a factor.

Sadat finally concluded the second agreement with the Israelis in September 1975, and for the fourth time his confidence in Kissinger produced difficulties for Egypt's relations with other Arabs. The move was greeted by a chorus of opposition from Qaddafi, Assad, the Baathist leaders of Iraq, and Arafat. Even King Hussein of Jordan was mildly critical. The Syrians characterized the Sinai Accord as an "Arab defeat." Assad refused to discuss the matter when Husni Mubarak, Egypt's vice-president, traveled to Damascus to explain the terms of the agreement to Syria's leaders. Typical of Arab politics, one of the early calls following the signing of the Accord was the proposal by Arafat that an Arab summit conference be convened. Here national perceptions would supposedly prevail and Sadat's actions could be judged accordingly. The tensions that the agreement produced clearly troubled the Egyptians. Subsequently they were to attribute the difficulty they experienced in acquiring economic support from the consortium of Persian Gulf oil producers to the attitude of certain Kuwaiti officials toward the Accord.

For a moment, let us go beyond Arab rhetoric and ask what was involved in the tensions that developed and how they related to Kissinger's diplomacy. In strategic terms, it can be said that any Arab advantage that might have existed in the struggle with Israel was maximized when Egypt, Syria, and the PLO approached Israel together. For the most powerful partner to strike a separate bargain clearly limited the negotiating capabilities of the others. Some hard feelings were to be expected. Actually much more was involved because the Arabs thought in terms other than cooperation among independent states having common interests. Sadat was not criticized for letting down his allies but for betraying the Arab nation.

And it was not just in press commentary from unspecified sources that the Egyptian president was attacked for his treasonous acts. Syrian Foreign Minister Khaddam leveled such a charge openly, as did Yasir Arafat, who declared that he would do anything to frustrate the evil design thrust on the Arabs by Sadat and the United States. From their standpoint, Sadat had taken a position that contravened common Arab rights. Punishment of Sadat was therefore due in the form of isolation with all it represented in the way of threat to an Arab leader.

During Kissinger's mediation, Arab national feeling could be held responsible for the long delays between agreements, even when an important segment of Arab leadership and opinion accepted a settlement with Israel. It also had an influence on the content of agreements. In defending himself against the charges of betrayal, Sadat was to assert that Egypt had never forgotten the interests of the Palestinians and Syria in negotiating the Sinai Accord and had, in fact, rejected an Israeli offer to return all of Sinai to Egyptian control in exchange for full and unequivocal peace. Sadat clearly sensed the limitations of Arabism. The same factor was apparent when Kissinger attempted to proceed with his step-by-step diplomacy beyond the Sinai Accord to a second agreement on Golan. By this time Israel was prepared to negotiate another interim agreement with Syria, but Kissinger found that Assad had now tied further negotiations on Golan to an Israeli willingness to hold parallel talks with the PLO. In so many words Assad was saying that he refused to negotiate outside the Arab context. It was a self-imposed limitation, but it was real. Assad's position placed negotiations beyond the Israelis' capabilities. Thereafter Kissinger's initiative languished throughout the sixteen remaining months of his tenure in office.

In retrospect, Kissinger and his aides might play down the significance of Sadat's response to Israel's alleged offer on Sinai or the meaning of Assad's refusal to proceed with the negotiations on Golan unless something was also done about the national claims of the Palestinians. Nevertheless, Sadat's and Assad's assertions pointed to the constraints Arab leaders experience in negotiating on national issues. Without a doubt, Arabism can impinge on the relations a leader of an Arab state may choose to have with non-

Arab governments. In Arabism an outside mediator or negotiator faces a vexing dilemma. If he does not press against the barrier that Arabism presents to communication and compromise, he may never achieve movement toward his objectives. If he presses too hard, however, the reaction sparked by Arabism may be counter-productive to his efforts. Kissinger's performance vis-à-vis the issue of Arab national sensitivities was not error free. His boldness created problems, but we must also acknowledge that it achieved results, however limited.

Almost as an epilogue, we should note the conflict between Sadat and his Arab antagonists after President Carter's Camp David initiative in September 1978. Their behavior was no different than during Kissinger's negotiations. Sadat sorely wanted an agreement with Israel, and during his meetings with Carter and Begin he took giant strides in this direction. The agreement that the Egyptian and Israeli leaders signed made it appear that peace was now a matter of a few protocols. The Arab response was the accusation that Sadat had betrayed the nation. This assertion was duly followed by a gathering of Arab chiefs of state (excluding Sadat) in Baghdad in October 1978 to formalize the isolation of the Egyptian leader. Sadat's reaction was as predictable as this well-established liturgy by his Arab counterparts. Whereas Carter had assumed that Sadat's and Begin's lieutenants would reach an early conclusion in the negotiation of details to the Camp David agreement, in fact the discussions were interminable. The Egyptians procrastinated. Long sessions were devoted to a formula that would firmly tie any treaty to a pledge by Israel to proceed with some plan for self-determination by the Palestinians on the West Bank. The Israelis objected to placing their negotiations with the Egyptians in an Arab context. They were prepared to do something about the West Bank someday, but once and for all time, they wanted to establish that they were negotiating with Egyptians as Egyptians. Sadat could not free himself from the compulsion to express Egypt's position in Arab terms as well. A link between any bilateral treaty and the core issue of Arab nationalism became a *sine qua non* for agreement. Thus when Sadat finally signed a treaty with Begin, the status of the West Bank and the Palestinians, rather than the steps for returning Sinai to Egyptian control, were set forth as the core problem in the continuing Egyptian-Israeli dialogue.

Negotiations on national issues in the Middle East are always an uncharted journey. Consequently, the best an outside mediator can do is to be ever mindful of the forces with which he is working and to recognize that each step constitutes a calculated risk. Positions that are reasonable within a bilateral setting can be questionable and even damaging in the context of Arabism. Mediators can encounter delays and pitfalls that have little to do with an Arab leader's good faith in negotiation. More often they stem from the two-level syndrome that leaves outsiders in the quandary of attempting to determine when an Arab leader in a particular instance is free to respond to state interests and when he must be guided by a national Arab perception.

A New Approach to Arab Politics?

We have reviewed the influence of nationalism on Arab diplomacy and noted both the continuity that exists and the changes that are beginning to take place in Arab politics. It is now possible to return to the question that was raised but not fully answered at the conclusion of chapter 1. If the Arabs simply seek national expression that is popular, powerful, and progressive, is it necessary for them to follow the practices of the past? Does political unity of the variety seen in Nasser's United Arab Republic provide the only answer to national fulfillment? Events that transpired after the 1973 war showed that other courses may also satisfy national needs. With a minimum of palaver about unity, Sadat and Faisal took more practical steps toward the national goals of Arabism during 1974 than the Arabs had taken in the preceding thirty years. For the first time the core of the united effort shifted away from incorporating Syria into the politics of either Mesopotamia or the Nile Valley and moved toward a coalition between Egypt and Saudi Arabia. The very nature of the entities involved in the Cairo-Riyadh axis gave the Arab initiative a more substantial base than one centering on Syria.

In Egypt, political continuity was well established. Sadat was part and parcel of *all* the Egyptian people. While some of his detractors questioned his dedication to Arabism, he actually accepted the Arab element in the Egyptian character that had been periodically restated and nurtured since the late 1930s. No question of national identity arose to weaken Sadat's resolve. It was just that he was intent on forging a *policy* from that identity. He wasn't satisfied, as other leaders had been, to believe that something was being accomplished simply by restating it. Neither was an issue of identity likely to arise in Saudi Arabia. Unlike the Arabs of the Mediterranean littoral or the Mesopotamian Valley, the only identity the Saudis could perceive was Arab and Muslim. The conflicting currents of minorities or the complexities of divisiveness based on an assortment of state loyalties did not yet exist among most people of the Arabian Peninsula.

In cases where national identity is weak, a leader launched on an undertaking such as Sadat's often attempts to strengthen his position by seeking public adulation and by forcefully silencing opposition. Sadat, in fact, was to resort to these tactics later. But in the negotiations with Kissinger, neither was a factor. The identities of Saudi Arabia and Egypt were not the same, but they were sufficiently stable to give Sadat and Faisal confidence in proceeding with their plans. Sadat was certainly worried at times, as other leaders tried to maneuver him into isolation. But with Faisal's support, he was able to persevere. Together Sadat and Faisal could swing a large segment of opinion in their favor. Their moves, in fact, were popular. The first element in the Arab national trilogy was in place.

The Egyptian-Saudi combination was also powerful. The Egyptian performance during the October War demonstrated that, despite the ability of Israel ultimately to gain the upper hand in the fighting, success was purchased at a cost in men and equipment that gave every Israeli pause in thinking about the future of his country in a belligerent Arab East. Likewise, the use of the petroleum weapon with embargoes on oil shipments to Europe, Japan, and the United States demonstrated to the industrialized countries that they could no longer proceed in shaping the world independently of Arab wishes. The Arabs must be taken seriously. For the first time, the world saw them as the possessors of power.

The Arabs' power rested not only on their ability to withhold oil from Western economies. It was also evident from the claim on resources that the fourfold increase in petroleum prices provided. The potential for dedicating these resources to vast development projects in Kuwait, Saudi Arabia, Iraq, and Egypt gave the Arabs confidence regarding economic and social improvement. A practical ethic, both progressive and popular, could realistically be established. In the presence of power, all the attributes of Arab nationalism were on hand. For the first time the purpose of the Arabs as a nation was amenable to a definition that could be widely accepted without being couched in terms of war and destruction. Moreover, in the form in which Sadat and both Faisal and his successors expressed it, this purpose was not likely to be thwarted by outside forces. Arab unity was still problematic, but now its absence did not deter the realization of national objectives insofar as these could be expressed in powerful, popular, and progressive themes.

Perhaps the most remarkable feature of Egyptian and Saudi leadership was that neither reached for the scepter of Arabism. Each demonstrated a modesty uncharacteristic of nationalist leaders. They were content with a new conviction tempered by power and dedicated to implementing a policy rather than generating the mass hysteria of acclamation. Generally policy was set forth by Sadat within the framework of an interpretation of Arab objectives found acceptable by the Saudis. The policy orientation was evident in the willingness of the Arabs to enter the give-and-take of negotiations with Kissinger rather than just to proclaim uncompromising demands and ignore the necessity of developing mutualities with Israel—a course that heretofore had been followed throughout the long and tortuous history of the Arab-Israeli confrontation. A new attitude also was evident among less moderate Arabs. The support of Boumediene was critical in the early days of the new consensus, and in no case was the negotiating mentality more evident than in the stance of Assad during events leading to the Syrian-Israeli disengagement agreement.

Because they approached the situation in terms of policy rather than acclamation, the Arab leaders were relieved of the burden of always implementing their intentions within the amorphous context of the Arab nation. Neither Sadat nor the Saudi kings were called upon to take any action that could not be initiated by Egyptian or Saudi officials working within the limits of the identity provided by their respective governments. Yet they worked on national issues. Because their outlook was inclusive rather than exclusive, they did not face the contradictions of Nasser when he attempted to assert his leadership over other Arabs while working through Egyptian deputies to the exclusion of other Arabs. In the past the very objective of players in the game of Arab politics had often been to isolate and perhaps destroy another Arab leader. Quite naturally this approach created antagonisms and fostered attitudes that divided Arabs to make Egyptians appear more Egyptian and Syrians more Syrian.

But this time there was no rhetoric aimed at vilifying as a traitor to the Arab nation any Arab chief of state who did not favor the Egyptian-Saudi initiative. Never had Arab leaders shown so much concern for the sensitivities of their fellow kings and presidents as at the conferences held during 1974 in Rabat, Algiers, and Tunis. The beginnings of accommodation were attempted even between King Hussein and Yasir Arafat. The Libyans and the Iraquis could separate themselves from the movement if they wished, but they were also welcome to participate. Little by little a practical unity was being forged among Arabs.

Faisal's untimely death was to demonstrate that however great the accomplishments of the Egyptian president and the Saudi king, their steps were still uncertain when compared to the changes that were necessary in order to assure a realistic relationship in Arab politics between actions and objectives. Simply because Faisal was a quiet and unassuming man who preferred to influence events from a position somewhat outside the spotlight of public attention, it was not always recognized that his influence was based on charisma and that in a traditional sense he was a leader to all Arabs. The first question to arise after Faisal's assassination in March 1975 was whether his successors could have the same influence on Arab affairs that he had enjoyed. The answer was critical to Sadat's actions and even to his longevity. Without effective Saudi support

Sadat would face isolation. In a Western setting such a transition would have rested more on the power the Saudi government derived from its oil than on the inclinations of the successor. The pressures of institutionalized political continuity would have assured steadiness of policy. The prospect of simply withdrawing from a prominent role in politics would have been unthinkable in Western terms, but some observers feared it was a real option for the Saudis.

For the eighteen months following Faisal's death, the bitterness and recriminations among chiefs of state that had become virtually a tradition in Arab politics appeared again. The pattern seemed to be more of the same dreary, dismal business that had existed in the past as Assad, Qaddafi, and the Palestinians attacked Sadat over the Sinai Accord and vituperation spewed forth from all sides over the roles of the Syrians and the Palestinians in the Lebanese civil war. Could it be that the new course plotted by Sadat and Faisal was already lost? Faisal's successor, King Khalid, made several efforts to resolve Syrian-Egyptian differences and to bring peace to Lebanon, but to no avail. Economic development based largely on American technology and the continuation of the Riyadh-Cairo axis in conjunction with Kissinger's mediation were well established in the thinking of the new Saudi leadership. But in addition, the Saudis also continued their symbolic allegiance to the cause of the Palestine Liberation Organization, even while they privately favored Syria's efforts to establish more control over the Palestinians through its intervention in Lebanon after June 1976. These contradictions were sufficient to render the Saudis ineffective.

Finally, in October 1976, conditions accommodated Saudi intercession. With Assad's degree of success against the Palestinians, with his budding Syrian-Jordanian association, and with Israel seeming unusually tolerant of Syrian gyrations in Lebanon, the Syrian president no longer felt as exposed as he did in the aftermath of the Sinai Accord. He was ready for a new inter-Arab understanding. Defeat at the hands of the Syrian Army in Lebanon had led the Palestinians to realize that they could not shape the future of Arabism single-handedly. Nor could the PLO be assured any longer that the Arab leaders who opposed narrow Palestinian objectives would meet political destruction through isolation from Arabism. Accommodation seemed the best route. Sadat was so beholden to the Saudis by this time, in both political and economic terms, that he could not afford the luxury of annoying them by devoting his energies to assuring that Assad's influence in Arab politics did not continue to increase relative to his own. At Khalid's invitation, therefore, Assad, Arafat, and Sadat were ready to travel to Riyadh to discuss their differences. The willingness of the Saudis and the Kuwaitis to use their oil wealth to underwrite the other Arab's activities was made more or less contingent on Sadat's and Assad's coming to some understanding on Syrian hegemony in the Arab Levant and on steps that each might take toward a settlement with Israel. The Palestinians were to have a secure place, but it was to be secondary to that of Syria and Egypt. There were even indications that it might also be secondary to peace with Israel. Saudi leadership and power had finally been asserted, even if in a quiet and somewhat unassuming manner. On this occasion a long-range unity of policy was not established, but neither was a single word uttered about the structural unity to which the Arabs had habitually been wedded. Here was the future of the Arabs' effectiveness if they chose to pursue policies.

The Arabs would continue to encounter contradictions between the governmental institutions under which they lived and the national goals to which they aspired. Unity of purpose was not complete. The Iraqis sniped at the Riyadh-Cairo initiative from the sidelines. Qaddafi continued to play his spoiler's role while the Rejectionist Front within the Palestinian movement maintained that at the appropriate time it would halt any drift away from the national perception that the Palestinians embodied. Indeed, Arab tensions were to reach other peaks when Sadat, without due regard for the sensitivities of his Saudi benefactors, travelled to Jerusalem in November 1977, participated in the Camp David meetings in September 1978, and signed a treaty with Israel in March 1979. The Egyptian's vision was too much for even the Saudis, who now became disaffected. Nevertheless, the interlude following the 1973 war had provided the first glimmering that, even with the complexities heaped on the Arabs by their unusual approach to nationalism, the differences between their states and their nation need not be irreconcilable after all. With power and policy, and with a new inclination on the part of some Arab leaders to reflect such factors rather than just to romanticize about Arab history, the thought of movement toward greater political satisfaction was no longer unrealistic. To predict success along the lines suggested here would still be imprudent, but at least a new way of achieving national objectives had emerged and had seized the imagination of many Arabs.

3

The Psychic Limits
of Negotiation

An often ignored aspect of negotiation is the psychological bounds within which it occurs. In dealings among Western countries, negotiators on both sides of the table operate with many of the same assumptions derived from similar cultural backgrounds. Individual and national outlooks that influence negotiating postures do not constitute unusual problems. Beyond Western Europe, considerable attention has been given to the effects of the psychic dimension on our relations with the Russians. George Kennan was one of the first to make an effort to explain such factors in "The Sources of Soviet Conduct" (*Foreign Affairs,* 1947). Since then Robert A. Goldwin, Adam Ulam, and Hendrick Smith have added their interpretations of Soviet diplomatic behavior.[1] With regard to China, Robert Lifton and Stanley Karnow have done similar work.[2] As for Arab conduct, Morroe Berger, Sania Hamady, and Raphael Patai have approached the matter of Arab psychology in general ways.[3]

It is indeed dangerous ground on which to tread. Many readers have considered the results of these efforts at explaining Arab psychology as being demeaning and superficial. There is always the risk of depicting a sterotyped *Homo Islamicus,* that creature of some orientalists' imagination who stands several cuts below Western mankind and is incapable of change in response to normal social stimuli. Nevertheless, Arab reaction to Western diplomatic initiatives cannot be fully appreciated unless the psychological factor is considered. Consequently, I will proceed, not with support from an array of scholarly sources, but quite frankly, on the basis of attitudes that Arabs have expressed to me and forces that my experience has shown to be significant in shaping the dynamics of political relationships between Arabs and Americans across national lines. In an admittedly selective fashion, I will consider various aspects of the Arabs' response to the great powers; and in a practical vein, I will attempt to provide material for answering two questions: When we approach Arabs with the traditional techniques of adversary diplomacy, how can we expect them to react and what are the sources of their response? In a final analysis, what does the Arab reaction tell us about the manner in which we can successfully negotiate in the Middle East?

Arab Weakness

The Arabs' perception of any relationship with a great power is shaped by their longstanding condition of relative weakness. The meaning of Middle East politics has always been conceptualized within a European political framework rather than in terms of the interests or the will of the people of the region itself. At the end of the eighteenth century, the European balance of power was linked to control of the Middle East land bridge from Europe to Asia and Africa. Similarly, domination of the region was believed by Great Britain and its various intermittent allies to be critical in preventing Imperial Russia from gaining the military advantage associated with access to a warm-water port. Somewhat later military occupation of Arab lands was viewed as necessary for safeguarding the communications links of the British Empire. Subsequently, in relation to Cold War containment policies, the issue was the West's requirements for military bases in support of regional defense.

Arabs also suspect that for close to a thousand years Western powers have been responding to an underlying theme of protecting Christian populations and religious places in the Middle East against the transgressions of Islam—a notion that strikes an antagonistic chord within the context of Arab national feelings. Even today Western concern for the region appears to the Arabs as a combination of the emotional and the material, with the United States assuming a commitment to assure Israel's survival as a Jewish state and simultaneously attempting to guarantee the flow of Persian Gulf oil that has become so vital to the economic growth and well-being of the West.

Whenever Arabs have taken an adversary stance against the West, they have invariably lost. In response, they have quite often seized on Western adversity with relish or attempted to concoct victory from actual defeat. Both attitudes have served only to emphasize their impotence. Early in World War II many nationalistically inclined Arabs—including Anwar Sadat—cheered Axis success only to have Germany and Italy ultimately defeated. In 1956 Arabs rationalized a victory for Nasser in the Anglo-French-Israeli attack on Suez from the necessity for the aggressors, under American and Soviet pressure, to relinquish their conquests. All Arabs knew, of course, that the Egyptian Army was virtually annihilated while the enemies' losses were insignificant. Along the same lines, the demise of any Arab regime friendly to the West has also been seen as a national victory. The overthrow of the Hashemite monarchy in Iraq in 1958 is a case in point. The demise of the Shah of Iran in February 1979 in a neighboring Muslim but non-Arab country was viewed in the same light.

The Arabs' ineffectiveness in their perpetual struggle with the West was vividly dramatized in 1967 when Nasser thought he could inflict great injury on his antagonists by refusing to clear the Suez Canal after the Israeli seizure of Sinai. An Arab could reason that perhaps the dislocations created for Western economies by the loss of access to this vital waterway would be sufficient to cause the United States and Europe to see the Arab point of view on the Middle East. As the situation developed, Western dependence on the canal, and therefore on Arab goodwill, proved to be fiction. Western technology rose to the occasion by building the supertanker that sailed around Africa, leaving Nasser, his strategy, and the canal high and dry. No doubt the greatest source of confusion has been Soviet arms, the acquisition of which was mistaken by the Arabs for an existing trained military force. The arms, however, could prevent neither the defeat of Arab armies at the hands of the Israelis in 1956 and 1967 nor the ultimate ability of the Israelis to seize large areas west of the Suez Canal and beyond the Golan Heights in 1973.

Even the union of Egypt and Syria as the United Arab Republic in 1958 was bitter fruit. Rather than an act of self-assertion, it proved to be a makeshift arrangement between two governments that were separated by a basic difference over an esential ingredient of Arabism—the place of individual initiative in public life. Dissolution of the union in 1961 only accentuated the fragmented state of Arab relationships and seemed to belie the very existence of an Arab nation.

Despite the fervent desire of Arabs to be masters of their destiny, the end result in each of these incidents appeared to be beyond the control of the people and governments of the Arab East. The frustrating thing for the Arabs was that, throughout all the tension and struggle, Western interests somehow continued to be served. Because of their weakness the Arabs had been compelled to generate hope by structuring favorable signs from symbolic rather than from tangible evidence of control and power. Impotence led the Arabs to see national achievement in events that brought little more than short-lived exhilaration, events that did nothing to change the Arab condition.

In 1973, the October War did not wholly follow this pattern. It is true that by the time the cease-fire was established Israeli forces were in control of the situation on both fronts. They could have destroyed the Egyptian Army's effectiveness had hostilities continued. Nevertheless, true to their practice of the past, the Arabs interpreted the outcome as a victory. When compared to earlier Arab-Israeli conflicts, the Arab performance was indeed better insofar as the Israelis had initially given ground and had suffered disastrous losses in planes and tanks. At least in terms of the size of their population, it had been necessary for the Israelis to incur heavy casualities in order to turn the tide of battle. It could be said, therefore, that the Arabs had at least tasted Pyrrhic victory on the battlefield. In addition they had demonstrated power through the exercise of the oil embargo. When considered together, these two aspects of the October War made the situation something different from the past. In the minds of the Arabs and their antagonists, the possibility of victory was now projected into the future. Henceforth Israel and her supporters would have to take account of Arabs who could inflict such a level of pain on an enemy. For the first time since the armies of Muhammad Ali had marched from Arab lands into Anatolia in the 1830s, Arabs showed evidence of possessing power.

Anwar Sadat characterized the new mood with his assertion, "The October War is a dawn that is breaking over every inch of the Arab World."[4] Typical of the Arab outlook was the comment of the then influential journalist and one-time confidant of Nasser, Muhammad Hassanein Haykal: "The Arabs discovered that they were not as weak as they thought."[5] Various Arabs interpreted the willingness of Sadat, Faisal, and even Assad to try for a negotiated settlement as a new outlook born of the October War. Haykal observed, "The Arabs had overcome their inferiority complex and [were] . . . ready to enter negotiations because they were sure for the first time of being able to influence the shape of the solution."

Many Arab officials saw the situation in terms similar to Haykal's. "Before the war the Arabs were weak and frustrated," one said. "Negotiations could not have been suggested without provoking a violent reaction from the Arab people."[6] The October War was also given credit for changing Arab official behavior. One delegate to the conference of kings and chiefs of state held in Rabat during October 1974 noted a decrease in the strident ideological expression of those who habitually attended these gatherings. "The focus is now on practical ways of achieving the desired ends. When Israel seemed invincible and the Arabs powerless, [we] . . . resorted to rhetoric." Another delegate, obviously savoring the new Arab importance, pointed out that a year earlier Europeans would never have noticed such a meeting in Rabat, whereas now the open plenary sessions were carried on live television in many Western capitals.[7]

The Western Essence of Israel and Politics

The significance of the change in attitude that seemed to emerge from the experience of the war was that the Arabs themselves recognized that they had a new outlook that contrasted sharply with their feelings of weakness and ineffectiveness of the past. This difference served to call attention to the conditions under which Arabs had heretofore related to the non-Arab world. Nothing demonstrated the nature of the Arabs' attitude better than their interpretations of Israel and international politics. First, Israel has not been just a state having strong ties to the United States and somewhat more tenuous relations with Great Britain, Germany, and France. According to the Arab view, Israel was meant from its very inception to embody a Western presence within the region which could serve as a means for frustrating the realization of Arab purposes whenever these were injurious to Western interests. The circumstances of Israel's founding, from the Balfour Declaration to the Truman policies, combined with the high level of official and private support that continues to pour into Israel from the United States, have been used to substantiate this essentially Arab interpretation of history. Israel's preemptive attack in 1967 and the longstanding Israeli practice of escalated retaliation as retribution for incursions by Palestinian guerrillas were seen until quite recently as being dictated from Washington. They have been accepted as evidence of evil Western designs rather than as a defensive posture by Israel toward Arab hostility.

At the first meeting of the Arab kings and chiefs of state following the October War, this view was set forth in the concluding communiqué. Israel's expansionist actions were portrayed as taking place within "the framework of imperialist strategy." Relations between Israel and the West were described as an "active complicity" of economic, technological, and military support for Israel from the imperialist countries, and above all from the United States. The danger constituted by Israel was equated with "a serious resurgence of the colonial system and its methods of domination and economic exploitation."[8] A mark of Kissinger's success in his shuttle diplomacy was, in fact, his ability to dissuade Sadat from this view. "My talks with Dr. Kissinger convinced me," Sadat said on one occasion, "that he rejects the simplistic notion of some of your strategists who see—or saw—Israel as the American gendarme in this part of the world."[9] The underlying problem for the Arabs has always been that Israel depicted in this light stood as a symbol of the inability of the people of the Middle East to control the fortunes of their own region.

The relative weakness of the Arabs' position has had another important effect that has influenced their perception of the West over the years. It has nurtured a popular belief in a hidden hand that works incessantly against them. No doubt Western influence exercised in a surreptitious manner has played a role in the contemporary Middle East. Under the mandate and during the period of British control in Egypt, the European powers had little difficulty operating through client politicians to penetrate and influence the workings of almost every indigenous political, economic, and social institution. Indeed, outside powers have used furtive and sometimes questionable means to effect political outcomes. But for many years now this capability has been much more limited than many of the politically conscious Arabs who subscribe to such a view could ever imagine.

The idea of a mysterious power working in some evil way can, of course, be derived from the omnipotent forces Arabs associate with their faith. More directly, the perseverance of the belief has stemmed from outward evidence of Arab ineffectiveness. The Arab charge is not just the old vacuum theory that weakness constitutes a circumstance that invites outside meddling. Rather, the Arabs assert that the meddling takes place in order to assure the continuation of a weakened condition that allows outsiders to achieve objectives that do not serve the people of the region.

As a result, Arab politics are characterized by a tendency to overinterpret, to see all kinds of hidden meaning in seemingly innocent and unrelated events. Innumerable suspicions are voiced and avidly believed whenever politics are discussed in the Middle East. It was the Americans, for example, who supposedly precipitated fighting between the Lebanese Christians and the Palestinians in April 1975 in order to further weaken the Palestinian claim to legitimacy, thereby denying them a place in the Geneva negotiations. Another claim is that somehow the Israelis were behind the assassination of King Faisal a month earlier. Arabs who subscribed to this view could reason that Faisal, after all, was a powerful figure who controlled the flow of oil, maintained the convictions of an Arab nationalist, and refused to compromise on control of Old Jerusalem. He stood in the way of the realization of Western interests. During 1976, when Assad saw advantage in restraining the Palestinians in Lebanon, a move that inadvertently served Israeli security interests, many Arabs became convinced of a grand design by which Israeli Prime Minister Rabin, Kissinger, and the Syrian leader intended to shape the future of the Middle East.

Essentially, therefore, outsiders are treated in a friendly but wary fashion. After years of association between an American and an Arab, for example, a question may still arise about the American's intentions. It is not that these intentions are always seen as being bad, but are they really what he claims? In a diplomatic sense this outlook translates into a basic objective of denying influence to those who would bend Arab policy to serve extraneous purposes. Positive formulations of the programs of Arab states are sometimes sacrificed for action that will frustrate Western intentions. Several times Arabs rejected American proposals for developing the Jordan River Valley because these plans called for tacit cooperation with Israel. Arabs can never fully embrace the possibility of working with outsiders for some mutual advantage lest it constitute a ruse while the underlying intent of the outsider's proposal is to injure Arab national purpose. Viewed from abroad, this tendency is interpreted as negativism by many Americans and Europeans.

The outsider who signals a desire to resolve a basic issue through negotiations, therefore, has little opportunity to escape Arab accusations of foul play if untoward events occur while negotiations are underway. Looking back on a series of negotiations that were not brought to fruition many Arabs are not inclined to see a simple and straightforward failure resulting from an inability to achieve an accommodation of interests. Instead, they often suspect that the negotiations were not for the stated purpose at all. Malevolence is attributed to the other side, which is accused of entering into negotiations to cover some hidden objective, generally seen as dividing the Arabs. The accusation of failure to deal in good faith is common in any negotiations between the Arabs and an outsider on matters that touch national sentiments. This attitude was evident in the Arabs' response to Kissinger's efforts during 1975 to negotiate an agreement between the Israelis and Egyptians over Sinai. Kissinger was finally able to get his agreement, but not without bearing the accusation of having worked consciously against Arab national interests.

Almost parenthetically, it is necessary to mention another dimension of the Arabs' sense of weakness—one that is more subtle than their feelings of inferiority when in direct association with the West. It is the inclination to be eclectic in their politics. Few observers grasp the significance of the negative influence of the Arabs' eclectic view. Eclecticism constitutes the practice of always borrowing ideas. It implies measuring your accomplishments by some alien standard of achievement as if the necessary criteria were not to be found in your own society. In the Middle East it dates to the late eighteenth century, when the Ottoman Turks, after experiencing defeat at the hands of European armies, began to emulate the West in order to overcome a comparative weakness on the battlefield—first by adopting Western military equipment and organization and then by following the West in production practices and education. The same outlook was assumed by the Arabs when they confronted the West outside the context of the old Ottoman Empire. The inclination to borrow was evident in the readiness with which Arab leaders embraced early twentieth-century liberalism. It was apparent again in their reaction to the failure of liberalism in the 1930s and early 1940s. Many Arab nationalists conceded that they modeled their attitudes after Germany and Italy during this period.

Gamal Abdal Nasser took pride in saying that his approach to politics was eclectic. The concept conveyed the idea, not just of borrowing from abroad, but also of the power to reject, thereby giving the actor a sense of control over his environment. Nasser did not seem to see that to be eclectic was also to be uncreative in that environment. Constantly selecting and mainipulating thoughts that are already well formulated leads to piecemeal political ideas devised from extraneous social prescritions. Within Arab politics, ideas are usually set forth as ethical imperatives—a means of giving them local coloration and social power through a device that is compatible with Islam. Quite often, therefore, it is in Arab leaders' professions of strength that feelings of weakness can be detected. Eclecticism gives much of Arab politics an ephemeral quality that is accentuated by the phenomenon of public affairs proceeding simultaneously on the levels of the nation and the state. Each interferes with the other, and a continuous stream of events derived from a single conceptualization is difficult to follow.

Cultural borrowing and the use of trial and error when established practices prove ineffective are totally acceptable techniques of innovation. But when a people that is otherwise satisfied with its societal values adopts new practices from an adversary—principally for the purpose of fixing a parity with that adversary—difficulties can arise. (Adopting values in this way recalls the old admonition against fighting a man on his own ground.) The Arabs indeed have had a disadvantage that induced a feeling of weakness, and when eclecticism spread beyond military organization and equipment to encompass modes of production and education, the feeling reached into virtually every aspect of Arab life.

In Response to Force and Threats

The Arabs' sense of their own weakness creates monumental obstacles for a negotiator attempting to establish mutualities on which an agreement with outsiders might be reached. The fix in the Arab mind is that because of this weakness, the West is always prepared to use force to achieve its purposes in the Middle East. The Anglo-French attack in 1956 and the landing of American troops in Lebanon in 1958 substantiate the Arab view. A less publicized incident of a similar nature occurred in 1963 when fully armed American fighter planes flew missions along the Saudi-Yemeni border at the time of Egyptian and Saudi intervention on opposite sides in Yemen's civil war. The purpose of the missions was to deter and even interdict Egyptian planes that had been bombing Saudi border villages from which supplies were being sent to the Yemeni Royalists. Measured by these events and by the Arab assessment of Western intent, one can accept Nasser's sincerity in his totally erroneous accusation at the time of the 1967 war that American pilots participated in Israeli attacks on Egyptian airfields.

The United States did not, of course, employ force during the time of Kissinger's intercession in the Middle East, but force was threatened in the American reaction to the oil embargo as well as to ascending petroleum prices. At the time the embargo was imposed in 1973, Kissinger alluded to the possibility that the United States might respond with unspecified countermeasures, adding that the United States was not "a total prey" to outside pressure. On this occasion, however, the American secretary of state revised his position when shortly thereafter he dismissed as "essentially an academic question" the possibility raised by Secretary of Defense Schlesinger of American public opinion demanding that the United States use force if the embargo were carried too far.

In July 1974 Kissinger had again taken a somewhat threatening stand within the confidentiality of diplomatic channels when he instructed American ambassadors to countries that held membership in the Organization of Petroleum Exporting Countries to inform the governments that the United States was "restless" over increases in petroleum prices. President Ford himself hinted at using force when he addressed the World Energy Conference in Detroit in September 1974. Throughout history, he noted, nations had gone to war over natural advantages such as water, food, and convenient passage of land or sea. Within the setting selected for this remark, it was probably clear to everyone, including the Saudi minister of petroleum in the audience, that interruption of oil shipments to the West was clearly indicated, if not specified, in Ford's list of reasons for resorting to force in the furtherance of national objectives.

All these statements had passed unchallenged by the Arabs largely because of the mood in international relations at the time they were made. During most of 1974 everyone had been preoccupied with Kissinger's success in negotiating the disengagement of forces in Sinai and Golan. But by the end of 1974, observers were growing apprehensive over the complexities of achieving some accommodation between Israel and the Arabs that would do more than simply separate their military forces. For Kissinger to succeed on his second round of talks, longstanding convictions would have to be changed and real concessions made. While engaged in the rather slow and tedious business of positioning participants so that negotiations could commence, Kissinger had turned his attention to the oil problem and had dramatized its seriousness on various occasions with pessimistic pronouncements regarding the threat high prices constituted to world economic and political order.

At this point the option of using military force as a solution to the oil problem began to be discussed by university professors, business leaders, and news commentators. Rhetoric sometimes replaced straightforward expression of concern as when a *New York Times* feature writer pointed out that the option of using force was being considered only because no immediate political or economic measures could promise to stop the financial hemorrhage in the industrialized countries caused by the quadrupling of oil prices. Policy makers felt equal despair, he contended, over alleviating the effects of a new embargo that was certain to be imposed in the event of resumption of Arab-Israeli hostilities.[10]

It was in this atmosphere that Kissinger commented during a magazine interview in December 1974 that he would not say that there were no circumstances under which the United States would not use force in response to the actions of the oil cartel. "But it is one thing to use it [force] in a dispute over price," Kissinger said; "it's another when there is some strangulation of the industrialized world."[11] In a way, Kissinger's statement was unnecessary. The Arabs were fully aware that the West was prepared to use force. History had taught them that much. They also knew that quite often otherwise repugnant action was preceded by intellectual rationalizing in its defense. For many Arabs the development of such justifications was viewed as one of the functions of the Western intellectual community. Perhaps nothing was more telling about Arab-American relations than the manner in which the threat incident had unfolded.

Common sense would seem to indicate that any suggestion for

using force to secure petroleum supplies would center on action against Venezuela, Nigeria, and even Indonesia, all of which were more accessible to attack than the countries bordering the Persian Gulf. From the American standpoint such sources would have been sufficient to guarantee the 6 million barrels of oil it imported daily. But Kissinger's academic speculation was directed toward saving the entire industrialized West from economic strangulation. Consequently, sources of oil outside the Middle East would not have been enough, and the Persian Gulf would also have to be controlled if total demand was to be covered.

But even within this region, various magazine articles on the subject appearing at about the same time as Kissinger's statement concentrated on the Arabs. In one case an author foresaw direct military action by the Americans to seize oil in Kuwait, Saudi Arabia, and Qatar. There was no talk of seizing Iran's oil. In fact, another article had the forces of the shah of Iran sweeping through the same area helping American armies secure Arab oil.[12] Clearly the Arabs were regarded as a more fitting subject for these aggressive flights of fancy than non-Arabs, even though Venezuela, Nigeria, and Iran had pressed the hardest for higher petroleum prices. The non-Arab countries, of course, had not participated in the embargo; that is, they had not related oil to a specific political issue such as Israel.

Some Arab leaders had thought that they were developing a close relationship with Kissinger, and quite naturally they felt consternation at his threatening remark. Even the moderate Cairo press asserted that the statement indicated that the United States could not be thinking clearly about the relationship between oil and a political settlement in the Middle East. A series of official responses from Arab governments was also forthcoming. Referring obliquely to the possibility of the Arabs' being prepared to provide better terms on oil in return for American support for Arab political objectives, a Kuwaiti cabinet minister observed that in relation to the West's oil imperative, whatever could be achieved by force could also be had in a cheaper and more peaceful way. Picking up the theme of Arabism, Algeria's Boumediene declared that the occupation of one Arab state would be regarded as an attempt to

occupy the entire Arab world. All other OPEC countries responded
by rejecting military threats against oil exporters. As a whole, however, the organization refrained from adopting the Algerian suggestion that any perpetrator of aggression against a member state
should be subjected to a worldwide oil embargo.

It was clearly the Arabs who felt the most threatened—a heritage
of their past and a reflection of their longstanding contention with
the United States and Israel. In no Arab's mind could Israel be
separated from oil. Kissinger's threat was somehow specific in spite
of the general nature of its expression. Whatever the intention of
the secretary of state, the Arabs' sense of weakness had been heightened. In this regard Sadat's comment was perhaps the most
poignant. Referring to Kissinger's statement as regrettable, Egypt's
president said that in the face of an imminent military threat the
Arabs would destroy their oil wells. While Sadat's assertion might
have suggested an effective means of dissuading the United States
from seizing the wells, it was a strategy born of weakness. As an
Arab, Sadat could see no possibility of protecting the oil. Only
in the destruction of their own source of wealth could the Arabs
inflict injury on an aggressor. Sadat's was a response that all Arabs
would prefer had not been necessary.

Kissinger and other Ford administration spokesmen attempted
to abate Arab fears and suspicions, principally by drawing a
narrow definition of economic strangulation. They did not, however, refute the possibility of using force. In a subsequent television
interview Kissinger said, "No nation can announce that it will let
itself be strangled without reacting, and I find it difficult to see
what people are objecting to. We are saying that the United States
will not permit itself or its allies to be strangled. Somebody else
would have to make the first move to attempt the strangulation. It
isn't being attempted now."[13]

Despite Kissinger's disclaimer, talk of using force was more than
idle speculation. Some attention had obviously been given to the
prospect by officials in Washington. Schlesinger and his military
advisors affirmed the feasibility of using force. Intelligence community assessments disputed the assertion that Arab attempts to
destroy the wells in the face of an attack would succeed. Modern

technology was held forth as a nostrum that could have damaged wells back in operation in a matter of days.

The Arab reaction made it clear that Kissinger's threat— however mild, hypothetical, and circumscribed—was a blunder. The response was not what he had wanted. No one ever doubted Kissinger's astuteness. For that reason observers were somewhat surprised that he had shown so little regard for Arab sensitivities on this issue. It was even more puzzling because on a previous occasion he had made the same mistake and had drawn the same negative response from the Arabs. In October 1973, when he negotiated the cease-fire between Egypt and Israel, Kissinger had been emphatic about the absolute necessity of avoiding any situation in which forces armed with American weapons (the Israelis) would appear to be less capable than those armed with Soviet weapons (the Arabs). Here was a reflection of global concerns of the great powers in regional affairs. From Kissinger's standpoint, high costs for the United States had been involved in the early Arab military success of the October War. The Israeli loss of 700 tanks and 150 planes was a blow to American military prestige. It could give encouragement both to the Soviet Union and to clients whom the Soviets had armed. It could influence the power considerations of various Third World states and be injurious to American international arms sales. A United States objective in the Middle East, therefore, was to see that the incident did not occur again.

The issue had some immediacy in November 1973 after the cease-fire. The Egyptians had massed virtually all available firepower around the Israeli salient west of the Suez Canal. Had hostilities resumed, the Egyptians were determined to make it a real contest. Whatever an objective assessment might have indicated about the situation, the Egyptians believed that they had a good chance of driving the Israelis back across the canal. Subsequently, officials in Cairo were to contend that the major Israeli casualties had not occurred in the initial Egyptian attack, nor even in the Israeli counterattack in Sinai. Rather, they took place in the fighting west of the canal. By no means did the Egyptians believe that they were in the desperate straits depicted in the American press, particularly after the suspension of the fighting on October 22 had allowed them time to regroup. Nevertheless, in pressing his point, Kissinger made much of the plight of the Third Egyptian Army, which was still trapped in Sinai, and he tied its extrication to Sadat's accepting the American stipulations for a cease-fire. By implication he was saying that otherwise the Israelis would be permitted to destroy the Egyptian force.

It was the wrong tactic to use with Arabs. Sadat interpreted Kissinger's position as an ultimatum, and he would not permit the Third Army to be used as a hostage. What ensued was perhaps the only tense and dissonant session between Kissinger and the Egyptian leader. Kissinger had interjected a threat into the negotiations and Sadat had bridled. It was conceivable that Kissinger, who prided himself on being attuned to the attitudes of others, might have fallen into this difficulty once, but to do so a second time as he did with his remarks in the magazine interview in December 1974—after a full year of dealing with Arab leaders—was indeed strange.

Kissinger's difficulty over the Third Army amply demonstrated that the conceptualization of the use of force in politics among the great powers does not serve the same purpose in a great power's relations with former colonies and client states. Kissinger's assertion that no nation could allow itself to be strangled made it clear that power was the essence of his thinking. Commentators pointed to statements from his days as a scholar that verified this characterization:

> If recourse to force has in fact become impossible, diplomacy too may lose its efficacy. Far from leading to a resolution of tensions, the inability to use force may perpetuate all disputes, however trivial.[14]

> As statesmen have become increasingly reluctant to resort to war, negotiations have become more and more ritualistic.[15]

Unlike the nuclear politics of ultimate destruction, no issue associated with United States diplomacy in the Middle East ever becomes discrete. For the Arabs, everything is related to everything else in a totally real world, and all diplomacy is viewed accordingly. The nuclear diplomacy to which the West has become accustomed in great-power politics takes on the abstract characteristics of gaming, largely because no single individual can truly grasp the meaning of nuclear war. It is much like the chessboard war and diplomacy of the seventeenth and most of the eighteenth centuries, when the principals neither experienced nor comprehended personal injury from their exercise of power. Within this milieu, diplomatic relationships are often defined by the West without full regard for all the factors that are at work in any set of circumstances.

For the Arabs the situation is different. How many Americans, for example, appreciate the problems of isolation faced by an Arab leader while negotiating with a Western statesman? From the Arab viewpoint abstractions do not prevail, particularly with regard to the problem constituted by Israel. The Arabs see the use of force by an outside power in the same concrete way they view their politics. They place the prospect of force in a totally tangible melange of past and present relationships. This practice precludes outsiders from using a hypothetical threat in order to win a point through elegant diplomacy. Any action by an outsider has a number of ramifications for the Arabs. While the perpetrator of a threat may intend only to alter Arab perceptions on a single issue, all sorts of spinoffs result from it. Diplomatic concepts that depend on the nuclear age's balance of terror have not been effective in dealing with Arabs because Arabs recognize no balance between themselves and the West.

In the modern era, therefore, Arabs have been poor subjects for psychological warfare or pressure tactics. The esoteric nature of the signal conveyed by Kissinger's threat fell outside the context of the Arabs' social reality. They interpreted it differently from the way he meant it. Actually, there has been little reason for the Arabs to adjust their behavior in the face of a threat. Within their own intimate and vivid image of the social and political environment in which they live, the benefits of acquiescence have been offset by an assortment of related negative effects. Conceivably, compliance with a threat could lead to even more demands within the complex of the Arabs' relations with outsiders. When confronted with force the Arabs have known that, because of their weakness, they would have to bear certain losses and indignities. But their strong sense of being a nation has prevented them in the past from accepting the alien reality that the outsider always seemed to be attempting to establish through threats and force.

Because of what amounts to the negative self-concept that Arabs sometimes assume when placed in the position of measuring relative strength with the West, they do not respond to threats from abroad. They know that they cannot win anyway, and as a result they tend to become immobile when confronted with a threat, almost as if they are in a state of conditioned helplessness. Threats of force by an outsider can have only one purpose within the Arab context—they are meant to be carried out in the knowledge that whatever gains are realized by the outsider will in all probability have to be maintained by the continued application of that force. This approach, in fact, has always characterized the Israelis' response to relations with their neighbors. The Arabs, therefore, can cite real application of the principle involved in a threat even while the principle seems quite hypothetical to the American, who makes the threat in the first place. The Arabs' attitude has begun to change since the development of the oil weapon has given them a counterforce.

Another factor that has contributed to the Arabs' defiance of threats is the mood both in international forums and among the informed and politically effective populace of the very countries that would suffer from being deprived of Arab oil. In 1974, at the time of Kissinger's utterance, the United Nations and the Western public displayed a moral sense that favored the weak whenever they defied the powerful. This outlook may have served as a restraint on the power brokers who looked approvingly upon the suggestion that force be used to secure the industrial countries' oil supply. An American army general alluded to this attitude when commenting on the possibility of seizing the oil wells: "We could do it all right, but would the country [United States] stand for it?"[16]

It can perhaps be seen as a credit to Secretary Kissinger's flexibility that thereafter he backed away from his threats of force. In testimony before Congress he set aside his strangulation analogy and linked the use of military force to some condition that would otherwise require American surrender. On a subsequent visit to the Middle East he publicly stated in response to a Saudi Arabian query regarding American use of force, "I would like to state categorically here that our relationship with Saudi Arabia is based on friendship and cooperation in which threats, military or otherwise, play no part, and we base our relationship on cooperation and not on confrontation."[17] Thus we have seen that the Arab sense of weakness does not allow for an adversary type of diplomacy by outsiders. To the contrary, the use of threats is counterproductive.

The Threat of Kissinger's Multilateralism

As an outgrowth of their sense of weakness, Arabs generally have not accepted the assumption of equality in negotiations with Western powers. Acutely aware of the West's potential for military, political, and economic action in any confrontation, Arab leaders have always contended that in entering negotiations with the West they face someone wielding vastly greater power than they themselves can command. One example of the frustrations of this inequality was the maddening situation prior to 1955 when the Arabs were dependent on their very tormentors, the United States and Great Britain, for military supplies. Negotiations over arms were a farce as long as the Americans or British could decide unilaterally not just whether to extend or to deny arms to the Arabs, but also the conditions under which any arrangement would proceed.

Equality among participants in any negotiations implies that all have options, including the choice of not entering into an agreement at all. It suggests that each participant has the opportunity to reject a proposal put forth by a counterpart in negotiations without being made to suffer undue privation. Or if privation is to be experienced by participants in unsuccessful negotiations, it will be shared. Perfect conditions of equity, of course, never exist. International politics is in fact devoted to seeing that whenever possible the scales on such matters are tipped against one's adversaries. In great-power politics of the nuclear age, however, everyone is allowed the minimal facility of a plausible and peaceful way out of any situation that becomes totally unbearable.

The problem for the Arabs has been an almost total absence of

viable options to the terms determined and offered by the West or
by Israel. In the Arabs' mind these terms have usually been intolerable. The distribution of privation has been consistently against
them. During the 1950s, it was not the West but only the Arabs who
suffered when the arms talks failed. When Nasser refused to accept
the Western proposal for regional defense, John Foster Dulles had
an alternative—the Baghdad Pact. At the same time, Nasser's
choice, the Arab Collective Security Pact, was ignored as if it did
not exist. Israel's longstanding insistence that the claims of the
Palestinians be settled by the Arabs themselves, or after 1967 that
any Middle East settlement permanently incorporate the Golan
Heights, Jerusalem, and the West Bank into Israel, also left the
Arabs without options. The difficulty of the Arabs, of course, is that
they have never had the power that normally affords alternatives to
a player at international politics. The one exception prior to 1973
occurred when the Arabs, in defiance of the West, acquired arms
from the Soviet Union. But even with the arms, the Arabs knew that
they were no match for the West in a military contest, even when
Western power was applied only through Israel.

The Arabs have always been sensitive to Western maneuvers
that maximize the West's power in its relationships in the Middle
East. The most common practice has been for the West in concert
to face an Arab leader acting individually. Implicitly, therefore,
Western proposals for multilateral consideration of a problem have
always incorporated a threat. Such was the case of the 1950 Tripartite Declaration on arms supply in which the West as a group
dealt with Arab states one at a time. The same practice was attempted with the MEDO defense plan and the Baghdad Pact.
Another multilateral proposal from the West was Dulles's 1956
Suez Canal Users Association. Again just prior to the 1967 war the
United States suggested a conference of ocean-shipping states, this
time to consider the freedom of passage through the Straits of
Tirana after Nasser declared the straits closed to shipping bound for
the Israeli port of Elath. From the Arab standpoint neither of the
initiatives on waterways amounted to anything other than stalling
tactics preceding surprise military attacks, and in 1956 such an
attack came in the form of a direct Western multilateral conspiracy
among Great Britain, France, and Israel.

In recent years the Arabs have seemed to favor multilateralism insofar as they have advocated for some time now a solution to the Middle East problem that would be imposed by the great powers. After the 1973 war they also pressed for French and British participation in any resumption of the Middle East Peace Conference that was to be orchestrated by the United States and the Soviet Union at Geneva. It would be a mistake, however, to generalize from these instances or to predicate a firm Arab approach to peace from what amounted to negotiating strategy. In fact, the Arabs have never supported multilateralism in the tradition of concerted Western action for achieving some purpose that the Arabs as likely as not could only equate with imperial objectives. The Arabs' proposals for great-power participation in Middle East politics have been specific and have had plenty of safeguards, a matter that will be considered fully in chapter 5, where we examine the limitations within which Kissinger was compelled to work as mediator. For the present we will explain how Arabs see Western multilateralism and why they resist it.

Events surrounding the marketing of oil following the 1973 war were to highlight the problem that a collective Western approach has always constituted for the Arabs. Immediately after the opening of hostilities in October 1973, the Arabs imposed an embargo on all oil shipments to the supporters of Israel, as well as a 5 percent monthly incremental reduction in production until such time as Israel evacuated the occupied territories and recognized the rights of the Palestinians. The intentions of the Arabs were clear. Sheikh Yamani, the Saudi minister of petroleum affairs who rapidly became the Arab spokesman on matters pertaining to oil, was solicitous of the West's fear of economic recession and unemployment in the industrialized countries for lack of oil. Yet Yamani said, "I am sorry, but we want your people to become concerned about our problem of enormous territories illegally occupied by Israel, and the fate of two million Palestinians who are forced to live in cold tents in the desert."[18] Sadat referred to the embargo as "a message to show the whole world that the Arabs after the 'Sixth of October War' deserve to take their place in the sun."[19] When the Arab producers finally lifted the embargo in March 1974 under conditions far more accommodating to the position of the United

States and Israel than those originally stated, they reiterated that the interdiction of oil shipments had been an effort "to draw the attention of the world to the Arab cause in order to create a suitable political climate for the implementation of Security Council Resolution 242"—that is, they wanted Israel to withdraw from the occupied territories and to accept some resolution of the problem of the Palestinians.

For the first time the Arabs themselves had acted effectively in concert. Because the production cutbacks were never more than 10 percent and because the embargo on most countries was lifted quite rapidly after their governments indicated support for the Arab position, the full force of the oil weapon was never tested. With the Arabs controlling 40 percent of free world production and 55 percent of known reserves, it was clear, however, that the international economy was highly dependent on Arab cooperation. Henceforth a new dimension might be added to relations between the West and the Arabs with both power and negotiating options more fairly distributed.

Actually, the embargo was a relatively crude use of the oil weapon. In December 1973 the world was to witness a much more dramatic development when oil, which just two years earlier had sold at $2.59 a barrel, was auctioned in Tehran at $17.40. A new set of international trading relationships was signaled for Western Europe and Japan. Both depended on the Arabs for about 80 percent of their petroleum products. The United States was better off. About 65 percent of its consumption was from domestic wells and only a third of the imports could be traced to Arab sources.

Following the shock of the Tehran auction, prices settled to $10.50 per barrel.* As long as this figure prevailed, the West could see a massive transfer of wealth into Arab, Persian, and Venezuelan coffers. Early estimates indicated that at this price, and with existing levels of petroleum consumption, oil would, by 1985,

---

*By June 1979, this figure had climbed to $18 with premiums raising the price of high quality and easily accessible oil to as much as $23 per barrel.

generate holdings for petroleum exporters of perhaps $600 billion, a figure that was later to be adjusted downward. Apprehension developed over how the exporters might use these resources. They would be earned in Western currencies and probably all amounts in excess of outlays for current imports would be maintained in Western bank accounts, equity, or property. Earnings of perhaps $20 billion annually would accrue to Saudi Arabia alone, $7 billion to Kuwait, and about $50 billion to the Arabs as a group. At this level, monetary earnings are not just claims on wealth; they constitute power. Discomfort was added to the Western position when the oil producers, through the Organization of Petroleum Exporting Countries, closed ranks to maintain their new advantage with an effective cartel arrangement. Multilateralism now seemed to be on the side of the Arabs working in cooperation with other Third World oil producers.

The situation provided all oil producers—particularly the Arabs, who had the largest balances in excess of current account—with an almost unconscionable opportunity to influence Western currencies, financial institutions, and perhaps even equity markets. Moreover, wealth was a medium through which the West could not easily counter Arab influence without damaging the free market system that provided the foundations of the European and American economies.

The response of the United States was consistent with the tradition of Western postwar multilateral diplomacy. With the outbreak of hostilities and the imposition of the embargo, President Nixon took a position that was ultimately dubbed "Project Independence." The United States was to opt for high-cost energy autarky in an effort to establish self-sufficiency in petroleum by 1980. On more careful consideration, the objective of the plan was changed to being "less reliant" on foreign oil and the date for achieving this goal was revised to 1985. Despite heroic rhetoric, the chimerical nature of the scheme was revealed by the somber assessment of geologists who reckoned that, even with the likelihood of many new oil discoveries in areas under U.S. jurisdiction, it was improbable that we had enough domestic oil still undiscovered and economically producible to meet more than a part of future American demand. At best, accuracy in predicting petroleum projections is illusive. Nevertheless, even in its revised and less ambitious form, Project Independence was unrealistic. What then was its purpose?

At a distinguished gathering in London in December 1973, Kissinger gave the answer when he proposed that a union of consumer countries form a energy action group that would formulate joint plans for conserving energy, developing new domestic oil supplies, and coordinating research. Kissinger's suggestions were made just prior to the escalation of oil prices. By the time the invitations were extended by President Nixon to Canada, Japan, and the six major European countries for a conference to be convened in Washington in February 1974, the full implications of the situation were clear. The American call for consumer action warned that the energy crisis "threatens to unleash political and economic forces that could cause severe and irreparable damage to the prosperity and stability of the world."[20]

Once again the Arabs were faced by the West in concert, and they were fearful. Along with other oil producers they saw multilateral action as the powerful industrialized countries "ganging up." Through their spokesmen the Oil Arabs warned that such an approach could provoke reprisals. Arab suspicions had been heightened by the tightly prescribed nature of the list of those invited to the Washington conference. It was virtually the same alliance that faced the USSR. Conflict was inherent in Kissinger's stance. Serving as the spokesman of the Arab oil interests, Sheikh Yamani warned that if the Washington conference was aimed at producing a confrontation, he foresaw trouble. Algeria's Boumedience characterized the American proposal as an effort to reestablish a new protectorate or condominium over the Arabs' raw materials, and he vowed to fight all such attempts.

Arab feelings were partially the result of Kissinger's failure to discuss his multilateral approach with Arab leaders before announcing the conference. He made his London speech, in fact, while en route to the Middle East. The Arabs could only wonder whether the timing of his remarks was meant to maximize the implications of Western power in his subsequent talks with the Arab leaders concerning a settlement with Israel. Kissinger firmly denied that his plans contained the seeds of confrontation, but when the Washington conference convened, the French representative pointed out that whatever the intent of the United States government, the Western powers were in fact inviting OPEC hostility by appearing to claim an exclusive position in defining new relationships on petroleum. M. Jobert cautioned other participants at the conference to avoid all attempts at establishing or imposing a new world energy order.

Kissinger's efforts resulted in the formation of a twelve-nation Energy Coordinating Group that in turn drafted a charter for the the new International Energy Agency. The purpose of the new organization, which came into being after seven months of negotiations among the Western countries, was to administer a program for reducing the industrial nations' dependence on OPEC oil and for taking policy measures that would create a downward pressure on petroleum prices. The group was also to devise oil-sharing arrangements in the event of another embargo.

Next, in November 1974, Kissinger unveiled his "safety net" proposal, a $25-billion facility from which member countries could borrow in order to retain financial and monetary stability when faced with an adverse balance of payments resulting from exorbitant oil prices. The fund would assure that, as oil producers recycled their earnings back into Western financial institutions, allocations would correspond roughly with the Western countries' payments for oil on a country-by-country basis. In return for this protection participants would agree to reduce their dependence on oil imports through consumption cutbacks and would follow responsible policies that avoided restrictive trade measures in any adjustments to the new international conditions. In this regard also, Kissinger displayed a power bias insofar as he objected to financing oil debts through the new "oil facility" of the International Monetary Fund to which the oil producers were lending and in whose affairs they were consequently having a voice. In announcing his proposals Kissinger set the tone he saw as appropriate for the West's position: "It is our liberty in the end that is at stake, and it is only through the concerted action of industrial democracies that it will be maintained."[21]

The birth of the new energy agency might have gone unnoticed had President Ford and his secretary of state not made simultaneous statements that had all the earmarks of an attempt to create a crisis atmosphere. For his part, Ford warned that "exorbitant prices can only distort the world economy, run the risk of worldwide depression and threaten the breakdown in world order and safety." Kissinger was somewhat more blunt when he told the General Assembly that existing prices were not based on economic factors but on "deliberate decisions to restrict production and maintain an artificial price level. . . . What has gone up by political decisions can be reduced by political decisions." Without price changes, Kissinger concluded, the United States could not help the Saudis or the Iranians develop their economies.[22]

The response of the oil countries was quick in coming. The Saudis protested officially. As a non-Arab offended by Kissinger's remarks, the shah of Iran warned, "No one could wave a finger at us because we could wave back."[23] It was Boumediene who captured the essence of the Arabs' legacy of weakness. In a lengthy letter to United Nations Secretary General Waldheim, the Algerian president contended that certain large industrial countries had launched a veritable offensive against the oil-exporting countries. He portrayed conferences of oil consumers acting in concert under the cover of coordination as a strategy to recover economic advantage at the expense of the Third World. Attempts to use economic and political power to dictate prices were reminiscent of the darkest days of colonialism. Such aggressiveness created perplexity, Boumediene said, mixed with a certain apprehension for the cause of international peace and justice. Moreover, it betrayed a determination on the part of the industrialized countries to continue the practice of cornering resources that belonged to other peoples.

The meaning of the OPEC pricing cartel for former colonies and client states can be appreciated only against the backdrop of Boumediene's words. Cartel members started from the assumption that gross inequity had always existed in their relations with the West. They were determined to protect their new position, which came closer to a just distribution of the world's wealth and perhaps eventually its power. Western statesmen did not always grasp the nature or intensity of feelings over oil prices. It was not a matter of resources but of justice. National independence was involved. From the Arabs' perspective of weakness, the cartel was not so much an offensive as a defensive mechanism that could provide a shield for uncertain Arab, Persian, or Venezuelan representatives during exchanges with the West, much as the Arab summit agreements had given cover to Sadat and Assad within the context of Arab-Israeli negotiations.

Kissinger's insistence on establishing the International Energy Agency, coupled with his remarks at the United Nations about the political origins of price increases, revealed his assessment of the situation. If it were simply a matter of economics, he could have followed a course similar to that of the French, who emphasized export promotion and worked for a healthy balance of payments through *bilateral* trade with the oil countries. Instead, Kissinger viewed unrestricted bilaterial competition among Western countries as "ruinous" and maintained that no single country could solve the problem by itself. For Kissinger the issues were those of power—forcing a reduction in oil prices in order to decrease the claims on wealth acquired by the oil producers and then establishing mechanisms that would permit the industrial countries to control the flow of oil earnings into Western banks, companies, and property holdings. In order to have power it would be necessary for the West to follow a unified policy in facing the oil producers.

Quite naturally, the Arabs saw the advantage for themselves in a series of bilateral arrangements. Bilateralism would help assure that they were not overpowered by the extensive technical knowledge and organizational skill of the industrial giants. It meant independence. In every Arab there was still the sense of weakness expressed twenty years earlier by Gamal Abdal Nasser when he opposed the West's regional multilateral defense proposal: "They [the Western powers] would have all the weapons. They would put forward the plans, and the rest of us would say, 'Yes Sir.' "[24]

Thus the dimensions of the struggle were defined. Kissinger hoped to unify the industrial consumers, who would follow common guidelines in dealing with the producers individually. The oil exporters, on the other hand, wanted to maintain the cartel pricing arrangement formalized through OPEC while allowing each producer to conclude bilateral deals within the limits set by their common purpose of assuring good prices. In effect, the game was that of each group working to maintain its solidarity and power while forcing the adversary countries into the fragmented and weak condition of competing with one another under bilateral agreements. In terms of conventional free market thinking, the issue was whether a consumers' or a producers' market was to prevail in the sale of petroleum products. Once again it was a matter of who was to have the negotiating options.

Kissinger's purpose was to encourage a market-induced decline in the consumption of OPEC oil throughout the industrialized nations. This approach required solidarity and determination. Unfortunately, these attributes were noticeably lacking among the Western consumers. France had failed to join the Energy Coordinating Group from the outset, and Norway declined full membership in the International Energy Agency. All European countries seemed to be pushing ahead on bilateral trade with the oil producers. At the very time that the charter for the new energy agency was being drafted, the European Common Market established a permanent joint commission with the Arab League for the purpose of enhancing long-term economic development and trade—all on bilateral terms.

A meeting of the finance ministers of the United States, Japan, West Germany, Great Britain, and France—called to coincide with the announcement of the International Energy Agency—ended without results when the European representatives decided the time was inappropriate for any action on oil prices. Responding to the American call for support of Kissinger's policy by instituting a 15 percent reduction in oil consumption, the British chancellor of the exchequer alluded to America's "waste of energy," which placed the United States in a different position from his country. The 10 percent retrenchment that had already taken place was all Britain could bear.

It is almost needless to point out that, in addition to following a relatively independent approach on oil purchases, all European countries disassociated themselves from Kissinger's remarks in December 1974 regarding the use of force to assure the West's oil supply. They uniformly denied that any danger of economic strangulation existed. Except for the United States, the industrialized countries did not want to participate in power politics or to risk precipitating an international crisis. With American prestige and through international conferences Kissinger could create the form of Western unity, but he could not create its content. Yet he persevered. His intention seemed to be the structuring of a Western consumer's alliance—however passive—with a set of relationships that exemplified power. His single hope was that in time, or when a crisis occurred, the Europeans would respond accordingly in spite of themselves.

But one question remained unanswered. If the Europeans were bearing the principal burden of the increase in oil prices, why was it the United States that stood alone and so far ahead of its allies in responding to the new situation in the petroleum market? One explanation was that the American stance was really aimed at freeing the United States from Arab pressures in order to maximize its bargaining potential in the Arab-Israeli negotiations. For the Europeans the new situation was tolerable; for the United States, it was not. The Arabs could reasonably conclude from Kissinger's behavior that the commitment to Israel was more important to the United States than any relationship with them, even when oil was inserted into the equation. Many Arabs wondered whether Kissinger's approach to oil marketing did not have more to do with assuring a continuation of the traditional domination of the West in the Middle East than with worldwide economic stability.

For Arabs, Kissinger's stance involved another problem based on the supposed avaricious nature of oil producers. Implicit in his outlook was the assumption that they did not have the discipline to conduct their affairs for very long on the basis of multilateral policy. Even though the oil producers seemed to be doing better than the West at the multilateral game, American strategists were calculating that, if demand for oil decreased and supply again exceeded demand, the oil producers would break ranks, abandon the cartel, and reduce prices unilaterally to engage in price competition with one another in order to maximize individual sales of oil to the West. In effect, Kissinger's strategy would have them grab for immediate advantage rather than work for the long-range group interests of all OPEC members. This attitude toward African and Asian peoples was very similar to attitudes existing at the height of nineteenth-century imperialism. For many Arabs it typified a lack of respect. They perceived that Kissinger did not intend to deal with them as equals. The element of power politics embodied in his multilateral approach could not be concealed. The apprehension over negotiations with the West appeared to be justified, at least in the minds of Arabs.

While maneuvering within the free market was satisfactory for Kissinger's strategy of depressing oil prices, it did not fit his grand design of explicitly defined relationships for an American version of world order. As early as the Washington conference he had proposed a meeting of oil consumers and producers to discuss prices and marketing practices. For their part, OPEC members could also see advantages to be derived from multilateral discussions. Their problem was the inflation that plagued the industrial countries. In 1974 inflation had cost the oil exporters perhaps 15 percent of their earnings as the currencies they accepted for their oil steadily lost purchasing power. This record was to be repeated in 1975 and was to continue. The petroleum exporters could compensate for these losses only by continuing to increase oil prices. In January 1975, when the OPEC members agreed to freeze prices temporarily, they had indicated that after September 1975 they would again raise the price of oil to compensate for up to 90 percent of inflation.

But continuous price increases were not satisfactory, and everyone appeared to have reasons for favoring multilateral discussions. As a means of assuring clarity in the issues and interests that would be raised at an oil conference, the United States proposed limiting participation to the Organization of Petroleum Exporting Countries and the International Energy Agency, with France also represented. Surely, an American diplomat could reason, these two groups commanded sufficient power to resolve the question of world oil prices, particularly with the Soviet Union taking an inconsequential role in international petroleum trade. At variance with the American approach was the OPEC proposal—supported by France and to some degree by other industrial states. According to this plan, representatives of some developing countries that did not produce oil would also be invited to a consumer-producer meeting. As oil importers they too were influenced by the international petroleum market, and under the pressure of higher prices their balance of payments situations had become precarious. Brazil and India were suggested for this role.

In terms of world economic stability the OPEC proposal made sense, but from the standpoint of political power it was detrimental to the West. If developing countries were included among representatives of oil importers, the interests of the importers would have to be interpreted in terms of a broad common denominator that did not exclusively represent the interests of the United States. The group would include countries that had customarily seen themselves on the opposite side of the power equation from the industrialized West. Consumers would not be able to speak with one voice. The force of Kissinger's arguments would be diluted by the necessity to consider factors for which the industrialized countries had little concern. In addition, the contrast between the consumption patterns of the West and those of the developing countries would highlight the waste, or at least the conspicuous consumption, of the former in its energy use. To the extent that attention focused on this matter during the proceedings of any conference, an invidious comparison could only embarrass the West and weaken its bargaining position.

The attitude of the oil producers was curious and even anachronistic. By insisting on the presence of the developing countries, they had indicated a lack of appreciation for their new and powerful position. They still viewed international politics as being the weak countries of the Third World, including the oil producers, facing the omnipotent imperialist West. In effect, the oil producers, including the Arabs, had rejected Kissinger's invitation to become partners in power. A conference of consumers and producers of oil never occurred.

The Arabs were to accept Kissinger's mediation of the Arab-Israeli problem, and through his negotiations the balance in Arab politics was to shift heavily toward more intricate ties with the West. But the interplay over oil was to demonstrate the complexities of the relationship. The nuances of Kissinger's conduct were not lost even on the moderate Arabs. Most of them could not and did not throw themselves into the American embrace.

In almost every respect Henry Kissinger's petroleum policies failed, largely because they were based on considerations of power that the world was not prepared to support. The Arabs opposed them because Kissinger's ideas would have stripped the Arabs of policy options in negotiations. The industrialized countries resisted them because Western Europe and Japan preferred to seek accommodation through bilateral trading arrangements. Finally, the American people were indifferent to them. The Ford administration could not demonstrate that a critical threat to the American economy that was beyond our control had arisen because of the new conditions in the petroleum market. The petroleum crisis boiled down to a matter of higher fuel prices, and there seemed to be sufficient surplus income in the hands of most American institutions and individuals to cover these in one way or another. Where then was the basis for Kissinger's oil policy? It was still far into the future. Unlike the case of his mediation of the Arab-Israeli dispute, on matters of oil he was not attuned to the political and economic environment in which he was operating.

Arab Reliability

More than Kissinger's inclination for power politics is revealed by an examination of American attempts following the 1973 war to achieve a Middle East accord and simultaneously to arrive at a new understanding on the marketing of petroleum. The American attitude included a continued questioning of the Arabs' reliability. The problem was not so much one of Arab intent or behavior as of Western perception. Western powers in their relations with Arab countries often seek assurances that cannot be provided under the conditions of insecurity and instability that prevail in Middle East politics. Any proposal that ignores this reality is difficult for Arab leaders to understand, and when they fail to provide the assurances sought by the West, prejudgments regarding Arab reliability are seemingly confirmed.

To a large extent it has been the Israeli viewpoint, reinforced with official interpretations by Western governments, that has shaped the popular American outlook on the Arabs. The transnational ties that ordinarily support a sympathetic view of one nation for another have not existed between the United States and Arab countries in the same way they have with Israel. Our narrow official experience has nurtured a generalized conclusion about Arab character that is often quite disparaging. Some of this sentiment no doubt has historic roots in the cultural differences that have been revealed since early Western incursions into the Ottoman Eastern Mediterranean. The upshot of the situation is that for a long time Arabs have been cast as an uncomplimentary stereotype in the popular American imagination.

During the negotiations that followed the 1973 war, evidence of the American attitude was ample. Nixon's Project Independence was part of it. While the United States was officially declaring the necessity of being independent of Arab oil, an upward trend was occurring in the degree of U.S. dependence. Our own petroleum production was decreasing. Non-Arab sources of oil no longer sufficed, and we were importing increasing and substantial amounts from the Arabs in order to sustain our industry. The best that could be said for the official United States position was that it reflected a certain incongruence; it signaled an absence of trust in Arabs as trading partners at the very time the American economy was becoming more dependent on them. The difficulty with the American policy during the Nixon and Ford administrations was that no shortage of oil existed, and the Arabs consistently offered to provide for American needs as long as they themselves were not threatened. Free market institutions responded accordingly, but the United States government continued to reserve its position.

Kissinger himself was one of the first to raise the question of Arab reliability when he said of the oil embargo that failure to end restrictions in a reasonable time "would be highly inappropriate and would raise serious questions of confidence in our minds with respect to the Arab nations with whom we have dealt on this issue."[25] The secretary of state was referring obliquely to the understandings he and the president thought they had reached with the Arab leaders for lifting the embargo; but he was also impugning the legitimacy of the Arabs' position.

Popular questioning of Arab trustworthiness took a variety of forms. A general fear was voiced that the Arabs might "overcompensate" because of their bitterness regarding the past transgressions of the West and seek retribution by steady increases in the price of petroleum products. In addition, a conflict over petroleum production schedules was foreseen, pitting the long-range welfare of the producing nations that might wish to conserve their exhaustible resource against the immediate demands of the industrial consumers whose well-being rested on its lavish use. At times commentators implied that the Arabs did not have a social conscience. Shmuel Yaari, director of the Israeli School of Petroleum Studies, asserted in a leading America daily that the real issue between the Arabs and the West was not Israel at all but whether "seven million desert Arabs could rightfully determine the level of petroleum production for the world at large."[26]

The question of Arab good faith was also raised with regard to the billions of dollars paid to the Arabs for petroleum and then recycled to American and European financial institutions. Noting the potential that bank deposits gave the Arabs for disrupting Western economies, even Kissinger asked whether the Arabs did not have a "money weapon" as well as an oil weapon that they could use against the West. The issue for Kissinger was the "enormous unabsorbed surplus revenues" that jeopardized the functioning of the international monetary system. The radical decline of the dollar on the international money market and the increase in the price of gold were said to be due to the movement of petro-dollars from one currency to another as much as to indigenous inflationary pressures in the American economy. It was also asserted that the tumbling of the British pound to historic lows in December 1974 resulted from the rumor that the Arabs would henceforth not accept sterling in payment for oil.

In neither case could evil motives be traced to the Arabs. Certainly the dollar was having difficulties prior to the oil crisis. Ultimately the incident over the pound proved to be a generalization inferred from narrow negotiations between Saudi Arabia and the Arabian American Oil Company (Aramco). The report was erroneously afforded credibility by the decline in the flow of petrodollars into British institutions and the resulting inability of Great Britain temporarily to cover its balance of payments deficit.

The questioning of Arab good faith was not limited to the issue of oil. It was also a major theme in the Israelis' justification for retaining territories they had seized in 1967. The paramount consideration of the Israelis had always been security, and like the Western powers, on this matter they sought a level of assurance from the Arabs that did not exist in this highly turbulent part of the world. This quest for assurance led them to reject Sadat's pledges at the time of Kissinger's March 1975 attempt to arrange an interim solution over Sinai. Israel wanted the formalities of nonbelligerency—a public commitment that would separate Egypt from the other Arabs in their common struggle for national rights. Sadat was prepared to offer the essence of nonbelligerency as long as it was called something else. The word raised the emotional issue of capitulation for many Arabs, and Sadat feared that its use would threaten his Arab identity. The Israelis saw deceitful intent lurking behind Sadat's position. Their underlying assumption over the Arabs' attitude toward peace was more difficult to veil than that of the United States over the Arabs' posture on oil, but essentially the question was the same: Could the Arabs be trusted?

As in so many of the West's relations with the Arabs, substantial psychological barriers accentuate existing differences. Sensing their weakness, confronted by outside powers that have always been prepared to achieve their purposes by using force, and rejecting the alleged equality of diplomatic exchange as a myth that only conceals the cruel facts of their subordination, the Arabs have had a tendency in their relations with the West to proceed with mental reservations. Certainly a careful scrutiny of relationships of the past century raises more questions regarding European and American reliability than about that of the Arabs. More often than not the very reservations the Arabs harbor because of this history are seen by outsiders as the absence of trustworthiness.

From the Arab position, if they cannot work their will with regard to their own future, they can at least frustrate Western purposes. Thus the Arabs' contribution to the disjunction in relationships has been their expression of a desire to inflict on the West the same psychic hurt that Europe and the United States have heaped on them over the years. In the West, we might interpret the Arabs' wars, their guerrilla raids on kibbutzim, and the oil embargo as an effort to force us to make political concessions on Arab national issues. There is, in fact, a basis for this supposition. But there is also another side to these events. If Israel could not be defeated, it could at least be denied the security it has always coveted. If Western influence could not be expunged from the region, Western countries could be denied both satisfactory regional defense arrangements within the context of the Cold War and a comfortable position from the standpoint of easy access to Middle East oil. The real difficulty is not some special Arab potential for treachery. It is an image that the Arab sense of weakness has reflected into Western perceptions, an image of Arabs seeking equality through the only means that in the past has been available to them—through the equalization of hurt.

The question of trust as it existed after 1973 was not one-sided. The legions of American and European business representatives who traveled to the Middle East in search of the petrodollar, as well as the flood of proposals these entrepreneurs left behind in Arab offices, contributed to a high state of confusion. Arab officials themselves were uncertain about the intentions of the aspiring contractors, and it was not uncommon for them to ask an American or European friend, "How do we determine whom we can trust?" Sheikh Yamani raised the subject in a talk to three hundred American officials and business executives when he informed the audience that the Saudi government would insist that American concerns competing for business in Saudi Arabia enter into joint ventures and contribute to the capital of development projects. In this way the sheikh hoped that the Saudis could ascertain that "you have an interest with us."[27]

The West and the Arabs have different problems in relating to one another. The question in the mind of the Arab constitutes a positive formulation aimed at selecting the best Western partners for economic and social development. The West's perception levels a blanket indictment of the most negative sort against the Arabs as a people. This point has never been missed by the Arabs themselves even though it is seldom discussed. It has become an integral part of their desire for respect and appreciation by all outsiders who approach their society.

Within the limits of the Arab-Israeli problem no one really had an occasion for assessing Arab reliability during Kissinger's diplomacy. Israel remained on guard and the United States demonstrated its support of the Jewish state with a massive supply operation during and after the 1973 war. The Arabs were given no opportunity to demonstrate trustworthiness. Syria and Egypt did renew the mandate of the United Nations peace-keeping force that served as observers along the Golan and Sinai cease-fire lines. This step alone signaled that the Arabs were content to give mediators a chance at arranging a peaceful settlement. But the doubts persisted. Detractors tried to depict the Arabs' refusal to enter into financial arrangements with American and European concerns doing business with Israel as anti-Jewish discrimination. Black humor came into its own as cartoons depicted heavily robed desert sheikhs ejecting someone named Finkelstein from a responsible position in an American or European corporation in which they had just purchased the controlling interest.

Much was also made of Sadat's decision to proceed with the opening of the Suez Canal after the failure of the March 1975 negotiations. He acted without Israeli withdrawals in Sinai, but also without permitting Israeli cargoes to pass through the waterway. American spokesmen questioned this decision in view of the understandings Sadat had accepted in January 1974 at the time of the disengagement of Egyptian and Israeli forces. In the American view Egypt was committed to allowing Israeli cargo to pass through the canal, and when it did not, a question of Arab reliability was raised. The Egyptians saw this interpretation as a typical Western abstraction. Sadat had placed the stipulations covering Suez firmly into the circumstance of steady movement toward a final settlement as it had been contemplated at the time of the first disengagement agreement. From the abortive negotiations of March 1975, it was clear that progress was not being made. The passage of Israeli goods, therefore, could not be allowed. The sincerity of the Egyptians was demonstrated within a matter of months when, as part of the Sinai Accord, Israel was afforded the use of the canal for its cargoes.

As this incident showed, Arabs regard action as taking place in a real setting. It was inconceivable that the Israelis be allowed to use the canal as long as a deadlock existed over further Israeli withdrawals in Sinai, and the Egyptians said so. Diplomacy that required any commitment beyond the framework of the assumptions under which that commitment was accepted proved perplexing for the Arabs. Once again Western diplomacy had taken on the characteristics of a game in which one player could structure a situation in such a way that another would be compelled to punish himself. As reasonable as their own attitude appeared to the Arabs, in Israel and the United States it was initially interpreted as evidence that the Egyptian leader did not stand behind his word. And when access to the canal was allowed under conditions the Egyptians understood, no amends were made by American or Israelis for their incorrect assumption about Arab trustworthiness. In fact, the existing doubts were as strong as ever.

Thus we have constructed the psychological limits within which any diplomatic initiative undertaken by an outsider must occur. Proceeding with mental reservations, always ready to overinterpret any small move made by the West in concert, seeing malevolence lightly concealed in the Western position, and dismissing equality at the negotiating table as an illusion, the Arab leaders in their attitude, if not in their intent, embody an obstacle to a general settlement in the Middle East. For its part, the United States has little to gain from continuing to employ threats or from structuring negotiations in ways that accommodate some relative advantage in power that we think we have over the Arabs. Above all else, we must examine and accept the real basis for the lack of trust in Arabs that has become almost a legacy of our relations with them. The results of any negotiations should be assessed in the first instance from the standpoint of success in erasing these images from the minds of Arabs, Americans, and Israelis.

4

The Conflict of Arab and Israeli Legitimacies

At the heart of the Arab-Israeli struggle has been a conflict so deep that each side has literally perceived its national identity as being threatened by the very existence of the other. Those of us who do not have a filial relationship with either the Arab or the Jewish nation sometimes consider one side or the other unreasonable because we do not experience the same sense of nationhood as either of these peoples. But in order to understand the complexities encountered by Kissinger and his successors in mediating between Israel and its Arab neighbors, it is necessary to view the situation through Arab and Israeli eyes and then compare these perceptions with those of the alien reality that is introduced by anyone who attempts to mediate between them. For an outside mediator operating as a trustee of peace to accept the conflicting perceptions of the Arabs and the Israelis as firm and unchanging is, of course, self-defeating. Nevertheless, to err by minimizing the importance of national feelings is perhaps to risk stepping into the path of impending disaster and experiencing the wreckage of months and even years of work devoted to a resolution of the Middle East problem. If we expect the Arabs and the Israelis to change their outlook, then we should have some idea of what we are asking of them. It is necessary, therefore, to probe the national consciousness of both Arabs and Israelis in charting a course toward peace.

The Land of Israel

From the outset of the Zionist movement, its purposes were not very different from the efforts of the anticolonial forces in Asia and Africa whose struggle the world was not to witness until fifty years after the first expressions of Jewish nationalism. The two Zionist objectives were to preserve a special Jewish identity and to achieve for Jews a status of dignity in the eyes of other peoples. An axiom associated with this latter aim was to free Jews from oppression and to shape a Jewish future in distinct and recognizably national terms.

The origins of Zionism are usually associated with Russian pogroms of the nineteenth century. But they are also linked to the prospect of Jewish assimilation into the societies of Western Europe. An early leader of the movement, Theodor Herzl, defined assimilation as "identity of feeling and manners"—clearly the denial of other nationality for those assuming this kinship. Indeed, Herzl saw anti-Semitism as a "national question" that developed as a result of Jewish zeal for maintaining a separate identity within other men's homelands.[1] Zionism is, therefore, a political movement. Its foundations in religious faith do not differentiate the Jews who embrace it from the Arabs who adhere to a nation that also rests on religious assumptions. The result in either case is the fervency associated with a national identity that is premised on God-given principles rather than on the collective pursuit of such individual goals as life, liberty, and property.

Early Zionists tied national dignity to a desire to erase from Jewish identity the derisive assertions of anti-Semitism—to obliterate those features that prompted Herzl to say, "We are what the Ghetto made us." By this Herzl meant Jewish association with finance to the exclusion of other types of economic activity.[2] Thus Zionist rhetoric hoped to remake Jews in another image. It was studded with intentions to establish them as agricultural and industrial workers, with allusions to brawny pioneers, and with the self-assertiveness of such questions as: "If I cannot help myself who will help me?"[3] Jews hoped to control their destinies in a real and vivid environment. The unidimensional image of a Jew fulfilling a specialized and hated role in an alien Western society was rejected, at least within the national ideal. In demanding the respect of the West, Zionists displayed an outlook that was similar to the Arabs'.

An outgrowth of any quest for identity and dignity is the seeking of national expression in a homeland. Zionist purpose could be achieved only within the context of an independent state. Early proponents of the creed asked that "sovereignty be granted us over a portion of the globe large enough to satisfy the rightful requirement of a nation."[4] The Jewish tradition in the Middle East also pointed to the objective of "a home in our country"—which could only mean Palestine.[5] Once the concept of the homeland was established, the Jews were capable of experiencing the suffering of imperialism in the same way as other peoples who have been denied access to or control over their land. Again, the Zionist perspective was no different from that of the Arabs.

The Zionists embraced the idea of a homeland with a totality that gave their movement a mood that can also be compared with Arab nationalism. In order to capture the sense of Arabism it is necessary to return to Muhammad, the prophet of Islam. In launching his movement, he was confronted by two distinct peoples other than his own—the Christian and Jewish communities in the Arabian Peninsula of the seventh century. The distinguishing feature of each was a divine book, and in his search for power and distinction, Muhammad saw an identification with God's revelation as the mark of "a people." However quaint this approach to nationhood may appear in the light of contemporary politics, it is critical to an understanding of Arab society. To this day the Quran has a place among Arabs that cannot be matched by the view of Holy Scripture in the West. As Muhammad perceived inferiority in the absence of a revealed text, so the Zionists saw it in the absence of a homeland. It is not a misplaced comparison to suggest that the idea of the Land of Israel has the same intensity of symbolism for Jews as the Word of God has for Arabs.

In a speech before the United Nations in November 1974, the Israeli representative developed the full force of this theme. "Jewish history," Yosef Tekoah said, "is the saga of a people which has remained one with its land through millenia of independence and foreign conquest, of uprooting and dispersion, of struggle to rebuild its statehood and of final restoration of national liberty. . . . To the Jewish nation, this land [of Israel] has been the very essence of its existence."[6] Historians may be able to rebut this interpretation of Jewish experience. But a rational refutation is unimportant because Tekoah's statement represents Jewish national reality, a controlling factor in any Israeli response to outside efforts at inducing a territorial settlement with the Arabs.

The situation following the 1973 war called to mind a further factor about the Israelis' concept of their land. It was not limited to the territory controlled between 1948 and 1967, nor simply to additional areas that may be necessary in the Israeli view to provide a minimum of security from military attack. Within popular Israeli consciousness is an irredentist feature of desiring to incorporate within the state all territories that constituted the ancestral homeland of biblical Israel. The right-wing Israeli parties of the Likhud coalition have always objected vociferously to any negotiations directed toward the separation of the occupied West Bank from Israeli authority. Such an act could amount only to the alienation of a part of Israel's ancestral homeland. The Likhud took this position in 1974 and 1975 when various options for an Arab-Israeli settlement were being explored through the good offices of Henry Kissinger. As a means of dramatizing their case, Israeli squatters occupied areas of the West Bank to the call of "God has ordered us here" and had to be ejected by Israeli troops. In April 1976, thirty thousand Israelis marched through the West Bank to emphasize Israel's claim to this divinely bestowed area. Such acts could, of course, be attributed to a small radical fringe, but deep undercurrents were astir on this issue. Sentiment over the ancestral homeland was sufficiently widespread that both the Meir and Rabin governments, in order to establish a working coalition in the Knesset, were compelled to pledge elections that would serve as a plebiscite on any plan that called for transferring a part of the West Bank to non-Israeli jurisdiction.

The election victory of the Likhud in May 1977 was not linked directly to popular Israeli sentiment over the West Bank. Nevertheless, the first act of premier-designate Menachem Begin was to visit a Jewish settlement on the West Bank that had been considered unauthorized by the former government. After assuming office, Begin confirmed the legality of three settlements whose establishment had been resisted by his predecessor, and he announced that additional Jews would be allowed to take up residence in the area. Previous governments had been circumspect about their intentions of incorporating occupied territories into Israel. The United States had hoped to keep the matter open because the future of the Arab lands, and particularly the West Bank, would be the crux of successful negotiations over a final peace. Risking tensions with the United States and hostility from the Arabs, Begin took his stand. Plans were formulated under which 2 million Jews would eventually share the area with its Arab inhabitants. What the rest of the world considered the occupied West Bank, Begin referred to as the "liberated" Israeli lands of Judea and Samaria. How, the Israelis asked, was it possible for them to occupy what was already theirs?

Nor is Jerusalem an easier issue to resolve than the West Bank as a whole. Observers such as the eminent Harvard political scientist Stanley Hoffman missed the point when they suggested that predominantly Arab portions of the city could be returned to Arab jurisdiction and the holy places of the three religions centering on the Dome of the Rock—originally a pre-Jewish Semitic high place of worship—could be placed under international jurisdiction.[7] Israelis responded officially to such proposals with the assertion that Jerusalem would never again be partitioned. It is necessary only to recall the scene of Israelis approaching the Wailing Wall for the first time after their capture of Jerusalem in 1967 to grasp the deep emotional sense Jews attach to the city. Faced with a choice, Israelis would probably prefer to surrender Tel Aviv before Jerusalem, and there is not much possibility that such a transfer could be achieved through diplomatic bargaining.

This is not to say that Jerusalem has any less hold over the feelings of Arab Muslims and Christians. The example of Jewish sensitivity cited here is only meant to provide a sense of the difficulties involved in dislodging the Israelis from any part of the city. Israel's national anthem states, "Two thousand years we cherished the hope to live in freedom in the land of Zion and Jerusalem." Like all anthems, that of Israel blends tradition and aspiration. It suggests what the Arabs or outside facilitators are really asking when they press for Israel to relinquish the West Bank and East Jerusalem. To surrender these areas is to abandon the purpose of the nation. Thereafter what would be left—for Israel to change its national anthem? As Kissinger initiated his shuttle diplomacy he faced a far more difficult task than persuading an intransigent Israeli government to take a chance and, for the sake of peace, to relinquish certain territories even though such a step might complicate Israel's defense strategy. At the heart of the matter was a nation that above all worldly things venerated a land of which Jerusalem was the most important feature.

The concept of the homeland has an additional dimension that complicates any effort to achieve a compromise solution to the Middle East problem. In a political sense, the founders of Zionism never supposed that all Jews would migrate to the homeland. That was a religious matter. At the same time, they could not conceive of their nation as being other than Jewish and therefore inclusive of all Jews. Consequently, even the earliest manifestos held forth the objective of binding together the whole of World Jewry and fostering Jewish national sentiment and consciousness.[8] In order to inspire a feeling of national unity among a people who would never live together, it was necessary to sustain the ideal of common habitation as being both possible and the ultimate aim of Zionism. Thus unlimited immigration to the homeland became part of the Zionist pledge. Any suggestion that as an element of Middle East peace the Israelis must suspend immigration amounts to a proposal for establishing barriers among the Jewish people and requiring denial of national expression. The Arabs, of course, see unlimited immigration as the basis for an expansionist Israeli policy. Periodically they have demanded its end as a quid pro quo for Arab acceptance of Israel's existence. Quite naturally, this proposal is characterized as absurd by Israeli officials.

The Israelis have habitually ignored Arab pressures on this matter. Even so, following the 1973 war immigration was impeded, much to the distress of all Zionists. In association with high defense spending, Israeli currency was devalued by 43 percent in 1974; inflation reached 57 percent; and taxation took more than half a worker's income. Conditions in 1975 and 1976 were similar. Inflation was between 35 and 40 percent each year and taxation of one form or another took 70 percent of an Israeli's income. Riots sparked by economic conditions occurred in the streets of Tel Aviv. All this had its impact on prospective immigrants. In 1976, 48 percent of the Russian Jews who were leaving the Soviet Union decided not to go to Israel. Between 1968 and 1973, less than 2 percent had made the same decision. Israelis were stung by the ridicule of the Arabs who asked why all Jews did not go to America. Already, Arab spokesmen pointed out, twice as many Jews lived in the United States as in Israel. Obviously America was the Promised Land.

Indeed the situation was agonizing. Israel was meant to serve the Jewish nation by providing a home for all Jews who were either uprooted or persecuted in their existing environments. Yet immigration dropped from fifty-five thousand in 1973 to thirty-two thousand in 1974 and twenty thousand in 1975. More seriously, in 1974, eighteen thousand Jews (the largest number ever) emigrated from Israel, and in 1975 the number reached nineteen thousand. Net immigration amounted to a scant one thousand. Several hundred Russian Jews were even trying to return to the Soviet Union. Considering the purpose of the Jewish state, this condition created almost as much distress for Zionists as the injury inflicted by the Arab armies in the 1973 fighting. Yet it all served to strengthen Jewish resolve to protect the homeland.

As we look deeper into Jewish national perceptions, we find even greater sensitivities over the efforts of Western countries to push Israel into concessions that would support a compromise solution with the Arabs. In this regard, perhaps nothing in Jewish experience has influenced the national consciousness more than the extermination of 6 million Jews by the Nazis. Although it is a relatively recent event for a people who see their national history spanning three thousand years, this overpowering experience is firmly embedded in the Jewish tradition. All Israelis, and prob-

ably most Jews, agreed with Prime Minister Rabin when he stood
before the shrine at the Bergen-Belsen concentration camp in July
1975 and said, "I am an heir of the Holocaust."[9] The Nazi concentration camps confirmed forever the Jewish belief in anti-
Semitism and attested to the wisdom of Herzl's view that short
of disappearing altogether through assimilation (or genocide),
Jews had no choice other than to seek a land of their own. Herzl
had even been perspicacious enough to see that a major force
favoring Zionist success would be the governments of countries
scourged by anti-Semitism. In order to relieve themselves of the
Jewish problem, he reasoned, these governments would be keenly
interested in helping Jews obtain the sovereignty they wanted.[10]

For that period of contemporary Israeli history during which
the Western World dominated international affairs and fully supported Israel, the future of the Jewish state was characterized by
determination and hope, despite the Arabs' threats. In the 1973
war, however, the Arabs demonstrated for the first time that their
armies could inflict pain on the Jewish nation and that their control
of the bulk of the world's oil could cause discomfort for Israel's
Western supporters. Thereafter images of disaster for the Jews reappeared. The Afro-Asian nations stood resolutely behind the
Arabs in opposing the Israeli presence on the international scene.
Europe wavered in its support, and in return for Arab oil gave lip
service to the "just nature of the Arab cause." Most European
countries had held this position for some time, but they now expressed it openly. Even the United States was urging an accommodation with the Arabs which many Israelis were convinced
would weaken their country's defenses. Jews and Israelis felt alone.
Another catastrophe was no longer unthinkable.[11]

The principal political feature to emerge from the situation was
the reaffirmation of the link between the state and the nation. The
fate of the Jewish people, wherever they might be, was seen as
being irrevocably tied to the Jewish state.[12] The conviction that
the people could not survive without the state was more than
rhetoric. After the long history of the Diaspora, the state had
finally been established with what many considered to be divine
guidance. If that state now failed, what lay ahead for the Jewish

nation? In the prevailing mood of pessimism, many Jews concluded that the demise of Israel would end the Jewish nation as well. It was not necessarily genocide that the Jews faced. Rather, it was the loss of national identity, with most of the individuals who embraced that identity fading into Western life through a form of assimilation that preserved only some minimal form of Judaic religious observance.

A dark side of reaffirming the state was an expression of shame over the Jews who fell victim to the Nazis. No one could forget that they had marched to their grisly fate without resisting. Out of a reexamination of their past the Jews could rightfully say, "Jewish society is today different. It has its own state. It has harnessed its courage to its own existence, and it can speak out and it can fight."[13] From this review and reassertion of national identity, the state assumed even greater importance in Jewish life. It erased the stigma of the Holocaust. The point is that for Jews, national extinction is as horrifying as the genocide of the Nazis, and they can be expected to react accordingly to any proposal for a settlement with the Arabs that would implant in Palestine anything less than the full manifestation of the homeland of the Jewish people.

However complex the relationship of the Arabs with the West, that of the Jews has been even more intricate. It is necessary to keep in mind that Jews have suffered more at the hands of Western society than have Arabs. Without a doubt, the contributions of Jews to Western culture have been of major proportions in science, music, literature, law, and commerce. Nevertheless, the decision was made long ago to opt for the Jewish nation over assimilation. Even though it has been rejected by some Jews individually, this sense of the Jewish nation prevails in Jewish communities throughout the world. As a result, many Jews see themselves as a special rather than an integral part of the West. Although they share its values and intellectual pursuits, they do not have what Herzl referred to as its "identity and manners." One of the great fears of Jewish leaders, in fact, is that a large part of the nation's younger generation living in the United States and Europe will lose interest in Jewish life.

Despite the impulse for a separate existence, Israel has continued to be identified with the West because of its dependence on Europe and the United States for the weapons and economic support that have meant survival. Survival, in fact, has depended on the ability of the Jews to compel the West not only to acknowledge but also to support Israel's right to exist in the form determined by Jews. Paradoxically, at the very time the dependent condition was becoming more evident, the core of Western support for the Jewish state seemed to be dwindling. On one occasion when the ambiguities of the Jewish nation's relationship with the West were discussed, Nahum Goldmann, president of the World Jewish Conference, asserted that, at a time when countries in which Jews live reject Israel's policies, conflicts could arise for the individual Jew. The only solution, he said, was to acknowledge double loyalties and to fight for their recognition.[14] Another view of the situation that developed after the 1973 war should be noted. Some observers have contended that the decline in Western support was not for Israel itself but only for uncompromising Israeli policies. From the standpoint of most Zionists, this distinction had little meaning. Israeli policies were seen as being tied to Jewish national survival, and any questioning of them was tantamount to denying support to Israel.

At a conference convened by Jewish academicians in March 1975 to review the meaning of the Holocaust, a discussion of the state of Jewish-Gentile relations quickly evolved into a consideration of Israel's relations with the West. In the light of changing Western attitudes toward the Arabs, this group concluded that, when confronted with Nazi extermination of the Jews, non-Jews had remained passive because "Jews weighed less than whatever other consideration was taken into account." The possibility was raised that after World War II the West rejected anti-Semitism not because of its evil but because it had accomplished so much in the way of eliminating Jews and therefore Jewishness from Western countries. As they considered Jewish survival, the conference participants saw Israel as its central feature and concluded that "delegitimization of Israel . . . is now equal to anti-Semitism."[15] The conference thereby denied that any difference existed between anti-Semitism and anti-Zionism. The participants seemed to be closing every argument that could be raised over Israel in its existing form. Their message was that, no matter how much difficulty the Arabs' oil weapon caused for the West, Europe and America were inextricably linked to the Jewish nation by the guilt of the Holocaust. For the West the burden was the passive acceptance of the mass murder of millions of Jews. For the Jews themselves it was Herzl's being "what the Ghetto made us" and proceeding to near-extinction at the hands of the Nazis without a struggle.

Even though Israeli feelings of ambivalence, anxiety, and perhaps sometimes even hatred toward the West are engendered by these circumstances, this outlook is not often considered by Western statesmen. Yet these attitudes add immeasurably to the difficulties of any Western negotiator attempting to move the Israelis toward a Middle East settlement. From a Jewish standpoint, the compromise and mutual adjustment necessary for a settlement can be interpreted as the West's insisting that Israel accept risks that could mean national extinction—all to accommodate Western economic convenience. Such a prospect is difficult for Jews to accept. The shared guilt of the Holocaust dictates that risk and privation be equally apportioned. Thus we encounter yet another similarity with the Arab outlook. In the last chapter we examined the Arabs' conviction that in negotiations the West expects them to shoulder most of the burden of privation that exists in any political situation. The Jewish view on this matter is no different.

Had Herzl been a man who developed the full dimensions of problems, he could never have provided the inspiration that led others to carry out his dream of a Jewish homeland. He anticipated the Palestinian question, but he limited consideration of this problem to the necessity of coming to terms with the "present possessors" of the territory of the contemplated Jewish state.[16] He saw the Jews offering numerous advantages to the existing inhabitants of the land to which Zionists would migrate. Jews would assume part of the public debt, build new roads, and increase cultivation. In addition, their presence would expand commerce and benefit adjacent countries. As a scheme of national expression, Herzl's approach was typical of the age in which he lived. It was imperialistic in form, and it did not vary one bit from the arguments of the British and French when they justified the extension of their authority over African and Asian peoples. It is indeed ironic that Herzl defended Zionism in terms of building and development when the Arabic word for imperialism conveys the idea of an outsider asking that things be built.

With regard to Palestine itself, Herzl could not have been expected to foresee that Zionist plans for a single vilayet of the Ottoman Empire would arouse the perpetual hostility of Arabic-speaking people from the Atlantic Ocean to the Persian Gulf. Nevertheless, the Zionist concept was marred by a serious flaw. In their exuberance over the realization of Jewish national aspirations, the Zionists failed to take into account that the "present possessors" of the land they hoped to occupy would also have national desires and that, by superimposing a portion of one nation on part of another, the Jews were creating a problem that might not be amenable to peaceful resolution.

One of the difficulties for Western observers in grasping the essence of the Arab-Israeli problem stems from the limited expression given to the nation-state in Arab and Israeli politics. In the established political system of the European tradition, pressures have been toward the nation and the state becoming coterminous. Efforts to extend a state's control beyond a single nationality usually encounter the cultural or historic limits of conflicting identities and result in resistance to what is seen as imperialism. A government's primary concern is viewed as being properly with the nation that it represents, and only this nation rightfully belongs under its jurisdiction. The contrivance of the nation-state gives Western politics a context for the definition of a state's function not found in the Arab world. Surely, the governments of Syria, Egypt, Saudi Arabia, Iraq, and so on must look after the interests of their respective citizens. But they must also respond to the concerns of the great, overarching Arab nation. Palestinians are part of that nation, and Israel occupies a portion of the homeland. It is not just Israel's policies that are repugnant to Arabs. Nor is the Israelis' conflict of interest only with the Palestinians whom they displaced. Israel by its very existence impinges on the national consciousness of all peoples residing in surrounding countries.

In a manner somewhat different from the Arabs', the Jewish

nation also transcends the boundaries of the Jewish state. Unlike the Arabs, who with few exceptions inhabit only Arab states, 80 percent of the world's Jews do not live in the Jewish state.[17] The dispersed nature of Jews precludes the state from claiming all areas in which they reside. Zionist doctrine has none of the flavor of manifest destiny found in Pan-Germanism, Pan-Turanism, or even Pan-Arabism. But when evil befalls Jews in any part of the world, all other Jews feel a sense of national hurt and believe they can legitimately respond and attempt to redress the situation with whatever influence they may have. Thus we are to witness an American senator (of Jewish faith) informing a Soviet leader that he will oppose the United States government's extending trade concessions to the Soviet Union unless Jews of Russian birth and citizenship are permitted to emigrate more freely to Israel. Here was the act of a Jewish nationalist. Because of the uniqueness of the Jewish concept of nationhood, Jews everywhere are more likely than not to be working for Israel's interests. Quite often Jewish nationalists living outside Israel generate tensions between Arab states and the country in which they reside.

Within Israel itself the concept of the Jewish nation gives rise to monumental problems. Because there is no *Israeli nation,* the three hundred thousand Christian and Muslim Arabs in Israel proper and the 1 million in the occupied territories cannot identify with the Jewish state and do, in fact, adhere to an Arab nation that Israel denies. This is not to suggest that more cohesion will be achieved by Israelis' giving up their ties to Jews living elsewhere. But Israelis should (and many do) recognize that it is their approach to nationhood that precludes their developing a closer association with Arab countrymen who carry the burden of being outsiders in their own land. The question, therefore, is whether a state can survive during the final years of the twentieth century when more than one-third of those living under its jurisdiction find themselves in a position in which they can only deny its legitimacy.

Palestinians: The Symbol of Arab Sacrifice

In the seventy-seven years between the formulation of Herzl's plan and the outbreak of the 1973 Middle East hostilities, the Jews incorporated virtually no change in their thinking on the matter of how Arab nationalism influenced their own destinies. They could not do so, because to recognize the legitimacy of the Arab nation—and its concept of a homeland—would necessarily mean a denial of their own justifications. Conversely, Arab acceptance of Israel would amount to the denial of Arab national aims insofar as it would ignore the Palestinians who—as Arabs—were either displaced by Jews and relegated to a squalid refugee existence or remained within Israel at the sacrifice of expressing full Arab nationality. The Palestinians, through their national loss, have become the ultimate symbol of Arab sacrifice and, therefore, of Arab purpose. What Nazi extermination camps had done for the Jewish nation, the Palestinian refugee camps did for the Arabs. Both peoples sought redemption through strength. For the Jews it was building a pioneer society that ignored the possessors of the land; for the Arabs the symbolic resolve was to compel the Israeli community to accommodate the Palestinians whatever the cost.

Any national symbol imposes discipline on a people who identify with it insofar as it implies their understanding of the nature of political order and illustrates their fundamental political assumptions.[18] Symbols themselves are generally passive. Their power comes from being used by leaders to capture the popular imagination and to create or maintain a national myth. Such was the condition of the Palestinians in the hands of Gamal Abdal Nasser prior to the 1967 war. But using a people as a symbol—or in this case, using a portion of a people for such purposes—involves the danger of that group's becoming active and influencing events in its own right as well as through the power it affords leaders who evoke its image. The period following the 1973 war saw such a transformation of the Palestinians from a disembodied symbol of nationhood to one of the forces that shaped the interlocking commitments that all Arabs impose on one another. The Arab attitude toward a settlement with Israel cannot be understood without a full recognition of the nature of this transformation and the role it gave to the Palestinians in Arab politics.

As early as 1954, guerrilla raids into Israel from neighboring Arab territory were linked to the Palestinians' affinity for the land from which they had been compelled to flee. In January 1964, the

Palestinian identity was given structure through the formation of the Palestinian Liberation Organization amidst the fanfare of the first summit conference of Arab kings and chiefs of state. This meeting had been convened to determine means for preventing Israel from unilaterally diverting the waters of Lake Tiberius. No practical answer was forthcoming. The Arabs simply did not have the power to do anything about it. The impotence of Arab states was only emphasized by the establishment of the PLO at this juncture.

In seeking redress for the many injuries inflicted by Israel, attention focused on the recourse available to a people but seldom to a government—guerrilla warfare. The struggle of the Algerians was supposed to provide an example for how Arabs would proceed against Israel. Much as the Zionists before them, the organizers of the PLO hoped to bring unity and form to a people through their resolve to regain the homeland. The PLO itself was little more than a composite or loose coalition of ever changing political and commando groups. For the PLO the Arab sense of individualism and political entrepreneurship was not just pronounced, it was rampant. Ideology and strategy varied widely from one group to another. Only in their ultimate purpose did the Palestinians agree. They were bent on establishing an Arab political identity in Old Palestine. Palestinian groups were compelled to maintain themselves by soliciting help from one or another of the Arab states. They thereby became clients of the warring governments of Egypt, Syria, and Iraq, which offered just enough support to permit each regime to have some influence within the Palestinian segment of the Arab nation. As far as anyone has been able to determine, the motives of these governments in supporting the Palestinians were tied more closely to the interests of their respective states than to broad objectives of Arabism. The arrangement served only to keep the Palestinians divided.

The 1967 war brought a dramatic change in Arab concepts of leadership and national intent, a change that thrust the Palestinians to the fore. Prior to 1967, Arab nationalists had worked to rid themselves of Western domination and to destroy the power of Western-oriented Arab governments and interests. They also pressed the national cause of the Palestinians against Israel. By 1967, some progress had been achieved on the first two objectives. Defeat at the hands of the Israeli armies proved, however, that Arab leadership, which centered on Gamal Abdal Nasser, was not capable of fulfilling the national goals associated with Palestine. As an Egyptian, Nasser thereupon shifted his emphasis somewhat. He acquired a new objective—regaining the Egyptian territory that Israel had seized in the 1967 fighting. United Nations Resolution 242, which prompted an end to the Six Day War, called for a return of the occupied territories and alluded to the refugee problem, but essentially it ignored the political rights of the Palestinians. In agreeing to this resolution, Nasser accepted Israel's existence. He was clearly giving precedence to the interests of the Egyptian state over those of the Arab nation. His step away from the Palestinian issue was affirmed in 1970 when he also accepted the proposal of Secretary of State William Rogers for a settlement with Israel based on compromise and mutual forbearance. At least in its general statement, the Rogers Plan signaled an abandonment of the Palestinians.[19]

From the standpoint of the Arab nation as defined by the mission of liberating Palestine, Nasser thereupon became anachronistic. Simultaneously, Palestinians who worked through the PLO seemed to be acquiring new recognition. In the months following the June 1967 war, armed Palestinian groups responded to the atmosphere of crisis by increasing their raids into Israeli-held areas. They even attempted—albeit unsuccessfully—to operate from within the occupied territory. Among the population of the West Bank there developed a deep sense of Israeli oppression—the outgrowth of Israeli punishment of Arabs who aided the guerrillas. For the first time there was resistance to the occupiers, and Israeli efforts to overcome it served to politicize all Palestinians.

Under the umbrella provided by the PLO, the various guerrilla units developed a new found sense of tolerance of one another. A small victory in March 1968 over an Israeli force that was staging a retaliatory raid against Karameh, Jordan, and minor successes at interdicting Israeli internal communications, emboldened the Palestinians and enhanced their reputation. Even though Israeli security measures shortly choked off the guerrillas' military potential, the Palestinians were seen throughout the Middle East as actively pursuing the national Arab struggle at a time when the leaders of Arab governments were either quiescent or working for the return of the territory of their respective states. The myth of the Palestinians' power, and with it their dedication to the national consciousness, seized the Arab imagination.

In common with Nasser, Jordan's King Hussein was ready to explore the possibilities for peace with Israel. Also like Nasser, Hussein restricted the activities of the Palestinian guerrillas. Out of frustration the Palestinians launched a campaign of plane hijackings, kidnappings, and shootouts at international airports. Little could be said for their tactics other than that members of the PLO had apparently decided to inflict indiscriminate pain on others until their own suffering ceased. From a somewhat misplaced sense of self-confidence, the Palestinian groups based in Jordan adopted an attitude of swagger and total disregard for Jordanian law. Ultimately, when the PLO challenged Hussein's authority in September 1970, the Jordanian Army proved more than a match for the guerrillas. The PLO was decimated. In what has since been known as Black September, three thousand persons were killed and eleven thousand were wounded, many of them the unarmed occupants of the refugee camps.[20] Subsequently the PLO shifted its operation to Lebanon.

With its activities terminated in Jordan, the Palestinian movement could easily have come to an end while the Palestinian cause once again assumed the status of a symbol to be manipulated by the leaders of Arab states. In most Arab capitals the Palestine Liberation Organization was regarded as an annoyance. The major concerns were to give the PLO a sufficient subsidy to demonstrate support for the national cause and to avoid the embarrassment of having terrorists land hijacked airplanes at the local airport. The Arab leaders had little choice but to offer assistance because the Palestinians were popular with the Arab people. Moreover, the head of state who did not make his peace with the PLO risked being castigated by his fellow leaders in the give-and-take of competition for national leadership.

The Palestinian movement managed to persevere. The debacle with Hussein and the growing alienation from Nasser coincided with an increase in Palestinian popularity and afforded the PLO greater independence. Arab nationalists applauded when the Palestinians asserted that they would not be subservient to any state. Black September destroyed the logic of whatever claim Hussein might have had to the West Bank and mitigated any allegiance the Palestinian people might have felt toward leaders of Arab states. After all, Arab leaders had done nothing to assist the Palestinians when Hussein undertook his bloody repression of their movement.

Within the popular Arab imagination, the Palestinians thereby acquired the characteristics of the Arab nation in its purest form. Certainly at this point they had no state interests of their own, and any to which they aspired were still synonymous with the objectives of the nation. In their political behavior Palestinian spokesmen suffered none of the stigma that many Arabs associate with leaders who carry the self-serving responsibilities of a state. The formulation of the Palestinian issue as a national cause gave Palestinians a unique status. In the national perception, they stood above the law. Their acts of violence were justified in terms of patriotism rather than condemned as outrageous crimes. The burden the situation placed on Arab heads of state was considerable. Thus, after the assassination of Jordanian Premier Wasfi Tel in a Cairo hotel in November 1971 and the murder of an American and a Belgian diplomat at a Saudi embassy party in Khartoum in March 1973, the culprits were eventually released. In a plot against the life of Hussein in mid-1973, the chief instigator was detained only for a short period, and it is safe to assume that others involved did not languish in prison for too long.

Arab leaders literally detested the perpetrators of these acts. Even Yasir Arafat, the leader of the PLO, found them annoying, but if he hoped to play an effective role in Arab politics he had to maintain some semblance of unity within the movement. His objectives could not be realized if he took a strong stand against the more radical elements within the Palestinian ranks. The PLO was not monolithic; it was an umbrella that attempted to coalesce all shades of Palestinian opinion. Unity was more important than discipline.

In their exuberance over the results of the Egyptian and Syrian attack on Israeli forces in October 1973, and particularly because of the sense of power derived from the West's response to the oil embargo, it was only natural for the Arab chiefs of state at their first summit conference following the war to affirm their support for the national cause—that is, the reestablishment of the full rights of the Palestinian people. No objection was raised when Arafat, on arriving at the meeting, declared his organization to be the "sole representative of the Palestinian people." While this self-assumed position was not explicitly affirmed by the chiefs of state at the time, Hussein, who attempted to represent the Palestinians living within the territory over which he claimed sovereignty (Jordan, including the West Bank), did not attend the conference, apparently to avoid a confrontation on the Palestinian issue.

The situation might have remained ambiguous had it not been for Faisal's and Sadat's receptivity to Kissinger's enthusiasm for a Middle East settlement. As part of the general movement toward peace, preliminary talks between Jordanian and Israeli officials were initiated in January 1974 with a view to winning civil jurisdiction for Jordan over portions of the West Bank. At this point, Hussein was purporting to speak for the Palestinians. An early reconvening of the Geneva Conference at which a general Middle East settlement would be considered appeared likely. The United States and the Soviet Union had agreed to make no provision for Palestinian participation in any resumption of the conference. It seemed sensible for the early moves toward peace to be limited to governments. Thus Hussein's presumptions in approaching the Israelis were not totally misplaced.

As painful as it was, the PLO leaders who heretofore had evinced a singular dedication to Arab national claims now had to recognize that Kissinger's exploitation of an Arab optimism resulting from the perceived success in the 1973 war had created new attitudes toward Israel. Intransigence no longer assured success in Arab politics. The Palestinians would have to develop a policy position on a settlement with Israel if they were to avoid being ignored in any reshaping of the Middle East.

Amid bitter splits over strategy, three of the six groups comprising the PLO agreed on establishing a Palestinian Authority in areas of the West Bank and Gaza relinquished by Israel. They also agreed to attend the Geneva Conference, provided the United States and the Soviet Union extended an invitation to the PLO in an identical manner as to other participants and then only if the terms of reference of the conference were amended to include consideration of the legitimate rights of the Palestinian people. Palestinians who could not countenance this implied acceptance of Israel separated themselves from Arafat to form the Rejectionist Front, and they retained as their objective the destruction of the Jewish state. The majority of the PLO leadership, still represented by Arafat, was careful to point out that its new position in no way compromised the movement's opposition to UN resolutions that considered the Palestinian question merely a refugee problem rather than an issue of national self-determination. Arafat and his colleagues still saw ultimate peace only in terms of a democractic secular state in Palestine in which Arabs and Jews would live as equals. At this point Arafat was apparently differing with the Rejectionists only on strategy.

As Kissinger succeeded in bringing even the Syrians into a disengagement agreement, the Palestinians became increasingly apprehensive. By fostering negotiations between Israel and one Arab state at a time, the American secretary of state had succeeded in operating on a bilateral basis. He was thereby circumventing the national issue with which the Palestinians identified. PLO leadership accused Kissinger of attempting to liquidate the Palestinian cause and of using pressure tactics to split the Arabs while "saving the Palestinian issue until the last." Thereupon the guerrillas—with Arafat standing by silently and equivocally—launched attacks against civilian communities in Israel, an action admittedly aimed at disrupting Kissinger's peace mission.

The Israelis showed no interest in the PLO as a negotiating counterpart. Golda Meir said that her government would never deal with Palestinian activists, whom she categorized as murderers. On becoming premier in June 1974, Yitzhak Rabin assumed an equally rigid position. The one hint of concession by the Israelis was the statement of Foreign Minister Allon that his government might not object to Arafat's coming to Geneva as a member of the Jordanian delegation. This suggestion was quickly refuted by Rabin, who asserted that he would not treat with the PLO even if Arafat appeared at Geneva in "Hussein's mask." The rapidity with which the Israelis dropped Allon's idea indicated that the acceptance of the PLO in any form was still an intolerable threat to Israel's own legitimacy. It was a view to be confirmed most forcefully by Menachem Begin when he became premier in May 1977.

Within this welter of confusion Sadat was striving for a position that would get Jordan, Israel, and the Palestinians all to the Geneva Conference. Without Jordan, Israel would be unlikely to negotiate over the West Bank. Without the Palestinians, Syria would probably decline to participate because of the slight their absence would constitute to the national cause. At this point Sadat's and Kissinger's purposes were somewhat askew. Kissinger, strengthened by his success at Syrian-Israeli disengagement, was pressing for Jordanian-Israeli talks on the West Bank. He clearly wanted the Arabs to confirm a negotiating role for Jordan and to set aside consideration of the PLO as a participant in any early moves toward a settlement.

Simultaneously with laying the groundwork for Geneva, therefore, Sadat had to allow for the possibility of bilateral talks regarding the West Bank under the aegis of Kissinger's shuttle diplomacy. The best the Egyptian president could do in these circumstances was to agree with Hussein in July 1974 that Hussein would negotiate for the Palestinians who lived in Jordan, while the PLO would represent those outside the country. The status of the West Bank was not mentioned and thereby left purposely vague. On a previous occasion Sadat had indicated that the legitimate rights of the Palestinians would have to be negotiated by the Palestinians themselves. But in his talks with Hussein the eventual participation of the PLO in a general Middle East accord was left an open question while Jordan's attendance at Geneva was assured. Under this arrangement, responsibility for the West Bank in any agreement with Israel would in the first instance fall to Hussein.

The Palestinians were not prepared to accept Sadat's ambiguities even for the sake of a disengagement agreement that would achieve an Israeli military pullback and the reestablishment of Arab (Jordanian) civil administration in areas of the West Bank. The Palestinian response was quick and sharp. The Sadat-Hussein agreement was castigated as an "Imperialist, Zionist, and Jordanian design against the Palestinian cause"; that is, it favored the interests of an Arab state over those of the Arab nation. King Faisal, who had publicly supported the Sadat-Hussein agreement, was also criticized and his sincerity questioned with the assertion that Saudi assistance to the PLO had been inadequate. The entire affair was seen by a PLO spokesman as another American-inspired scheme for dividing the Arab people.

The most important element that the leadership of Sadat and Faisal had brought to Arab politics was a practical sense of unity. If the moderates opposed the Palestinians openly, they would split Arab leadership, and without a unified position, the thought of successfully negotiating with the Israelis seemed hopeless. It was no longer possible to ignore the views of the Palestinians while using this people as a symbol of Arab national sacrifice. Like it or not, the Arab leaders had maneuvered themselves into a position in which the Palestinians served as the national conscience. Palestinian spokesmen were coming close to acquiring the power to define things Arab.

Sadat had been surprised by the intensity of the Palestinian reaction. He attempted to modify his position by suggesting that his failure to mention the West Bank specifically in his agreement with Hussein carried no veiled meaning. In a practical vein, he asserted that only Jordan would be acceptable to Israel as a negotiating partner. No matter what arrangement was made with the Israelis for the return of the West Bank to Arab control, Sadat said, the Jordanian position would only be that of holding a trust for the Palestinians. In attempting to equivocate, Sadat created new problems for himself. Heretofore Hussein had demonstrated flexibility on the West Bank issue by seeming to have an open mind about such ideas as a Palestinian-administered autonomous West Bank affiliated with Jordan or the possibility of Palestinians joining Jordan's delegation at the Geneva Conference. But now Hussein reacted negatively by refusing to accept Sadat's interpretation of their agreement. Sadat had been unsuccessful in his efforts to straddle the issue of conflicting state and national interests.

The United States did not respond to these developments. With some progress having been made on the Sinai and Golan fronts, a disengagement agreement covering the West Bank seemed to be the next logical step, and Kissinger urged the Israelis to move in this direction. Somehow it was assumed that if Israeli-Jordanian negotiations were initiated, the Palestinian issue could be shoved into the background. If attention were permitted to focus on the Palestinians, on the other hand, the whole negotiating process could lose its flexibility. By talking to Hussein now, the Americans reasoned, the Israelis could possibly preclude further consideration of the PLO claim to authority over any of the occupied territory that Israel might relinquish to the Arabs. The necessity of negotiating with the Palestinians later could thereby be avoided. In reality, by August 1974, it was too late to hope for unified Arab support of a Jordanian-Israeli understanding. The Arab conscience had been aroused. Following the Palestinian attack on the Sadat-Hussein agreement, the Egyptians displayed little enthusiasm for Jordanian-Israeli talks. In late September, Sadat restated his recognition of the Palestinian Liberation Organization as the sole representative of the Palestinian people.

Within weeks of the abortive Sadat-Hussein agreement, Kissinger virtually capitulated on the matter of West Bank talks, clearly the loser in his struggle against Arab nationalism. In a joint news conference held with Sadat in Cairo in mid-October, the American secretary of state feebly defended his preference for negotiations over the West Bank by surmising that Jordan and Israel could still negotiate at any time, but he acknowledged that it was a decision that "must be made by all concerned." For his part, Sadat said that the Palestinians would have to be represented at Geneva.[21] The possibility of Jordanian-Israeli talks short of Geneva was left open, but there was very little possibility that such an approach would result in anything tangible as long as the Palestinians remained influential in Arab politics.

Faisal and Sadat now recognized that their freedom to speak for the Arab nation was limited. Momentum was clearly with the Palestinians, and it seemed quite appropriate to all Arabs for the Arab League to seek inclusion of the *Palestine Question* on the agenda of the 1974 session of the United Nations General Assembly. During the preceding ten years the issue had been incorporated into general consideration of the *Middle East Problem* in such a way that it did not impinge on Israel's legitimacy. This time a new force was at work. The Palestine Liberation Organization in its own right sent representatives to a number of non-Arab countries urging support for the Arab League proposal. At an early session of the General Assembly the Arabs' request for a debate of the Palestine question won easy acceptance, even over impassioned Israeli assertions that consideration of this issue would only deter a general Middle East settlement.

The Arabs were now ready for the next step and immediately proposed that Yasir Arafat, the leader of the PLO, be invited to address the General Assembly as the "representative of the Palestinian people." Some Arab governments were uneasy with this proposition. Sadat could see it destroying the basis for a continuation of Kissinger's initiative in seeking a Middle East settlement. At the General Assembly itself the Jordanian representative pleaded that his government had a special relationship with the Palestinians, thereby implying that through Jordan the Palestinians were already represented at the United Nations. Nevertheless, both Jordan and Egypt supported the Arab bid to bring Arafat to the United Nations. In each case considerations of the Arab nation overrode those of an Arab state.

In a General Assembly vote, 105 members of the United Nations favored Arafat's presence for the debate and 20 abstained. Although the United States had not objected to consideration of the Palestinian issue, it did oppose any step that would enhance the position of the Palestinian leader in the international forum. Joined by the Dominican Republic and Bolivia, the United States and Israel cast negative votes on the proposal. The outcome was particularly bitter and foreboding for Israel. Fifty of the resolution's supporters maintained diplomatic relations with the Jewish state. Israel's sense of isolation deepened. The invitation to Arafat was indeed an unusual move for the United Nations. No nonmember other than Pope Paul in 1966 had even been given this honor, and the comparison of Arafat with the Pope was ludicrous to many supporters of Israel. The Israeli spokesman at the United Nations heightened the contrast with his assertion that the PLO represented only itself—"ten thousand murderers, trained and paid for the slaughter of innocent human beings."[22]

Within a formal diplomatic context, the position of the 105 supporters of the Arab resolution is difficult to sustain. In defense of their stand, it could be said that those who voted in favor of the Arab resolution had concluded that there could never be peace and stability in the Middle East until Palestinian interests were taken under consideration. But the gesture had an additional dimension. The core of support for the Arabs came from former colonies and client states in Asia and Africa. They were seeking a new world order of their own making that would parallel politically the position they were attempting to assume in economic matters when they pressed for greater equity in the distribution of income among countries. The Afro-Asian countries obviously saw the Palestinians' desire for national expression as being legitimate, even to the point of overlooking their politically inspired killing of innocent human beings in terrorist activities. Perhaps the problem was that imperialism had transgressed too long on their own innocence for the former colonies to register disapproval of violence employed in the cause of national self-determination.

Arafat's appearance before the United Nations introduced a new phase of activity for the Palestinians. The PLO leaders apparently concluded that their objectives could not be achieved merely by calling attention to the suffering of their people with notorious acts of terrorism. Emphasis thereupon shifted away from such activities. Indeed, legitimacy seemed to be the objective of the PLO when it opted for a Palestinian Authority in any part of old Palestine evacuated by Israeli forces. Legitimacy moved them to support a Middle East peace conference at Geneva, where they would talk with the Israelis. Any form of recognition from other nations strengthened the Palestinians' position and raised questions about the legitimacy of Israel in the form Jewish nationalists would have it.

More than any other event, the invitation for Arafat to address the United Nations signaled that Palestinians had to be reckoned with. Shortly thereafter, the General Assembly further recognized the Palestinians by accepting their right to nationhood and to their homes and properties in Israel. In this case eighty-nine countries favored the Arab cause, while thirty-seven opposed it and eight abstained. Many observers dismissed the vote as meaningless to any Middle East settlement. It was significant, however, because it demonstrated that, over the objections of the United States, the Arabs had sufficient power in the General Assembly to strip the moral value from those UN resolutions that over the years had relegated the Palestinians to the status of refugees. Two-thirds of the governments of the world at least nominally favored an expression of the rights of the Palestinian people—a position that the Israelis considered totally incompatible with their own interests.

Maneuvering at the United Nations was not the only sign of the Palestinians' acceptance. The PLO received observer status in UNESCO; the French foreign minister met with Arafat; and American representatives admitted that high-level contacts with Palestinians constituted a real possibility. The PLO readily conceded that it was seeking a public meeting with Kissinger. Congressmen and various prominent Americans met intermittently with Arafat or his aides. Following Arafat's appearance at the United Nations, representatives of the PLO were to receive full diplomatic status from scattered states, including India. Only in the Arab League's economic coordination with the European Economic Community did the Arabs fail to gain acceptance of the Palestinian entity. Economics, the Europeans reasoned, was a concern of *states,* and as a people the Palestinians did not qualify for representation in deliberations between European and Arab governments. Nevertheless, even in this case the Palestinians were not turned away. The issue was resolved by having negotiations between two delegations—the European Economic Community and the Arab League—with individual Palestinians taking part.

Increased international recognition of the PLO had two results. In all probability, it strengthened the moderate forces within the organization and moved the leadership toward a political solution —at least as a strategy if not yet as a way out of the Arab-Israeli dilemma. At the same time, it sparked a sudden upsurge in national feeling among the Palestinian people themselves, a development that could only contribute to additional Israeli doubts with regard to the Arabs' ultimate intentions. At the time of Arafat's UN speech, demonstrations occurred for six consecutive days throughout the West Bank. Crowds of Palestinians took to the streets to demand the end of Israeli occupation amid chants of "Palestine is Arab. Long live Arafat!"[23] (During the spring of 1976, when the Israelis allowed municipal elections in the occupied West Bank, candidates who openly favored the PLO were victorious in what was close to a clean sweep.)

From these developments the PLO had acquired the status of a government in exile without having claimed this distinction for itself. To have done so would have splintered the Palestinian movement even further. The radical and ideological forces would have interpreted such a step not just as a move toward legitimacy but as acquisition of the accouterment of a state and betrayal of the cause of the nation. The radicals were particularly sensitive to Arafat's acknowledgment of conventional morality when he established prison camps and threatened to mete out punishment to Palestinians who hijacked airplanes and engaged in acts of international terrorism. To the radicals, a government in exile could only have the purpose of negotiating toward the "partial solution" that many Palestinians abhorred. The establishment of such an identity would accommodate Kissinger's stey-by-step diplomacy. It would serve the purpose of leaving Israel intact, thereby negating the rights of Palestinians to return to their homeland. As it was, the Palestinians were moving toward the norms of international behavior in a way that usually avoided such questions.

Even though the legitimacy of the PLO was gradually being established, the Arabs themselves had not yet formally adopted a unified position on the role of the PLO in international diplomacy. The Israelis had made it clear that they would not negotiate with the PLO. Arabs who wished to proceed toward a settlement with Israel found themselves in a quandary. What formula would permit negotiations and still affirm ultimate PLO control of the West Bank and Gaza?

At an Arab summit conference convened in Rabat in late October 1974, the issue was addressed. Hussein pressed his case by arguing that Israel would relinquish the West Bank only to Jordan and that return of the land to some Arab jurisdiction should be the first tactical objective. Negotiations should proceed, therefore, through a Jordanian delegation. Sadat openly favored an approach that was compatible with Hussein's purposes because it would mean a continuation of Kissinger's step-by-step negotiations with Israel. But Sadat also felt the national compulsion to confirm the Palestinian position—a move that could have meaning only within the limits of the separate Arab sense of reality.

Middle ground between the state of Jordan (with which Israel might negotiate) and the Palestinian expression of the Arab nation (which the Israelis rejected) could not be found. Even though it was a retrogressive step in terms of negotiating an agreement that could satisfy some claims of both the Arabs and the Israelis, the Arab leaders at Rabat—including Hussein—recognized the PLO as the "sole legitimate representative of Palestinian people on any Palestinian land that is liberated."[24] In return, the PLO agreed to coordinate its policies with Syria, Egypt, and Jordan. The formalities of unity had been preserved, largely through the efforts of Faisal, who offered participants lavish subsidies.

Initially Hussein attempted to conceal his bitterness. By agreeing to an Arab position as opposed to a Jordanian one, he had contributed to a unified stance—and he had also avoided isolation. But in the days following the conference he expressed his intention to modify the Jordanian constitution in order to separate the West Bank formally from his sovereignty and to remove all West Bank Palestinians from his government. He also rejected the idea of a Jordanian-Palestinian confederation. Hussein even stated that he would refuse to attend the Geneva Conference if the PLO represented the West Bank. All such intentions were, of course, symbolic. Ultimately Hussein let them drop, no doubt because of the complexities they would have added to American efforts to retain him as a negotiating partner for Israel.

The ascendency of the PLO within the ranks of the Arabs did not mean that the influence of the Palestinians would dominate in all matters pertaining to the Arab nation. Admittedly the PLO was becoming the conscience of the Arabs. But like all social bodies, the Arab body politic was not always willing to be guided by its conscience. The Palestinians were still a symbol, and their treatment at the hands of the leaders of Arab states indicated as much. Events following Arafat's appearance at the United Nations were to demonstrate that the moderate forces had seized the initiative in shaping Arab perceptions and that the Palestinians could not always use Arab symbolism to counter moderation.

Within weeks of the Arabs' acceptance of the PLO as the negotiator for the Palestinian people, the PLO Executive Committee rejected Kissinger's step-by-step diplomacy. Yet Sadat held to his course of working through Kissinger toward the Sinai Accord. During the summer of 1975 a move, inspired by the PLO, was launched to suspend Israeli participation in the United Nations General Assembly. This action was incompatible with the Egyptian-Israeli negotiations that were at a critical stage. Sadat openly opposed the PLO at meetings of the Arab and nonaligned states and did so with impunity. Ultimately the radical Arabs and the PLO dropped their initiative. At the conclusion of the Sinai Accord in September 1975, Arafat denounced the agreement between Egypt and Israel and asserted that it should be overturned. His statement implied that perhaps Sadat should be overturned as well. The PLO invective became so sharp that Sadat ordered the suspension of Palestinian programs over the Egyptian Broadcasting System. In so doing he was showing the world that he was not sufficiently imbued with the Palestinian cause to be prevented from expressing and acting on his own ideas.

The attitude of other Arab leaders was similar to that of Sadat. Despite his acceptance at the Rabat summit conference of the PLO as the negotiator for the Palestinian people, King Hussein refused to allow Palestinian guerrillas to operate against Israel from his territory. Although the Palestinians pressed for the isolation of Hussein from the Arab nation, Syrian president Assad proceeded to work with Hussein on matters pertaining to Arab politics. Arafat was open in expressing the fear that Assad's maneuvers might be directed toward having the PLO superseded by Hussein, who would again be charged with authority to speak for the Palestinians and to negotiate with Israel on the future of the West Bank.

In Lebanon Assad's stand was even more threatening to the Palestinians. As the civil war that had begun early in 1975 wore on into 1976, the death toll climbed toward thirty-five thousand. The war was precipitated by the Christian Lebanese response to "the state within the state" that the PLO maintained in Lebanon. Contrary to the wishes of many Lebanese, the PLO attacked Israel from Lebanese territory, resulting in Israeli retaliatory raids against Lebanese towns and villages. Ultimately Assad was drawn into a common cause with the Lebanese Christians because he too saw disadvantages in a freewheeling radical Palestinian movement that could goad Israel into seizing South Lebanon, thereby starting another Middle East war. Nor could Assad tolerate Palestinian carping over whatever plans he might have for political accommodation or even confederation with Jordan and conceivably Lebanon. As Syria became involved in the civil war, Assad did not hesitate to confront the Palestinians, to arm their Christian enemies, or to take direct military action against PLO forces. The confidence of the Palestinians that the Arab national conscience of the Syrian people would be so offended that they would not tolerate such behavior from their leader proved to be ill-founded. Predictions of an early coup d'etat in Damascus were inaccurate. Most Arab leaders are usually in some danger of overthrow, but in the case of Assad in 1976, more than his actions against the Palestinians would apparently have been required to cause it.

Against this backdrop of something less than deference to Palestinian national perceptions, and Arab leaders demonstrated repeatedly that they would continue to embrace the Palestinian cause as the symbol of Arab national realization. At the height of the Palestinians' verbal attacks on the Sinai Accord, the Egyptian representative at the United Nations emphasized Palestinian rights as he restated the position of the Arabs on a Middle East settlement. Moreover, in the same forum, the Egyptians proposed that the PLO be invited to any reconvened Geneva Conference "on equal footing" with other participants. Again and again Sadat urged that the United States establish a dialogue with the PLO. After the conclusion of the Sinai Accord, Kissinger attempted to capitalize on the Arab desire for a Geneva Conference and at the same time meet Israeli objections to PLO participation by suggesting a preliminary informal gathering of those who had been invited to the original conference in 1973. At least at the outset the PLO would have been excluded under this formula. In this case, it was the Saudis who countered that the next step toward a settlement should be a resolution of the Palestinian problem. The unasked question implied by the Saudi position was: How could the Palestine question be discussed without the Palestinians being present? Arab insistence on PLO participation in a new Geneva Conference was to persist and to frustrate all attempts by Kissinger to move negotiations beyond the Sinai Accord.

Nor did Arab support for the Palestinians end here. In November 1975, Assad made it clear that his renewal of the United Nations peacekeeping mandate on Golan depended on Palestinian participation in Security Council debates. The United Nations met Assad's terms, and for the first time a PLO representative took part in the proceedings of the Security Council. All Arabs supported resolutions in the General Assembly and other international bodies in defense of Palestinian rights. On only one such occasion did an Arab representative not declare support for the Palestinians. During intense fighting in Lebanon, the Lebanese representative to the United Nations laid the full blame for the civil war in his country on the Palestinians, whom he accused of inflicting an injustice of inhuman proportions on the Lebanese people. But the form of Arab unity was to prevail even while the content was missing. In September 1976, the Arab states unanimously gave the PLO full membership in the Arab League. The curiosity of this affirmation of PLO status was that it occurred at the very time Syria was preparing to launch another attack on Arafat's forces in

Lebanon. Other Arab leaders may have looked with horror on Assad's killing of his Palestinian brothers, but no one really did anything about it.

The key to the somewhat perplexing attitude of Arab leaders with regard to the PLO was that support for the Palestinian cause met the conditions of Arab reality. It represented the national orthodoxy that no Arab leader could totally deny. Yet the Palestinians as such were not permitted to dictate state policies. More and more, the moderate Arab leaders chose to define things Arab themselves and not be swayed by the pronouncements of Arafat. They were attempting, quite forcefully, to return the Palestinians to the status they had held prior to 1967—a mute symbol of the Arab nation's sacrifice rather than a vocal element in its leadership.

If there was an issue on which the Arab leaders deferred to the Palestinian viewpoint it was the West Bank. They ignored the Arab national conscience, however, on other political questions even when these pertained to Israel. As a national issue, the Arab leaders related to the Palestinian cause through acclamation. But under the aegis of Kissinger's diplomacy, they began to brush aside contradictions this created with state policies. Confusion developed over the Arabs' real position, leading to prognostications in the United States that Arafat's influence on the course of Arab politics was declining. But whatever foreign observers might have thought, throughout Kissinger's diplomacy and into the era of President Carter's efforts to mediate the Arab-Israeli dispute, the Arabs were a long way from abandoning the Palestinian cause.

In recent years Palestinian perceptions have become so distinctive that some observers have identified a budding Palestinian nationalism distinguished from that of Arab consciousness. This view can be pursued through all sorts of strange byways while being supported with a conglomeration of events drawn from the broad perspective of current history. But in terms of a balanced view of the Palestinians' self-concept, it is well to keep in mind that the sense of being Palestinian has thus far been expressed only in an Arab context. In all probability it appears to be more intense than the comparable sense of being Egyptian, Syrian, or even Algerian because the Palestinian cause currently stands at the center of Arab national expression. In a broader time frame the possibility of the Palestinians' ever remaining distinct from other Arabs seems remote. As a result of the Lebanese civil war even many Lebanese Christians were compelled to acknowledge that they could not escape their Arabness, and it is unlikely that the Palestinians can ever do so. If the bonds of the Arab nation are weakened and replaced by more parochial feelings of nationality, all Arabs, not just Palestinians, will lose their sense of Arabism. But in this case, where will the Palestinians get the strength to reclaim the lands of the "Palestinian nation"?

One important factor of course gives the Palestinians a somewhat different view of the Arab nation than that held by others who have an affinity for it—the client relationship into which Palestinians have been forced with fellow Arabs. Even with Arafat and the Palestinian cause given a symbolic role in Arabism, the Palestinians have found themselves subservient. During the Lebanese civil war, Palestinian units controlled by the Iraqi, Egyptian, and Syrian armies were committed on different sides of the fighting when Assad moved against the PLO. It was revealed that even Hussein still maintained an all-Palestinian unit in his army. Despite their best efforts, the Palestinians were not charting their own destiny, and the relationship with Arab benefactors was often no different from that which the Egyptians, Syrians, and Iraqis had experienced with the imperial powers during the nineteenth century or under the mandates. Palestinians, therefore, have an understandable yearning for a separate identity, but contemporary politics have not allowed for its expression. Even a Palestinian state would not mean a separate national fulfillment. Militarily, politically, and economically it would be dependent. As in the case of the Egyptians and their pharaonic vision of the 1920s, if the Palestinians sought a separate (Canaanite?) identity, to what would it relate in the present world? They would not even have the egress from Arabism of the Lebanese Christians who emphasize their religious and cultural ties with Europe while toying with the imagery of the seafaring Phoenician.

The Alien Reality of Negotiation

The circumstances surrounding the drive for Palestinian legitimacy served to accentuate an unusual aspect of the Middle East situation. Americans, Israelis, and Arabs were launched on a coincidental venture in diplomacy in which each had an entirely separate sense of reality. The Arabs and the Israelis both claimed legitimacy, and in effect asked the world to judge their respective cases according to a set of premises that included absolutely no regard for the frame of reference of the other. The third reality—that of the Americans—was only slightly less parochial. Certainly at the beginning of Kissinger's initiative, U.S. officialdom was bound by a conventional view of diplomacy. In January 1974, just prior to the beginning of his famous shuttle diplomacy, Kissinger said, "The purpose of the negotiations is to bring about positions which both sides can accept because they reflect the just aspirations of both sides, and this is the role which the United States is attempting to perform."[25]

The disengagement accords Kissinger arranged for Israel with Egypt and then Syria could rest on this supposition because the order of military units constitutes a physical situation in which disputes can be confined to how much security each side gains or loses by redeploying its armed forces. The negotiating parties can use a common yardstick for determining advantage and disadvantage. But what about a political settlement in which many Israelis literally see the agenda as a realization of the Old Testament and the Arabs insist on refiguring the institutions of government in the territory of Old Palestine in a way that totally denies the Talmudic tradition? Could one side or the other be persuaded to abandon its concept of the nation?

The trick in the Middle East, a mediator could easily conclude, was nothing less than convincing the two sides that one solution could serve the interests of each within its separate and unique sense of reality even though this reality was in direct contradiction to that of the other negotiant. Middle East perceptions indeed make mediation a complicated business. With the Israelis' rights based on the suffering of the Holocaust, in which Western society shared the guilt, and with Arab legitimacy linked to retribution for the pain of historical Western transgressions (including the establishment of Israel), the area for third-party maneuvering was indeed narrow. It was not just that neither side would accept the reality of the other.

Neither would tolerate even a modicum more of Western-imposed suffering—a phenomenon that was easily equated in Arab and Israeli minds with Western-proposed compromise. There was to be compromise in Kissinger's diplomacy, but it was not easy to come by.

Diplomacy, of course, is an unusual art. To ignore problems altogether is to risk unrealistic solutions and to court disaster. Yet to pay excessive attention to problems rather than solutions is to stymie all action. A third party extending good offices often hopes to impute to the two sides comparable scales for measuring negotiated outcomes and to convince the antagonists that the issue is one of finding piecemeal solutions through mutual adjustment until each side has no options other than accepting the arrangement that has been achieved. With the negotiating environment found in the Middle East, the mediator who employs such diplomatic practice assumes that the forces of Jewish and Arab nationalism can be overcome and that the participants can be persuaded to approach problems from the standpoint of a nation-state pursuing so-called rational interests. Herein lay the crux and also the weakness of Kissinger's *third reality*.

The issue of the third reality became apparent in Kissinger's initial consideration of the West Bank. After observing the outcome of the Sadat-Hussein agreement of July 1974, it was difficult to see how he could assume, as he apparently did, that Israel could avoid negotiations with the PLO and instead settle the disposition of the West Bank with Jordan. Kissinger's approach concentrated on the state and ignored the nation. This was the very problem that caused the Sadat-Hussein accord to be defective. In his understanding with Hussein, Sadat was attempting to establish conditions amenable to the notions of the United States regarding the place of the state as contrasted to that of the nation. Sadat's approach to the West Bank issue was indicative of the difficulties an Arab leader can encounter within his nation by responding to the pressures of an outside negotiator who does not share or perhaps fully understand the Arabs' concept of national reality. As in the case of Kissinger's urging Sadat in January 1974 to press other Arab leaders to discontinue the oil boycott, the Sadat-Hussein agreement served only

to weaken the position of the Egyptian leader in Arab national
politics. By focusing attention on the role of the state (in this
case Jordan), Sadat actually created a situation in which the popular reaction to his efforts strengthened support for the nation (in
this case the Palestinians).

Nor was the American position on the Jewish nation and its state
much more perceptive. Kissinger made it clear that "the United
States—and in the last analysis Europe—will not negotiate over the
survival of Israel." Israelis considered the statement itself to carry a
threat. What range of modifications in the Jewish state could be
covered by Kissinger's term "survival"? Did it approach the Palestinians' concept of a "secular" state in Palestine? Israelis found
Secretary of Defense Schlesinger's pledge to support Israel's
"security" much more reassuring. Schlesinger's formulation implied
that the power of definition would remain largely with the Israelis
themselves. Survival carried the connotation of a passive Israel
grateful simply to exist. On one occasion when Tel Aviv demon-
strators protested against American pressure on Rabin to be more
forthcoming in making territorial concessions, they carried ban-
ners that echoed the call of those Jews who ninety-three years earlier had issued the Manifesto of Bilu: "No others will determine our
fate. We shall do so ourselves."[26] Such are the sensitivities when
diplomacy encounters the force of national feeling.

Moreover, what conclusion was to be drawn from the assertion
that the United States would not bargain over Israel's survival?
Kissinger maintained that the United States would not recommend
to the Israelis that they negotiate with the PLO until it "accepts
Israel as a legitimate state." Rabin, however, had already rejected
the possibility of negotiating with the Palestinian group—even if
it recognized Israel. The quid pro quo for such recognition, the
Israelis feared, would more than likely be Israeli acceptance of a
Palestinian entity, presumably on the West Bank.

Indeed, Kissinger was implying a set of relationships that were
not to the Israelis' liking and that they could not be expected to
accept freely. The Israeli prime minister characterized a Palestinian state as a "time bomb." Israelis clearly saw the "rights of
Palestinians" as a call for the destruction of their own state. They

continued to maintain that the solution to the Palestinian problem should be found in the context of negotiations between Israel and Jordan, with Palestinian national identity being satisfied in a single state with Jordanians. The Israeli foreign minister tipped the Israeli hand slightly when he foresaw a Palestinian state coming into existence but being expansionist at the expense of Jordan, not Israel. The posture that gained acceptance in Israeli circles was for establishing a "Palestinian Arab State of Jordan" east of Israel, and perhaps even east of the West Bank. One interpretation of the Israelis' longstanding position on the refugee question had been that they refused to recognize the Palestinians as an identifiable people. It now seemed that Israel might acquiesce to a Palestinian identity, but, inexplicably, never within the confines of Old Palestine. In effect, the Israelis were still telling the Arabs to solve the refugee problem themselves.

The Israelis said they were prepared to include within their state all "settled Arabs" who would have full and equal rights of citizenship with Jews. This proposition had little meaning for Christian and Muslim Arabs, who could not identify with that citizenship. Considering the Israeli outlook on security and the affinity for the Jewish homeland, it did not appear likely that Israel would be prepared to relinquish more than a small portion of the West Bank. Many of those living in the occupied areas were not, of course, "settled Arabs" insofar as they had come from villages and towns incorporated into Israel in 1948 and had lived as refugees in Gaza or the West Bank thereafter. The ideal solution from the Israeli standpoint would have been for this group to express its Arab identity by moving on to Jordan. Even some outside observers concluded that it was a line of reasoning that had a lot to do with the Israeli insistence on negotiating only with Hussein over the West Bank. It could even have been the basis for Allon's suggestion, noted earlier, that Israel might accept the PLO in the Jordanian delegation at Geneva. Such an arrangement would have been the first step toward creating the Palestinian Arab State of Jordan.

It was such fears, suspicions, and veiled intentions that confronted Kissinger as he approached the West Bank disengagement issue in late summer 1974. His position was beginning to approximate that of Dulles, who twenty years before had hoped to find some means of providing arms to Nasser in spite of Arab-Israeli rivalry and U.S. support for Israel. Indeed, an appreciation of a situation becomes valueless or even counterproductive if it leads a negotiator to ignore those views of the other negotiating parties that cannot be reconciled with his own idea of reality.

Nor was this the only complexity that plagued the American negotiations. Unless Arab and Israeli perceptions of reality were altered radically, Kissinger's bilateral or step-by-step negotiations between Israel and one Arab state at a time for limited objectives would eventually run their course. The view that prevailed in 1974 and 1975 was that all participants in the negotiations would then be required to meet at Geneva and try for a general settlement if they hoped to avoid renewed tension and more fighting. Not wishing to face a group of divided and bickering Arabs, and apparently still confident that the moderate forces led by Sadat would carry the day, the Americans advised that a common Arab position on the outstanding issues would be necessary if a Geneva meeting was to be fruitful. This advice was given, of course, before it was clear that Hussein would not be sustained by other Arab leaders in his desire to negotiate for the West Bank. But by suggesting that the Arabs adopt a common position, the Americans had structured a situation that could only culminate in the Arab leaders' opting for national aspirations over state interests. National aspirations they held in common; many of the state interests were competitive. The Arab chiefs of state followed a totally predictable route in October 1974 by confirming the PLO, both before the United Nations and at the Rabat summit conference, as the sole representative of the Palestinian people.

In so doing the Arabs actually moved away from an accommodation with Israel. Again the third reality of the United States in suggesting a common Arab position had led to a counterproductive situation because the Arabs had treated an idea derived from an outside viewpoint according to their own perception of reality.

During the emergence of the PLO, casual observers of the Middle East scene often misconstrued Arab attitudes. Generally, they failed to grasp the subtleties of Palestinian power. Some gave undue weight to the distaste and contempt many Arab officials expressed privately for Arafat and his followers because of their self-seeking opportunism. Others read the intensity of the Syrian, Jordanian, or Egyptian desire to regain the occupied lands as an inclination to abandon Palestinian rights if this act would assure the return of the territories. Such assumptions were based on the alien reality of outsiders.

In any test of the propositions associated with this reality, the conclusions proved doubtful. If Israel agreed to return Golan to Syria, the West Bank and Jerusalem to Jordan, and the Sinai along with Gaza to Egypt, but made it all contingent on the denial of the Palestinian personality, would peace come to the Middle East? In the answer to this question, outsiders can see the meaning of the Palestinian issue to the Arabs. To suggest that such a solution had appeal to Arabs was to maintain that the Arabs' attitude of the past generation could be changed if conditions existing prior to the 1967 war were reestablished. At least during 1975, the momentum of Arab politics was all in the other direction. A sense of growing Arab power sharpened a national consciousness that was not likely to be muted simply by territorial exchanges. Such a development could lead only to a greater desire for the achievement of the Arabs' national aspirations. Add to this difficulty the Jewish concept of a biblically sanctioned Land of Israel in what the Arabs consider their own national homeland, and the complexity of negotiations becomes clear.

Perhaps nothing summarized the dilemma of conflicting legitimacies better than the exchange between the Palestinian leader, Yasir Arafat, and the Israeli representative, Yosef Tekoah, before the United Nations General Assembly on November 13, 1974. While acknowledging the legitimacy of the Jewish faith, Arafat rejected the state of Israel, identifying it with the colonialist Zionist movement. Israel amounted to the conquest of Palestine by European immigrants who in fact were being exploited to serve the interests of Western imperialism. It was the forces of imperialist, racist, and neocolonial Zionism, Arafat asserted, that were clinging to Arab territory and attempting to convince the world that Palestinians were disembodied spirits—fictions without a tradition, a present, or a future. On the contrary, Palestinians did have an identity and a homeland, Arafat declared. They always dreamed of returning to their land, and nothing would persuade them to forsake it. Defending his organization, Arafat stated that the Palestine Liberation Organization acquired its legitimacy from representing all factions among Palestinians and from the support of the entire Arab nation. In concluding his remarks, the Palestinian leader proposed the abandonment of the theocratic state of Israel and in its place the creation of a secular state in which Jews, Christians, and Muslims could live on equal terms.

The rebuttal by Tekoah had even more of a historical perspective than the statement of Arafat. When the Arabs stormed out of the peninsula in the seventh century to pursue the acquisition of territory by war and conquest, he said, only the people in the Land of Israel refused to shed their national identity before the onslaught. Those who pushed the Palestine question in the twentieth century hoped to annul the rights of this same Jewish people. In fact, the PLO convenant that was announced in 1964 denied that the Jews are "one people with an independent personality." As for the PLO, Tekoah saw it as being nothing more than "a gang of murderers who thrive on Jewish blood."

Refuting the Arab assertion that contemporary Jewry has no particular association with the Middle East, Tekoah stated that throughout history the Jewish people have remained one with their land. The land has been the very essence of their existence. Despite the Diaspora, Jews retained the customs, holidays, and language of that land. They were, in fact, the only people who saw this particular land as a separate entity or who thought of establishing an independent state in it. Tekoah saw peace being achieved by the Palestinians expressing their identity in the Palestine Arab State of Jordan, but not in an independent base east of Israel (the West Bank), from which a terrorist campaign would more than likely be pursued against the Jewish state.

When only the essentials of their remarks are considered, the positions of Tekoah and Arafat appear strikingly parallel. Each asserted the legitimacy of his own nation while denying that of the other. Their respective solutions represented extremes. For Arafat, Israel should disappear and in its place should be a state that accommodated all those who claimed the land. He did not, however, address himself to the issue of nationalities. Arafat's formulation, in fact, would result in the inconceivable arrangement of two transcendent nationalities being on equal footing in the same state. Those who heard the address could only conclude that, at least in Arafat's mind, one of these nations would ultimately disappear.

Takoah's answer was equally unrealistic. The Palestinians would simply be absorbed into Jordan. Presumably those in Gaza and the West Bank who maintained an Arab consciousness would disappear just as Arafat hoped Jewish consciousness would evaporate in the secular Palestinian state. In effect, Tekoah called on all Arabs to wipe from their memories any association with Palestine.

As these speeches demonstrated, statesmen and politicians will resort to rhetoric. Perhaps this is why diplomats are inclined to listen more to what national leaders whisper in closeted session than to whatever they choose to say from the podium. Nevertheless, it is in the latter that the force and compulsion of national commitment are expressed. Since the establishment of Israel in 1948, many would-be mediators have not faced their real task in the Middle East—changing what is said from the podium, that is, the perceptions of political reality held by the Jewish or the Arab nations—while maintaining approximately the same boundaries and population patterns as existed in 1967. Such was the purpose of Henry Kissinger.

Prior to the emergence of the oil weapon, Western statesmen did not have to confront the issue of conflicting legitimacies. Some European governments might have questioned Israel's right to retain any of the occupied territories, but how effective was that challenge? To the extent that the United States supported Israel, the Jewish state only had to assure that it was militarily capable of holding the territory under its de facto jurisdiction and that it could continue to acquire enough outside support to sustain its economy. This posture was based on ignoring Arab legitimacy, an attitude that was possible because the Arabs could inflict no injury on the West. After the 1973 war and the oil embargo, the West could see that, in order to maintain its tack, it would have to give the Arabs hope of some resolution of the Palestinian question. Otherwise the oil weapon might be used again. To cope with this situation, American leaders projected publicly that within ten to fifteen years newly discovered oil and a variety of sources of energy would alleviate them of dependence on Arab oil. Thereafter American policy could proceed independently of Arab sensitivities. At this point American diplomacy in the Middle East assumed a "Thousand and One Nights" quality, with Western supporters of Israel telling the Arabs one tale after another in order to put off the day of reckoning. Such was the path of the alien reality.

5

The Confines
of the Mediator

In assuming the role of a trustee of peace, Henry Kissinger had implied that the United States was prepared to act, not only as an honest broker working for a disengagement of forces, but also as the guardian of a more fundamental accommodation. The premise of mediation is that sufficient respect and goodwill exist toward the mediator for the antagonists to be amenable to his interpretations of their differences and mutualities. They must be prepared to accept his suggestions regarding areas in which they might profitably modify their respective positions. Necessarily, it means that the go-between has the powers of flexibility and communication that the belligerents lost when they entered combat.

When the role of a mediator is changed to that of a trustee, much of the responsibility for achieving peace shifts from the combatants to the interceding party. Trusteeship includes a clear commitment to preserve and nurture whatever understanding the facilitator is able to induce. Responsibilities are long range. The trustee must persevere. In accepting the obligations of a guardian, the mediator indicates that his may not be the beneficent position of disinterest normally associated with mediation. The commitment of energy, time and resources required for the task suggests that the trustee also has interests separate and distinct from those of the parties for whom he is mediating—interests that will be served by the accommodation he hopes to reach and to sustain. A trustee in the Middle East, therefore, does not stand apart or have the qualities of a public-spirited benefactor. He is a player in one of the more difficult contests to be found in contemporary diplomacy.

In the Middle East any friendly outsider experiences limitations in his quest for mutual understanding. Within the context of conflicting Arab and Israeli legitimacies, neither side can see the concessions asked of the other as being comparable to its own. An even greater limitation is the inclination of each side to view almost any initiative by an outsider as being on behalf of its antagonist. As a consequence, an overly ambitious move on the part of a mediator is seldom accepted as equitable. Both Arabs and Israelis insist on controlling their respective destinies.

Clearly the maneuverability allowed by these attitudes is restrictive. Yet, for many years prior to the 1973 war, and also in the aftermath of hostilities, the Arabs expressed a distinct predisposition for a solution imposed by the great powers. The Israelis' position was also preplexing. While insisting on complete independence of action, they hoped to preserve the "special relationship" with the United States that afforded them military equipment, economic assistance, and political support on the international scene—all vital to their country's future. In effect, the Israelis counted on the United States to impose conditions that favored this relationship. The nature of the trustee's role, in fact, carried the implications of a guarantor. But to use an old expression, both the Arabs and the Israelis wanted it both ways. Thus the guardian of peace was constantly being pressed to act, only to encounter resistance when he did.

Another problem for the trustee was that action in the negotiating arena was not confined to what he alone might do, even within the limits set by Arab and Israeli attitudes on comparability of concessions, trustee initiative, and guarantees. Neither the Arabs nor the Israelis were restricted simply to reacting to the moves of the trustee. Both were capable of initiatives on their own. These were not just explicit acts that the trustee as well as the other side could counter. Each had the ability to influence implicitly the perceptions of the trustee himself by working within the milieu of

America's domestic politics and economy. Such were the conditions Kissinger encountered when he assumed his role in Middle East negotiations. They constituted definite but often murky confines within which he was compelled to work.

Comparability of Concessions

Throughout his efforts to achieve a more stable set of relationships between Israel and its neighbors, Kissinger was confronted by the firm conviction on the part of each side that nothing the other could offer would come close to matching the sacrifice that it was being called upon to make. The Israeli leaders feared that almost any concession, even a limited withdrawal from Sinai, would only encourage the Arabs to press Kissinger even harder to force Israel to meet their demands. The problem was popularly characterized in Israel as Kissinger's "salami tactics"—little by little the American secretary of state would slice away at Israel's bargaining position by urging piecemeal territorial concessions for which the Arabs would offer little in return. Israeli Defense Minister Peres expressed this aspect of his government's attitude in July 1975 at the time of the negotiations over the Sinai Accord. In referring to the Egyptians, Peres said, "Actually they want us to give them a tremendous amount for absolutely nothing on their part. . . . We have gone far, very far, and we have made it clear that our suggestions are final. It is hard to believe that we shall be able to concede any more."[1]

For the Israelis the second Sinai accommodation, which Kissinger failed to achieve in March 1975 but finally brought about in September of that year, involved territorial concessions that detracted from their defense capabilities. In return for the transfer of a substantial area, with the security it represented in Israeli minds, Sadat wanted to do no more than give his "word" not to resume hostilities for three years. From the outset of the negotiations the Egyptians had attempted to depict any agreement with the Israelis as nothing more than an extension of the January 1974 troop separation. Sadat maintained that he was ready to consider additional aspects of military disengagement but not political concessions. Admittedly, Sadat's qualified position may have reflected

nothing more than his desire to ward off Arab antagonists who
would question his loyalty to the nation if he sought a political
accommodation with Israel separate from one that might be
arranged by all Arabs working together. Nevertheless, his attitude
contributed to Israeli suspicions about the sincerity of any Egyptian commitment to a long-range compromise solution. For this
reason, the Israeli leaders concluded in March 1975 that despite
the tension their refusal to accept Egyptian assurances was likely
to create in relations with the United States, there was no basis
for a limited agreement with Egypt.

Sadat had a similar sense of being asked to make the major
concessions. When Prime Minister Rabin demanded that Egypt
accept a state of nonbelligerency in return for Israel's relinquishing
territory in Sinai, Sadat could see nothing the Israelis were offering that was equivalent to such a momentous step on his part.
From a logical standpoint, how could Egypt be expected to affirm
nonbelligerency with a country that still occupied Egyptian territory? Following the failure to achieve Israeli pullbacks in the
Sinai in March 1975, Sadat was known to have felt cheated for
having taken the risks an Arab leader associates with negotiation,
only to have the Israelis refuse to make the concessions he could
hold forth publicly as justification for his decision to defy Arab
national sentiment by treating with the enemy.

In conventional Western diplomacy, such stands would be considered as bargaining positions that are taken along the way in the
give-and-take of negotiations. In the Arab-Israeli struggle they are
based on far different premises. The Israelis saw the possibility of
national extinction in any subsequent Arab military effort that
found them at a disadvantage. The political future of Sadat and his
supporters—and perhaps their lives—were at stake if the radical
Arabs could successfully paint the Sinai Accord in the colors of
betrayal of the Palestinian cause with Sadat as an archtraitor to
the nation. Could there be any wonder that each side saw a lack of
comparability between its own concessions and those offered by the
other?

In strictly military terms Sadat had very little to offer the
Israelis in exchange for his minimum position of Egyptian control

of the Sinai mountain passes at Gidi and Mitla and the return of the Abu Rudeis oil fields. He could give some assurances on easy renewals and perhaps extensions of the cease-fire, but only to the point where such actions did not totally alienate him from Arabism. Within a strict military framework, Sadat could also accept the demilitarization of any occupied territory that was returned to Egypt and also allow inspection of this territory by UN forces. But the Israelis would not negotiate for such meager concessions. If bargains were to be struck, Sadat had no choice but to pay in political terms.

In September 1975 Sadat granted political concessions in the Sinai Accord, including passage of nonmilitary Israeli cargoes through the Suez Canal and a pledge to resolve all disputes by peaceful means. He was also prepared to keep the peace under the accord until it was superseded by a new agreement. In an allusion to the Palestinians' activities, he would refrain from paramilitary as well as military action. Portions of the understanding that were meant to remain unpublished covered selective termination of the Arab boycott in Egypt against firms dealing with Israel and a toning down of anti-Israeli propaganda. As a demonstration of its good faith, and to the frustration of the radical Arabs, Egypt opposed resolutions to expel Israel from the United Nations when they were introduced at both the African Solidarity Conference in Kampala and at the meeting of the nonaligned states in Lima. Egypt did, however, join other Arab delegations at the United Nations in October 1975 to vote for a resolution that labeled Zionism a racist doctrine.

Because of conflicting legitimacies and the unusual configurations of the Arab and Jewish nations, Sadat's political concessions could not, in fact, be equated in the Arab mind with the territory Israel relinquished. Saudi officials assented to Sadat's move. The Iraqis avoided the issue by pointing out that they were not a party to Egyptian-Israeli negotiations. They were not, however, "against any Egyptian or other Arab land being liberated from occupation."[2] Otherwise the accord was greeted in Arab lands with indifference or hostility. Many Arabs asked what Sadat had achieved from the second Sinai withdrawal. In the narrow sense used by his detractors, Egyptian troops regained a few miles of desert. In addition, critics conceded that the Egyptian economy would benefit from the return of the Abu Rudeis oil fields. They also noted, however, that the annual income from Sinai oil was no more than the amount Saudi Arabia could provide with just two days of its oil earnings. In objecting to the accord, the Syrians ridiculed Sadat for having given so much for so little.

In response to these attacks, Sadat attempted to convince his constituents within the Arab nation that the accord with Israel was in the interest of all and that Egypt was not abandoning the Arabs' confrontation policy. To this end, and even while Sadat was accepting many aspects of nonbelligerency, the Cairo press maintained that Egypt was moving ahead within the context of a comprehensive Arab settlement with Israel: "This strategy does not hinge on the Egyptian position alone, but on the solidarity of the Arab stand as a whole."[3] Sadat's leadership among Arabs did not prevail, however, as it had in other cases during the previous two years. If an Arab position could be discerned, it was that Egypt had given much more than it had received in the accord. Certainly during the summer of 1976 the author found this view to be prominent among Egyptians, even editors of government-supported newspapers and many officials.

In spite of Sadat's political concessions, the Israelis were not enthusiastic. Former prime minister Golda Meir advised her countrymen to accept the Sinai Accord with neither fanfare nor mourning. Publicly the Israeli officials put the best face possible on the accord by pointing to Egypt's readiness for the first time to agree with Israel to work toward a final and just peace and to forgo the use or even the threat of force. The difficulty for the Israelis was that Egypt's political concessions were a certainty for only one day at a time. At any point Egypt could interdict Israel-bound cargoes transiting the Suez Canal, take punitive action against friends of Israel under the Arab boycott, or resume boisterous propaganda attacks. If Egypt ever reneged on its commitments and Israel attempted to redress the situation by reclaiming the relinquished territory, hostilities would almost certainly result. Possibly the United States government, which had become Israel's most important benefactor, would be alienated by such an act. The Israelis could only conclude that Egypt had the preferred position. Each side was paying in a different coinage, and equitability of payment could not be easily established.

The effect of this situation on the negotiations was that Israel placed a virtual premium on all concessions. When the Egyptians would not pay the extra charges, the trustee of peace did. Thus we were to see the emergence of a pattern in which Israel bargained over American largesse, not over Arab concessions. To a lesser extent the Egyptians did the same. Both Egypt and Israel, in fact, saw their gains from the Sinai Accord in some commitment undertaken by the United States rather than in any concession made by the other. Kissinger was obviously limited as to how far he could proceed if each step involved substantial costs, not for the Arabs and the Israelis, but for the mediator himself.

Virtually the same scenario was replayed in 1978 as part of the Camp David accord and again when the two states signed their treaty in March 1979. In these instances, with the President of the United States personally involved in the negotiating process to offer "sweetners," Begin and Sadat reached agreement. Thereafter, when lower level Israelis and Egyptians met to develop the details of the agreements, the sense of a lack of comparability of concessions would emerge and wrangling would ensue. Even when Sadat and Begin met in December 1977 at Ismailia, there was sharp disagreement over which side would be getting the better deal from the various proposals that were put forward. Without the American presence to assure personal understanding at the highest level, agreement proved impossible.

The Mediator's Bias

Over and above the problem of comparability of concessions, the stance of a "trustee of peace" taken by Secretary Kissinger made it difficult for him to determine how either the Arabs or the Israelis might perceive his initiatives. Because of the long-standing inability of Arabs and Israelis to respond positively to one another's moves, any third party that attempted to persuade first one side and then the other to yield was ultimately viewed with suspicion by both sides and likely to be accused by each of supporting the other.

The Arabs were open and direct in acknowledging that their use of the "oil weapon" was the result of the United States' favoring Israel. From different Arab perspectives variations on this theme were expressed, but they all rested on the assumption of an American bias in favor of the Jewish state. Even for the Egyptians this feeling appeared on occasion to lie just beneath the surface. In March 1975, following Israel's refusal to conclude any agreement that did not contain a pledge of Egyptian nonbelligerency, Egypt's foreign minister saw in the situation evidence that the United States was a prisoner of Israeli actions. Despite the inclination of the Arabs to view the Geneva Conference in a positive light, at times they suspected that it was a contrivance to be used by the United States to lengthen negotiations and permit Israel to delay returning the occupied territories. Throughout the negotiations that culminated in the Sinai Accord, the Syrians and Palestinians were suspicious to the point of paranoia. They believed that Kissinger was trying to pressure Egypt into a separate agreement on Sinai in order to split the Arabs. They saw his policy as avowedly hostile. When the Accord was finally concluded, the Syrian delegate at the United Nations said, "The latest agreement arranged by the United States . . . has proved that the main aim of Zionism and colonialism is to freeze the status quo in the region, to perpetuate the Israeli occupation, and to sow the seeds of dissension and discord among Arab forces of the confrontation prior to their liquidation one after another."[4] At a later date the same Syrians might again accept American mediation, but it does not take too much imagination to see the limitations this attitude placed on Kissinger's flexibility while he was negotiating the Sinai Accord.

Kissinger was fully aware of the difficulty such attitudes created for his relations with Arabs, and he did what he could to prevent the feelings from becoming too negative. Yet the problem of an American bias continued to arise. Such an incident occurred in June 1975 when the American ambassador-designate to Israel informed the press that, in any peace arranged in the Middle East, some rectification away from the 1967 borders would be necessary in order to satisfy Israel's legitimate requirements for security. The State Department was compelled to disassociate itself from this proposition in order to maintain what appeared to be an impartial position while serving as mediator. The new ambassador was well versed in the ways of European diplomacy from a long and distinguished career in that area. He was unfamiliar, however, with Middle East sensitivities. The delicate nature of relationships was reflected in the fact that he was the first American official since the October 1973 war to comment on Israel's ultimate borders. The mere suggestion that adjustments might be in order was proof to all Arabs of an American bias.

Nor were the Israelis less convinced than the Arabs that the U.S. posture favored their adversaries. From the outset of the negotiations, the Israelis complained that Kissinger was pushing them too hard and that he should seek more from Sadat. A popular Israeli view was that the United States wanted them to make concessions in order to shore up the American position with the Arabs. Perhaps the most common theme in Israeli commentary was that the Jewish state would respond to no American pressure to accommodate the Arab position whether that pressure be procedural in the form of deadlines for concluding phases of some agreement, or substantive in terms of withdrawing from specified occupied territory.

With the strain in U.S.-Israeli relations that followed the failure of the March 1975 negotiations, Kissinger himself contributed to difficulties by contending that it was not so much American pressure as it was Prime Minister Rabin's failure to be sufficiently forthcoming that caused the breakdown. Immediately the Israelis claimed that they could sense a shift in the American position toward the Arabs. When negotiations were resumed, Kissinger was compelled to pay the price. Rabin sought a wide variety of assurances that were more closely related to U.S.-Israeli relations than to Israel's future relations with its neighbors. If the Geneva Conference were to be convened, Israel wanted a coordinated policy with the United States; and if an interim agreement happened to be reached on Sinai, the Israelis wanted a pledge that the United

States would not apply pressure for a subsequent partial agreement with Syria. The Israelis went so far as to ask for explicit assurances that the United States would not side with the Arabs, and they openly asserted that they would work to protect Israel's "special relationship" with the United States. In effect, the Israelis wanted to preclude the United States from exercising any latitude in its Middle East policy if it implied that the United States did not side unequivocally with Israel. Any change was seen as an American bias in favor of the Arabs.

Kissinger did, in fact, accept the incorporation of Rabin's stipulations into the unpublished memoranda that accompanied the Sinai Accord. In addition, he agreed that the United States would seek to keep all substantive negotiations at Geneva on a bilateral basis, presumably to preclude Israel from being required to face representatives of the Arab nation—including the Palestine Liberation Organization—as opposed to those of individual Arab states. No delegation heretofore not specified as a party to the negotiations was to join the conference without Israel's approval, and the United States would neither recognize nor negotiate with the PLO as long as the Palestinians did not accept Israel's right to exist. According to the confidential memoranda, American representatives at the United Nations were obligated to oppose, and if necessary to vote against, any effort to change the resolutions that had terminated the 1967 and 1973 hostilities and that were to serve as the framework for a settlement. The allusion here was to the Arab-sponsored resolution passed by the General Assembly in October 1974 by which the status of the Palestinians was changed from that of refugees to "nationhood." The United States' flexibility as a mediator between the two sides was obviously limited by its commitments to Israel.

Kissinger accepted these undertakings in order to offset what Israel viewed as the inequitable concessions it had been required to make in Sinai. They were also meant to assure the Israelis that an American bias toward the Arabs was not developing. At the conclusion of the Sinai Accord, President Ford even felt called upon in a congratulatory telephone conversation with Prime Minister Rabin to say, "you can count on us to continue to stand with you."[5]

Despite all such assurances, Israeli leaders could not overcome the fear that the United States would eventually serve as an Arab advocate. There was apprehension that perhaps Kissinger had offered Syria greater concessions (which he hoped to formalize through further negotiations) than Israel was prepared to make. In guarding the "special relationship," Israelis could never acknowledge that there might be a convergence of Arab and American interests on certain matters. Such a supposition would lend legitimacy to the Arab position. The Israelis did, however, admit to a growing realization that their power to resist American wishes was limited— a sense that served to strengthen their resolve to retain complete independence in policy making. Following the signing of the Sinai Accord, a senior Israeli official who wished not to be identified sounded the same theme that had been voiced by Israelis in 1974 when Kissinger first looked beyond the mere disengagement of forces. "The most pernicious aspect," the Israeli said, "is that after this agreement [the Sinai Accord], the appetite will grow among the Arabs and in Washington."[6] In the eyes of this official, the Arabs and the United States at least had a common end, if not a common purpose. Thus an inherent American bias was perceived by many Israelis.

Israeli sensitivities over any evidence of an American bias toward the Arabs reached even into ceremonial matters, with results as restrictive for the trustee of peace as they were on issues of substance. When Sadat requested during his visit to the United States in November 1975 that he be permitted to address a joint session of Congress, arrangements could not be made until it was agreed that the same courtesy would be extended to the Israeli prime minister. Much of what Kissinger hoped to accomplish with the Arabs depended on mood; the form of an occasion was sometimes as important as the content. The impact that could be achieved with the Arabs through special attention was vitiated because no favor could be permitted to appear distinctive when compared to consideration given Israel. Indeed, as a mediator Kissinger had to contend with a variety of constraints.

The attitudes of the Arabs and the Israelis suggested that the decision on the part of either to enter negotiations did not constitute an inexorable step toward compromise with the other side. The Israelis hoped to accommodate the American as opposed to the Arab perception of Middle East conditions, and then only to the point of assuring the continuation of the support that made their economy and defense viable. Arabs were concerned with enlisting U.S. help in moving Israel to return the occupied territories, if not to acknowledge the Palestinians' rights. Sadat remained convinced that the United States had the influence to force Israel into an accommodation that was acceptable to the Arabs. The Egyptian purpose was made clear in the assertion of the official who stated after the announcement of the Sinai Accord that "America is no longer Israel's unconditional supporter."[7] Kissinger's mission, therefore, was not the usual mediation. Each of the Middle East antagonists devoted as much time to changing his outlook as to changing that of its counterpart across the bargaining table. Under these circumstances, an honest broker was likely to find himself immersed in Middle East affairs, but possibly without the influence necessary for achieving a settlement.

An Imposed Solution

While the Arabs were ever on the alert for evidence of outside interference in their affairs, even before 1973 they had sought a solution to the Middle East situation that would be imposed by the great powers. Perhaps the most important underpinning for this position was the Arabs' sense of weakness. In the past, their negotiating stance had never been sufficiently strong to permit them to deal independently and forcefully with Israel. Thus they avoided direct negotiations and invited intercession by outsiders. At the same time, they resented any independent attempt by an outsider to refigure Arab affairs. What the Arabs were after was the power or strength of an outside force working in their behalf, but without paying the full price of compromise inherent in such an arrangement.

Sadat had expressed an interest in a negotiated settlement and stood in alliance with Saudi Arabia, a major oil producer with which the United States had always maintained good relations. For its part, the United States was motivated by a growing dependence on Arab oil to give special attention to a Middle East settlement, especially to one favored by the Saudis. The coincidence of interests regarding oil and peace was sufficient to make the United States receptive to Arab blandishments regarding techniques for achieving a settlement. Following the 1973 war conditions did, in fact, favor an imposed solution. The United States and the Soviet Union seemed to be searching jointly for a peaceful way out of the Middle East problem. Each had stopped giving unqualified support to one of the two contending sides. Moreover, for the first time in many years, a basis existed for communication between the United States and the Arab states that were in direct confrontation with Israel. But despite a somewhat favorable situation for the assertion of great-power initiative, perceptions varied considerably over what an imposed solution entailed.

Immediately after the cessation of hostilities, the pattern preferred by the Arabs was set when Egypt looked to the United States to press for Israeli concessions. At that juncture the Arab objective was to get the Israeli Army moved to the east bank of the Suez Canal and to extricate the Egyptian forces that had been trapped in Sinai when the Israelis crossed the canal near Suez City. Through American intercession these goals were achieved. Thereafter, Sadat remained steadfast in his conviction that only the United States could dislodge Israel from the occupied territories. The Soviet Union did not have sufficient influence with Israel, and the Arabs themselves did not have the strength. Sadat, therefore, focused his attention on the United States as the point of negotiation with Israel. Herein lay the route of the imposed solution.

In addition to the matter of Arab oil was the tantalizing prospect for the United States that a closer working relationship with Arab governments would lead to a decline of Soviet influence in this critical part of the world. The one danger against which the Arabs had to guard in seeking outside intercession was that considerations of great-power diplomacy not override Arab political objectives in any imposed solution. Competition between the Soviet Union and the United States was regarded by the Arabs as an important factor in avoiding this pitfall and keeping the United States on course. The Arabs did not object to American influence if it could be used to squeeze concessions from Israel. They were confident that the Soviet Union could again be made into a willing advocate if American influence turned against them. It appeared at times as Kissinger's diplomacy proceeded that the Soviets were being ignored. For the Arabs, however, the USSR had an important if benign part in the game. At this point, Egypt's relations with the Soviets had not yet deteriorated to the level of hostility that was to be reached in 1975.

While great-power intercession was adopted by the Arabs, the rationale for their position rested largely on the United Nations. Since the establishment of Israel in 1948 the Arabs had based the legality of their case on the contention that from its very inception the Jewish state had lived in violation of United Nations resolutions that called for some redress in favor of the Palestinian refugees as well as Israeli withdrawal from some of the territory incorporated within Israel's original boundaries. More immediately, the Arabs pointed to the United Nations resolutions that terminated hostilities in 1967 and 1973 and required Israel to withdraw from the occupied territories. The logic of the Arab argument was that, as great powers and permanent members of the Security Council, the United States and the Soviet Union should compel Israel to honor various international pronouncements made through the United Nations.

The announced Egyptian position as Sadat entered the negotiations sponsored by Kissinger in December 1973 was that "the real threat to peace is Israeli refusal to implement the United Nations resolutions."[8] The first Egyptian-Israeli disengagement agreement was justified by the Egyptians, in fact, as furtherance of the will of the international body. The happy circumstances of growing pro-Arab sentiment within the United Nations as more and more new African and Asian states of the Western colonial heritage were added to the membership assured UN support for Sadat's position. It explained the Arab insistence on, as well as the Israeli resistance to, the interjection of the United Nations image into the post-1973 negotiations. The issue first came to the fore in a dispute over UN Secretary General Waldheim's role at the Geneva Conference. With the UN imprimatur, Sadat could contend that the real business of

the conference was to implement United Nations resolutions stipu-
lating Israeli withdrawal from occupied Arab lands and to investigate means of satisfying various UN calls for the recognition of
Palestinian rights. Despite Israeli grumbling, Waldheim did preside
over the first session of the conference, but Soviet-American sponsorship of Geneva, with U.S. and Russian representatives serving
as permanent joint chairmen, precluded Sadat from achieving even
a superficial advantage from this event.

Thus the Arabs proceeded along the course of a solution imposed
from the outside. Kissinger's shuttle diplomacy, in fact, was quite
complementary to this position. Every time he traveled to Jerusalem
and extracted another concession from Israel it could be depicted
in Arab capitals as an imposition at the Arabs' behest. At the same
time, the shuttle itself, consisting of repeated consultations with
Sadat, Assad, and the Saudis, conveyed the impression that the
political dynamics of the region, rather than the alien interests of
the great powers, were at work. Moreover, shuttle diplomacy required none of the direct contact with or acknowledgment of
Israel that the Arabs were loath to accept.

Sadat was convinced of the United States' sincerity when its
representatives stated that ultimately Israel must surrender a great
deal of the occupied territories. Quite logically, he continued to
press for greater American initiative. At his meeting with President
Ford in Austria in June 1975, the Egyptian leader argued that
mediation was no longer sufficient to assure progress on a Middle
East settlement. The time had come for the United States to
announce its position on the basic issues. Ford could not agree
completely, but in order to relieve Arabs of the fear that the United
States and Israel were conniving through delays and obscure positions to permit Israel to retain the Arab lands, he responded that
the United States would not permit a stalemate in the negotiations.

In working toward the Sinai Accord of September 1975, U.S.
officials nudged the Israelis along by implying that eventually the
United States would have to propose a plan of its own if progress
were not made. An American plan would supposedly be sufficiently
even-handed to expose the differences between the positions of
Israel and the United States, thereby damaging the "special relation-

ship." At the same time, Kissinger consistently denied that the United States would ever try to impose a solution. The prospect of the overt imposition of a settlement by the great powers therefore seemed unlikely. Nevertheless, the type of behind-the-scenes pressure that was being exerted on Israel, and the American threat to announce a unilateral but unimposed position, did have the potential for moving the Middle East toward a solution induced by the United States.

The Israelis' position was virtually a reverse image of that of the Arabs. They were adamant in rejecting any *pax Americana*. The mediator was seen as little more than a facilitator of direct negotiations. Israeli Foreign Minister Allon contended, "It is counter productive for governments outside the region to try to draw the future map of Israel in advance. The future boundaries should be drawn in negotiations between the two parties to the conflict. Efforts by foreign governments to define the boundaries can only encourage Arab intransigence and make negotiations more difficult."[9]

As for the United Nations, the Israelis were rapidly coming to regard it as a curse. Security Council Resolutions 242 (1967) and 338 (1973) called for the termination of all claims of belligerency and for all parties to respect "the sovereignty, territorial integrity and political independence of every state in the area and their right to live in peace within secure and recognized boundaries free from threats and acts of force."[10] In accepting these resolutions the Arabs had for the first time recognized the fact of Israel's existence. Yet this advantage was of little consequence to the Israelis because the Palestinians had also been acknowledged in the United Nations resolutions. Any solution of the Palestine question that was acceptable to the Arabs could only be viewed by many Israelis as making demands on the territorial integrity of biblical Israel. Moreover, a Palestinian state on Israel's borders could constitute a threat to its security.

Israeli dissatisfaction with multilateral channels increased as the Arabs succeeded in having the status of the Palestine issue changed before the General Assembly from a question of refugee compensation and settlement to a matter of a right to nationhood.

The international legitimacy afforded the Palestine Liberation Organization when Yasir Arafat was invited to address the General Assembly was also a bitter experience. The attempt in the UN Social, Humanitarian, and Cultural Committee to label Zionism a racist doctrine that had inflicted injury on the Palestinians, much as South Africa's apartheid was used against black Africans, only accentuated Israeli antipathy toward the international body. As we have seen, during the critical 1975 negotiations the Arabs even mounted an effort to have Israel suspended from participation in various UN activities. Only when Israel responded that any such move would result in its termination of the UN Truce Supervisory Organization stationed in Sinai and Golan did support for the idea of ejecting Israel dwindle.

The Israeli outlook on these gyrations was expressed by Abba Eban, former foreign minister and member of the Knesset, who saw the United Nations becoming the world center for anti-Semitism. "The horrifying truth," Eban said, "is that Hitler himself would often have felt at home in a forum [the General Assembly] which gave applause to a gun-toting Yasir Arafat and an obsequious ovation to the murderous Idi Amin."[11]

To the extent, therefore, that the Arabs succeeded in having an imposed solution phrased in terms of the compelling necessity to implement United Nations resolutions, and in moving the United States toward this position, Israel would lose. If great-power intercession was to be beneficial to Israel, it must be bilateral and take the form of military assistance enabling the Jewish state to protect its borders against hostile neighbors.

The Israelis, of course, also talked about the implementation of UN resolutions, but in so doing they emphasized different things and held different interpretations from the Arabs. First, the Israelis wanted an unqualified peace, and second, they interpreted Resolution 242 as not requiring them to return all occupied territory. What placed the Israelis at a disadvantage in the proceedings of the United Nations was the atmosphere that prevailed after the 1973 war. The Arabs were successful in creating the impression through General Assembly votes that virtually the entire world stood with them. The Israelis were protected in the debates only by the United

States's veto in the Security Council. Maneuvering within the United Nations tended to strengthen the impression of Israeli intransigence, placing the Jewish state on the defensive in negotiations with the Arabs.

As in other aspects of his position, Kissinger's ability to employ an imposed solution was limited. In negotiations with the Arabs he could indeed consider such an approach, but only to the extent that the specifics of the outcome could be portrayed as falling within the context of a series of United Nations resolutions. As for the Israelis, they were intent upon determining their own future. Their preferred route toward a settlement was face-to-face negotiations, and they were opposed to any international prescription emanating from the United Nations that could influence either the process or substance of such negotiations. Because of the "special relationship," and the critical nature of American support for Israel's survival, Israeli leaders were susceptible to American coercion. At best, however, Kissinger could only apply pressure gingerly if he hoped not to disaffect from his efforts the many supporters of the Jewish nation to be found within his own domestic constituency.

A Great-Power Guarantee

Many commentators, observers, and statesmen coupled the idea of an imposed solution with the belief that the great powers must affirm that they were prepared to guarantee any peace resulting from the negotiations. Otherwise the agreement might not stand the strains of the Arab-Israeli legacy that would still exist after the conclusion of a treaty. Generally, the formulas set forth for this purpose followed the United Nations resolutions and cited the necessity to guarantee the territorial inviolability and political independence of every state in the area. Most outsiders concerned with the Middle East scene perceived guarantees as a precondition —as the basis for a final settlement. Prominent features in such schemes were a guarantee of borders by the great powers, some formula for demilitarizing the region, and the stationing of international forces astride the Arab-Israeli boundaries. Most of the hypothetical solutions placed these boundaries close to those that had existed prior to the 1967 war. Through the implementation of such proposals the great powers would actually have served their own interests by not permitting smaller countries to endanger world peace with regional wars. They gave little attention to the wishes of the parties to the Middle East dispute, and in this regard such solutions were truly meant to be imposed.

But again, limitations existed for a trustee of peace who hoped to build a settlement on guarantees. A specific United States commitment to Israel's security, for example, in exchange for an expressed Israeli willingness to negotiate over the occupied lands was viewed by many Arabs as further American interference in the area. Because of the yet unfulfilled nature of Arab aspirations, an outsider who became the guarantor of a status quo was seen as little more than a neocolonialist in disguise. The guarantor's position stood in direct contradiction to the Arab assertion that the shape of events must emerge from the dynamics of the region itself.

Once Kissinger's shuttle diplomacy was underway, the Arabs did show occasional interest in guarantees that were of a limited duration or that gave them an exclusive advantage. Sadat, for example, suggested a U.S. guarantee to maintain the peace while Egypt and Israel worked toward a Sinai Accord. The Syrians spoke of the desirability of the United States's and the Soviet Union's guaranteeing that Israel would ultimately withdraw from the Golan Heights. At the outset, therefore, the Arabs had no clear-cut proclivity for a set of guarantees that would give the participants in the negotiations certain permanent minimum positions from which they could bargain. In fact, a review of the public record indicates that the Arabs assiduously avoided the subject of guarantees.

The underlying factor that fed Arab suspicions of a guarantor role for the United States was the part the United States played both in Israel's founding and in its subsequent well-being. The situation had not improved with time. In fact, the Nixon administration had provided more aid to Israel than all previous presidencies combined. This relationship served to confirm the popular Arab belief that Israel was just another Western imperialist influence thrust into the Arab breast. A guarantee would ensure not so much that Israel survived—because many Arabs were beginning to accept their neighbor as a fact of life—but rather that it would continue to exist as a Western, or more accurately an American, enclave from which Arab national expression could somehow be frustrated.

In the aftermath of the Sinai Accord, sensitivities over guarantees were clearly revealed. The Egyptians found themselves in the position of attempting to justify the agreement to other Arabs in terms of its having committed the United States "as a basic party to the Arab-Israeli conflict"—an affirmation of the trustee role with heavy overtones of the United States's also becoming a guarantor. Almost immediately, criticism of the Accord from Syrians and Palestinians became so severe that Sadat felt compelled to deny that he favored the United States's playing such a part. He was emphatic in asserting that Egypt had not thrown itself into the American embrace. "We do not accept trusteeship from anyone," he said.[12]

The generally unstable condition of Arab politics leads to a compulsion on the part of each Arab leader to give public assurances that he remains loyal to the larger Arab principles. Protestations usually take the form of an affirmation of "just Arab demands" and the castigation of anyone, including the counterpart in the negotiations, who stands in the way of their realization. Even Sadat felt compelled to attack both the United States and certain aspects of the Sinai Accord he had just signed. In reestablishing his bona fides as an Arab leader he went so far as to charge the United States with sending technicians as well as weapons to Israel during the 1973 war. "When I accepted the cease fire on October 22, 1973 —and I want my brothers in the Syrian Ba'ath Party to hear this— I was facing both the Americans and the Jews, America with its strength and its weapons that had never before left the United States."[13] Looking to the future, the Egyptian leader contended that the United States policy of continuing to arm Israel did not fit the new American role in the Middle East, and he threatened that the Arabs would continue to arm themselves if the United States and Israel persisted. There could be little doubt that deep suspicions remained in Arab hearts even as Arab leaders accepted American mediation.

In this essentially negative response to his own agreement, Sadat had laid the groundwork for accusing the United States of betrayal if that eventuality ever proved politically expedient. He also attempted to assume an Arab as opposed to an Egyptian position by getting other members of the Arab League to join Egypt in warning the United States that American policy encouraged Israel "toward new aggression as well as maintaining her expansionist policy."[14] If Egypt, as the United States's principal negotiating partner, felt the necessity to make such statements and take such positions, how could Kissinger ever hope to further his mission by proposing the United States as the guarantor of Middle East peace? Kissinger himself was hesitant to do so.

It was also difficult for the Israelis to contemplate a solution buttressed by guarantees from the great powers. Even though such a solution was identified by outside observers with secure and recognizable boundaries, the Israelis viewed it as a limitation on their freedom of action. Within the context of a guarantee was always the possibility of American restraint on the implementation of Israeli policy. It would seem that safety for a small country such as Israel would lie in having outside powers feel a responsibility for its welfare. This condition actually existed in America's unilaterally adopted policies on diplomatic support and military assistance for the Jewish state, but with not quite the same possibility for American pressure as with formal guarantees. For that matter, Israel could not even acknowledge this implicit American guarantee, for to do so would contradict the heroic myth of total independence to which Israelis clung so avidly. During the 1975 negotiations Kissinger, in a moment of exasperation, was to refer to this sense of independence as the "Masada complex"—self-reliance to a point of martyrdom. It was a feature of Israeli national character, a reaction to the condition of having been subjected for so long to a dominant gentile society that had considered Jews to be subservient by nature. It was an aspect of the Jewish revolt against Herzl's concept of "what the Ghetto made us."

In a pragmatic vein, the Israelis could also argue against the efficacy of guarantees. They recalled that in exchange for Israeli withdrawal from Sinai in 1957, Secretary of State Dulles had provided Israel with a letter of understanding that the United States would maintain the freedom of the seas in the event of an Arab blockade of Israel's oil supply line through the Gulf of Aqaba to the port of Elath. Yet in 1967 when Egypt declared, but did not impose, a blockade, the Israelis found the United States slow to act. Again in 1970 the United States refused to acknowledge that Egypt's relocating missiles nearer to the Suez Canal was in violation of undertakings with Israel that had been achieved through U.S. intercession. Israel saw little value in guarantees in view of American reaction—or perhaps reaction time—to their contravention. The essence of the situation was that Israel refused to be relegated to small-power status. Kissinger was among the first to recognize that the Israelis would not accept any effort by the United States to substitute great-power guarantees for Israel's own independently derived concept of security. In this atmosphere guarantees and imposed solutions as a means of spurring the negotiants on to a settlement appeared to be a dead letter.

Thus the proponents of guarantees failed to give due attention to some of the basic attitudes that could lead the Arabs and the Israelis to resist both international guarantees and a truly imposed solution to the Middle East problem. Another weakness in the thesis was that it called for joint U.S.-USSR action. To the extent that they rested on detente, guarantees depended on extraneous conditions. If the United States undertook to guarantee the status quo unilaterally, the Soviet Union could be inspired to support the Arabs more firmly in whatever change they might hope to induce. In such a case very little would be guaranteed.

How good, in fact, was any guarantee? If international forces were placed along the borders, they could also be precipitously withdrawn just as they were in 1967, when Nasser's request for removal of UN forces set the scene for the Israeli attack. Few observers could conceive of Israel living with an American garrison or even a United Nations force on its territory. Such a situation would be totally contrary to Jewish self-reliance. It was precluded because of an important psychological dimension to political behavior so often ignored by those who are imbued with international legality. As for demilitarization guaranteed by the great powers, the Middle East had witnessed this device in the 1950 Tripartite Declaration when the United States, Great Britain, and France attempted to control the flow of arms to Israel and the Arabs. Anyone familiar with the period could testify to the declaration's ineffectiveness. Self-defense was too much a part of national existence for either the Arabs or the Israelis to forgo weapons and simply trust pledges from abroad. On a number of counts, therefore, the idea of a guarantee appeared suspect.

Kissinger fully understood the situation. He acknowledged the necessity for an American assurance of Israel's survival and security, but he saw it coming at the end of negotiations and being supplemental to an overall accord rather than as the groundwork for one. Because negotiations would presumably bring peace, a commitment by the United States at this juncture need not be offensive to either the Israelis or the Arabs.

In taking this position Kissinger was influenced by the Arab perception of what a guarantee constituted. If, for example, it appeared to be an obligation assumed unilaterally by the United States without prior consultation with the Arabs, it would have the characteristics of a guarantee of Israel's security rather than of regional peace. In this light it would be seen as a move taken in defiance of the Arabs. The problem was amply covered at the time of the negotiation of the Sinai Accord. At the outset of the negotiations, President Ford was careful to make it clear that, while he saw a substantial relationship between U.S. and Israeli security interests, and while he agreed that a guarantee of Israel's borders could not be ruled out, real progress on an Arab-Israeli accommodation would have to precede such an assurance. In effect, Ford had straddled the issue. Eight months later, when the accord was announced, he took the same position, this time to deny that the assurances given Israel in the memoranda that accompanied the accord actually constituted a security treaty with the Jewish state. There were, of course, domestic considerations that prompted such a position. The fears of excessive foreign commitments engendered by the Viet Nam experience lingered on. Nevertheless, Kissinger still had a long way to travel before he could broach the idea of guarantees to Arabs and Israelis. His latitude in employing a variety of tools to induce a settlement was quite narrow. Despite the power and influence an American mediator brought to the negotiations, neither was sufficient to allow him to impose a solution or in all probability to declare credible guarantees unless such formal assurances were preceded by a settlement that both sides accepted.

The Arab-Israeli Struggle for Implicit Influence

In maneuvering through the Middle East labyrinth Kissinger had to be ever mindful of the reaction of the American public to the tactics he might employ and concessions he might suggest for moving the antagonists toward peace. Between the establishment of Israel in 1948 and the war in 1973 there had been no comparability between the places Arabs and Israelis occupied in the minds of the American people. The segment of the Jewish nation residing in the United States had little difficulty generating support for Israel through such domestic institutions as the major political parties, labor unions, and Congress. Israel's strength was *implicit*. That the United States would stand by the Jewish state was determined from internal considerations. The policy was expressed in terms of American advantage and not as favors to a foreign state. A pro-Israeli lobbyist put it succinctly when he stated, "If we have to make a case solely on the basis of the interest of Israel, we've had it. Basically I think we are effective because we have a good case—what is good for Israel is good for the United States."[15]

The Arabs were at a disadvantage because they did not have the same access that would allow them to influence the American equation from within. In any contest for the popular conscience, the Arabs had to rely on *explicit* requests or demands. They shared no identity drawn from common experience with American society. As a result, their objectives in relations with the United States could be achieved only in terms of American official generosity or perhaps by means of whatever pressure they could exert on the free world through the dynamics of the West's bipolar competition with the Soviet bloc.

In October 1973, when the Arabs introduced oil into the Middle East struggle with embargoes, production cutbacks, and price increases, the situation was altered. The Arabs were no longer required to make explicit pleas for support or to realize their aims by playing the Soviet Union off against the United States. Because of Western dependence on Middle East oil, the Arabs now had another means of influencing American and European thinking. Henceforth, only implicit factors—oil and the wealth it produced versus Jewish national influence—need be brought into play. The latitude of the American secretary of state as an outside facilitator of any Arab-Israeli agreement necessarily became more limited than when he only had to take account of Jewish sensitivities on the American homefront. The situation amply demonstrated that the United States was indeed a player rather than an honest broker in the Middle East struggle.

Despite certain advantages that they enjoyed, leaders of the Jewish nation were concerned. At the meeting of the World Jewish Congress in 1975, speakers noted that relations between Israel and non-Jewish countries were deteriorating, compelling the Jewish state to rely even more heavily on its special relationship with the United States. Over the years the American people had provided the principal outside support for Israel. Since 1948 the United States government had given it $5.2 billion in direct assistance, including $2.2 billion in emergency aid following the 1973 war. The United States was Israel's largest trading partner; its financial community purchased 85 percent of Israeli bonds; its business firms in 1973 provided 53 percent of total foreign investment; and the American public contributed by far the greatest portion collected abroad for Israeli charities and social development.

Unusual consideration was given to Israel under U.S. foreign assistance programs. Of the $2.2 billion in aid that was provided Israel in fiscal year 1975, 68 percent had been declared a grant. Once the Sinai Accord was concluded, the Ford administration was prepared to continue with this pattern of expanded support. In fiscal year 1976, an additional $2.2 billion was appropriated, and in 1977, the figure was $1.8 billion plus $200 million to cover the transition involved in the United States's changing the cycle of its fiscal year. As in 1975, two-thirds of the aid provided Israel was for military equipment, with the likelihood that virtually all of it ultimately would be classified as grant and therefore not subject to repayment. Moreover, the United States demonstrated major con-

cern for Israel's defense problems by assuring that its army's equipment was always comparable in quantity and sophistication to anything acquired by the Arabs. When the Soviet Union provided Syria
with a short-range ballistic missile, the United States agreed to
transfer to Israel larger numbers of a better one; when Syria and
Egypt acquired a Soviet-built fighter that was deemed slightly
faster than the American F-4 Phantom, the United States initiated
procedures for providing Israel with the far superior F-15 warplane.
In the reequipping and buildup of the Israeli army after 1973, the
United States government took the unusual step of diverting to
Israel tanks, missiles, laser bombs, and late-model aircraft from
U.S. Army units that were already short in the established quotas
of these items. In a technical sense, Israeli defense requirements
were permitted to supersede those of the United States.

Despite the solicitous nature of American response to Israel's
needs, the Israelis were uneasy with the special relationship. Kissinger was pressing them to make concessions to facilitate a partial
settlement with Egypt. Israeli officials found Kissinger's efforts not
to their liking, and they worried lest the United States decide, in
the event of increased tensions in the Middle East, that Israel was
an expendable client rather than a valuable ally to be defended at
all costs. Kissinger's diplomacy sparked a petulant outlook on the
part of many Israelis. Illustrative of their lack of confidence was
the stoning of the American Embassy in Tel Aviv in July 1975—the
type of outburst normally associated with Third World populations
that harbor a deep sense of weakness and feel that because they
have no implicit means of influencing a great power they must
resort to symbolic gestures that accomplish little more than fulfilling
a short-run need for some form of explicit expression.

American support for Israel has been attributed to a variety of
factors—the shared guilt of the Holocaust, an affinity on the part
of Bible-belt Americana for Old Testament Israel, easy identification with the pioneer spirit of the Israeli settlers, and common
interests with a bastion of democracy in an alien and antagonistic
part of the world run by dictators. All these factors no doubt contribute to the "special relationship," but it is America's Jewish

community that provides the organization and energy that keep the relationship intact. A full 40 percent of world Jewry resides in the United States as compared to 20 percent in Israel, 18 percent in the Soviet Union, and another 15 percent distributed among France, Argentina, Britain, Canada, Brazil, and South Africa.

In describing the relationship of American Jews with Israel, former Foreign Minister Abba Eban said, "The role of the American Jewish community is to do everything for the common interest of the Jewish people everywhere in the economic arena. We are all partners in this arena."[16] This particular appeal was economic in nature. In effect Eban was asking American Jews to accept voluntarily a portion of the financial burden of the Jewish state. Normally nationals meet this obligation through taxes, but in the relationship between Israel and the Jewish people this practice was not possible. Quite emphatically, Israeli spokesmen have contended that U.S. government assistance could never be a substitute for support from Diaspora Jews. Certainly if the enthusiasm and commitment of world Jewry ever waned, or if Jews themselves became complacent about the future of Israel, non-Jewish sources of support for that state would soon disappear.

The link between Jews in America and Jews in Israel was thus regarded as being through the nation of which the Jewish state was the embodiment. On the question of whether Jews living outside Israel had any voice in the political decisions affecting the future or security of Israel, the chairman of the Zionist Organization of America contended that American Jews could not "accept unconditionally every decision of the Israeli Government. . . . We must keep our freedom of action. We have a right to express our opinion about events and policies in Israel because the Jewish state belongs to all Jews."[17] The head of B'nai B'rith, on the other hand, while conceding the right of American Jews to intervene in the use of their donations to economic and social activities in Israel, maintained that only the government of Israel and its people could determine the foreign affairs of Israel. In less critical times such debate need never occur. It served only to emphasize the problems associated with any attempt of a people to function out-

side the context of the nation state or to operate with what the
president of the World Jewish Conference had referred to as double
loyalties.

Certainly the role described by the head of B'nai B'rith was the
easier to perform. While it fell somewhat short of the full implications of double loyalties, it was totally compatible with American
pluralism. The Jewish community in the United States could justi-
fiably press for an American policy on the Middle East that
reflected its concerns and interests. In this regard, the role of the
American Jewish community went beyond what Abba Eban saw as
the economic arena. American Jews worked to assure that the
American people perceived an identity of interests between Israel
and the United States. Herein lay the meaning of the special relationship, and Jews were apprehensive lest this relationship might
weaken in the face of growing Arab power and influence.

The cause of Jewish concern was amply revealed in a Harris
Poll conducted in January 1975. At that time 52 percent of the
American people supported Israel while only 7 percent favored the
Arabs. The imbalance in sentiment was apparent, but the important
point was that the remaining 41 percent of those polled did not care
about Israel, and if this proportion increased, the future of the
special relationship could become clouded. The Arabs did not have
to achieve a favored position in the United States in order to end
the preference that was afforded Israel. Nor did sympathy for
Israel among the American people have to disappear. It was only
necessary for this sympathy to be rendered secondary to such overriding considerations as the security of the West's oil supply.

The prospect of erosion in American support for Israel may
have seemed unlikely to a non-Jew, but for a people who had a
long history of persecution and who were now being pressed—however tenuously—by their principal benefactor to come to terms with
what they considered an unrepentant enemy, very little could be
taken for granted. Jews themselves accounted for a bare 2 percent
of the American population. Support for Israel, therefore, rested
in the hands of people who did not share the Jewish experience. Yet
the Jews were organized, and they worked prodigiously. As one
Israeli policy maker put it when a difference occurred between

Washington and Jerusalem, "What is Ford going to do; suddenly decide to abandon Israel and have the whole Jewish community on his neck? That hardly seems likely."[18]

American Jews certainly have influence with regard to American policy, both domestic and foreign, and they have the capability to use this influence to modify the actions of any trustee of peace. Quite often, however, the nature of Jewish influence within the body politic is misunderstood. Many Jews themselves see their influence working through the liberal intellectual community. Intellectualism has long been associated with Jewishness and has been depicted by Jews as the secularization of the emphasis on religious study that was prominent in the European ghetto. High status was afforded the religious scholar, an attitude easily transferred to anyone engaged in intellectual pursuits. The second feature of Jewish political proclivities has been a liberal outlook stemming from interaction with gentiles that had cast Jews in subservient roles. Many felt that they were pushed by circumstances into a social position of discontented skepticism, a characteristic of both intellectuals and liberals. In terms of Jewish liberalism itself, historic patterns of discrimination had disposed Jews to oppose the conservative politics with which discrimination was generally indentified in Western democracies. The cultural and social conditions of Jewish life, therefore, helped shape an identification between American Jews and an intellectual and liberal point of view.[19]

Jews have not simply followed the liberal intellectual trail; they have had a major role in determining both the meaning of liberalism and the content of intellectual life in contemporary America. Survey data collected in 1969 by the Carnegie Commission on Higher Education suggested that, while Jews constituted 2 percent of the population, they accounted for 9 percent of academicians. One-third of these academicians were in high-quality schools that accommodated only 12 percent of the entire academic community. It was particularly the liberal Jews who congregated at the elite schools. They proved to be the most active group in publishing and were high in research accomplishments. Jews, in fact, were disproportionately represented among the country's distinguished scientists and scholars. Generally they showed less interest in applied fields of study (agriculture, engineering, earth sciences), which were marked as the most politically conservative groups identified in the survey. With the exception of physics, medicine, and medically related fields (bacteriology and biochemistry), Jewish faculty concentrated in the social sciences and law. In every respect, therefore, Jewish academicians are so positioned that their views can attain prominence—their career interests are directed toward areas that impinge on questions of public concern, and their location at major universities assures a platform from which their pronouncements will be heard.

The case of academic intellectuals can reasonably be generalized to nonacademicians. To a large extent, the views of Jewish liberals are those of non-Jewish liberals as well. Thus Israel is assured a significant and powerful group of advocates who take positions out of conscience and not just to serve the interests of a political movement, Zionism, or a foreign state. A link exists between public policy and the views of academia insofar as the government looks to academicians, well-known and obscure alike, for a variety of services related to the formulation and implementation of policy. Since the mid-fifties the Washington bureaucracy may well constitute the largest collection of individuals having intellectual pretensions to be found anywhere in the world.

Support for Israel among liberal academicians remains evident, but it has been eroding. Survey data collected in 1975 suggested that between 70 and 75 percent of all academicians favored continued U.S. support for Israel in such areas as economic and military assistance and in the political battles at the United Nations. Only about half, however, believed that the United States had a moral obligation to prevent the destruction of the state of Israel and only one-third felt that the United States should provide ground troops or air support if Israel were ever threatened with defeat.[20] The post-Vietnam reaction to U.S. involvement abroad and the inclination of liberal academicians for a foreign policy of peace over international power indicated the limits of the intellectuals' support for Israel.

The advent of anti-Semitic fascism during the 1930s and early 1940s had the effect of intensifying Jewish proclivities for liberal politics and the parties of the left. Nevertheless, Jews associated with the left experienced some discomfort because of radical opposition to Zionism as an outmoded expression of nationalism that was counterproductive to the objectives of international socialism. Essentially, however, an accommodation between the liberal-leaning Jewish community and the left, even into the post war era, was stable. The horror of the Holocaust and the nature of its perpetrators were powerful forces binding together all opponents of fascism whatever their differences. But during the 1960s the situation began to change. Support by the left for the anti-imperialistic Third World (of which the Arabs were a part), opposition to any "Establishment," and Israel's close ties to official circles in the United States all worked to decrease support for Israel among members of the intellectual left. After the Six Day War, Israel no longer served the need of liberals to rally to the oppressed. The war in Viet Nam and civil rights became the causes of the left as it was joined by large numbers of young people. For the New Left, Zionism was not a cause. It was the advocacy of the interests of Israel, a state that stood with the imperialistic West and against weak and downtrodden peoples. At least in the more radical fringe of liberal politics, attitudes toward the major political purpose of the Jewish community cooled.

Simultaneously, support for Israel had been developing in more conservative political circles. Non-Jewish conservatives came to admire Israel as an American ally that had succeeded in military operations against the Arabs, who were viewed as clients of the Soviet Union. The phenomenon of "ethnic succession" also became a factor as black Americans pressed to replace Jews, first in the leadership of the civil rights movement, then in ghetto small business, and finally through affirmative action in social services to poverty-stricken blacks. The Jewish-black tensions that resulted from ethnic succession created advocacy for Jews among conservatives who were uneasy over black militancy.[21] Indeed, in the 1975 survey of academicians, Israel had a high level of support among 61 percent of non-Jewish faculty heretofore characterized as conservative as compared to only 42 percent of non-Jewish faculty in groups known for their liberal views. The point was that, while support for Israel was decreasing marginally, it was also becoming more generalized throughout the political spectrum.

Here then was the basis for the influence Jews could exert on policy, and Congress proved to be a major target for those who wished to assure that American policy favored Israel. The principal organization through which this influence was brought to bear during Kissinger's diplomacy was the American Israel Public Affairs Committee which claimed twelve thousand members and was registered to lobby in Congress on issues of interest to Israel. The strength of the committee came from its association with fourteen Jewish organizations representing 4 million individuals. Each group maintained representatives in Washington, where they met weekly under the direction of the committee to review any matter that might affect Israel.[22] The principal argument used by this group to influence Congress was that the interests of Israel and those of the United States coincided.

The effectiveness of the committee could not be doubted. At a time when foreign assistance was otherwise receiving less support from Congress than ever before, the House of Representatives by a vote of 362 to 54 approved legislation by which Israel received emergency assistance in December 1973. The American Israel Public Affairs Committee claimed credit for this vote. Another example of the committee's influence occurred in 1975, when the Ford administration submitted to Congress the proposal for providing Jordan with a defensive missile system. Within days congressmen were deluged with phone calls and mailgrams opposing the transaction. Almost all were inspired by the committee. Ultimately the missile proposal was delayed, refigured, and finally permitted on terms acceptable to Israel. With similar tactics, a request by Saudi Arabia in 1976 to purchase 1,900 air-to-ground missiles was reduced through the committee's intercession to 650. Both Arab requests had been viewed favorably by Ford and Kissinger.

A third instance of influence in favor of Israel occurred in the wake of Rabin's refusal in March 1975 to make concessions on Sinai. In response, Ford had announced his intention to withhold new assistance from Israel until a review of U.S. Middle East policy could be completed. Almost instantaneously the American Israel

Public Affairs Committee was able to generate a letter signed by seventy-six senators calling on the administration to consider Israel's urgent military and economic needs. Congress was indeed the focus of the pro-Israel movement. In conjunction with visits to the United States in support of annual United Jewish Appeal fund-raising campaigns, prominent Israelis gave high priority to calls on congressmen. Congressional visits to Israel were also popular. In one three-week period during 1975, for example, Prime Minister Rabin met with sixty American legislators.

Many Congressmen were quite confortable in their support of Israel, while others were not. Some legislators admitted that they were afraid not to sign the letter sent to Ford by the seventy-six senators. They were hesitant to talk about the American Israel Public Affairs Committee because it could deliver votes, not just in heavily Jewish constituencies but through the channels of both parties in most parts of the country. The same point applied to campaign contributions. A few congressmen were less than proud of their signature on the letter, not necessarily because of its content but because they had succumbed to the lobby's pressure. One such congressman said, "The lobby wants to do Congress's thinking on Israel. They don't want any independent judgments."[23]

At the same time, many Americans who were feeling the growing influence of the Arabs had concluded by late 1974 that Israel could no longer count on the automatic support of a Senate majority. Some congressmen were openly saying that the time had come for Israel to face up to the Palestinian problem, and public debate in the United States was beginning to be phrased with a view to the Arab position. Sen. Charles Percy, for example, asserted that the United States could not give unlimited support to "Israeli occupation of Arab lands." What followed was meant to be a show of strength. Within a few days Percy received twenty thousand pieces of mail denouncing his position. Some congressmen privately said that their hold on the voters was not sufficient to take this kind of battering. But the supporters of Israel were worried—if one politician could say such things and escape unscathed, would others be far behind?

The letter signed by the seventy-six senators made it clear that

Israel had not lost support in Congress. The argument in the message to Ford was a classic statement of the position held by the friends of Israel: "We believe that a strong Israel constitutes a most reliable barrier to domination of the area [the Middle East] by outside parties. Given the record heavy flow of Soviet weaponry to the Arab states, it is imperative that we not permit the military balance to shift against Israel."[24] This expression of senatorial concern over a possible delay in arms deliveries to Israel countered Kissinger's efforts to use arms in bargaining with Israel. In exchange for military supplies, he had wanted Israeli concessions to facilitate an agreement with Egypt over Sinai. Thus the implicit influence exerted on Israel's behalf within the United States helped mark the confines within which the trustee of peace was compelled to work.

Congress was only one of the channels used by the Jewish nation. In addition to the American Israel Public Affairs Committee, there was the powerful Anti-Defamation League of B'nai B'rith. Its target was the American mind, and its concern was viewpoints that appeared to be anti-Semitic. Generally anti-Semitism takes the form of an irrational attack depicting Jews as a conspiratorial force extraneous to the country in which they live and accusing them of using surreptitious means and hidden influence to work for some dark and evil (but unspecified) purpose. Anti-Semitism as a hate thesis can spark damaging and discriminatory acts or even persecution of Jews involved in nothing more than the same economic, social, or political activites that are considered legitimate and even worthy for non-Jews.

The usual accusation underlying an anti-Semitic appeal is that Jews control or manipulate some institution that is a vital source of national power and ultimately their work will result in the destruction of the country. The most common assertion is of the kind expressed by the chairman of the Joint Chiefs of Staff, Gen. George Brown, in November 1974, when in an outburst against the Israeli lobby he suffered a lapse of judgment and charged that Jews controlled the banks and newspapers. He then went on to imply that with these vehicles they unduly influenced American policy. Whatever Brown's intent, no Jew could fail to draw the comparison between such remarks and those that had gained credence in Germany after 1930.

In the aftermath of the 1973 war, Jewish spokesmen identified what they considered a new anti-Semitism—that is, any questioning of the legitimacy of Israel or the validity of Zionism as the political expression of the Jewish national movement. As we have already noted, the position of Jewish groups was that "any delegitimization of Israel . . . is now equal to anti-Semitism."[25] With this assertion an important extension of anti-Semitism had taken place. The articulate Israeli spokesman Abba Eban saw classic anti-Semitism as denying "the rights of Jews as citizens within society." Anti-Zionism, or a refusal to accept Israel, on the other hand, denied "the equal rights of the Jewish people to its lawful sovereignty within the community of nations." Eban saw a common element in these rather divergent cases. That element was discrimination.[26]

To the Arabs, on the other hand, no discrimination was evident in anti-Zionism, which was simply an expression of opposition to the Law of Return for Jews who did not originate in Palestine. Arabs contended that Zionist theory violated the rights of the Palestinian people who had been driven from their land by Jewish settlers. Within this context, it was Israelis who were denying another people lawful sovereignty within the community of nations. For some observers the anti-Zionism of the Arabs was not so much a case of discrimination against Jews as it was a matter of conflicting legitimacies. Two nations had rested their national claims to the same homeland on the absolute principles of religious faith, thereby precluding either side from accepting compromise.

Following the 1973 war the efforts of the Anti-Defamation League were not directed toward exposing classic forms of anti-Semitism so much as countering the critics of Israel. Those whom the League identified as proponents of new anti-Semitism included the New Left (a radical student-based group that opposed the "Establishment" in the United States and came to favor all other challengers of the status quo, including the pro-Arab Third World), columnists (Evans and Novak) who asserted that Jewish pressure groups controlled U.S. Middle East policy, any group (the American Friends Service Committee) or newspaper (*Christian Science*

Monitor) that favored a solution in the Middle East that appeared
to consider the Arab position favorably, Senator William Fulbright
for his charge that pro-Israel efforts in Congress did not reflect U.S.
interests, and clergy who on occasion labeled the Israelis as oppres-
sors and equated the murder of Israeli athletes by Arab terrorists
at the Munich Olympics in 1972 with the deaths of Lebanese vil-
lagers whose homes were shelled or bombed by Israeli military
units attempting to ferret out Palestinian guerrillas in South
Lebanon. Major oil companies, ex-diplomats who happened to be
Middle East experts, and some university faculty and students
were also depicted by the Anti-Defamation League as part of an
elaborate Arab campaign "to indoctrinate the American people
against Israel."[27]

Having identified the "adversaries of Israel," Jewish organizations that were concerned with the issue took what they considered appropriate action. Perhaps the most noteworthy, if not
effective, weapon of the Arabs had been their boycott of firms that
maintained business relations with Israel. The Anti-Defamation
League and the American Jewish Congress contended that the boycott amounted to discrimination against individuals of the Jewish
faith. In response, the Arabs patiently explained that neither ethnic
nor religious considerations had anything to do with their attitude.
The boycott of Israel did not discriminate on the basis of the
nationality of the companies or the religion of their owners. It was
simply a matter of wishing to avoid profit-making undertakings
that could possibly result in Arab-generated funds being funneled
through a Western company into the Israeli economy and military
establishment. After all, the Arabs maintained, a status of belligerency with Israel still existed, and the boycott was a legitimate
means of self-defense in accordance with the rules of international
law and the principles of justice. The Arab point of view hinged to
some extent on the supposition that Jews individually could be distinguished from supporters of Israel, a proposition the proponents
of Zionism could not concede.

Unable to counter the Arabs directly, the Anti-Defamation
League and the American Jewish Congress hoped to pressure
American companies that cooperated with the boycott—that is,

those firms that operated in accordance with Arab trade requirements to the extent of ascertaining in their letters of credit to Arab customers that they had no business with Israel. Moreover, Arabs also required assurances that no components of items sold to them were processed by firms having Israeli ties. Herein lay the grounds for the contention that American firms who so indicated were engaged in a secondary and even tertiary boycott against companies that traded with Israel. The United States government was urged by the Anti-Defamation League to protect American companies from "Arab boycott pressures and to defend the principle of free trade and nondiscrimination which are fundamental to the American system."[28]

This move was also pressed through Congress, where Secretary of Commerce Rogers Morton was brought before an investigative subcommittee and requested to divulge the identity of the American concerns complying with the boycott. The 1965 Export Administration Act had required that such information be revealed to the Department of Commerce as part of a *policy* "to oppose restrictive trade practices fostered or imposed by foreign countries against other countries friendly to the United States." Simultaneously, the American Jewish Congress filed suit on behalf of twenty-five members of the House of Representatives, accusing the secretaries of commerce and interior of acting to hinder congressional policy. The court was asked to enjoin the cabinet officers from frustrating the 1965 act and from promoting or encouraging trade between the United States and the Middle Eastern and North African countries that participated in the boycott.

The legal basis of the suit was doubted by many lawyers, because no *law* had been contravened by those honoring the boycott. The friends of Israel had raised the issue of American companies' operating contrary to a congressionally proclaimed *policy*. Some businessmen questioned how the information demanded of Morton might be used. Finally, faced with a contempt citation in December 1975, the secretary of commerce agreed to reveal to Congress the identity of the American concerns. The names were not made available to the public, however, until October 1976, at the height of the presidential election campaign. The principal purpose of these moves seemed to be to draw attention to the boycott and to work on the American sense of fair play—even to punish companies that complied. One congressman declared that if companies had been guilty of flagrantly violating the enunciated public policy of the United States, the reasonable course was to expose such acts to their stockholders, customers, and competitors. His statement fell just short of proposing a counter-boycott. In response to the uproar, President Ford announced plans to introduce legislation that would prohibit a business enterprise from using economic means to coerce any person or entity into discriminating against a United States citizen or company on the basis of race, color, religion, national origin, or sex. The Anti-Defamation League viewed Ford's suggestion as failing to come to grips with the full scope of the boycott.

Thereupon Jewish groups took their own initiative. Through Sen. Abraham Ribicoff, the Tax Reform Act of 1976 was amended to deprive taxpayers who agreed to participate in or cooperate with any international boycott of the benefits of various tax credits and deferrals. Reports were required of all companies that either did business in a boycotting country, had been requested to participate in an international boycott, or had heretofore cooperated in a boycott. In addition to the usual prohibition against discrimination on the grounds of nationality, race, or religion, the tax law defined a boycott as refraining from doing business with companies, the government, or nationals of a boycotted country; refusing to do business with American companies that did have such trading partners; or purposely avoiding shipping or insuring with companies that appeared on the Arab blacklist because of their trade with Israel.

Through the Anti-Defamation League's influence, six states had already passed antiboycott legislation and others were considering it. Next came a move on the national scene to give antiboycott measures the force of law rather than merely the sanction of congressional policy. Amendments to the Export Administration Act were passed that paralleled the tax legislation, and also made it illegal for an American company to furnish information to a boycotting country with regard to the race, religion, nationality, or national origin of any United States person. It also became illegal to inform a boycotting country with regard to any company's or person's business relationships in a boycotted country. Thus it was unlawful to provide information on subcontractors as Arab countries required.

In a suit filed in January 1976 for violation of the Sherman Anti-Trust Act, the Justice Department contended that in operations outside the United States, American companies could enter into agreements having boycott stipulations as long as they did not attempt to enforce discriminatory behavior within the United States itself. On such fine points of interpretation and with much uncertainty over what compliance with the boycott actually involved, the friends of Israel proceeded. Some businesses that already had lucrative arrangements with the Arabs concluded that the real purpose of all this pressure was to interdict American commercial relations with Arab countries sufficiently to preclude major transfers of modern technology until the Arabs were no longer a threat to Israel.

The campaign against growing American-Arab ties had another aspect. Amid fears that sizable Arab investments in the United States would lead to Arab control of critical sectors of the American economy, and with warnings that Arab investment might bring discriminatory policies against Jewish employees, the Anti-Defamation League supported a bill requiring that the true identity of ultimate owners of corporate equity be revealed and that notice be given to the Securities and Exchange Commission by foreign entities attempting to acquire 5 percent or more of a major company. In addition, the president was authorized in any instance to bar foreign investment altogether. In one publicized case, an effort was made to prevent a Saudi Arabian businessman from gaining a controlling interest in a California bank. Commenting on the situation, the executive director of the Jewish Federation of San Jose said, "We naturally view this with deep concern. . . . What's happening with Arab oil money is touching all Americans. Whether Arabs are going to use this for political purposes remains to be seen."[29] Actually, overwhelming Arab investment in the United States did not materialize. By the end of 1976, total investment of

Arab countries in diversified common stock amounted to about $3 billion. Not a single effort was made to take over a major American company or even to buy a substantial block of stock in one. What the supporters of Israel did not wish to notice was that they were raising emotional questions and generating fear about the supposed intentions of individual Arabs in a way almost identical to the practice of classic anti-Semitism.

Another concern for Jewish groups was oil. They feared that the energy crisis would be blamed on Israel's refusal to reach an accommodation with the Arabs, thereby arousing anti-Semitic feeling throughout the United States. With some justification, the proponents of Israel claimed that America's energy problems had nothing to do with Middle East politics. Jewish organizations did note the generally pro-Arab stance of many oil companies and the benefits these companies acquired from the existing configurations of the oil industry. The American Jewish Congress took the lead in urging the U.S. Congress to initiate tax reform designed to end windfall profits that petroleum companies would reap from an oil shortage. In support of this tax modification, the charge was leveled that oil companies had been able to exempt profits from U.S. taxation by "developing foreign rather than domestic sources of energy."[30] Another example of the organized Jewish response to the oil companies occurred when three hundred Jewish leaders meeting as the Conference of Presidents of Major Jewish Organizations endorsed a boycott of Gulf Oil because of its contributions to Arab public relations activities in the United States. It was indeed difficult to distinguish between the merits of this action and those of the Arab boycott.

The influence of the Anti-Defamation League and the American Jewish Congress was great, but now it was pitted against the growing influence of Arab oil and wealth. To some extent the tables were being turned. The advocates of Israel found it increasingly necessary to become explicit in their appeal, while the Arabs for the first time began to operate through implicit influence. Without their having entered the contest directly, the Arabs' position was being pressed by Kissinger, who feared that harsh legislation would jeopardize his mediation efforts, and by business houses that wanted no impediment in the way of growing Middle East trade. Even in an election year, when Jewish influence was supposedly at its zenith, Congress did not act on the antiboycott and oil taxation proposals before it. Most of those who followed these events assumed, however, that eventually the proponents of such legislation would have their way.

A final arena of the Arab-Israeli battle for implicit influence on the American scene was higher education. Several oil-rich countries, particularly Saudi Arabia, looked to the United States for assistance in developing their educational systems. Not only were thousands of young Arabs enrolled in American universities, but teams of American academicians were also invited to the Arab countries to offer advice on the formation of new universities and technical schools. The issue was whether Jewish academicians would be permitted to participate. It had been the Saudi practice to deny visas to individuals from Jewish families, no matter what reason they gave for desiring to enter the country. The policy was seldom officially acknowledged; visas for certain individuals simply were not forthcoming. Quite often the situation became self-policing, as when American institutions participating in the projects simply did not nominate Jews as participants. The exclusion the Arabs practiced in such cases was tied to assumptions regarding religious persuasion rather than to any aid that might have been provided Israel. Thus anti-Semitism was at work.

In one case the Midwest University Consortium for International Activities withdrew from a project sponsored by the University of Riyadh because of Saudi refusal to provide a visa to a Jewish professor. A similar situation developed over participation by the Massachusetts Institute of Technology in a Saudi water resources project. Harvard also refused to take part in a Saudi project. In response to a solicitation from the American Jewish Congress, more than 100 colleges and universities gave assurances that they would not accept discrimination against Jews as the price for receiving lucrative development contracts from Arab countries. Some Arabs obviously felt that they could not allow individuals who might support their enemy to take part in sensitive development activities. In so doing they were inadvertently accepting the Israeli contention that no distinction could be made between a Jew and a Zionist. The upshot was that Arabs were denied the services of many of the best academicians—Jews and non-Jews alike—in the United States.

As contention over the boycott, oil taxation, and educational contracts demonstrated, the work of the Anti-Defamation League against the new anti-Semitism had more than one facet. Basically, the supporters of Israel wanted to maintain among the American people a sympathetic attitude toward the Jewish state. But another result—intended or not—was the introduction of an element of friction into official and unofficial associations of the United States with the Arab countries. This friction proved to be a serious source of complexity for U.S. policy toward the Middle East. As we have seen, the special relationship with Israel influenced the shape of agreements that Kissinger was able to negotiate. Through Congress the Israelis could limit the quantity of arms shipped to Jordan and Saudi Arabia and assure the supply of weapons to Israel, even after the Ford administration had opted for another course. By questioning the legitimacy of the boycott, the institutional arrangements of the oil companies, the inclination of the Arabs to invest their untold billions in the United States, and a role for the American educational establishment in Arab social development, the various groups that worked for Israel against the new anti-Semitism emphasized disjunctions in Arab-American relations. A growing affinity of Arabs and Americans for one another had resulted from the increasing Arab contact with the United States. But this feeling was being undercut somewhat by a suspicion among Arabs with regard to American intent. They could not help but wonder about the real meaning of the obstacles they were beginning to encounter in the areas of arms supply, trade, finance, and education.

Divergence also occurred between the positions of the Arabs and the United States in various international bodies, and each time the issue was Israel. In November 1975, the American delegation to the International Labor Organization, under pressure from representatives of the AFL-CIO, brought the United States to the point of withdrawing from the ILO over the granting of observer status in that body to the PLO. The same year, the United States government suspended financial support to the United Nations-Educational, Scientific, and Cultural Organization when the Arabs succeeded for a one-year period in having Israel barred from participation in UNESCO activities. On two occasions when virtually all Security Council members were prepared to condemn Israel for air raids that killed scores of women and children in Lebanon, the United States exercised its veto because the resolution did not also mention the terrorism undertaken by Palestinian guerrillas against Israeli civilians.

The Arabs were sufficiently sophisticated not to respond to the campaign rhetoric during the American presidential election in 1976, despite pledges by Ford and Carter not to tolerate another oil embargo—which incidentally no Arab leader had even remotely suggested. The pronouncements of support for Israel by Ford and the assertion of biblical sanction of its legitimacy by Carter were permitted by the Arabs to pass uncontested. Nor did the Arabs make much of Ford's decision at the height of the campaign to lift the ban on the sale of advanced weaponry to Israel, including the particularly deadly antipersonnel cluster bomb. Such actions did have their effect. From the Arab standpoint these were American institutions conducting business purported to be for the public good, and American leaders speaking for their people. Domestic pronouncements in the heat of a political campaign may be regarded as different from parlance among diplomats or from propaganda wars among contending states. The nature of official American behavior, however, could only increase Arab reservations because it raised questions about the actual purpose of the United States. Any mediator had to overcome this outlook in order to assure a continuation of Arab confidence in his own personal integrity and in the political dependability of the United States.

In addition to dispelling Arab misgivings, Kissinger had been forced to contend with severe restrictions on the leverage he might have been expected to exert over Israel. Rabin had made it clear in public statements that quite often he could afford to ignore much of what Kissinger said.[31] After all, seventy-six senators had supported Rabin's position over that of the secretary of state. When critics of step-by-step diplomacy charged that Kissinger's negotiating design was flawed insofar as it permitted Israel to procrastinate in returning the occupied territories and thereby to vitiate the effect of the American effort, the secretary of state angrily responded that any attempt on the part of the United States to force Israel to return the territories would bring the two countries to the point of rupturing relations. This remark was, of course, an overstatement. Nevertheless, its implication was clear. Israeli influence in the United States made it impossible for Kissinger to press the Jewish state constantly toward a settlement. Kissinger's position was circumscribed. He knew it. The trustee of peace was indeed a player, not a referee, and he was operating within definite and sometimes uncomfortable confines.

6

Israel's Defense Policy

Perhaps nothing limits the activities of a Middle East mediator more than the Israelis' approach to their country's security. Seen almost totally in physical or strategic terms, the concept emphasizes "secure and recognizable boundaries that are defensible." Following the 1967 war this formula was utilized by Israel to justify retention of the occupied territories in Gaza, Sinai, the West Bank, and the Golan Heights. In its election platform announced shortly after the 1973 hostilities, the Labor Party affirmed the necessity for defensible borders and asserted that "Israel shall not return to the lines of June 4, 1967 which had invited aggression."[1] The essence of the Israeli position was that the mere act of relinquishing the occupied territories would automatically reestablish the conditions that assured another war. Four years later, as Israelis and Arabs were maneuvering for position in response to President Carter's insistence at one point on reconvening the Geneva Conference, Foreign Minister Moshe Dayan responded to secret Jordanian proposals on the disposition of the West Bank with an expression of concern over the effect the establishment of Jordanian authority on the West Bank would have on Israeli security. Whatever the Israelis' intent, they always focused on the security aspects of negotiations.

A clear-cut concept of defensibility is complicated by Jewish nationalism. First, on the issue of the ancestral homeland, many Israelis contend that Jews have a historic right to all land between the Jordan River and the Mediterranean. The Labor Party was somewhat more circumspect in its claims to the West Bank than its successors in the government of Prime Minister Menachem Begin. Labor Party leaders did not stress their irredentist position. They had maintained that they were willing to negotiate with the Arabs over parts of the West Bank while retaining areas that were critical to Israel's security. On coming to power, Begin did not hesitate to declare Israel's right to the entire West Bank.

For political as well as security reasons, successive Israeli cabinets were unswerving in their opposition to the creation of a Palestinian state in the area west of the Jordan River. When asked to take a position on the West Bank, the Israelis proposed ideas that were often incomprehensible. Essentially, all propositions combined Israeli security with Arab administration. Most Israelis, led by Moshe Dayan, thought that a string of armed Jewish settlements along the Jordan River with some type of Arab administrative supervision of the West Bank population should satisfy both sides. Ultimately the Begin government adopted this proposal for negotiations with Sadat following the Israeli-Egyptian Treaty of March 1979.

In one configuration, Jordan and Israel would share the governing role on the West Bank, which itself would be autonomous but federated with Israel. Under this scheme the political aspirations of West Bank Arabs would supposedly be satisfied by permitting them to vote for representatives in Amman. A more rational Israeli alternative that lost popularity under the Begin government was to have a truncated Palestinian West Bank incorporated into Jordan.

While the Israelis had proceeded with the construction of the fortified Jewish settlements along the Jordan River, the political aspects of these schemes remained tentative. All proposals lacked reality, a fact that was highlighted by the Israeli position that under no circumstances should West Bank leadership fall to the Palestine Liberation Organization. The tension in the unusual mutations that appeared in each successive Israeli suggestion stemmed from the knowledge that a Jewish state could not function with a million alienated Arabs in its midst. A way must be found to exclude Palestinians from the body politic. Yet Israelis did not trust the Palestinians enough to leave them to their own devices in a separate state on the West Bank.

The schemes proposed by Israelis for a West Bank solution involved two techniques for resolving the dilemma of the alienated Arab. Both were eccentric and could only have come from the Israeli mind. First, armed Jewish settlements in the tradition of the Yishuv would somehow provide the security for which all Israelis yearned. Second, the Palestinian identity would be denied, or at least effectively subsumed in a Jordanian presence. Even with the best of luck, these suggestions would give a mediator very little that could be useful in any effort to work toward a Middle East solution.

The other complicating factor associated with Israeli defense related to agricultural settlements and applied principally to the Golan Heights, where the Israelis had established a number of kibbutzim. Early in 1974, it was even announced that plans were underway for building the first Israeli city on the heights. Initially, Israel's interest in Golan had been a straightforward security consideration. One of the early disputes following the establishment of Israel concerned Hula, an area of perhaps 100 square miles that lies below Golan and that the 1948 armistice declared to be demilitarized. While Syria contended that the disposition of the area had not yet been resolved, the Israelis interpreted the provisions of the armistice to mean that Hula would remain devoid of military emplacements but under Israeli sovereignty. The usual troubles occurred between Arab cultivators and Israeli officials as kibbutzim began to encroach on Arab property rights. When Israel drained the lake in Hula, more tension developed. Palestinian refugees on the Syrian side of the line, and Syrian forces themselves, responded by firing on Israeli installations, a practice that continued intermittently until 1967. Typically, the Israelis ignored the political ramifications of the dispute and considered only the matter of security—the necessity to compel Arabs to stop shooting at Israeli settlements.

The arrival of Jewish settlers in Golan changed the rationale for Israeli occupation of the heights. One leader of the Golan Israelis expressed the revised position in the statement, "Israel is a country without borders. No two people in Israel or abroad agree on the borders of Israel. What we have is where Jewish people have settled. The only solid thing is that in the last eighty years the Jewish people have not willingly given up a settlement. The people feel that by coming here they have made this the border."[2] A solution of the Golan problem that would be acceptable to even the most forthcoming of Syrian regimes would require Israel to relinquish not just territory but the settlements as well. Clearly, this could not be popular in Israel.

The three concepts involved in Israel's territorial integrity—defensible borders, ancestral homeland, and Jewish settled areas—were not coterminous. What the advocates of one concept would be prepared to surrender, proponents of another would consider unthinkable. Thus successive Israeli governments were required to work within the context of a complex situation. During the Kissinger negotiations the Israeli leadership was reluctant to provide the ultimate map of Israel, a step that some critics of Israel's policy urged them to take as a means of breaking the impasse in negotiations and paving the way for a final settlement. Usually Israeli officials in their talks with Kissinger would go no further even in informal exchanges than to commit themselves to relinquish most, if not all, of Sinai while keeping most of Golan, all of Jerusalem, and retaining military control over the West Bank and Gaza. Begin, of course, went a step further at the Camp David meeting in September 1978 and agreed under certain conditions to surrender all of Sinai including the Jewish settlements that had been established there.

In any event the Israelis were not prepared to return to the 1967 borders—a position they expressed to the Egyptians when representatives of the two governments met at the first convening of the Geneva Conference in December 1973. The Arabs found this position unacceptable. Kissinger was faced, therefore, with what appeared to be an irreconcilable tangle of vague but rigid territorial claims that the Israelis could not define because of political problems at home. For the Israelis it meant contested borders, a situation that they had experienced since the inception of their state and that the country's leaders over the years had said they hoped to change. In terms of a negotiated settlement, therefore, the Israelis themselves constituted a major obstacle to arriving at the conditions that Egypt, Syria, and Jordan had pledged to recognize under United Nations Resolutions 242 and 338—that is, to accept Israel's existence with "secure and recognized borders free from threats or acts of force."

The Policy: Regional Dominance

Defensible borders proved to be a matter not only of self-definition but also of self-fulfillment for Israelis who were intent on defending the occupied territories against Arab claims. With massive American assistance and draconion domestic economic measures, the Israelis were able, within a year of the cessation of hostilities, to establish a stronger military position in relation to Egypt and Syria that they had held prior to the 1973 war. Thereafter they returned to the practice of assessing their position vis-à-vis their neighbors in terms of military balance, a concept the Arabs had found repugnant since it was first introduced in the early 1950s. Prime Minister Rabin could tell the World Jewish Congress in February 1975 that Israel's rearming had guaranteed that the balance of military power had not changed to his country's disadvantage. Israel could take care of itself, he said, and need not make concessions to the Arabs! The basis of Arab dissatisfaction was evident in this Israeli perception.

The Arabs were greatly annoyed at having their every act measured by this military balance with the implication that Israel must initiate some countermeasure for whatever they happened to do. Thus when Syria obtained shipments of Soviet arms, some Israelis asserted that President Assad was about to acquire the capability of launching a full-scale attack on Israel independent of Egypt. For the Israelis the conclusion was inescapable that they would need even more and better weapons from the American arsenal. Defense Minister Peres applied the concept again when Syria did not rebuild and repopulate the Golan city of Quneitra, which it had regained as an outcome of the 1974 disengagement agreement with Israel. Supposedly a bustling Syrian city just a few hundred yards from the border would give the Israelis some assurance that the Syrians would not again attack the occupied portion of Golan. The Syrians' refusal to rebuild the city aroused Israeli suspicions and was used to justify requests for additional military assistance from the United States. Syria's paving of the roads on Mount Hermon was also viewed in terms of its influence on the military balance, and Jordanian-Syrian talks on coordination of military policy— one of the oldest and perhaps most futile gestures of Arab unity— was immediately seen as a threat. Even Arab recognition of the PLO as the sole legitimate representative of the Palestinian people was interpreted by the Israelis in this light. Yet despite all of the anxiety these incidents represented, Israel maintained a preponderance of military power that the Arabs could not hope to match for years to come.

From Israel's inception, "balance" had meant a capability of turning away all Arab armies simultaneously. Now Israel went further and moved to achieve not just defensible borders but rather a position of undisputed military superiority over the region as a whole. On a smaller scale, it reached for the same position in the Middle East that the United States had attempted to achieve in the world during the early 1960s. One factor that led Israel to this strategy was the growing involvement of distant Arab countries in the Palestine problem as Arab solidarity assumed more reasonable and less rhetorical proportions. An indication of the change was seen in 1974, when Arab League members made financial and material commitments to the national struggle. In an unambiguous response Defense Minister Peres threatened Israeli military retaliation against any Arab countries that sent armies to attack the Jewish state. Kuwait, Morocco, Libya, Saudi Arabia, and Abu Dhabi were singled out in this warning. The capability for carrying out this threat was verified in July 1976 by the Israeli raid on the Entebbe Airport in Uganda in order to rescue passengers of a plane hijacked by terrorists. Entebbe was as far from Israel as the most distant Arab state. Who could doubt that the Israelis were serious about such threats?

A second matter was the question of Red Sea shipping. Egyptian intentions to interdict movement from the Red Sea through the Gulf of Aqaba to the Israeli port of Elath helped precipitate the Six-Day War when Israel attacked Egypt. Subsequently, Israeli officials asserted that the Jewish state must maintain a presence in and continuity with Sharm es Shiekh, the tip of the Sinai Peninsula controlling access to Aqaba. During the 1973 war, however, Egypt imposed a blockade at Bab el Mandeb at the southern terminus of the Red Sea—six hundred miles from Israeli territory. The use of this vantage point was formalized in 1974 when the Arab League arranged for the lease of Perim Island from South Yemen, and Egyptian troops were stationed there. The Sharm es Sheikh position was thereby rendered useless as an assurance against the interruption of the flow of Iranian oil that was so vital to Israeli economic and military performance.

Under the disengagement agreement of January 1974 and the Sinai Accord of September 1975, Egypt agreed not to press a blockade. Nevertheless, as a potential counter against such an eventuality, Israel reconstrued its occupation of Sharm es Sheikh as a position from which it could dominate the shipping lanes of the reopened Suez Canal if Egypt hoped to continue traffic through the canal while imposing a blockade on Israel from the straits at Bab el Mandeb. One factor slipped from sight, namely, that Israeli forces in March 1973 had temporarily occupied some of the islands at Bab el Mandeb in what appeared to be little more than a training exercise. The Israelis thereby demonstrated the military capability of seizing a commanding position at Bab el Mandeb if that eventuality ever proved necessary. It was indeed a thin line that divided legitimate defense from regional dominance. By 1979, when the Israeli-Egyptian Treaty was concluded, conditions were such—particularly with regard to the sources of Israel's oil supplies—that Sharm es Sheikh had lost much of its importance to Israeli security. The area was relinquished to Egypt, but not before arrangements were made to have it occupied by United Nations Forces.

As real as defense requirements were for Israeli, they were devastating to any effort by a mediator to achieve an Arab-Israeli understanding. In successfully assuming a posture of regional dominance, as opposed to a more moderate defense concept, the Israelis placed the Arabs in the position of always attempting to resolve problems with their antagonist as the weaker of the two sides. From the standpoint of Israel's military preponderance, Rabin was correct in his assertion that his country need not make concessions. This almost total absence of moderation added to the Arabs' frustrations and made them more rigid for fear that any concessions they made in an accommodation with Israel would be interpreted by their people as evidence of weakness rather than as justified steps toward the realization of national interests through a peaceful settlement. For several decades the Arabs had centered their attention on eliminating feelings of weakness in the presence of the West, and it was not likely that they would suddenly change their outlook and willingly accept impotence in a peace agreement with a country they considered to be the West's surrogate.

Critics often suggested to the Israelis that security had political as well as strategic connotations and that to base their position solely on defensible borders that incorporated occupied territories amounted to the "delusory security of acreage."[3] On a visit to Israel in November 1974, the French foreign minister developed the theme that security depended not so much on conquered territory as on "a whole series of peace undertakings and guarantees," including the implementation of United Nations resolutions.[4] Harvard professors Stanley Hoffman and Nadav Safran, both experts in international politics, raised related issues. The former proposed that emphasis be placed not on the strategic necessity of holding territory but on the dangers of hostile armies ever again being deployed in that territory. Hoffman's plea, of course, was for demilitarization. Safran questioned whether over the long run 2 million Israelis could sustain a physical military balance with 60 million oil-rich Arabs.[5] Implicit in this query was whether the time had not come to achieve some equanimity in Israeli thinking between strategic and political considerations.

At the root of the Israelis' refusal to accept political over strategic security was their inherent distrust of Arabs. In a poll conducted by the Israeli Institute of Applied Social Research two months after the October War, 80 percent of the respondents expressed the belief that destruction of Israel and not the return of the occupied territories constituted the real Arab purpose.[6] The Israelis argued that agreements offered by their neighbors did not guarantee in practical terms that at some future date Arabs would not renew pressure against the original 1948 boundaries, even after Israel had relinquished the occupied territories. Thus we confront the real basis for the Israelis' obsession with security—they did not trust the Arabs.

Writing in the American press, Defense Minister Peres pointed out that, even if Israel gave what Egypt wanted, the Egyptians would press Syrian claims, and when Israel reached a settlement with Syria, both Egypt and Syria would press the claims of the Palestinians, who would establish themselves on the West Bank and in turn press for the liquidation of the Jewish state. The Israelis too were caught in the two-level syndrome of Arab politics in which the position of the leader of an individual Arab state could not be separated from his aspirations for the Arab nation. Kissinger's task was not just to reach an equitable agreement between the two sides. First he had to change this Israeli perception —an outlook engendered by the Arabs' view of their nation. The issues were those of the mind, and they were intertwined to a point where a solution sometimes seemed impossible.

Using typical strategic thinking, the Israelis always assumed the worst possible position for themselves and attributed optimum strength to their adversary. The Israeli ability to respond was invariably minimized in such exercises, and attention was devoted to overcoming what amounted to hypothetical Arab military excellence. Strategic thinking, in fact, lay at the root of Israel's insistence on maintaining a favorable balance of military power. The outcome was a compelling necessity for greater and greater military capability and ultimately for regional dominance. One of the principal measures of a mediator's success would be the extent to which he could persuade the Israelis to move away from their strategic approach and toward a political settlement in which all shared the risks of peace. Repeatedly Kissinger urged the Israelis to take this chance.

Throughout each negotiating sequence, however, the Israelis held tenaciously to their strategic concept. In September 1974, in talks with President Ford that were meant to be preparatory to the resumption of negotiations over Sinai, Prime Minister Rabin insisted that any territorial concessions by Israel must be matched by concessions on the part of the Arabs that would *increase Israel's sense of security.*[7] In subsequent talks with Israeli leaders, Kissinger agreed that any accord must embody "some kind of non-belligerency" in exchange for additional territory. The Israelis translated Kissinger's terminology into political concessions by the Arabs that would strengthen their *sense of well-being and security.*[8] In rejecting the final Egyptian position in the abortive March 1975 attempt to reach an interim agreement over Sinai, Rabin expressed the hope of resuming the talks, but only "under circumstances that will *protect Israel's security.*"[9] Indeed, security rather than peace appeared to be the Israeli purpose.

The Tactics: Massive Retaliation and Preventive Attacks

Beginning in the mid-fifties, whenever an Arab government participated in the planning or execution of guerrilla attacks against Israel, or even permitted its territory to be used for this purpose, the Israelis responded with massive retaliation. Over the years Syria, Jordan, and Egypt were to feel the pain of such retribution. The United States had come to accept this Israeli response to transgressions against the Israeli people, even though it sometimes aggravated the situation and contributed to an Arab desire for further vengeance. At the time of Israel's disengagement agreement with Syria, the American position was formalized by Kissinger's giving confidential assurances to Israel that his government would condone and politically support antiguerrilla countermeasures taken in self-defense.

In the aftermath of the 1973 war, this American and Israeli position did not rankle the Arabs as much as might be expected. Hussein had driven PLO forces from Jordan in 1970 for the very reason that he wanted to prevent terrorist attacks launched from his territory and thereby avoid the inevitable Israeli retaliation. Sadat's policy was similar in intent, even though he was never called upon to be as antagonistic toward the Palestinians as Hussein in its application. In the Sinai Accord, Sadat took an additional step when he agreed to preclude all paramilitary attacks on Israel from areas under Egyptian jurisdiction. As an article of Arab faith, Assad refused to undertake such a commitment in the Golan disengagement agreement, but after the October War, the PLO was seldom active against Israel from Syrian territory.

If not peace, the Arabs had accepted a *modus vivendi* with their Jewish neighbor. Limits on Israeli expansion and bounds on the Arabs' hostility had been set. Only the situation along Israel's border with Lebanon remained ambiguous. As controls had been placed on their activities elsewhere, Palestinian forces had concentrated in Lebanon, which served as a refuge from less-than-friendly Arab regimes and also as a base for operations against Israel. The Israelis behaved accordingly. Throughout 1974 and 1975, massive sea, air, and ground thrusts were made against Palestinian military sites and refugee camps in Lebanon following each raid into Israel. Israeli forces roamed at will over South Lebanon, destroying any village suspected of harboring guerrillas. Lebanese noncombatants suffered as much as Palestinian fighters.

In effect, Israeli policy offered Lebanon peace and coexistence if it rid itself of the Palestinians, but circumstances would not permit the Lebanese to accept. Lebanon was immobilized by a confessionally organized population and government. The heads of two Muslim communities (Sunni and Shia'), as well as the leader of the Druz (a group of Islamic origins), saw their identity in Arab nationalism. On the other hand, four distinct Christian communities grasped at the independent image found in Crusader roots. The two categories—Muslim and Christian—were divided among themselves insofar as the Shia' population was at best half-hearted in its commitment to Arabism, while many Christians of the Greek Orthodox and Protestant communities rejected the tendency among the Maronite Christians to isolate themselves from the Arab nation. The Christians, particularly the Maronites, drew resources from a prosperous emigrant population located in West Africa and North and South America. They nurtured their ties with the West and most would gladly have cleansed themselves of the Palestinian intruders to live in peace and prosperity as the bankers and entrepot merchants of the Eastern Mediterranean.

Muslim Lebanese, despite their greater number, found themselves operating at an economic and political disadvantage in relation to their Christian countrymen. In order to redress this balance they looked to Arab national power and rhetoric, arousing fears among Christians, who could see themselves being overwhelmed by a wave of Muslim might receiving its impetus from the great Islamic hinterland of the Middle East. Because Lebanese Muslims perceived security in Arab unity, they were not in a position to repudiate the Palestinian presence in their country. But the Muslim leadership did not want its Lebanese identity lost in a larger Arab state either. Even among Muslims, the enterpreneurial spirit of the Lebanese was too strong and life was too good for that. Muslim leaders saw their Arab policy as a means of gaining a greater share of the fruits to be distributed in Lebanon. Tensions between the two communities led to periodic bloody outbreaks that some times reduced commerce to a trickle and resulted in innumerable deaths. The most serious disturbances occurred in 1958 and 1975 —76 when, because of the fragmented nature of the population, the situation got beyond the control of any combination of domestic political and security forces.

As Lebanon became the target of an Israeli retaliation sparked by Palestinian acts of terrorism, Christian-Muslim tensions steadily increased. Quite naturally, differences centered on the right of the Palestinians to operate independent of Lebanese authority. An effort had been made in 1969 through the intercession of other Arab states to arrive at an understanding that would permit the Palestinian presence and mission to be accommodated in ways that were not offensive to the local sensitivities of Christian Lebanese. But the arrangement proved to be less than adequate. Not only in the refugee camps, but throughout much of South Lebanon where the PLO forces were concentrated for attacks on Israel, Palestinians refused to operate within the context of Lebanese sovereignty. PLO directives actually superseded the power of either the Lebanese government or security force in large parts of the country.

The Lebanese civil war, which reached dreadful proportions in 1976, had started in April 1974 when Christians murdered twenty-six Palestinians in a bus ambush. To the extent that the fighting that ensued was between Lebanese Christians and Muslims, it was depicted as being over the distribution of economic and political resources among the respective confessional communities. But the Christian purpose was not just to retain the status quo; it was also to end Palestinian power and influence. In one brutal decimation of a Palestinian refugee camp, it was actually Palestinian Christians and not Muslims who suffered at the hands of Lebanese Christians. Christians or not, they were Palestinians, and they symbolized Arab and Muslim power that threatened Lebanese Christian identity. Moreover, the Palestinian factor caused many Shia' Muslims to join Christian forces as the fighting continued. The PLO leadership liked to explain the war in secular and sometimes Marxist terms—as a struggle between the haves and the have nots. Arafat maintained that his operations were still against the Israelis, and at first he interceded in the communal strife only when Muslim forces seemed to be suffering excessively. After all, it was the Muslims who assured the PLO sanctuary in Lebanon. But with time, the Palestinians found that they could not ignore Christian hostility. Little by little, Palestinian forces were withdrawn from the border region and moved north to Beirut, Tripoli, and Sidon, where the future of Lebanon was being decided. A formal commitment to the fighting had been thrust on the PLO, because from Lebanon it had no place to which it could transfer its operations and still avoid becoming the captive of one or another Arab state. Even if they opted for such captivity, the Palestinians choices were limited. In order to pursue its objectives, the PLO had to conduct its activities from a country that bordered Israel; otherwise its claim to a role in Arab politics would not be credible.

Eventually the Syrians were drawn into the fighting against the PLO for fear of what Palestinian/Muslim success could mean in terms of Israeli intervention. PLO domination of the Lebanese state and countryside would run counter to Assad's growing affinity for a confederation to the east and north of Israel. To Assad, therefore, Palestinian interests were secondary to those of Syria, and he was not about to permit Lebanon to become dominated by the PLO.

Israel had long held that it could not be indifferent to what took place in Lebanon. Over time the Israelis had moved closer to enunciating a policy of having Lebanon neutralized. When the PLO had asked Arab governments for missiles to protect its refugee camps from air strikes, the Israelis had warned that they would destroy such weapons and that Lebanon itself would become a battlefield if Arab armament or armies were transferred to that country. In any resumption of Arab-Israeli hostilities, a military drive up the interior Bekaa Valley of Lebanon would involve few difficulties for Israeli forces and could offer the ultimate prize of splitting Syria with the capture of the transportation center at Homs. Syrian forces amassed in the defense of Damascus would thereby be denied access to most sources of supply.

In the back of everyone's mind was the knowledge that, if Lebanon's Christian population were pressed too hard, it would eventually opt for partition with the idea that a smaller Christian state would prosper under Western protection. Such a prospect was in fact presented to a French envoy by Christian leaders at the height of the fighting in 1975. From the standpoint of the Syrians, Palestinians, and Muslim Lebanese, partition was a horrifying thought. It would alienate part of the Arab homeland, possibly introduce new Western interference into the affairs of the region, and result in the creation of what would amount to a "second Israel." In any final battle between Christians and Muslims, the Arabs could see Israel intervening to facilitate partition insofar as it would be an effective means of sealing off Israel's northern border from Palestinian terrorists. When Syria finally intervened in Lebanon in June 1976, its purpose was to freeze developments short of a point where these events could logically occur. Thus no contradition really existed between the Syrian decision to use force first against the Palestinians and then, after establishing some control over the PLO, to turn its guns on the

Christians who had never retreated from the objective of ending the influence in their country of the Arabism that Assad represented.

As the civil war in Lebanon continued, Israelis perceived a growing threat to their security. The arms buildup by the contending forces in Lebanon had been enormous and rapid. Artillery, rockets, and armored vehicles were deployed. Both sides were well financed, sometimes from the same source. At one point both Syria and Saudi Arabia saw their interests being served by this double game. The Israelis did not stand idly by while the Palestinians and their Muslim allies pressed for political dominance in Lebanon. Israel interdicted the delivery of arms to Muslim forces and even sank ships carrying supplies to the PLO. Conversely, it openly armed the Christians to a point of sending shiploads of materiel to the Christian enclave north of Beirut. Yet too much was at stake in relations with the United States and Egypt to go further. In arguing the case for more overt intervention, Israel would have had to establish that events in Lebanon constituted a clear and present danger to its security. It was a case that would have been difficult to sell to the United States. Moreover, a general Middle East war at this juncture would have set back Israel's efforts to achieve an impregnable defense. Some doubt was also expressed over the Israelis' ability in a general war to hold fronts on the Golan Heights, along the Jordan River, and in Sinai while pressing a campaign in Lebanon. The Israelis, therefore, had little choice but to allow the carefully executed movement of troops into Lebanon that Syria undertook in support of Lebanese integrity in April 1976.

But when Syrian forces in Lebanon reached thirty thousand troops the problem for Israel changed. The danger of guerrilla raids across the Lebanese border was superseded by the possibility of a conventional military attack of the type that had been launched from Golan and the Suez Canal in 1973. The United States brought great pressure on the Israelis to refrain from taking action. In addition, American channels served as liaison between the two enemies in order to assure that Israel did not misconstrue a single Syrian step and that Syria went no further than Israel could

allow. The American purpose was to see that the short-run interests of both Syria and Israel were met. Kissinger's reasoning was
straightforward—Syria was viewed as the force that could bring
an end to the fighting in Lebanon, thereby reducing the chances of
the Arabs' and the Israelis' stumbling into a war over the affair.

When Syrian forces turned against the Palestinians, Israel found
some solace in developments. Its leaders ultimately concluded that
their security was not being threatened from Lebanon as long as
Syrian forces did not move into the area fifteen miles or so beyond to the Lebanese-Israeli border and large numbers of Palestinians were not permitted to reestablish themselves in South
Lebanon. After October 1976, when the fighting subsided, conditions prevailed that were complementary to Israel's security. The
Syrians had no taste for confrontation, and they controlled Palestinian access to the border region. As an added precaution, the
Israelis armed and aided Christian forces near the border as a
deterrent to the Palestinians. A buffer zone was thereby created
without the partition of Lebanon. Out of the Lebanese civil war
the Israelis could say that they had achieved at least a temporary
accommodation along their northern border.

Over time a PLO buildup did occur in the area, and after a particularly murderous attack on Israeli citizens in March 1978,
Israeli forces temporarily occupied south Lebanon in a move to
destroy the Palestinians' bases. The introduction of UN forces
along the border again established the minimum security conditions demanded by the Israelis who thereupon withdrew their
forces.

In addition to massive retaliation, Israel had from time to time
undertaken preventive attacks. The most noteworthy was the as-
sault that launched the Six Day War in 1967 after Nasser ordered
the United Nations forces out of Sinai and declared, but somewhat
ambiguously executed, the closing of the Straits of Tirana to
Israeli shipping. Less dramatic were the attacks against Palestinian refugee camps in Lebanon in 1975. The Israelis claimed in
this case that by taking the initiative they had forestalled PLO
raids that were meant to disrupt the negotiation of the Sinai Accord. Another justification for the Israeli stance was that it kept

the antagonists sufficiently off balance to preclude them from taking action that would really hurt. The all-out war of October 1973, when Israel sustained heavy losses by not acting sooner, justified this aggressiveness in the minds of virtually all Israelis.

But as the incursions into Lebanon so amply demonstrated, Israeli policy toward the Arabs conveyed a sense of moral punishment. As such, it heightened Arab feelings of weakness and created severe problems for Arab leaders whenever they contemplated direct negotiations with Israel. The Israelis' position was one of studied disregard for Arab dignity. It could be argued that somehow Israeli retribution meted out as specific retaliation in areas just across its borders did not involve the same blatant insult that was to be found in the December 1968 attack on the Beirut Airport. Israeli troops landed in helicopters, fired a few shots, routinely destroyed several planes belonging to Middle East Airlines, and then calmly departed. Another such case was the operation of April 1973, in which Israeli commandos rode along the corniche of Beirut in rented taxis to kill their Palestinian quarry in some of the city's nicer apartment buildings and then escaped with few losses. The same could be said of the revelation that, during the 1975 Lebanese communal strife, Israeli snipers slipped into Beirut and took advantage of the chaos to assassinate certain Palestinians. The Israelis seemed to enjoy such dash, and they believed their acts were highly proper. However dazzling, and no matter how much these operations heightened the concept of Jewish self-reliance, they could never contribute to a Middle East settlement.

The Negotiating Objective: Settlement or Security?

Another difficulty for any mediator in the aftermath of the 1973 war was the implication in almost every Israeli act that Israel had less interest in a long-range settlement based on compromise and concessions than in weakening the military capabilities of the Arab enemy: security took priority over a negotiated settlement. Israel's military strategy rested on the premise that, without Egypt, the other Arab countries—Syria, Iraq, and Jordan—could not possibly initiate a successful attack. If Egypt could be neutralized in any future hostilities, Israel would have the advantage—but only if the fighting was of short duration. Otherwise the pressures of Arab nationalism would almost certainly draw Egypt into the fighting. Thus Israel not only had to be able to defeat the Syrians but also had to have the power to do the job quickly.

An obvious purpose of the Sinai Accord—discussed openly in Tel Aviv and Jerusalem—was to weaken Egyptian-Syrian solidarity and reduce Egyptian willingness to undertake military action in support of Syria in the event of Syrian-Israeli hostilities. It was clear even at the time of the unsuccessful negotiations over Sinai in March 1975 that, if Prime Minister Rabin hoped to win acceptance of an accord from the Israeli polity, he needed concessions that would remove Egypt, at least temporarily, from participation in any new fighting. An elaboration of this theme was seen in the idea of turning the Egyptians to domestic problems—persuading them to be less Arab. Instead of regional politics, they should devote their attention to matters of economic and social development at home. An element of this approach had been present during the early 1960s in the heyday of the American foreign assistance effort when aid to Egypt was justfied to some extent as a means of taking pressure off Israel. Again after the 1974 Sinai disengagement agreement, aid became a prominent feature of the American undertaking to Egypt, with an initial commitment of $250 million followed by a pledge of $750 million at the time of the Sinai Accord. In justifying the few concessions Israel had made to Egypt in the Sinai agreements, first Prime Minister Meir and then Rabin pointed to the rebuilding of the Canal zone cities, Port Said and Suez, as significant steps portraying Egypt's turning away from war—and presumably from the Arabs. This strategy continued. It was still evident after the Camp David agreements in 1978 when Israel insisted on a separate peace with Egypt. Insofar as the Israeli-Egyptian Treaty did not assure peace with Syria, Jordan, or the other Arabs, it had much more significance for the Israelis militarily than it did politically.

Quite naturally any move that served to preoccupy the Egyptians was counterproductive from the standpoint of Syrian and Palestinian perceptions because it left their issues—Golan and

Palestinian rights—unresolved. Because of the American role in achieving the Sinai Accord, Arabs quickly identified Israel's security objectives with American purpose. Syrian President Assad spoke directly to the point in saying, "It seems to us now that the policy of the United States has three goals—to strengthen Israel, to weaken the Arab nation and to divide it, and to weaken or eliminate Soviet influence in the Middle East. The pursuit of these goals makes it difficult, if not impossible, to accomplish a just and lasting peace in this area, and the goals explain why so little has been achieved since the war in October 1973."[10] In effect, Assad was asserting that the American intention was not peace at all. Rather, it was the enhancement of Israel's security and the achievement of great-power objectives that left the goals of the people of the Middle East largely unattended. It was not a climate conducive to an overall settlement. To the extent that Israel's concept of strategic security was served, the mediator's task seemingly became more complex.

The Israelis' concern for strategic considerations had actually been intensified by the outcome of the 1973 war. Their conviction as Jews that they could determine their own destiny in terms of the Promise of the Passover had been badly shaken. Many Israelis admitted that the losses in the fighting—the mere thought that Arabs could kill 2,600 Jewish soldiers and destroy 750 Israeli tanks and 150 jets—left them feeling that they had lost control of the future. Israeli defense had always rested on the resilience and sense of direction possessed by the individual soldier. This feature had been reflected in the almost nonexistent military code of dress, the casual response to command while the army was in garrison, and the careless approach to formal discipline within the ranks. Officers led—they did not direct. Army leadership, in fact, had always been one of the more cohesive and respected institutions in the land. In the aftermath of the war, the army lost some of its luster, particularly as then Defense Minister Moshe Dayan, Chief of Staff Daniel Elazar, and hero-turned-politician Gen. Ariel Sharon sniped at one another throughout the official judiciary hearings that were held to assess whatever blame might exist for the reverses experienced at the hands of the Arabs early in the fighting. For the first time Israelis were to ask: Does military elan provide a sufficient basis for defense?

The Israelis had little difficulty determining the steps that must be taken to overcome their military deficiencies. Failures had occurred in intelligence, assessment, and materiel. The army had not detected the full extent of the Arabs' war preparations; the government had been unduly confident that the Arabs would not attack; the population had not responded rapidly to the call for mobilization of reserves; and the economy had not provided the supplies necessary for the defense of the homeland. Structure was tightened all along the line. The army was to become more traditional, the government less complacent, and the public more alert. But within the economy the response was less certain. In the postwar military buildup, inflation had been rampant, foreign exchange reserves had dropped to new lows, and public expenditure —particularly for defense—was taking the lion's share of the national product. The economy had given its utmost. Yet by mid-1975, the Israelis calculated that, left to their own devices, they could sustain military operations at the level of the 1973 hostilities for only twenty-one days.

When Israelis looked beyond their borders they saw an equally grim set of circumstances. Despite the efforts of Henry Kissinger, the tacit accommodation with Hussein, and the disengagement agreement with Sadat and Assad, the Arabs still had a "next time" mentality. The attitude was evident in Arab newspaper editorials, magazine articles, and the statements of second-echelon leadership. The Arabs seemed to accept Israel's military superiority, but they looked forward to improving their own position and eventually being able to hold the kind of advantage they had seized at the outset of the October War. All the while the United States was counseling Israel to set aside its strategic concept of security and take a chance on peace by entering into political commitments that rested largely on mutual trust and understanding with the Arabs. Kissinger's advice notwithstanding, when the Israelis considered the situation confronting them, they saw a need for more arms, not a compromise. In January 1975 Defense Minister Peres was to assert that Israel had the greatest need in its history for military strength.

If Israel was seized with a national mania it was the necessity to control its own future. As symbolic and as unimportant as this issue may have seemed to Middle East peace, national morale required the Israelis to find some means for asserting their self-reliance. The logic of their purpose led to the necessity for freeing themselves from the pressure the United States placed on them to make concessions to the Arabs. Concessions could only increase the sense of having lost control of their destiny. While evading American pressure and establishing their independence from the United States, the Israelis still hoped to obtain from the Americans the arms and assistance that would permit them to repel hostile Arabs. Despite the contradictions inherent in this resolve, increased independence from the United States did, in fact, become an open feature of Israeli policy. No other course would meet the Israeli test. Jewish self-reliance was more important than negotiations, and at least for the time being the two were mutually exclusive. If self-reliance could be translated into policy, it meant greater emphasis on the strategic concept and even greater military power in relation to the Arabs. Once and for all the Jewish homeland must be secure, and it was along this path that the Israelis headed—in exactly the opposite direction from the one publicly charted by the trustee of peace.

Rabin amply expressed Israel's position on the eve of the March 1975 Sinai negotiations when he said:

> We want to be able to defend ourselves with our own force, and therefore we want defensible borders and a strengthening of our military forces, which, together with such borders, will enable us to stand alone.
>
> But if it comes to the threat of intervention by any power, we expect, like the rest of the free world, that the United States will fulfill its duty and prevent military intervention by that power.[11]

Strategy and Time

For the Israelis the critical element was time. The task was to assure the United States that a relatively stable situation could be created in the Middle East for a considerable period even without an Arab-Israeli settlement. In the short run the Arab armies were no match for the Israelis. The Egyptians were not sufficiently equipped for sustained military operations, and Syrian forces were not yet effective with the new weapons provided by the Soviet Union. Officials in Cairo and Damascus conceded the accuracy of this assessment. They were particularly apprehensive over Israel's growing edge of superiority, which could make its position unassailable within a few years.

One problem for the Arabs was the refusal of the Soviet Union to provide Egypt with the arms Sadat desired. Difficulties had begun prior to the 1973 war when the Egyptians in July 1972 expelled several thousand Soviet technicians who worked with the Egyptian Army. For two years before the expulsion, Soviet and Egyptian officials had been engaged in an acrimonious debate over the capability of Arab forces in the event of a resumption of hostilities with Israel. At issue was the Egyptian request that the Soviet Union provide the sophisticated weapons needed for an Arab offensive. The Soviets feared that any such military undertaking would lead to disaster along the lines of the 1967 fiasco. They said so, and they refused to associate themselves with any canal crossing by the Egyptian forces or to supply the equipment Sadat believed he needed for such a venture. This official Soviet attitude rankled Sadat, who as a new president had attempted to gain popularity by promising that 1971 would be a "Year of Decision" in regaining Sinai. At the operational level Soviet-Egyptian relations already carried the burden of the heavy-handed style of individual Russians in dealing with Egyptian officers. It took only a small incident to trigger Sadat's decision to ask that the technicians be withdrawn. The occasion presented itself when the Egyptian chief of staff arrived unannounced one day at Cairo West, a major Soviet military installation, and the Russians refused to allow him entry to the base. Egyptians regarded the event as a calculated insult.

In addition, Egypt's abandonment of the Soviet-supported heavy industry strategy as the best means of developing its economy, and the rise under Sadat of liberal forces more attuned to a mixed economy than to socialism, made an association with the Soviet Union less compelling. Then, after the October War, the United States moved to the center of the Middle East stage with Kissinger's shuttle diplomacy. The Soviets saw a sharp diminution of their influence and attributed this development to Sadat. They could see little reason to continue a basic commitment to any government that followed policies so injurious to Soviet interests. The Soviets did not terminate their military ties with Egypt altogether, however. Spare parts and new equipment arrived intermittently during late 1972 and early 1973. In the months before the October War larger quantities were made available, although critical offensive weapons—bombers and surface-to-surface missiles—were withheld. The Soviets did not participate in the planning or initiation of the 1973 war, but they did provide Egypt as well as Syria with massive amounts of supplies and equipment during the fighting and subsequently covered most of the losses incurred as the result of the action. But the military situation in the Middle East was dynamic, and the Soviets would not meet what Sadat saw as his postwar requirements. Relative to Israel's growing military strength, Egypt was rapidly slipping behind.

The Soviet decision not to provide Egypt with large quantities of arms was profoundly important to Israel. Arab military success rested on simultaneous attacks against Israel from the north and the south. As long as Egypt had no offensive capability, the Syrians were not likely to initiate hostilities. Soviet policy, therefore, was a deterrent to Arab aggressiveness and contributed to Kissinger's success in persuading the Syrians and the Egyptians to enter into negotiations. The Arabs simply did not have the option of fighting.

In order to overcome his military supply problem, Sadat contemplated shifting to Western Europe as a source of arms. Experts argued over the ability of the Egyptian forces to incorporate European weapons into what was essentially a Soviet system. Even the most optimistic estimates of Egypt's success in acquiring weapons from Europe and in training its forces to use them projected that at least seven years would be required to ready the Egyptian army for even minimal combat.

Barring a change in the Soviet posture, the Israelis knew that they could count on this lengthy respite before being called to battle again for their national survival. They hoped to use this time in two ways: to decrease the sense of imminent disaster that drove the Americans to seek an early settlement and to develop for themselves a military position the Arabs could never again match. With this strategy, major concessions, such as relinquishing the West Bank, could be forestalled and perhaps ultimately avoided altogether.

American policy worked both for and against the Israelis' use of time. As the American commitments embodied in the Sinai Accord were to demonstrate, the United States probably wanted the agreement more than Egypt, and certainly more than Israel. The accord represented the culmination of sixteen months of American effort. In pointing out the dangers of the situation, Kissinger foresaw the United States becoming involved, "at least indirectly given the international situation," in any war that resulted from a breakdown in negotiations. In addition to preventing a war, he also wanted to develop a stronger relationship between the United States and the Arabs while eroding the position of the Soviets in the area. The implication was that Israel should be sufficiently forthcoming in seeking an accommodation to avoid war and to serve America's regional interests. At a minimum, Kissinger wanted a negotiated outcome that would safeguard American prestige and protect his personal reputation. No agreement at all would be damaging to both. These considerations restricted Israel's strategy of using time.

The other dimension was the West's dependence on Arab oil. Presumably the United States—the only major Western power still supporting Israel with arms, financing, and political backing —would bear the brunt of any future oil restrictions the Arabs might decide to impose. In addition, in any extended bipolar struggle, Western defense was not viable without Arab oil. U.S. leaders hoped that, over the long run, the American economy could free itself of Arab oil by converting to other types of energy and by reducing consumption of petroleum products in home heating and in use of the internal combustion engine that powered the

American transportation network. The energy policy of each administration after 1973 was directed toward this end.

The Israelis fashioned their arguments to correspond with efforts by Washington to achieve independence from Arab oil. In pressing for additional arms assistance from the United States, Israeli officials emphasized that with arms they could assure stability in the Middle East for ten years. The supposition was that, with a strong Israel, the Arabs would not be in a position to start another war, or even to increase international tensions by using the oil weapon. Israel, in effect, would give the United States the time it needed to implement its energy policy. In order to serve the common purpose of independence from the Arabs, the Israelis emphasized the necessity for joint planning on future diplomatic moves. But they did not assume for a moment that negotiations could cease short of the neutralization of Egypt, nor did they hope to avoid costs. The costs were clear—marginal transfers of occupied territory in exchange for time. As one senior Israeli official put it, "We need time and we may have to buy it with real estate."[12] This aspect of U.S.-Israeli strategy proved ineffective in the long run. As time passed American dependence on Arab oil was to increase.

In order to determine Israel's short-term success in protecting its strategic concept, it is necessary to assess the Sinai Accord of September 1, 1975, in terms of Israeli security objectives rather than just from the standpoint of Kissinger's efforts to achieve a partial settlement of the Arab-Israeli struggle or the Arabs' aim of regaining the occupied territories and realizing the rights of the Palestinian people. In most respects the accord suited Israeli objectives. The security considerations Israel received from the agreement and its accompanying annexes, memoranda, and addenda were:

1. A resolve by Egypt to settle the Middle East conflict by peaceful means and a commitment to keep this pledge until some other agreement superseded the accord.

2. A commitment by Egypt not to resort to military blockades and a U.S. pledge of support in assuring the use of Bab el Mandeb by Israeli shipping.

3. An assurance from Egypt that it would refrain from para-

military activity, which in effect precluded Palestinian guerrilla attacks against Israel from Egyptian territory.
4. An early warning and sensor system installed in Sinai with
   U.S. assistance to permit Israel literally to detect Egyptian
   planes warming up on airfields in the Cairo-Delta area.
5. A confirmation of continued U.S. air reconnaissance over
   Sinai.
6. A limitation on military forces in Sinai, precluding Egypt
   from bringing across the Suez Canal any heavy weapon
   that could fire into Israeli lines.
7. The assignment of 200 American technicians to operate
   the early warning system, which provided an American as
   well as a United Nations deterrent to a surprise attack by
   either side.
8. An assurance from the United States that it viewed the
   accord binding even if UN forces were withdrawn.
9. A U.S. pledge to be responsive to Israel's defense, energy,
   and economic requirements by—
   a) sending an annual request for assistance to Congress,
   b) engaging in periodic consultations on Israel's long-term
      military supply needs,
   c) developing a contingency plan for providing arms in
      the event of an emergency,
   d) continuing to maintain Israel's defensive strength with
      high-technology items and within this context to con-
      sider providing jet aircraft yet to be deployed by the
      U.S. Air Force (F-16s) as well as missiles (Pershings)
      capable of bearing nuclear warheads,
   e) reimbursing Israel annually for the loss involved in re-
      linquishing control of the Abu Rudeis oil fields ($350
      million),
   f) increasing Israel's petroleum storage capacity from six
      months to one year,
   g) making available through purchase all petroleum needed
      for normal requirements in the event Israel was unable
      to secure suitable supplies, and applying the Inter-
      national Energy Agency oil-sharing plan to Israel if

the United States itself was prevented by an embargo from procuring the oil to meet its own requirements. (This stipulation included the shipping necessary to transport the oil as well as the oil itself and was limited to a duration of five years.)

10. An agreement by the United States not to press Israel for a second interim agreement with Egypt (which in effect would preclude the relinquishing of further territory in Sinai without a final treaty) and not to view the accord as being conditional on developments with other Arab states—that is, not to exert pressure on Israel to make concessions to Syria.

11. An understanding with the United States to regard negotiations with Jordan as a part of the overall peace settlement. (This point was tantamount to permitting Israel to ignore the Palestine Liberation Organization in the disposition of the West Bank.)

12. Diplomatic support from the United States in blocking all United Nations proposals detrimental to Israel; vetoing any Security Council resolution that contravened the accord; opposing any initiative to alter the UN resolutions that terminated hostilities in the 1967 and 1973 wars; and consulting immediately with Israel on appropriate steps to be taken in the event of threats to Israel's security or sovereignty by a world power (the Soviet Union).

13. An acceptance by the United States of Israel's position on the Geneva Conference to the extent that the United States would—

    a) seek to concert with Israel on strategy for the peace conference, which would be reconvened only at a time coordinated between the two governments,

    b) not recognize or negotiate with the Palestine Liberation Organization so long as the PLO did not recognize Israel's right to exist and did not accept Security Council Resolutions 242 and 338 (which affirmed Israel's pre-1967 borders but were vague about the return of all the occupied territories; resolutions also referred to

the Palestinian issue as the "refugee problem" rather
than a national cause),

c) accept the participation at Geneva of additional states,
groups, or organizations only after Israel itself had
agreed,

d) make every effort to assure that the substantive negotiations at Geneva were conducted on a bilateral basis
(this stipulation would allow Israel to face one Arab
state at a time and avoid any multilateral negotiations
that centered attention on an Arab position and brought
into play the concept of the Arab nation),

e) coordinate its actions with Israel to assure that the conference was conducted in a manner consonant with
these understandings.[13]

It could not be said, therefore, that Israel's security interests
had been neglected in the Sinai Accord. They were, in fact, the
most prominent feature of the document and its appendages, and
they afforded Israel both time and room to maneuver. As long as
the United States honored the agreement, it would be virtually
impossible to move Israel away from the objective of regional military dominance within defensible boundaries—a position that in
Arab parlance was equated with the hated status quo. In assertions
paralleling those made by Arab nationalists, American critics of
Kissinger's diplomacy maintained that the accord left Israel with
no incentive for an overall settlement. It stripped Sadat of authority with Syria and Jordan because through the accord Egypt
stepped back from Arab unity and at least temporarily was neutralized. Finally, it froze the Middle East situation in a condition
that was essentially unstable and explosive. Speaking for Syria,
President Assad said much the same. He did not see how Israel
could be pressured into further concessions. The Syrian representative at the United Nations rhetorically asked what the price of
liberating the remaining 99 percent of the occupied territory might
be if so much had to be paid for Mitla and Gidi passes. Actually,
one means of moving Israel incrementally was to emerge—bold
initiatives by Sadat that energized the United States to bring pressure on the Jewish state.

United States officials were almost certainly aware that they were contributing to the conditions critics described. In relation to the accord, the Ford administration presented to Congress a foreign assistance request of $3 billion—$2.3 billion for Israel, $750 million for Egypt, and smaller amounts for Syria and Jordan. From the total proposed for Israel, $1.8 billion was earmarked for military purchases. Just a few months earlier Secretary of Defense Schlesinger had said that this amount was double what was needed in order to preserve Israel's dominance in the Middle East military balance. When the American multiyear commitment assumed in the Sinai Accord was taken into consideration, along with the declared Israeli intention to engage in a rapid military buildup in excess of $2 billion annually for three years, the significance of the accord was clear. Israel's military domination of the region was intended to go unchallenged for the decade or even for the generation to which Israeli spokesmen often alluded.

Dominance Through Technology

Perhaps the most important feature of the memoranda that accompanied the Sinai Accord was the emphasis they placed on providing Israel with the most advanced military technology. These stipulations signaled Israel's intention to shift the image of its defense effort away from the "derring-do" and heroics of individual Israeli soldiers. Israel had always relied on current technology, but now the technology of modern warfare was to become the focus of its defense. Most significant in this regard was the Pershing missile, which was capable of delivering a nuclear warhead over a radious of 450 miles. The Israelis had already devised with their own resources the Jericho missile, which could deliver a 1,000-pound warhead 300 miles. Their defense industry had worked on this project for a number of years. Technical problems were not insurmountable, but economic exigencies made the acquisition of the Pershing far preferable to production of the Jericho.

For some time intelligence reports had indicated that the Israelis could also produce a nuclear device at their highly secret installation at Demona and had, in fact, developed the necessary components for a bomb. In December 1974 the Israeli government confirmed such a capability and announced the intention to proceed with the assembly of a bomb if it were needed. Prime Minister Rabin emphasized that Israel need not be the first to use nuclear arms in any future war in the Middle East, but a surprise attack would not catch Israel unprepared. Syria, Egypt, Iraq, and Algeria were reported to have Soviet-trained nuclear warfare sections in their military forces. They did not, however, have nuclear weapons. In response to the Israeli announcement, the Arabs indicated that they would seek assurance regarding nuclear capability from the Soviet Union at any time it appeared that Israel actually possessed a bomb.

Broad hints of escalation were in the air, therefore, when the United States agreed to a joint study with Israel of high-technology and sophisticated military items, including the Pershing missile. The United States had previously provided Israel with a nuclear delivery system in the form of the Lance missile. With its seventy-mile range, however, this weapon was of limited strategic significance. The Pershing, on the other hand, could reach all of Lebanon, Jordan, and Syria as well as the Egyptian Delta, Cairo, and Egypt's industrial complex at Helwan.

Kissinger attempted to respond to critics of this part of the accord with the assertion that the United States had no actual commitment to provide the Pershing missile. Anyway, he said, the Pershing had appeared on Israeli shipping lists as early as August 1974. Israeli Defense Minister Peres quickly announced that his government was prepared to guarantee that the Pershings would be armed only with conventional warheads. Peres attempted to convey the impression that the Pershing would offset missiles already in the hands of the Arabs.

All such protestations defied logic. The Arabs had no warheads, and the Soviet missile in their possession was more like the Lance than the Pershing. The United States was on the verge of giving Israel the capability of continuing its strategic domination of the region no matter what conventional weapons the Arabs might acquire. The moment its new weapons went into place, Israel's independence from American pressure would be achieved. In September 1975, the Israeli timetable for achieving this independence seemed to be the three years involved in its announced military buildup. Continued negotiations and limited Israeli concessions could probably be expected during that period. Thereafter, the homeland would be secure; Jewish self-reliance would be reestablished; and any further step toward an accommodation with the Arabs need not be taken if it raised the slightest doubt about Israel's security.

When questions arose about the advisability of introducing into the Middle East a weapon with such a clear nuclear potential, the Israelis adopted a fallback position. If not the Pershing, then the United States should provide Israel the conventional weapons that would give its forces a first-strike capability—more sophisticated planes, more laser bombs, and tactical missiles that were not suitable for nuclear warheads. A subtle threat was interposed in this request, namely, that any time Israel's qualitative superiority was overtaken by the Arabs, the Jewish state would have no choice but to consider nuclear arms—and it had the capability of developing them independently.

Presumably as long as Israel had the ability to launch a preemptive attack of such magnitude that the Arabs could not respond militarily, the qualitative superiority of Israeli forces would have been preserved and they could forgo the acquisition of the Pershing. In effect, the Israelis were willing to bargain over the full development of nuclear weaponry and conceivably delay the fateful step into this area of technologically advanced armament if the United States would play the game by their rules—that is, leave Israel full freedom of action (as the Middle East countries worked their way toward a settlement) and limit military discussions between the United States and Israel to the consideration of how Israel could best achieve a first-strike capability and retain regional military dominance. In the Israeli mind the United States must forgo any effort to tie military assistance to the political aspects of a Middle East settlement.

Commenting on the matter of advanced technology, a Jordanian spokesman said, "These weapons would put Israel in a position to dominate and threaten the whole area by remote control without actually conquering the territory."[14] Consideration of missiles in the Sinai Accord did seem to deemphasize the importance of the occupied territories to Israel's security. Nevertheless, the sanctity provided existing kibbutzim by Israelis who had established themselves in Golan, the importance of much of the West Bank for those with an affinity for the "historic homeland," and the firm opposition to any expression of Palestinian nationalism in an independent state between Israel and Jordan all indicated that, even with the enhanced security provided by either the Pershing missile or a first-strike capability, Israel would not easily make the concessions the Arabs considered necessary for a settlement.

What, then, of Kissinger? Where did all this leave him? Had he taken the gamble that, by giving the Israelis ten years of security defined in their own terms, he could persuade them to relinquish the occupied territories? Or did he so despair of even concluding an Arab-Israeli settlement that he had succumbed to the Israeli argument that the best to be expected for the Middle East was military stability achieved through Israel's strategic superiority under conditions of a nonsettlement? Certainly Kissinger was dedicated to aiding Israel. When his critics noted that even without additional arms Israel would have qualitative superiority through 1980, the secretary of state took the amazing position of casting doubt on this conclusion by questioning the capability of his own intelligence agencies. In 1973, he said, they had been erroneous in their assessment that Israel would win easily, and they could be wrong again. Perhaps the pressure of Israeli influence in the United States was so great that the Ford administration found it impolitic to resist Israeli claims. One thing was certain. Israel's reliance on strategic security had not been diminished by the Sinai Accord. With the possible exception of Sadat, the principal figures in the Arab-Israeli confrontation had not changed their minds about the situation. All the issues separating the Arabs and the Israelis were alive and virulent. If anything, the Sinai Accord had made the mediator's task more difficult.

7

The Mediator's Assets

The obstacles Kissinger encountered in the Middle East negotiating environment were indeed formidable. Virtually irreconcilable Arab and Israeli legitimacies within the context of long-standing U.S. support for Israel; the frustration and fears of the Arabs as they observed the Israelis moving toward an indomitable defense; the bitter legacy of American involvement in the West's years of supremacy in the region—all provided questionable ingredients for the fabric of peace Kissinger hoped to produce. Such problems raised the question whether "good will for America" was not too fragile a structure to bear the weight of negotiations that much of the world hoped would be guided to success by the United States. Actually the situation was not sufficiently negative for the mediator's efforts to be viewed as futile from the outset. The United States did possess certain assets, and full advantage would have to be taken of these if the Arabs and the Israelis were to be edged toward a settlement.

But the mediator could not assume that some technique of negotiation might succeed in the Middle East simply because it had achieved good results in resolving problems among states in other parts of the world. The standards of the craft of diplomatic exchange were of questionable value. The implied threat, the hard bargain, a multilateral format, the exploitation of an adversary's domestic weaknesses, any exchange based on a *quid pro quo* that ignored national aspirations and concepts of justice—none of these could be counted on to produce the desired results. Then too, it must be remembered that the mediator himself was at times the most avid player in the game. He also had interests to serve, and any move he made in the name of mediation could be rejected by Arabs or Israelis as self-serving. If total failure was to be avoided, it would be necessary for the trustee of peace to plan his moves with precision.

The United States ties with Israel placed serious limitations on the mediator's initiative, but at least the nature and extent of the restrictions were known. In addition, no one could miss the ever present Arab-Israeli hostility. It was only the many aspects of the third side of the triangle—the Arab-American relationship—that remained unexplored. The central question for Kissinger, in fact, was the dynamics of the links between the United States and the Arabs. What tools were available to the mediator in this area? When Arabs looked toward the United States, what did they see that was positive? Could these views be used to bridge the chasm created by U.S. support for Israel? Or was it predetermined that the supposed path to peace charted by Kissinger was a dead end that led into the barren wastes so typical of the Middle East landscape?

Policy Assets

The most obvious asset possessed by the mediator was the view of many Arabs that only the United States could facilitate an Israeli withdrawal from the occupied territories. This conclusion was first expressed and acted on by Anwar Sadat when he accepted U.S. intercession to bring about a cease-fire in the fighting along the Suez Canal in October 1973. His ready acceptance of American efforts to achieve Israeli pullbacks caught many Arabs by surprise. Even if the United States had the ability to pressure Israel, what made Sadat think that it would do so? The simple response was that for the short run Egypt had no alternative. The Egyptians were quite blunt in asking their Syrian, Iraqi, and other Arab partners, "What other country can force Israel to withdraw?"[1]

As tenuous as this argument seemed, it prevailed even among

the Palestinians until the time of the Sinai Accord. Thereafter discord developed, but Sadat persevered. His confidence in American intercession had never flagged, even in March 1975, when the negotiations that ultimately led to the Accord in September 1975 were suspended due to Kissinger's inability to squeeze concessions from the Israelis. Upon the conclusion of the accord itself, Sadat responded to his critics with the assertion that he had finally succeeded in making the United States a party to the Arab-Israeli dispute. In Sadat's mind this achievement was sufficient to offset the security gains realized by Israel. His outlook rested on a conviction that the United States could, and ultimately would, move the Israelis toward relinquishing the occupied territories and perhaps even bring the Palestinians and the Israelis to a grudging acceptance of one another.

The United States did what it could to encourage this belief in its mediating capacities. While supporting Israel with military and economic aid and refusing to deal with the Palestinians until they accepted Israel's existence, American officials never totally closed the door on an eventual understanding with the Arabs over their national aspirations. Kissinger maintained that Israel would have to be more forthcoming if peace were to be achieved. Ford asserted that the United States would not permit a stalemate to develop in the Middle East. American officials asserted that they did not lack understanding and sympathy for the "very real concerns" of the Palestinian people. One State Department presentation to Congress, which Kissinger reportedly had a hand in preparing, stated, "The issue is not whether Palestinian interests should be expressed in a final settlement, but how. There will be no peace until an answer is found."[2] Under the Carter administration, the United States was to persist in this position. Carter maintained that Israel must surrender virtually all of the occupied territories and that there must be a homeland for the Palestinians.

Kissinger and his successor, Cyrus Vance, implanted a positive view of the American position in Arab minds. On one occasion Sadat went so far as to tell an American journalist, "This is the first U.S. Administration with a true vision of your interests in the area—the most dangerous problem spot in the world. And I trust

Henry Kissinger. He is a real strategist who has succeeded in revolutionizing American policy in the Middle East."[3] Yasir Arafat was more reserved, but even he was compelled on one occasion to note, "All that we can say is that there has been the beginning of a verbal, not practical, change in the position of some American personalities who are beginning to see that the Palestine question is the key to the Middle East crisis."[4]

In addition to its negotiating powers, the United States also utilized the full range of policy initiatives available to it on economic and military assistance. Egypt was provided with $250 million in economic aid in 1975. The Ford administration acquired from Congress a two-year authorization allowing Egypt $1.45 billion for 1976 and 1977. Sympathetic consideration of Egyptian projects by the Export-Import Bank and shipments of wheat valued at $336 million were added to this amount. The United States Navy took the lead in clearing the Suez Canal of the mines and unspent bombs that had remained in its channel since the Six Day War of 1967. As for other Arab countries, Jordan was provided economic aid of $135 million during 1976 and 1977, and the administration proposed that close to $100 million be made available annually to Syria.

In the area of military supply the United States was also active. Sales to Saudi Arabia in the two years following the 1973 war ran close to $1 billion. In 1976 this figure reached $4 billion with an additional $5 billion pending. The United States remained the principal source of military equipment for Jordan. Military items were also made available to Kuwait, North Yemen, and Oman. Late-model aircraft, air transport, missiles, radar installations, and armored vehicles were all included in these transfers. Such deals were desirable from the American standpoint because of their salutary effect on the U.S. balance of payments. They also demonstrated the United States' willingness to arm certain countries that were avowedly hostile to Israel.

To be sure, care was taken that arms sold to the Arabs did not unduly influence Israel's defense posture, particularly after Saudi Arabia sent American-acquired jets to engage in joint maneuvers with Syria. At Israel's insistence American limitations placed on the installation of a Hawk antiaircraft missile system in Jordan proved to be so rigid that the Jordanians considered them an insult to their national dignity. Nevertheless, American officials were as responsive to Arab overtures as the special relationship with Israel would allow. The United States was inching closer to the proposition that, while Israel should have the capability of defending its borders, it need not amass the capacity on an item-by-item basis to balance the entire military might of all Arabs from the Atlantic Ocean to the Persian Gulf.

The United States stance on arms supply in the Middle East must also be assessed in terms of Soviet-American relations. Previously the United States had precluded the Soviet Union from developing any appreciable influence in the Persian Gulf. Beginning with the establishment of a British presence in the gulf during the nineteenth century, the West had maintained good relations with and watchful guidance over the states of the area. An atmosphere of friendly cooperation prevailed between the West and the gulf states, with the exception of Iraq. For the 1970s and 1980s, great-power strategic considerations required the protection of whatever advantage might exist for the United States in the Persian Gulf. Consequently, various minimal risks had to be assumed by Israel as the United States was confronted by growing Soviet interest in the area and a simultaneous demand by Saudi Arabia, Kuwait, and Oman for military hardware. This supposition was well established by 1978 when the United States, over Israel's objections, agreed to make the most advanced military aircraft available to Saudi Arabia. Even among Israel's supporters the mood was changing as no less a figure than Senator Abraham Ribicoff supported the sale.

The case of Egypt was somewhat different from that of the Persian Gulf governments insofar as it was a confrontation state bordering Israel. Nevertheless, early in 1976, President Ford proceeded to acknowledge that the United States had an "implied commitment" to sell military equipment to Egypt. An informal pledge to this effect had been made by Kissinger in his efforts to conclude the Sinai Accord. On his visit to the United States in October 1975, Sadat had raised the possibility of acquiring weapons, and Kissinger had assured the Israelis that any consideration of Egypt's military requirements would be held in abeyance until a more stable situation had been achieved in the Middle East.

The affair was finally brought into the open in March 1976, when the Soviets blocked an effort by Egypt to purchase from India spare parts for its Soviet-made fighters. Sadat's military capabilities were rapidly slipping. His army was reportedly restive. The Egyptian leader thereupon pressed the United States more actively for "defensive weapons" and took the position that he could not afford to negotiate further with Israel until his country had a credible defense posture. The Arabs had already been in too many negotiating situations in which they were the weaker party. They knew that without power they could achieve nothing.

In a move that was highly complementary to Egypt's new Western orientation, Sadat responded to the Soviet freeze on military shipments by unilaterally abrogating the Soviet-Egyptian Treaty of Friendship and Cooperation. It was now Kissinger's move. In order to meet Sadat's needs and to reestablish a situation in which negotiations might proceed, the United States took what its spokesmen alluded to as a "first step." It agreed to sell Egypt six military transport planes. Israel's objection was quick in coming. But Sadat's claim on American consideration had indeed become compelling. President Ford openly resisted efforts of the American Jewish community to prevent the sale, even when its representatives warned of repercussions in his fund-raising capabilities in the forthcoming presidential election campaign. Ford's policy was continued by the Carter administration which arranged to provide Egypt with F5E planes. While this aircraft was inferior in performance to equipment in the hands of the Israelis, the pending transfer was a further demonstration to the Arabs of American goodwill.

Economic and military assistance are ever-present elements that the United States introduces into just about every possible foreign policy equation. In the case of Egypt, however, the United States went a step further. Over the years Egypt had amassed a debt to the Soviet Union in excess of $4 billion. As in the case of a much smaller sum owed to the United States from the assistance program of the early sixties, debt service on Soviet loans constituted a problem for the Egyptians. Unlike the United States, the Soviet Union was unwilling to reschedule payments and thereby give relief from this burden. In structuring its assistance effort, therefore, the United States took the initiative to help Egypt with its problem. At Kissinger's suggestion, a coordinated plan was developed with Saudi Arabia, Iran, some of the Western European countries, and Japan to give Egypt the foreign exchange that would release it from some of the stringencies embodied in the Soviet attitude. The initial $250 million of American assistance was provided in this context. The United States's conduct, therefore, included more than a willingness to respond to Egypt's requests for aid. It also incorporated a spirit of cooperation and concern—the impression of working together. More was involved than just dollars. The United States was making the most of its assets.

The Intangibles

As useful as policy moves may be in improving the atomsphere for Arab-American exchange, they do not fully explain the nature of the relationship that has existed between the United States and Arabs. This relationship is unusual insofar as a persevering cultural propinquity between the two has withstood the battering of political antagonism. No one would deny that over the years we have made one another uncomfortable, but the readiness with which Arabs— particularly Egyptians—approach Americans to whom they have access demonstrates that the links are compelling and even inextricable. Such ties have a healthy legacy. Even while the Arabs were rejecting Western institutions in the late 1930s, most of them continued to embrace European culture. The Egyptian educator and author Taha Hussein expressed this affinity in 1938 when he asked, "Is the Egyptian mind Eastern or Western in its imagination, perception, comprehension, and judgment?" Hussein went on to assert that Egypt's experience had given it a clear Western orientation. He believed that Egypt could adopt the "motive forces" of Europe and still retain its Egyptian and Islamic character. Hussein's appeal was not exclusively Egyptian. He saw Egypt as part of "our Near East" and identified the controlling factors in Egypt's destiny as its geographical situation, Islam, and the Arabic language, as well as its heritage of pharaonic art and its unbroken history. Indeed,

Hussein was very much an Arab and stood among the precursors of Nasser when he depicted Egypt's objective as the achievement of an equal status in civilization with Europeans. He forcefully stated the Arab condition when he wrote, "I do not want us to feel inferior to the Europeans because of our cultural shortcomings. . . . It is obnoxious for a man who is sensitive to dignity and honor to be compelled to acknowledge that he is not yet deserving of either."[5]

The Arab inclination to prefer things American over those European is, of course, a finer delineation than that made by Taha Hussein. Sheikh Zaki al Yamani, the Saudi minister of petroleum affairs, alluded on one occasion to a "sense of fair play" as the appealing feature of American society. An Arab technique in working toward a Middle East settlement, he said, was to play on this theme by attempting to jolt the United States into an awareness of the justice of Arab grievances. In effect, Yamani hoped to draw on similarities in American and Arab societies to achieve this purpose. He was saying that in important ways Americans and Arabs are alike. In Yamani's view it was reasonable for Arabs to hope that they could get Americans to acknowledge the Arab sense of justice insofar as American perceptions of equity corresponded quite well with those of the Arab people.

Perhaps the set of attitudes in the American makeup that the Arabs find most appealing, and that corresponds most to their own values, is our populism. This aspect of the American outlook has been described as a lack of class consciousness, a sense of particularity, and a scorn for privilege.[6] These attitudes are all prominent in Arab thinking as explained in chapter 1. Such concepts reinforce the belief in both Arab society and American populism that the nation really belongs to the people. Society may not be classless, but it lacks class consciousness and has a certain horizontal equivalency of structure that is more important than the special interests of pluralism or the idea of hierarchical organization in which a participant in society performs a specialized function that eventually determines his viewpoint.

This outlook is not without its shortcomings. It contributes to an absence of effective institutions for achieving functionally defined goals, and it is the source of both Arab weakness when confronting the West and ultimate populist failure in American politics. Neither the Arabs nor the populists have learned to apply a precise sense of integration that makes every participant an efficient contributor to society's product. At the same time, this void has left the individual intact. He is totally identifiable in each system. The abstractions that have reduced a person to an interchangeable digit in the mainstream of industrialized society are not yet present in Arab countries or in American populism.

In each case the real circumstances of the individual give him a preoccupation with a variety of social justice that cannot be assigned to the impersonal institutions of government. He cannot pursue personal interests in the self-assured knowledge that public institutions will take care of others. The wealth and riches from which privilege is derived are seen as the agents of pride that turn men from ethical considerations and ultimately from God. For both the populist and the Arab, social cohesion rests on a strong sense of the divine sanction of equality with moral controls outweighing public enforcement as the operating principle. The unusual occurrence of particularity without privilege forges the theoretical social consolidation of the egalitarian mold that is so admired both by American populists and in Arab Islamic society. The two viewpoints also share a high respect for authority, but only on the premise that the possessors of power are dedicated to the ideal involved in the concept of social organization to which the followers adhere.[7]

These attributes may appear to refer broadly to Islam rather than precisely to Arab society. But as Maxime Rodinson has said, subtle arguments over whether Islam embodies or only canonizes such concepts need not be addressed.[8] The point is that, in the twentieth century, even though these ideas may be identified with Islam, they also constitute the element of faith found in Arabism, and a similar element of faith is present in American populism. When this faith is combined with particularism (called a proud history in one setting and patriotism in the other), and also with the real circumstances into which each system places the individual, the American condition produces a social context that an Arab finds comfortable. Perhaps most important is the emphasis on equality. For Arabs it makes America a society devoid of the traits that convey inferiority to those who approach it.

At times an observer is reduced to the startling and almost un-believable conclusion that many Arabs believe literally in the American ideal that still stirs in populism. One gets the feeling that in their quest for national sufficiency the Arabs most of all want our acceptance. The question for the American mediator, then, was that of translating into negotiating style the similarities of Arabism and populism that would allow for the mutual trust necessary for the Arabs to be persuaded to accept the American viewpoint on a settlement.

The most obvious, but also the most ephemeral, means of reaching this end is to establish an Arab leader's equivalency with American leadership through explicit gestures indicating honor, respect, and acceptance. This approach was utilized in October 1975, when Sadat was invited to address Congress. The second technique concerns the Arabs' sense of the individual operating within a real environment and therefore in his own name. Going beyond honorific display, it is well to remember that the heroic concept of the individual is very much alive in Arab life. Moreover, the personal commitment and zeal of populism are found attractive. A high degree of independent and individual initiative on the part of their leaders is totally acceptable to the Arab people as long as it occurs without violation of the norms that have been identified here as being similar to those of populism. Any mediator, therefore, can advantageously engage Arab leaders in the variety of personal contact that stresses an egalitarian and open ethic.

Here was the heart of Kissinger's shuttle diplomacy, and he practiced it well. Despite the antagonistic configurations of much of American policy, both the Saudis and Sadat expressed personal trust in Kissinger. The Saudi foreign minister, the late Omar Saqqaf, would address him as "my friend Henry." In greeting Mrs. Kissinger on her first visit to Cairo, Sadat said, "You're among Henry's family." In Arab etiquette these were meant as clear signals to the informed public and to other Arab leaders that policy accom-modations with the United States, as well as good personal relations with Kissinger, were in the offing.

Even for observers who followed the course of shuttle diplomacy through the press or on television news, cordiality between Kissinger and the Arab leaders was marked by none of the stiffness (possibly excepting King Faisal) that characterizes normal diplomatic exchange at this level. In addition to Sadat, Kissinger developed contacts with Algeria's leaders, Boumediene and Bouteflika. In the case of Syria's President Assad, the personal element was also at work. When it appeared that efforts to achieve a disengagement on the Golan Heights would fail, it was reportedly Assad who expressed remorse over the apparent outcome in view of the energy that he and Kissinger had already expended on the draft agreement. Kissinger suggested that together they make one final effort. An agreement was achieved almost wholly from personal commitment. Officially each man had already done everything that could have been expected of him.

Arab leaders clearly experienced satisfaction in personal relations with Kissinger. As he traveled from capital to capital, exchanges took place in a medium that was visible and that Arabs understood. Kissinger was among them and was apparently willing to deal with them on an equitable basis, with none of the latent hostility to be found in negotiations through long-range telegraphic communications or the coldness of official conferences that sometimes seem to be convened for the very purpose of making distinctions that can be bargained over. American power was never forgotten by the Arabs in any of Kissinger's exercises. Yet in view of the way he generally used that power, Arab leaders could only gain prestige in the eyes of their people from their association with him. The Arabs were not permitted to feel superior with their oil weapon, but the style of the American secretary of state was such that they did not feel inferior, either. The sense of weakness the Arabs customarily carried to the negotiating table was not present in shuttle diplomacy.

The personalized approach to negotiation does, of course, place additional burdens on the American representative. Can he activate the intangible forces that are conducive to understanding and still not mislead Arabs with regard to our purpose or the limitations on our ability to accommodate some of their positions? At the outset of the United States mediation, it was not uncommon for a secretary of state or a special envoy from the president to get caught up in the style of relationships characteristic of Arab society, only to be compelled by pressures from Israel to put some distance between himself and his congenial Arab hosts upon returning to the United States. In December 1968 it happened to William Scranton, whose favorable inclinations toward an "evenhanded" policy were disavowed by Richard Nixon's spokesmen when they refused to associate the president-elect with any policy change and asserted that Scranton's mission as a special envoy had been fact finding, not floating new policy initiatives.

Kissinger himself slipped into similar circumstances on an early visit to the Middle East. With the outbreak of fighting in October 1973, the world had witnessed an Arab hostility toward the United States that led to the oil embargo. Within a month, however, Kissinger was in Cairo and Riyadh engaged in an easy working relationship with the same leaders who had expressed this hostility. From his personal efforts, he was able to formalize the cease-fire and arrange the Geneva Conference, the first occasion on which any Arabs had agreed to meet openly with the Israelis on political matters. A startling change in mood had occurred. Kissinger's success was attributed largely to the personal rapport he had developed with Arab leaders, and some observers speculated over American policy modifications that might ensue from the new relationship.

On the same trip Kissinger traveled to China, where he took time to meet formally with the newsmen who accompanied him. Surprisingly, the topic of discussion was not China but the Middle East. The meeting seemed forced insofar as Kissinger had had ample opportunity for discussions with journalists about the Middle East on the flight from Cairo to Peking. He had, in fact, talked to them at some length. But now Kissinger had another purpose. In a statement meant for the American public and for Israel, the secretary of state asserted in a somewhat pointed fashion, "while we are highly respectful of the views of the Arab world, it is not possible for us to be swayed in the major orientation of our policy by the monopoly position or the temporary monopoly position enjoyed by a few nations."[9] Distinctions between Arabs and Americans had been made. Balance was restored. It could not be said that Kissinger's personal relations with Arab leaders signaled a policy change that would offend Israel.

Power and Technology

Personal appeal alone cannot be expected to carry the day in diplomatic exchange. Nor is its application universal. In a European diplomatic milieu, for example, Kissinger's Middle East activities might have been viewed as clownish. In shaping a negotiating approach, social practice and culture cannot be ignored if a diplomatic representative, particularly a mediator, hopes to exploit whatever potential a situation may have for him. The critical feature of any diplomatic relationship, however, is how the participants see one another's strengths and weaknesses in terms of the ability of these attributes to influence a political outcome on matters of common concern. Inequality in power had always been a major irritant in relations between the Arabs and the West. European and American superiority has usually been ascribed to Western military and industrial technology, a conviction that prevailed even among the Ottoman Turks prior to Arab independence. While the influence of Western power in the Middle East may be abhorred, its basis is admired. The acquisition of Western-style power has always been a major objective of Arab leaders. With technology, and the power ensuing from it, the Arabs have hoped to participate in certain aspects of the Western experience with what Taha Hussein called an equal status in civilization.

In the aftermath of the fourfold increase in petroleum prices, the oil-producing Arab countries had the wherewithal to buy what they wished. The additional income seemed to signal a new dedication to economic development—to the acquisition of power. Outlays for development increased many times more than the jump in oil prices. In 1974 purchases from abroad by OPEC countries reached $50 billion. Through 1978 the oil producers of the Persian Gulf had committed upward of $300 billion for imports, largely for development. In Saudi Arabia a five-year development plan encompassing expenditures of $140 billion was announced. Implementation at a somewhat lower level was expected by most experts.

Nevertheless, commitments for the industrial complex at al Jubayl ($10–12 billion), the electrification and water desalination project (up to $40 billion), gas treatment facilities ($4 billion), and telecommunications ($500 million) seemed likely. It was enough to confound the imagination.

Countries such as Saudi Arabia and even Algeria had always depended on the West for trading partners. During periods in which the radical Arabs were alienated from the West, several countries had relied on Soviet trade and technology. When these same countries acquired the resources to deal again with the West, however, the changes in trading patterns were dramatic. Between 1972 and 1974, the Soviet bloc's share of Egypt's imports from industrialized countries fell from 41 percent to 10 percent as Sadat took advantage of funds made available by the oil-producing Arabs to move his country away from the radical outlook of Nasserism. In Iraq the decrease was from 36 percent to 14 percent, and for Syria the decline was from 32 percent to 22 percent. In a comparative sense, the Arabs had found the Soviets' products and technology wanting.

Within the Western orbit, European rather than American products had always been dominant in Middle East trade. Long-standing commercial relationships with Europe, pricing considerations, and the lack of concern on the part of many American companies for Middle East business all served to limit the United States to a modest share of Arab imports. The trade in which the Americans did engage was highly concentrated in Saudi Arabia and Kuwait. With the beginning of the Arab drive for economic development that accompanied the increase in oil prices, however, the Arab fascination for American products and technology revealed itself. As one wag put it, even a box of bananas labeled "Product of Central America" sells twice as fast if the word *Central* is blocked out. By 1976 American participation in Arab import programs with the noncommunist world stood at about 20 percent of the rapidly expanding market. Some European countries had entered into long-range, semibarter, state trading arrangements with Arabs by which complete factories were literally exchanged for long-term oil commitments. The refusal of the United States to engage in this practice, along with the traditional factors cited above, constituted the only limitations on additional American sales.

Even then, the United States, by working in select developmental sectors, was able to sell more to the eighteen Arab states than any other industrialized country. Heretofore, its sales had lagged behind those of France and about equaled the level of the Soviet Union. By 1976, American companies were in the forefront of construction activities associated with Saudi Arabia's multi-billion-dollar industrialization program. The United States also took the lead in Egypt's trade, largely because of the economic assistance it extended to Sadat. In addition, Americans were increasingly prominent in the business of Algeria, Kuwait, and the United Arab Emirates. The United States' exports to Syria increased fourteenfold between 1972 and 1976 when they reached $275 million. Despite the vehement Iraqi and Libyan reactions to U.S. Middle East policy, American businessmen were well received in Baghdad and Tripoli. Iraq's purchases from the United States increased from $23 million in 1972 to about $382 million in 1976. For Libya the increase was from $85 million to $277 million.[10] In fact, it was in Arab countries whose governments had the reputation for being radical that the United States's proportion of the market seemed to grow the fastest.

Various explanations can be offered for the Arabs' proclivity for American technology. Clearly the United States had long maintained a special position in Saudi Arabia through political support for the House of Saud and through its military supply and training arrangements. The considerable influence of the Arabian American Oil Company also gave U.S. business an edge. With regard to investment by Arabs for the expansion of their petroleum production capacity, the United States had the advantage over European countries because most of the aggressive major multinational oil companies were American dominated. But what about areas of industrial development outside the petroleum sector? The size of the American industrial establishment in itself would lead to a substantial share for American concerns in the economic expansion of the Persian Gulf. A final explanation often suggested by Arabs themselves is that American technology is preferred because it is superior to that of Europe and Japan. But any reasonable test of this assertion would hardly establish its veracity. What we are dealing with here is more than American capabilities. It is the Arab preference for things American.

An underlying factor that is often overlooked is that American technology is preferred because it fits the Arab mood. When Nasser and the leaders of Iraq and Syria once came together to issue a manifesto reflecting Arab aspirations, they declared, "unity is a revolution—a revolution because it is popular, a revolution because it is progressive, and a revolution because it is a powerful tide in the current of civilization."[11] In chapter 2 we identified these factors as the mainspring of Arab nationalism. But they also apply to the American approach to technology. In the American sense, technology sparked a revolution, and it is indeed popular, progressive, and powerful. It is not the special domain of any single group among the populace. The implicit assumption in American society is that everyone can and does apply the technical arts. Everyone is expected to tinker with his own automobile; just about everyone has a tool chest in his home. Technology is the engine of our concepts of equality and progress, and with its power we sometimes assume that we can overcome almost any social ill. This popular and optimistic element in the American technological experience makes the Arabs feel that it can be their own. In this respect they want to be like Americans. In the absence of foreign domination and with a new sense of power derived from their oil income, the Arabs for the first time in the technological age permitted themselves to think magnificent thoughts. Nothing demonstrated the new outlook more than a conversation between two educated, radical, and socially sophisticated Arabs of my acquaintance over the possibility of an Arab someday walking on the moon. Heretofore such feats had been reserved in the minds of Arabs for Americans, Russians, and eventually perhaps Europeans. Unless a mediator grasped the dynamic found in Arab society after the 1973 war, opportunities for applying the intangible assets afforded Americans in the Middle East would in all probability be lost. Kissinger's strength was that he had the intellectual powers and the intuition to see this aspect of the situation.

Perhaps the best example of Arab pursuit of the American technological ideal has been their desire for American education. Anyone who has spent time in the Middle East has noted the Arab mania for education. The Egyptian minister of state for planning once told me that it didn't matter what young people studied as long as great numbers of them were educated. From this popular phenomenon, he reasoned, economic and social progress were bound to emerge. The American practice of allowing individual choice in selecting a program of study and our belief in upward social mobility through education correspond quite well to the Arab outlook. For the individual it is the key to social participation, progress, and power.

By 1976, close to 20,000 Arabs were studying in American universities, many of them in engineering.[12] Even the antipathy of Libya's ideologically oriented Qaddafi for the United States could not dampen this desire for American technology acquired through our education. In 1974 alone more than 1,000 Libyans were sent to the United States for graduate education, and American instructors were avidly sought to staff the technical, public administration, and English departments of Libya's universities.[13]

The Way of Peace or the Road to War?

This rush to things American would seem to raise problems for the Arabs. Technology cannot be transferred by machines alone. Transfer takes place only through the presence of individuals who possess technical knowledge. Thus, along with production units must come the Western experts who supervise the installation and operation of facilities while Saudis, Kuwaitis, and Iraqis become familiar with the new technology. The dimensions of the situation were particularly dramatic in Saudi Arabia. With a work force of 1.6 million, the Saudis already employed 1 million aliens—mainly Yemenis, Egyptians, and Pakistanis in unskilled, semiskilled, and lower-echelon administrative categories and Europeans and Americans in technical positions. The indigenous Saudi population was not large enough to staff and manage the industrial establishment that was being planned for Saudi Arabia. More aliens would be required, and the infusion of an additional half million was considered likely. To build the gas treatment facilities alone, close to 2,000 technicians and 20,000 craftsmen would have to be brought to Saudi Arabia from abroad. Under the best of circumstances the massive influx of foreigners would be socially unsettling. In addition, might not the Saudis and other Arabs who entertained large numbers of Western technicians view them as a threat—even as instruments of their respective governments? Generally, they did not. As individuals, and as employees of Arab concerns or foreign contractors, Westerners constituted no threat. It is only when confronted with Western politics that the Arabs become uneasy.

The United States did, therefore, have a valuable asset that could induce much more diplomatic assent on the part of the Arabs than threats of force or the implication that we could apply our power through Israeli aggressiveness. This asset was technology set in a popular context, and it was much more influential than anyone cared to say. Within days of the termination of the fighting along the Suez Canal and on the Golan Heights—at a time when the full force of the oil embargo was beginning to be felt in Western countries—Zaki al Yamani, the Saudi minister of petroleum affairs, said, "We require that two basic conditions should be satisfied before we agree to produce our oil at rates higher than are strictly necessary to cover our own economic and financial needs. One is the establishment of the right political atmosphere. . . . The other is that the West should provide the requisite assistance to help Saudi Arabia industrialize itself."[14] Kissinger had, of course, labored mightily to meet the first condition, and events were to prove that American industry was equally ready to fulfill the second. The symbolic aspect of American compliance with Yamani's condition of technological assistance was formalized by an official joint economic commission between the United States and Saudi Arabia. Working groups were established under the commission's auspices to assure that the best the American economy had to offer would be available for Saudi Arabia's plans in industrialization, manpower development and education, application of advanced technology, and agricultural growth.

The political meaning of the high priority the Saudis and many other Arabs placed on American technology was evident in the violent reaction of the radical forces in Arab politics to efforts by the United States to achieve "partial" solutions on the issues that separated Israel from its Arab neighbors. The radicals' response was particularly strong at the time of the Sinai Accord because this agreement appeared to set the scene for an Arab-Israeli compromise that would ignore the Palestinians' objectives. Many Arabs concluded that "Arab" policy was inexplicably being frustrated at a time when the Saudis had only to tighten the valve on oil in order to squeeze concessions from the United States and Israel. A popular belief among the radicals was that treasonous Saudi leaders were again permitting the United States to control its policy, and as a result Arab power was being rendered ineffective. Somewhat more realistically, it could be said that the guiding force in Saudi thinking was not just "Arab" policy. There was also a commitment to economic development and a desire for American technology. These factors could be viewed as being important to the support the Saudis provided Sadat as he took a moderate position on Arab national issues that sometimes appeared more compatible with American thinking than with the perspective of many of his Arab brothers.

Some insight into the forces at work in this situation was provided by Egyptian Foreign Minister Ismail Fahmy, who remarked that ideally Egypt would be armed by the Soviet Union but would take advantage of the influence the United States had with Israel to work for peace. In effect Fahmy was saying that relations with the Soviet Union represented an Arab potential for war; those with the United States for peace. When the Soviets would not lend themselves to the Egyptian design, Sadat moved even closer to the United States and in so doing enhanced the opportunities for a negotiated settlement. Economic activity and the application of American technology were important aspects of a peace policy. The relationship was accentuated when the United States government, during Sadat's visit to the United States, agreed to sell Egypt two nuclear power reactors. For the Egyptians the reactors had a symbolic importance that far exceeded their practical value; they signified access to American technology and indicated that the United States was willing to see an end to Arab weakness and inferiority.

The question arises, therefore, whether the Arabs wanted development and equalization of status with the West more than they wanted an early resolution of the national cause as expressed through justice for the Palestinians. Neither the Syrians, Iraqis, Libyans, nor Algerians were immune from the influence of the American technology. The American asset did not completely offset the dynamics of Arab national politics, which tended to pull the Arabs toward confrontation with Israel as long as the Palestinian cause remained the core issue. The technological factor was, however, a moderating force that had some influence, even beyond the councils of Sadat and the Saudis. It was useful, therefore, for any American mediator to introduce technology into his relations with the Arabs.

The Case of Boumediene

An example of the new American influence was Houari Boumediene, the late president of Algeria. His popularity at home dated from his uncompromising stand against Israel at the time of the 1967 war and was tied to the imagery of Arab radicalism which had a profound emotional impact on the Algerian people. At the same time, Boumediene had a broader view of power than that allowed by the dimensions of the Arab-Israeli struggle. He followed a policy that gave priority to developing a strong economic base from which Algeria could play a role in the world and not just in the Middle East. For this purpose he relied on Western technology, and despite the bitterness of the period immediately after the 1967 Israeli victory, he entered into a wide variety of arrangements with American as well as French companies for the development of Algerian industry. After 1973 Boumediene's vision was broad enough to see the significance of the oil embargo and the latitude it allowed for a new diplomacy based on the control of raw materials. He assumed a position of leadership in pressing the industrialized West for a new economic order that would sanction a more equitable distribution of income throughout the world. His concern was not only for producers of oil but also for those who provided the world's supplies of bauxite, copper, tin, and other materials on which industry depends. He was pragmatic enough to see that, even with industrialization, Algeria and the Third World could never equal the West's power under existing terms of trade, and he did not wish to pretend that Algeria could become part of the West. His ties to the Arabs and to Africa were too strong for that.

On the Arab-Israeli issue, Boumediene did not underestimate the importance of the great powers. On a visit to Moscow after the 1973 war he was impressed by what he considered to be Soviet cynicism over the inability of the Arabs to move the Israelis toward an equitable settlement, even with Soviet arms. He concluded that the Arabs had no choice but to work through the United States in order to pressure the Israelis into withdrawing from the occupied territories. In 1973 and 1974 he considered the course laid out by Sadat as the only viable one for the Arabs to follow. While he looked on the Saudi regime as a despicable anachronism, and an anathema to the progressive nationalism that constituted his domestic strength, he knew that Saudi wealth and financial support for the Arab cause meant Saudi influence in Arab councils. Other Arabs had little choice but to accept it. He did not believe that much could be gained from the invective and vituperation often used by competing Arab leaders against one another.

Finally, Algeria's own revolutionary experience shaped Boumediene's views on the Palestinians. He saw no substitute for their gaining legitimacy—albeit with Arab material and political support —through military operations against Israel from territories adjacent to the Jewish state. Whatever the consequence of Palestinian operations in terms of Israeli retributions, the Arabs should accept it and respond to aggressiveness with aggressiveness. Boumediene did not consider all guerrilla pressure as incompatible with negotiations conducted through the United States.

Avid nationalists might accuse Boumediene of being cynical. He assumed a radical Arab posture for domestic purposes, yet his behavior on the international scene was comforting to the Arab moderates. Actually, Boumediene was only recognizing that the influence he could bring to bear on the Arab-Israeli struggle was limited. Anyway, the future of the Arab nation need not hinge solely on an immediate resolution of the Palestine problem now that the Arabs had the power with which to play a role at the international level. It was this new outlook typified by Boumediene, an otherwise radical Arab leader, that permitted Sadat at the outset of his negotiations to explore peace without experiencing a national outcry from all Arab lands against what the radical Arabs considered to be a traitorous attitude. An observer could only speculate whether the influence of Boumediene and those like him did not work to diminish the significance of the Palestinian question. His broader view of power was born of a concern for technology, a resource that could only be acquired from the West. By the end of 1976, the United States had become the principal customer for Algerian crude oil and was consuming one-quarter of its natural gas production. Seventy American companies held contracts for $6 billion in housing, irrigation, institutions of technical education, gas processing plants, mining, and the production of television sets. Additional billions of dollars in contracts for construction and the installation of industrial capacity were in view.

Any diplomatic initiative takes place against the backdrop of a social dynamic that sets the tone of international relationships. When negotiators or mediators are dealing with precisely prescribed matters such as trade, finance, or the physical aspects of relative power, this dynamic can sometimes be ignored for short periods while an agreement is being hammered out. But even in great-power relationships, mood can be important—witness the effort devoted to detente by the United States and the Soviet Union during the Kissinger era. In the Middle East, where problems are often of the mind and Arab affinity for the West is strong but mixed with doubt, the use of intangibles to create an environment conducive to mutual appreciation assumes great importance. The case of Boumediene demonstrated how technology influenced the politics of a pragmatic but otherwise radical Arab.

The broad social aspects of relations between peoples that have been described here as the intangibles of negotiations are usually formalized in diplomacy with programs of cultural exchange, educational opportunities, press relations, and the like. In the institutionalized setting within which they are placed, these activities assume an adjunct character and become lost in major diplomatic thrusts on critical issues. At least in the Middle East, the intangibles have such great value in the type of personal diplomacy Arabs practice and enjoy that they should not be taken for granted. Western statesmen can use them directly to establish the context of good feeling that relations between peoples can provide. Such a tactic gives negotiators a wider view of their endeavor and establishes a real sense of working together. When immediate negotiating objectives differ, it can yield the essence of compromise.

Implicit Arab Influence on America

Herein lay a possibility for the success of the Last Crusade. Curiously, it depended on Arab initiative in pressing for American assistance in development rather than on anything Kissinger or his successors could devise themselves. All they could do was assure the conditions that would permit American technology to flow to the Arab countries. In view of the level of resources involved and the free-enterprise nature of the American economy, no American official could hope to tie the pace of technological transfers to successive steps the Arabs might take toward a settlement with Israel. The profit motive and business judgment of private concerns would control that. Likewise, the government could not hope to limit the growth of the implicit influence that business relationships with the Middle East would afford the Arabs in American society.

Even before American involvement in large-scale Arab development that began in earnest in 1975, implicit Arab influence was evident in the United States. The increase in oil prices elevated the oil-producing Arab countries to the level of the world's power brokers. Initially economists were concerned over the havoc the Arabs could bring to Western economies and money markets with the large amounts of capital they would accumulate but could not spend. But as it turned out, the Arabs' main interest was development at home, not controlling businesses abroad. Attention centered on the purchase of European, Japanese, and American products and machinery. The Arabs clearly wanted legitimacy. They wanted their wealth and power cast in Western terms.

The Arabs readily adopted themselves to the new relationship with the United States by attempting to make inroads into American consciousness much as the Israelis had done. Admittedly without too much success, the Arabs attempted to reach the public through information offices in New York, Washington, Chicago, Dallas, and San Francisco. The Palestine Liberation Organization had opened an office in New York in relation to its observer's role at the United Nations. In December 1976 the PLO attempted to do the same in Washington, but the lameduck Ford administration preferred to have any decision on PLO presence in the nation's capital made by its successor. President Carter and his advisors, in turn, began their diplomacy on too conservative a note for such a gesture to seem appropriate. But the Palestinians were not silent. Despite travel restrictions placed on their UN representatives by the U.S. government, the PLO initiated a mailing operation and sent those speakers who were permitted to travel to just about any public gathering—including those sponsored by Jews—to which they could get an invitation. The Palestinians' message was usually low-key and reasonably devoid of threats and thunderbolts. In August 1977 the PLO was finally permitted to open an unobtrusive information office in Washington.

To facilitate their affairs through the channels of power, the Arabs retained the law firms of various prominent individuals, including former cabinet members from both political parties. In addition, a lobbying operation was mounted by the National Association of Arab-Americans. One of the association's monumental tasks was to get an estimated 3 million Americans of Arab ancestry to show concern for the Arab cause. In one early effort, eleven representatives of the Arab community conferred with President Ford and Secretary of State Kissinger to plead the case of the Palestinians. A small group of perhaps a half dozen congressmen openly asserted that the Arab cause should be heard.

The Arabs' message was not very different in tone from that of the Israelis. They too attempted to establish that the interests of the United States were virtually identical to their own. Only on Israel was there a difference in outlook. Probably because their nascent efforts were of marginal influence when compared to those made on behalf of Israel, the Arab-Americans were less exclusive in their appeals than Jewish-Americans. They did not advocate that the United States adopt an anti-Israel stand. In fact, they accepted continued U.S. support of the Jewish state. Their plea was for a more reasonable approach to the Arab-Israeli issue in terms of what they identified as "actual American interests." The representatives of Arab governments buttressed this call by asserting that they were only looking for "evenhandedness." Illustrative of the Arabs' approach was a full-page newspaper advertisement meant to justify the oil boycott, saying that the decision to suspend oil shipments to the United States had been taken "more in sorrow than in anger."[15]

This attitude was to persevere and ultimately be institutionalized in what was called the First Arab-American Dialogue that was held during November 1978 in of all places, Libya. The gathering was not sponsored by the United States's traditional friends in the region but by those who had stood against American policies. Over 100 Americans, including former senator William Fulbright, former airline executive Najeeb Halaby, and retired U.S. ambassadors attended. Qaddafi himself addressed the group to declare that the enmity of the United States could someday push him into joining the Warsaw Pact. The Americans argued that President's Carter's initiative in the Egyptian-Israeli peace negotiations could also provide opportunities for the Palestinians. Hot and heavy exchanges took place over terrorism and air piracy. But despite what was essentially an airing of differences and a drawing of distinctions between radical Arabs and the United States, most of those from the group of states and leaders (including Libyans) who rejected a negotiated settlement with Israel sought understanding and a closer relationship with the United States. The Arab attitude is mystifying to many, but there can be little doubt that whatever sins against the Arab nation might be laid at the door of the United States, Arabs are sufficiently fascinated by America to allow us access to all circles of power in the Middle East.

Such were the mediator's assets—the conventional tools of economic assistance and military supply combined with a conviction on the part of the Arabs that only the United States could move Israel to make the concessions necessary for peace. Just as important were the intangibles—a certain like-mindedness in social outlook between Arab egalitarianism and our own streak of prairie populism, combined with the Arabs' admiration and desire for American technology. The impetus for change was a new Arab perception that amounted to a broader view of the world and that suggested to some Arabs that national objectives were to be found in peace and not in the grinding of bayonets. Only through the subtle exploitation of all these factors could a mediator lead the Arabs toward an acceptance of Israel and at the same time convince Israel that this new Arab position was marked by none of the mental reservations Israelis had heretofore assigned to Arab expressions of peace.

8

The Structure of Negotiation

Having surveyed the environment created by the Arab and Jewish quests for national legitimacy and reconnoitered the undercurrents generated by Arab feelings of suspicion toward the West, after assaying his assets and cataloging the limitations under which he must operate, Kissinger might well have blenched at the thought of what lay ahead. But once he disregarded the example of angels, who would have feared to tread this path, his first task was to position the participants in some structure that would be conducive to working toward a settlement.

The Setting for Negotiation

Looking back over the first year of negotiations, Muhammad Hassanein Haykal, one of the Arab world's most astute political commentators, was to observe that Kissinger had lost his chance for peace because of the way he had proceeded. Haykal pointed out that, at the time of the cease-fire, the superpowers were equally involved in the Middle East situation. The military supply operation that each had undertaken on behalf of its client during the fighting had been critical to the survival of both the Arab and the Israeli armies. Consequently, the United States and the Soviet Union were in control of the situation. Israel had momentarily sensed that, without American supplies, it would have been in trouble. Its leaders were sufficiently aware of their tactical weakness to be receptive to American insistence that they accommodate peace.

On the other side of the battle lines, the Arabs, for just an instant, saw that with their oil weapon they had a strategic advantage. While losing on the battlefield, they had overcome their sense of weakness sufficiently to allow them to negotiate a settlement with Israel if prodded by their great-power benefactor. Had Kissinger opted for an immediate and total settlement rather than for a cease-fire and a disengagement of forces, Haykal reasoned, had he dealt with the situation in terms of regional dynamics at that moment, an early peace might have been achieved. But the relatively passive attitude assumed by the Soviet Union during Kissinger's shuttle diplomacy presented the possibility of the West's regaining its influence in the Middle East at the expense of the Soviets. Kissinger thereupon diverted his purpose from bringing about an Arab-Israeli settlement to establishing advantages for the United States. The combatants were given time to consider issues of national legitimacy. Positions hardened. As a result, Haykal concluded, the opportunity for peace was lost.[1]

Haykal's analysis captured some of the salient conditions that existed at the time of the cease-fire. But it also collapsed some important events into a few generalizations, thereby permitting them to be ignored. As the Egyptian and Syrian positions began to crumble in the face of Israel's counteroffensive, Soviet Premier Kosygin had hurried to Cairo on October 17, 1973. Upon his return to Moscow, the Soviet government invited Henry Kissinger to join them in pressing the combatants for a cease-fire. Following meetings in Moscow on October 20 and 21, and a subsequent visit by Kissinger to Jerusalem on his return trip to Washington, a joint resolution sponsored by the United States and the Soviet Union was passed by the Security Council on October 22 calling for negotiations and the implementation of Security Council Resolution 242 which had effected the termination of hostilities in the Six Day War of 1967.

For thirty-six hours after everyone had supposedly agreed to the Security Council resolution, Israel had taken advantage of the confusion on the battlefield to complete its encirclement of the

Egyptian Third Army. Seeing the best of his forces faced with destruction, Sadat frantically called for immediate and direct intervention by the Soviet Union to preserve the cease-fire which the Egyptians now claimed they had accepted on Russian assurances of the protection of Egyptian interests. Reviewing the situation later, Egyptian officials contended that Sadat's intention was not to introduce Soviet troops into the crisis, but only to acquire more sophisticated weaponry from the Russians.

The Soviets had been placed in an embarrassing position by the Israelis' action and by Sadat's call for help. An appeal to the Security Council would appear to demonstrate Soviet ineffectiveness; and additional or more-advanced Soviet arms would probably not change anything. Taking virtually the only course open to them, the Soviets approached the United States on the possibility of joint intervention to restrain the two sides. The Soviets also alluded to the prospect of their proceeding alone if the United States demurred.

Some observers have concluded that Sadat's appeal to the Soviets for help was actually at Soviet urging and that the entire affair was a Russian ploy to introduce its troops into the area, thereby gaining a dominant role in the negotiations that everyone assumed would follow. Kissinger must have seen the situation in much this way. Whatever the origin of the Soviet suggestion for either joint or unilateral intervention, the American response was an immediate worldwide alert of its forces as a signal that it would tolerate no unilateral action by the USSR. Further talk of great-power intercession ended as the small powers of the Security Council presented a resolution calling for a UN peacekeeping force that would exclude American and Russian participation. By this time the Israelis had reached their objectives. Suez City was surrounded, and the Egyptian Third Army was trapped east of the canal. The situation began to stabilize.

Kissinger's concern at the time was that joint intervention—or worse still a unilateral Soviet operation—would be to the disadvantage of the United States. Several situations could have arisen from the introduction of Soviet forces. Fighting might have occurred between the Israelis and Russians. Or Israel might have capitulated and withdrawn from the occupied territories as the

Soviet forces entered the battle zone.[2] A variation of the second possibility was joint United States-Soviet pressure on the Israelis to relinquish the occupied lands. As unlikely as this possibility seemed in 1973, U.S. and Soviet pressure had forced the Israelis to return to their borders after the occupation of Sinai in 1956. Thus there was precedent for what the Russians had initially suggested.

If events proceeded in any of these directions, the results could be undesirable and dangerous, not just from the standpoint of Israel but also for the United States. The Soviets would gain immensely in prestige, and the Arabs, savoring the success of their military operations—albeit limited and transitory—would in all probability be less interested in an equitable settlement. After all, Nasser had fashioned victory for the Arab mind from a similar set of circumstances in 1956, and Kissinger had no assurance that Sadat might not be tempted to do the same. Thereafter, all pressures would be for the realization of Arab national aims and the humiliation of Israel. In view of the history of the U.S.-Israeli relationship, it was not likely that Israel could submit without damaging the prestige of the United States in the process. In these terms, the risk of confrontation with the Soviets involved in the military alert was justified.

Other forces were also at work. Kissinger had just negotiatied a face-saving withdrawal in Viet Nam, and he would not have relished doing the same thing in the Middle East. In addition, an Arab-Israeli settlement was on his mind, even before the October 6 Arab attack. Kissinger's unusual meeting with the Arab foreign ministers at the General Assembly on September 25, just two days after he became secretary of state, seemed to signal that his next concern would be the Middle East. He was an activist and a negotiator, and here was a situation that needed negotiating. The outbreak of hostilities was an opportunity to be seized. When confronted with the conditions of October 23, 1973—the Israelis nearing victory and the Soviets threatening to intervene—he quite naturally opted for the course that would be conducive to negotiation. He wanted a stalemate because it would give a mediator the most leverage.[3]

It can be said, therefore, that the U.S. military alert declared on

Kissinger's initiative on October 24, 1973, achieved the results he desired. The Soviets were stopped in their tracks; the United States appeared to be in command; and the Israelis were left in a position of maximum advantage but not dominance. Sadat's willingness to accept a cease-fire under the conditions that had triggered the Soviet proposal for intervention—that is, Israel's seizing and holding territory beyond the October 22 cease-fire lines—made the Russians look even worse. The advantage was clearly with the United States. It was at this time that Kissinger first referred to the United States, and to himself, as the trustee of peace.

Haykal's criticism of Kissinger's effort was that in its objectives it was set firmly within the context of great-power rivalry and in its techniques it relied on partial solution. But was it reasonable to suppose that the larger interests of the United States or the Soviet Union could ever be separated from the Middle East situation? What Haykal obviously meant by the United States or the USSR working to achieve a resolution of the problem in terms of the dynamics of the region itself was an imposed solution requiring Israel to relinquish all or virtually all of the occupied territories and perhaps even to accept a Palestinian state on the West Bank. The joint intervention proposed by the Soviet Union would have set the scene for this eventuality, but the United States was not inclined to follow such a course.

In Haykal's view, a certain equilibrium existed both in terms of the adversaries' feelings of strength and weakness and from the standpoint of the degree and nature of great-power involvement. The essence of his suggestion was that this condition would have supported the apportioning by the great powers of the sacrifices and benefits that were inherent in peace. It called for a structure in which the United States and the Soviet Union moved in tandem, each imposing the great-power solution on the side it had heretofore supported in the Middle East struggle. From the perspective of the parties to the conflict, this organization of the peace effort would have been confusing and contradictory—even illogical. The United States would be acting on behalf of the Arabs while the Soviet Union acted for the Israelis! Haykal assumed no freedom of maneuver for the Arab and Israeli recipients of this treatment.

Actually, it was not likely at this point that the United States and the Soviet Union could have been any more successful than their clients in arriving at some solution that both sides found acceptable. Soviet and American interests were clearly different in the Middle East, and neither country could be expected to sacrifice its position. A more dramatic, and by this time thread-bare, supposition was that Kissinger and the Russians should have set aside immediate political interests and been motivated solely by the desire to avoid World War III. Russian and American statesmen always keep an eye on this prospect, but it is simplistic to suggest that considerations of relative power advantage, as well as a desire to avoid war, are not also involved in every other crisis with which the great powers have been concerned. Not for a minute could someone of Kissinger's inclinations have forgotten this dimension of the state of affairs.

Questions can also be raised about Haykal's preference for a total solution. In the atmosphere that prevailed when the cease-fire finally went into effect, what was a mediator to do? Certainly, taking steps to reduce the likelihood of renewed fighting appeared essential. Assuming that success is nurtured by success, Kissinger declared his preference for achievable goals—disengagement rather than settlement. Hopefully, limited Israeli troop withdrawals would symbolize for the Arabs the ultimate return of the occupied territories. The trustee of peace, therefore, opted for a partial solution acceptable to both sides rather than a total solution that the great powers might try to impose to everyone's dissatisfaction.

The Problem of an Agenda

Thus was Kissinger to enter into his first venture in Middle East mediation. From October 31 until November 3, he served as a go-between for Israeli Premier Golda Meir and Egyptian Foreign Minister Ismail Fahmy, who had come to Washington to discuss the cease-fire. On November 2, the Syrian deputy foreign minister, who was attending the United Nations session, joined Kissinger in an exchange of views. Immediately thereafter, Kissinger flew to Cairo and Jerusalem, and on November 11, he managed to bring the warring parties to an understanding on how they might work toward the implementation of the Security Council resolution. Perhaps most important from the standpoint of future negotiations, Kissinger won approval from the two sides for direct discussions between Egyptian and Israeli generals on matters pertaining to the separation of forces in the highly complex battle-field situation around Suez. These talks began on November 13 at kilometer marker 101 on the Cairo-Suez road. The first step had been taken. The trustee of peace had bought an undetermined amount of time to consider how best to organize his peace effort.

In a situation such as that in the Middle East, popular imagination generally centers on two aspects of an effort to achieve peace. First, people assume that the resolution of problems will occur as the result of negotiations at a single gathering—a peace confer-ence. The refusal of the Arabs to engage in such a meeting after the 1956 and 1967 wars had been one factor that left the international community puzzled over the Middle East. The Israelis had con-sistently insisted that without such an event the Arabs would never really acknowledge the existence of the Jewish state, and any commitment to peace on the part of the Arabs would be under-taken with all those reservations that the West and Israel had long associated with Arab diplomacy. The symbolic meaning the Israelis imputed to the structuring of negotiations was of prim-ary importance to any mediator who hoped to urge the two sides toward peace. In 1973 Sadat and Hussein readily accepted a peace conference. The Syrians toyed with the idea and ultimately the Palestinians found it attractive. Nevertheless, when tactics were set aside and attention was focused on the simple act of sitting down to talk with the Israelis about peace, great pressures mili-tating against a general conference arose among the Arabs. Even a glance at Arab national perceptions on the matter of Israel should have been sufficient to demonstrate to Kissinger that his chances of getting *all* Arabs to a general conference were limited. Within the next few years the Arab and Israeli views on a con-ference vacillated as the meeting was converted in the Arab mind into a vehicle by which they hoped to get the Israelis to recognize Palestinian legitimacy by having them sit down at the same nego-tiating table with representatives of the PLO. In December 1973, this perception had not yet emerged.

A second feature of public expectation in peace negotiations is that attention will be devoted to the conditions that have disturbed tranquility. Because a settlement is considered the ultimate objective of a peace conference, observers often surmise that its immediate purpose is the resolution of problems related to peace. The Middle East situation demonstrated, however, that negotiants are often guided by other purposes. The demand of each side for recognition of its legitimacy by the other while avoiding a comparable acknowledgment on its own part was clearly as important as peace to the principals in the Arab-Israeli struggle.

The problem this attitude constituted for a conference was that of formulating an agenda. Great difficulty could be expected in getting the belligerents to agree on: (1) the issues that could fruitfully be discussed, (2) how the issues should be phrased, and (3) the order in which they might be considered. But even before an attempt could be made to achieve Arab-Israeli agreement on such matters, it would be necessary to overcome the complication of the Arabs' not being able to agree among themselves on how to proceed. A reconciliation of Arab views on the question of an agenda for a peace conference did not occur in the aftermath of the 1973 war. At the meeting of Arab chiefs of state in Algeria in November 1973, the difficulty was only temporarily and partially swept under the rug with allusions to the acceptability of "a conference," leaving the divergent political forces in the Arab world free to interpret the situation as they wished. Some, like Sadat, openly recognized the difficulties to be confronted in arriving at an agenda acceptable to all sides. The more strident nationalists at least said publicly that they assumed the agenda would be headed by consideration of Israeli withdrawal from all occupied territories and an acknowledgment of the rights of the Palestinians. This attitude conveyed a sense of right and wrong with the former quality clearly identified with the Arab cause. Could Israel be expected to concur with such an agenda? Unequivocally not. But Sadat's reservations were brushed aside by radical elements. The Arabs were separated by political disagreement and drawn together by the forces of nationalism. They could neither agree on a common agenda nor formulate separate agendas. What then were the prospects for a peace conference?

From the Israeli standpoint, any agenda must serve the purposes of Israeli security and reaffirm the concept of the historic homeland. After repeatedly defeating the Arabs on the battlefield, it would have appeared that Israel could impose its will—a phenomenon not unknown in international politics. In eighteenth-century diplomacy such imposition was common, and the United States and its allies had even applied it after the two world wars. But because the Arabs had never acknowledged defeat, the Israelis had not been able to impose their will. The great powers, in fact, had never permitted Arab defeats to reach the point of subjugation. Moreover, it was doubtful whether the Israelis had the capability of bringing the Arabs to their knees, even if they had been free to do so. Israel only had the ability to destroy the Arabs' war-making capability temporarily. Its victories had none of the biblical quality of cataclysm that the Israelis sometimes attributed to their battlefield exploits against the Arab enemy.

In 1967 the Israelis had overlooked their limitations when, as a result of the resounding defeat their armies had inflicted on the Egyptians, Syrians, and Jordanians, they assumed that the Arabs would have no choice but to seek a settlement. Implicit in Israeli thinking was the belief that they could dictate the agenda. When this proved not to be the case, their euphoria over battlefield accomplishments turned to bitter frustration, sustaining the conviction that they must retain the occupied territories. Certainly in 1973 it was clear that Israel's achievements on the battlefield were not great enough to permit it to shape the agenda for peace and unilaterally determine the conditions under which it would live in the Middle East. Yet the Israelis seemed to persist in this belief. The Arab and Israeli viewpoints assured that the trustee of peace would find it difficult to arrive at an appropriate agenda for peace and therefore to convene a successful conference. From the outset, therefore, the usefulness of a general conference could be questioned. But because general conferences are a well-established diplomatic practice, Kissinger knew that he might have to proceed in this way.

The idea of the Geneva Conference was first mentioned publicly by Sadat in a speech before Egypt's National Assembly on October 16, 1973. Kissinger was to comment later that Sadat had signaled

on several occasions during the fighting that he had limited objectives linked to creating a situation that would prompt a negotiated
settlement in the Middle East. This interplay attracted Kissinger
to the Egyptian even before he met him. It set the scene for the
relationship that was to develop between them during Kissinger's
venture in Middle East diplomacy. The statement before the National Assembly was one of the more overt of Sadat's signals. It
came on the eve of Kosygin's visit to Cairo and after Israel had
gained an upper hand in the fighting. It was compatible with
Israel's inclination to use any occasion for pressing the Arabs to
engage in direct talks. Heretofore, Arabs had always been loath
to take such a step because of the element of recognition for the
Jewish state that could be inferred from any such meeting. Kissinger took the idea for the conference with him when he traveled
to Moscow on October 20 and 21 to negotiate a cease-fire with
Communist Party leader Brezhnev. On October 24, having returned to Washington, he discussed a general conference with the
soviet ambassador to the United States. The idea was fully acceptable to both the United States and the Soviet Union even prior to
the crisis that led to the U.S. military alert.

While Sadat favored the idea, he preferred a conference under
the aegis of the United Nations rather than one dominated by the
United States and the Soviet Union. Great-power sponsorship carried too great an implication that political outcomes were being
determined by factors other than the dynamics of Middle East
politics. True, the Arabs were still attracted to the idea of an imposed solution, and they knew that only the great powers could
make such an imposition. Nevertheless, they were partial to a setting in which the great powers were under some constraints. They
wanted a means of appeal if the outcome was not to their liking.
As we have seen in chapter 5, sentiment for the Arab cause among
United Nations members made the international body ideal for
Arab purposes. The Arabs could get an agenda to their liking if
a conference were linked to the purpose of the United Nations and
defined in terms of the Security Council resolutions that had formalized the end of the fighting in 1967 and 1973. Moreover,
United Nations auspices seemed to avoid the full connotations of
direct talks with Israel.

The Arabs' preference for United Nations sponsorship was set aside largely because of urging by the Soviet Union that they not insist on this stipulation. On November 28, 1973, the great powers reached an understanding to convene the conference in Geneva as soon as possible. By coincidence, on the very next day, the Israeli and Egyptian generals suspended the talks they had been holding at Kilo 101. Agreement on how best to separate their forces or how to avoid shooting incidents along the cease-fire line had proved impossible.

As a result of the meetings with Golda Meir and Ismail Fahmy in Washington in early November, Kissinger had established himself as the point of contact between the Arabs and the Israelis. The Egyptians had already seeen the possibilities in a strategy of relying on the United States to squeeze concessions from Israel. On his first trip to Cairo in November, the secretary of state had exploited this hope on the part of Sadat to gain Egyptian approval for the meetings at Kilo 101. Now with the Israelis refusing to raise the seige they had established around Suez City or to withdraw their forces to the approximate battle lines of October 22, there was some concern in Arab circles that Sadat, in agreeing to the military talks, had been duped. Where was the American pressure on Israel? The negotiations at Kilo 101 might have saved Sadat's army, but they had also brought him into direct contact with the Israelis. So far he had nothing to show for it. Sadat was in a dangerous position for an Arab leader.

Kissinger was personally committed because the Egyptians had apparently agreed to the discussions at Kilo 101 after receiving oral assurances from him regarding a reasonable view of what might be expected from the Israelis. Kissinger had stipulated that the discussions of the generals were "to settle the question of the return to the October 22 positions."[4] When the Israelis refused to accept Egypt's demand that they withdraw to these battle lines, the feeling spread that he was playing with the Arabs. Kissinger now made his second trip to the Middle East with the idea of having the military phase of the discussions superseded by the more comprehensive treatment of problems that was expected at a general peace conference. In effect, the military discussions would continue, but at Geneva. After visits to Algeria, Egypt,

Saudi Arabia, Syria, Jordan, and Israel, Kissinger felt confident that a general conference could be convened. The breakdown that had occurred in the military phase of the talks was no longer a threat. He had managed to focus the attention of the negotiants on discussion at a higher level. Here was an example of how a shift in the structure of negotiations can get participants to shrug off an event that could otherwise lead to a crisis. It permitted all to perceive that progress was still possible even when negotiations were deadlocked.

The first session of the Geneva Conference opened on December 21, 1973. It had a slow start. The Israelis objected to a role in the proceedings for the United Nations secretary general because of the negative implications they associated with negotiating under UN auspices. Syria, a major participant in the fighting and a necessary party to any settlement, would not attend despite considerable pressure from the Soviet Union. Assad had not yet been able to persuade his colleagues to sanction publicly the idea of Arabs talking about peace with Israelis. The Egyptians and the Jordanians did face the Israelis across the bargaining table. Following the inevitable wrangle over seating, and after devoting an entire day to venting their spleens before television cameras with regard to one another's alleged crimes against humanity, the two sides did manage to get along somewhat better at a subsequent closed session. The best that could be achieved, however, was to transfer the stalled military truce talks from the tent in the desert west of Suez to the Palace of Peace in Geneva and to reaffirm the importance of these talks. The two sides also exchanged ideas on various functional committees that might be useful as the conference progressed. Neither the Israelis nor the Egyptians, however, were prepared to go further, and they agreed that until Syria was present and the December 31 Israeli elections were concluded, it was preferable to postpone further consideration of political matters.

The Arabs and the Israelis were finally talking, but the results were meager. In addition, difficulties developed between the United States and the Soviet Union over whether the great powers would attend the sessions of the military working group. Kissinger apparently hoped to emphasize contact between the Arabs and the

Israelis in terms of the direct negotiations the Israelis had always wanted. He insisted that neither the United States nor the Soviets be represented in the working group. The Soviets, on the other hand, wanted the great powers to be an integral part of all phases of the negotiations—the approach the Arabs had always favored. Nevertheless, Kissinger's view prevailed. He asserted that there would be no great power participation and departed from Geneva for Washington. The Soviets were left hanging. The fact that the working group proceeded without Russian and American representatives was a mark of the relative strength of the American position.

In considering this difference in outlook between the United States and the USSR, it is necessary to keep in mind that the United States had already established a position for itself in the negotiations while the Soviets had not. The question of participation in the working group was probably secondary. What Kissinger's action had avoided was the presumption that during the negotiations the United States and the Soviet Union would always be paired. The move had succeeded in protecting and also in exploiting the advantage achieved for the United States when Kissinger, on his two trips to the Middle East, had established that he was acceptable to the two sides as a mediator. He saw no need to share this role with the Soviets. It was apparent that the trustee of peace was not prepared to engage in negotiations independent of the considerations of great-power politics.

Shuttle Diplomacy

By early January the talks between the Israeli and Egyptian generals at Geneva had reached their limit. To bring about a separation of forces, territory would have to change hands. Such negotiations would center on political rather than military considerations. The parties appeared to favor dealing with Kissinger rather than confronting one another at the negotiating table. A personal touch was necessary if the situation was not to revert to the standoff that had already existed for twenty-six years. Thus Kissinger decided to visit the Middle East again and try his hand at reviving the momentum that had led to the initial meeting at Geneva.

Kissinger could not know, of course, that his new effort at mediation would lead to the pattern of negotiations that the world now calls shuttle diplomacy. His trip to Egypt in January 1974 did have the clear objective of facilitating a disengagement of the military forces of Egypt and Israel. The very fact that he was prepared to undertake another tour indicated his appreciation of the importance of structure. If progress could not be made on substantive matters with one form of negotiations, perhaps it could be made with another. While the visit was coordinated with the Soviet chairman of the Geneva Conference, the Department of State spokesman emphasized that Kissinger's trip was to be an American venture. The Middle East situation had reached a critical juncture, he said, and without a rapid disengagement of the Israeli and Egyptian forces, any small incident could trigger full-scale conflict. The Soviets deferred to the United States's dominant role and "good offices." In turn, Kissinger complimented the Soviets on their cooperation. He publicly noted their "responsible" attitude and affirmed that in its various initiatives in the Middle East the United States always "kept in touch" with the Soviet Union.[5]

At the outset Kissinger had said that he did not envision functioning as a courier between the Arabs and the Israelis. His plan was to help stimulate ideas while leaving it to the American ambassadors to work out the details. He assumed that official negotiating proposals would be conveyed to the teams at Geneva where final agreement would be reached on discrete segments of an overall settlement. As Kissinger looked to the future he saw negotiations occurring in several phases, each with limited objectives. For a beginning, the disengagement of Egyptian and Israeli forces was a sufficiently attractive target to be worth the time and effort to achieve it. It appeared, therefore, that he intended to modify the structure of negotiations only to the extent that he would insert a new catalytic agent—an agent that was to be Kissinger himself.

The first semblance of Kissinger's approach to structuring negotiations had begun to emerge. Talks were to be conducted on two levels and seemingly in a spaced sequence. Much of the spadework would be done through bilateral diplomatic channels with the United States serving as a facilitator. After issues had been explored and a prescribed agenda agreed on, the two sides could proceed to Geneva with some assurance that they would be talking about the same thing and that the items before them were negotiable. At no time would the negotiants' proclivity for settlement be overtaxed. Step by step the Arabs and Israelis would proceed toward peace. If the pace flagged, Kissinger would step in as he had done in December and as he was now about to do in January. He would also appear at Geneva at critical times to give the negotiations the impetus required for agreement. The only slightly presumptuous aspect of his scheme was that many of those who were involved had not agreed to it. He had not yet enticed to the conference table all the Arabs who must participate if there was to be peace. But as we have already seen, he was faced with the difficult question of agenda, and the structure implied by his actions was a means of getting around it.

The implications of Kissinger's third trip were to be more far-reaching than perhaps even he realized. His mission was not a simple exchange of views between Israel and Egypt on disengagement. The trustee of peace had said that he hoped to "stimulate new ideas." Here we were to catch our first glimpse of a mediator resorting to the techniques of an academic mentor operating through a seminar. For his purposes, a give-and-take situation would be necessary, but without all participants being located at a single place. After talking with Sadat on January 11 and with the Israelis on the following day, Kissinger saw the need for a second round of discussions. As his plane was about to leave Aswan, where Sadat was in residence, a senior State Department official said to the journalists who were accompanying Kissinger, "Welcome aboard the Egyptian-Israeli shuttle."[6] Shuttle diplomacy was born. Up to this point Kissinger's purpose had been to provide the impetus for a return to Geneva. Now he decided to be more ambitious. Something new was in the air. Egyptians were talking informally to American officials and newsmen who half an hour before had been engaged in similar discussions with Israelis. Each had an opportunity to ask what the other side was really thinking at that very moment. Those who took part have testified to the excitement of the occasion. As long as he retained the option of modifying the structure of negotiations in order to respond to new perceptions on the part of the negotiants, Kissinger could maximize his effectiveness as a facilitator and mediator.

Kissinger himself gives Sadat credit for suggesting that they strive for an agreement of some sort rather than be satisfied with an exchange of proposals to be negotiated at Geneva. After four meetings with Sadat in Aswan and four with the Israelis in Jerusalem, Kissinger had an agreement. He was to utilize the shuttle on three subsequent occasions. In April and May 1974, he spent thirty-two days traveling between Damascus and Jerusalem to facilitate the disengagement on the Golan Heights. In March 1975 the shuttle was the means by which he attempted to bring the Egyptians and the Israelis to an understanding on Sinai. In August 1975 it was reactivated when he finally achieved the Sinai Accord.

With the shuttle Kissinger had found a way of getting Arabs and Israelis to do something that American diplomats had wanted for a long time—to feel an incentive for working together toward a common end. Perhaps if the Middle East problem were approached in small segments, a common agenda at each step of the way could be devised. This aim was not to be achieved by some complex project based on common economic interests such as the opening of the Suez Canal for Arab and Israeli use, the joint development of the full potential of the Jordan Valley, or the use of nuclear power to desalinize seawater for a common agricultural project in Israel's Negev and Egypt's adjoining Sinai. These approaches had been suggested in the past but had solicited little interest, particularly as a route to an overall settlement. The new element Kissinger brought to the situation was the drama, the personal urgency, and above all, the human contact that shuttle diplomacy conveyed. As a Jordanian diplomat put it, "The formula is not the problem but rather the willingness to move."[7]

The shuttle involved the challenge of staying ahead of the game with the same type of imagination and flare for innovation that the Arabs had always admired in American technology. It incorporated the Arab sense of progressiveness, and it appealed to Arab leaders. Structure, therefore, was a feature of negotiating style. Perhaps for another mediator the same advantages could not be derived from the form that Kissinger found so complementary to his method of operation.

In assessing the delicate task that confronted the trustee of peace in structuring negotiations, it is necessary to remember that he was actually dealing with two issues. He must move the Middle East toward an Arab-Israeli settlement and simultaneously give the industrialized world a more comfortable position vis-à-vis its oil supply. Perhaps the most productive imagery for achieving his purpose would be that of the United States dragging Israel along to treat with the Arabs. The United States could thereby pose as a true mediator concerned for Arab as well as Israeli sensitivities, and in turn the Arabs would be more forthcoming on matters pertaining to oil. Ideally, the Soviet Union would play the passive role of pressing the Arabs for concessions on cue from the United States. Kissinger was to have remarkable success in constructing and retaining this image of his activities, at least until after the Sinai Accord.

Despite the outward asymmetry of this approach, it had the merit of establishing as counterparts those who were concerned with the two strands—oil and regional accommodation—in the skein that lay before the negotiants. Neither the Israelis nor the Soviets were of the same importance to the oil question as the Arabs and the United States. To be sure, Kissinger was to maintain that peace and oil were not linked. At the time of the ceasefire, however, he could not operate under the assumption that the two questions were separate. The Arabs controlled the oil, and they would be a party to any Middle East settlement. They had initially demanded, in fact, that Israeli withdrawal from the occupied territories take place before assurances were given on oil. The best Kissinger could do was refuse to acknowledge this Arab perception and work for the separation of the issues as the negotiations proceeded. In the meantime, he had to create the illusion that the United States was dealing equitably with the Arabs while nudging along a reluctant Israel. Shuttle diplomacy admirably served this purpose.

The Specter of Geneva

In launching his shuttle diplomacy, Kissinger had indicated a new structure for negotiations. Now he would engage the leaders in their capitals, and secondary issues that emerged from the discussions would be considered at Geneva. The general conference was to be of less importance to the negotiations than originally planned. In his actions and statements Kissinger was conveying a point of view about negotiating. He was clearly questioning the assumption that the purposes of peace would be served by confining efforts to a formal set of negotiations taking place within a specified time frame at a single locale. Good will of the opposing sides in the Middle East conflict toward one another was nonexistent. A general conference could serve only to concentrate all the suspicions of a malevolent past at one place and in one group of negotiators.

The first meeting at Geneva was indicative of this phenomenon; so were the sessions of the United Nations at which the Middle East situation was reviewed. The various international meetings sponsored by Kissinger or the French during 1974 and 1975 to consider questions of world energy consumption, resource allocation, and the national distribution of wealth also fell into the same pattern. Indeed, such gatherings were characterized as dialogues of the deaf. They could not provide a satisfactory means for working toward a settlement that required concessions on such vital issues as security and national legitimacy.

Even though Kissinger's major initiatives during 1974 and 1975 took place through shuttle diplomacy, all events seemed to be marked by the specter of a final general conference. Everyone assumed, or at least talked as if, it would ultimately occur. The perseverance of the idea had both positive and negative aspects for the negotiations. On the positive side, a general conference represented the norm of international behavior. Consequently, it was a logical and useful concluding point. The idea of a conference captured public attention, thereby attuning concerned parties to negotiations. Acceptance of the device by the Israelis and by some Arabs affirmed a commitment to negotiate rather than to fight. It demonstrated the readiness of the parties to seek a settlement. It had symbolic value. Perhaps more important was the discipline that the expectation of returning to Geneva imposed on those who were involved in the Middle East affair. Indeed the myth, not the reality, of the conference dominated thinking on negotiations. This aspect of the conference was useful to Kissinger insofar as it provided an element of stability that permitted him to carry out his own design through shuttle diplomacy.

For the Soviets the conference represented an opportunity to regain the influence they had lost to the United States as the impetus of Western-oriented economic development and the prospect of Kissinger's extracting concessions from the Israelis turned a large segment of the Arab nation toward the West. Neither private exhortations through diplomatic channels nor blasts in the Soviet press were sufficient to forestall the Arabs from this westward movement. The Russians saw the conference as an opportunity to show the Arabs that the Soviet Union stood by them while American sympathy was a chimera created by the Kissinger style. Consequently, the Soviets avoided the extreme positions and the denunciation of Israel that would have destroyed their potential for using Geneva to become active in Middle East diplomacy.

The Israelis were also affected. Throughout the negotiations over Sinai, Kissinger could threaten that, without progress in his shuttle diplomacy, there would be no alternative but to go to Geneva where the United States would be compelled to take a position on the occupied territories. Kissinger's threat carried the implication that the United States would differ from Israel on this basic issue, thereby increasing Israel's sense of isolation and undermining its ability to resist concessions. Israel, therefore, sought to coordinate its strategy on Geneva with the United States, and at least in Kissinger's view made certain concessions at the time of the Sinai Accord in order to achieve this aim.

The Palestinians too were disciplined in their anticipation of Geneva. Once they decided that they could achieve legitimacy by attending the conference, the PLO leaders were driven to seek international recognition through fairly normal representational techniques rather than by means of international terrorism. They even sought official talks with the United States on the future of the Middle East. The prospect of Geneva moved the PLO to take its first step toward enunciating the desirability of a "Palestinian authority" on the West Bank. As time passed, there was also some muting of the Palestinian demand that Israel be dissolved and a secular state of Muslims, Christians, and Jews be established in its place. Rather, the Palestinians limited their comments to proposals involving the West Bank and Gaza. Admittedly, the Palestinian position was vague and totally unacceptable to Israel. Nevertheless, the Palestinians had moved away from the symbolic stand of rigid nationalism embodied in the secular state. Their solicitous attitude toward Kissinger allowed him room to maneuver.

Finally, Geneva also influenced the attitude of the Arab chiefs of state. During June and July 1974, when the conference seemed imminent and the Arab leaders appeared to be taking steps in preparation for it, a greater degree of unity appeared in their relationships. Kissinger considered a unified Arab position vital to the success of a peace conference. Otherwise, amidst the charges and countercharges of this or that leader having betrayed the Arab nation, there was little possibility that the conference would produce anything useful—or for that matter that Kissinger could move the Arabs toward an accommodation through shuttle diplomacy.

The idea of a conference was of value, therefore, in creating the environment for negotiations. But the problems associated with transition from the idea to the reality were tremendous. The sessions held at Geneva in December 1973 had demonstrated little more than the willingness of Israelis and some Arabs to face one another in the same conference room. No real organization of the conference had taken place. If and when the conference ever reconvened, Kissinger's first task would be to develop a structure that met at least the minimal requirements of all parties for assuring that their interests were not ignored.

Unfortunately, each party had a different view of how the conference should be organized, and in each case it was derived from an individual assessment of what should be achieved from negotiations. For those Arabs, such as Sadat, who appeared to accept Israel's existence and who hoped to negotiate some type of settlement, any such meeting could easily have the detrimental effect of accentuating Arab-Israeli differences and requiring a symbolic defense of national goals, particularly on the Arab side of the table, where representatives would be eyeing one another for any betrayal of the Arab cause.

For Sadat, therefore, Geneva was to be avoided as long as there was a possibility of gaining concessions through Kissinger's shuttle diplomacy. He assumed that at some point the conference would convene, and he chose to see it structured as a working conference having a number of committees that dealt with specified issues while plenary sessions were brief and for purposes of ratification. Sadat's position was consistent with organizing the conference through bilateral channels prior to its opening, thereby avoiding the detrimental posturing that would take place if this task were left to the first sessions. Moreover, Sadat was not doctrinaire about how the structure of the conference might redound on national issues. After the signing of the Sinai Accord, he was among the few Arab leaders who were prepared to meet the Israelis for the purpose of discussing Middle East problems without the Palestinians present. His one stipulation was that prior to such a meeting it must be understood in principle that the PLO would participate in the major work of any conference.

For the radical Arabs the purpose of the conference was to achieve national legitimacy through international acceptance of the Palestinians. They envisioned the gathering as being similar to the forum constituted by the United Nations, where the Arabs had succeeded in winning international support for their case. They would place organization and the agenda firmly in the hands of the conferees. The great powers would neither select nor avoid issues on pragmatic grounds as Kissinger had done in his self-initiated shuttle diplomacy. National sensitivities would be served even if agreement were not reached; and toward this end many Arabs, including Assad of Syria, saw value in a united Arab delegation in which states would not be distinguished. The radical Arabs tended to see the conference as a tactical maneuver in the continuing struggle with Israel. Their attitude was not the stuff of compromise or agreement.

The Israelis also approached structure from the standpoint of what they considered to be the conference's real purpose. They did not trust the Arabs to keep a peace; therefore why negotiate for one? The prevailing Israeli mood was against the return to Geneva except perhaps as a tactic to win delay while working toward their strategic security objectives. If they were compelled to attend a conference, the Israelis wanted it to be little more than a framework for bilateral negotiations with individual Arab states. Within this context, the Palestinians need not be acknowledged. Diplomatic bargaining between states would be emphasized. Accession to large and necessarily vague principals—the real work of any conference—could be minimized. Israel need not have its position measured by the Security Council resolutions which had declared the unacceptability of the acquisition of territory by the force of arms. In a bilateral setting, each side would be called on to make comparable concessions, and Israel could deflect some of the American pressure to be more forthcoming or to "gamble" that peace could be achieved by accepting a Palestinian entity on its borders.

There was another theme in Israeli thinking, particularly among liberal Knesset members and certain political commentators. This secondary Israeli perception was held by those who might be prepared to see their country move toward a settlement even at the cost of some security risks. The proponents of the alternative were concerned because Israel's attitude was depicted as the obstacle to peace. The liberal position was not so much an inclination to sacrifice Israeli interests as it was a desire to avoid negative international connotations associated with Israeli negotiators' constantly being lectured by Kissinger to be more pliable in making concessions. For once, this group wanted to see Israel on the high road. They would have devised a "take it or leave it" proposal that contained some elements of compromise. Geneva could provide the face-to-face setting that they considered necessary for the presentation of such a proposition. They hoped it would then be the Arabs who would be pressured by the great powers to move toward an accommodation.

In effect, the liberal elements in Israel would have assumed a unilateral rather than a bargaining stance on peace. The reward for doing so could be less tension with the United States—if it were made to appear that Israel had offered much and the Arabs had conceded little. The important difference between the outlook of these Israelis and the official position taken by the Rabin government was that the former probably regarded peace as more of a possibility and they were more concerned over the isolation in which Israel found itself because of its outward appearance of obstinacy. Within the scenario of the Israeli liberals, the structure of the conference would be of secondary importance. In fact, after a few sessions at which the Israeli position would be presented, the conference need not meet until the Arabs were in substantial agreement with the Israeli proposals. The work of negotiation would be conducted outside the conference, between Kissinger and the Arabs.

When examined carefully, the liberal position had much of the Israeli mentality in it. It was the obverse of the elation that had swept over the country after the 1967 victory. It too was an effort by Israelis to create a situation in which they could say, "Once and forever we have done it." The liberals' approach allowed for the full expression of Jewish self-reliance. And what if the Arabs did not accept Israel's final position and the United States pressed for more concessions? Then there was the other face of self-reliance— fortress Israel, what Kissinger had called the Masada complex. The liberals were not so different, therefore, from the government. They were only more heroic. They emphasized the virtue of a positive position over the negative image of constant haggling over security issues. For those who knew the Middle East, the approach seemed unrealistic. Nevertheless, because the liberals wanted Israel to set forth proposals under the guise of compromise and accommodation, they constituted a force to be used by the trustee of peace in getting the Israeli government to make concessions. Consequently, liberal tendencies in Israel were watched carefully.

The Israelis who were the most liberal on the Palestinian issue were dubbed "doves." Throughout Kissinger's diplomacy they generated a curious response among so-called Middle East experts. In any review or analysis in which the doves were not mentioned, one expert or another would solemnly note the omission and cite the growing attention that the doves were attracting in Israeli politics as evidence of an improved climate for peace. But to what purpose? Certainly some Israelis had always been critical of their country's internal security policy to the extent that Israeli Arabs were denied certain rights of travel, the purchase and sale of property, and membership in various official institutions. This policy made the Arabs second-class citizens. For the government's critics it was a matter of civil rights. Many Israelis who held this outlook were prepared to talk with the PLO, apparently in the belief that the two sides could reason their way toward an accommodation. Optimistic observers believed that the growing voice of this group indicated a decrease in rigidity on the part of the Israeli public. This development was depicted as portending popular pressure on hawkish Israeli leaders to be more forthcoming on the Palestinian issue.

Inexplicably, the same experts who made so much of the doves criticized Kissinger's diplomacy because it could only have long-term results, and time, they said, was of the essence. Were they suggesting that Israeli doves could have other than a long-range influence on the situation? A careful examination of events will lead any observer to wonder whether the doves could ever have a significant influence on Israel's negotiating policy. Contacts began between private Israeli citizens and the PLO as early as 1970, but until 1973 these were made only by anti-Zionist Jews and Israeli communists. In 1974 some Zionists from the international Jewish community held talks with PLO members, but these were disavowed by Prime Minister Rabin. A change did occur in 1976 when several contacts were made by members of the Israel Arab Peace Council. Those involved included a prominent Hebrew University professor, two or three Knesset members, a well-known Israeli editor, and a retired general who was a friend of Rabin himself. The group was small but it could point to certain accomplishments insofar as the government dropped the pretense of making such contacts a criminal offense. Rabin was reported even to have known in advance of some of the meetings, and perhaps to have given his blessing to talks between unofficial Israelis and PLO representatives. Moshe Dayan, a hawk on Arab matters but also a maverick, went so far as to say that he too was prepared to talk to Arafat's representatives. In November 1976 the Knesset actually debated the propriety and wisdom of such a course.

While these developments were of interest, during Kissinger's diplomacy the Israeli doves constituted little more than a straw in the wind. In practical terms they could be disregarded in the long-term equation of Arab-Israeli negotiations. The most that could be said of their influence in the short run was that they were a minor but vocal group favoring a Geneva Conference that included the PLO. Other than that, their inclinations on the negotiations shaded off into those that have been identified with the other Israeli liberals.

The election victory of the Likhud in May 1977 ended most of the talk about the influence of the Israeli liberals and doves. Israeli opinion coalesced around the firm stand of Prime Minister Begin. As Kissinger's successors pressed for a comprehensive solution and the reconvening of the Geneva Conference, Begin reasserted Israeli policy and added a few embellishments that were meant to make Israel appear more forthcoming. The Arabs could have a single Pan-Arab delegation that included Palestinians, but only as long as known members of the PLO were excluded. Israel would not, however, negotiate with the Pan-Arab delegation, which would be composed simply for the ceremonial opening session. Thereafter negotiations would take place between Israel and the individual delegations of the Arab states. If Palestinians were to participate, perhaps they could join the Jordanian delegation. This structure was, of course, unacceptable to the Arabs.

A return to Geneva, therefore, was not simply a matter of cajoling recalcitrant Arab and Israeli leaders into participating. Each had ideas about what they hoped to achieve from a conference, and these ideas in turn influenced how they wished to see it organized. Kissinger could not assume that structure was a neutral factor on which easy agreement could be reached. The success of the entire peace effort could hinge on this issue.

Perhaps an even greater difficulty for Kissinger was the influence the conference was likely to have on Arab perceptions of the United States. The Arabs were fully aware of the features of American policy that were antagonistic to their interests. Kissinger's near confrontation with the OPEC countries over oil pricing, his organizing the International Energy Agency with the announced intention of breaking the oil cartel and reducing Arab power, and the varied threats to seize the oil wells by force all demonstrated imperfectly controlled feelings of antagonism. Also offensive to the Arabs was Kissinger's idea for an exclusively Western-dominated "safety net" oil payment scheme which evoked images of nineteenth-century financial imperialism.

The American record was much the same on the Arab-Israeli

problem. Its votes against PLO participation in the 1974 General Assembly debates and its various vetoes of Security Council efforts to condemn Israel, both for raids into Arab territory and for treatment of Arab populations on the West Bank, reaffirmed the impression that the United States was standing with Israel rather than serving as a mediator. Between 1972 and 1976, five such vetoes were recorded. The American threat to withdraw its financial support from the United Nations and even to cancel its membership if the Arabs succeeded in a move to suspend Israel from that body was equally vivid. Finally, the Arabs were mindful of the American commitment to Israeli security with enormous grants of military equipment. The U.S. position was placed in bold relief by its contrast with the course followed by America's European allies, who either abstained on critical UN votes or occasionally supported the Arabs. The Europeans were prepared to sell sophisticated weapons to the confrontation Arab states—Syria and Egypt. They were less determined than the United States to form a united consumer front on oil prices.

Nevertheless, the Arabs' tolerance for the American position seemed greater than could be expected just from the hypothetical ability of the United States to pressure the Israelis into concessions. Certainly, by the time of the Sinai Accord, the logic of the Egyptian argument that the Americans could move the Israelis to make concessions was beginning to wear thin. The Arabs' attitude could be explained only by the mediator's assets—the Arab affinity for American progressiveness and popular technology. But even in the presence of this bright (if mystifying) aspect of the situation, American officials were horrified by what could actually transpire at the sessions of a reconvened Geneva Conference. It would indeed be difficult for the United States to avoid the U.S./Israel–Soviet/Arab dichotomy. Those who doubted this prospect needed only to review the Sinai Accord to see how far the United States could be drawn in the Israeli direction when negotiations approached the point of culmination in a formal agreement. At any general peace conference, the Arabs would be faced by the United States and Israel. The congenial aspects of the "special relationship" would no longer be concealed as they were in shuttle diplomacy. Most American officials conceded, therefore, that even under Kissinger's guidance positions at a conference would harden. The parties to the dispute would themselves be incapable of moving toward a settlement and the trustee of peace would lose the flexibility of the shuttle.

To a large extent, a general conference was identified with an overall settlement, while shuttle diplomacy was tied to negotiating for limited objectives. Among Kissinger's aides were some who favored a conference. But even they acknowledged that if partial solutions were abandoned and a comprehensive settlement attempted, something would have to precede the Geneva Conference. They recommended that as a preparatory step the United States return to the tradition of "quiet diplomacy." This approach was the structure advocated by some country desk officers in the Department of State and ambassadors in the field. It was the antithesis of the flamboyance Kissinger had interjected into negotiations. The question raised by the suggestion was whether by inclination Kissinger could follow such a course. Even if he could, would reverting to the practices of pre-Kissinger diplomacy also mean a return to the dismal results that had characterized twenty-five years of futile efforts to achieve a Middle East settlement?

As early as the summer of 1974, following the conclusion of the Golan disengagement agreement, pressures for a general conference had begun to increase. Difficulties had arisen over which question the next shuttle should address, and some of those around Kissinger had concluded that the only recourse was to return to Geneva. These same officials surmised that, if an agreement was to emanate from a conference, the United States would probably have to put forth some sort of American plan for peace. The problem with an official American proposal was how the Arabs and Israelis would view it. One indication was the Israeli reaction in 1974 to the statement by the chief U.S. delegate to the United Nations that the fate of Jerusalem could not be determined by a single state and that the establishment of Jewish settlements in Arab-occupied lands constituted an obstacle to peace. These assertions were enough to bring official protests from the Israelis and a blistering response from the Jerusalem press that the United States had disqualified itself as a mediator. On the other side, many Arabs inferred an Israeli bias on the part of the United States and expressed serious misgivings about Kissinger's mediating qualifications, even within the guarded context of shuttle diplomacy.

How then could the United States hope to float an American plan? And if such a proposal would be the natural outgrowth of a general conference, how could anyone be sanguine about reconvening the meetings at Geneva? In retrospect the seriousness of the problem could be gauged by the reaction to a plan set forth by President Carter at a news conference in March 1977. The Israelis opposed his suggestion that they surrender virtually all the occupied territories, while the Arabs found unacceptable his idea of having Israeli or international security forces located for an extended period in the Arab West Bank beyond Israel's final borders.

Despite the currents and countercurrents that swirled around Kissinger on the issue of a general conference versus shuttle diplomacy, certain things were clear to all. Those who favored a conference with its American plan were thinking in terms of strong and determined pressures being brought to bear on the two sides (particularly Israel) to make concessions. Yet this was a position spawned by frustration. While many urged Kissinger to set forth a plan and move toward an overall settlement at a conference, almost everyone on both sides of the issue admitted that there was very little chance of the Ford administration squeezing from Israel the concessions that would be necessary to make this approach viable. Any such tendency was offset by counterpressures that Israel could exert with the implicit influence it had through the American Jewish community. On one occasion a senior American official conceded that the United States had not even been able to formulate clear positions on such issues as the seating of the Palestinians at any conference, the location of Israel's ultimate borders, or the disposition of Jerusalem. In another instance Ford vehemently denied to members of the American Jewish community that the United States had a position on Sinai or that he favored total Israeli withdrawal from the occupied territories. Much of the criticism of Kissinger's diplomacy stemmed from an inability or a refusal on the part of his critics to think clearly about the relationship between negotiating structure and an approach to a settlement that seemed likely to produce good results. Critics took positions without regard for the domestic political environment within which Kissinger and Ford were required to operate.

One advantage of shuttle diplomacy over a general conference was that, within this negotiating format, Kissinger could attribute all negotiating positions to the parties in the dispute. The United States need not be identified as the author of any proposal. Its role was based on Security Council resolutions that had been sufficiently vague in the first place to satisfy the Israelis and the more moderate Arabs. Kissinger appeared to be totally aware of the subtle relationship between structure and approach. His judgment was evident in the great lengths to which he went to avoid an overt American position on the principal issues that separated the Arabs and the Israelis. As his role of mediator unfolded, uncertainty over the American position actually contributed to whatever success he was to experience. In the absence of mutualities between Arabs and Israelis, any position taken by the mediator was viewed by each as favored treatment for the other. It was imperative that he avoid this accusation. Throughout the two years of negotiations that followed the October War, Kissinger managed not to reveal an American position on most questions. Herein lay a key factor in his ability to retain a negotiating relationship with both sides. The necessity of having less than lucid and far-reaching goals dictated the type of negotiating structure that Kissinger had developed in his shuttle diplomacy. It seemed to indicate his doubts about the viability of a general conference where all the forces of the Middle East situation—including the American position—would necessarily become explicit.

Geneva: Final Recourse or Residual Issues?

Despite the difficulties inherent in a general peace conference, it was undeniably part of the negotiating picture, and one route to a relatively fruitful conference lay open. If Geneva was to be successful, the participants would have to see it as the logical continuation of shuttle diplomacy along the lines Kissinger had suggested when he first launched his shuttle and developed the idea of negotiations on two levels. In this regard, he had noted the subtle distinction between viewing the conference as a *final re-*

course and approaching it as a means of resolving *residual issues.*
The success of the conference depended on what had preceded it.
If the negotiants were driven to a conference as a final recourse
following the failure of bilateral shuttle diplomacy, the atmosphere
would be sufficiently bitter to assure failure for the conference
itself. On the other hand, if the conference were preceded by a
successful set of negotiations, and the negotiants proceeded to
Geneva to formalize their accomplishments and to deal with residual issues, then the conference would have a better chance of
being concluded successfully. The complexity of outstanding issues
was less important than how the parties viewed the work of the
conference. The trustee of peace was playing with mood, not
substance.

The implication of Kissinger's position was that shuttle diplomacy should be continued as long as there was a possibility of
achieving anything through this technique. A critical element of
judgment was required in defining the scope of the succeeding
phases of shuttle negotiations. If the chances of failure were great,
and if the conditions of any failure were likely to preclude further
attempts at shuttle diplomacy, then Geneva would almost certainly become a final recourse and its future would be bleak. Such
was the logic of Kissinger's step-by-step approach.

His purpose, therefore, was to arrive at an outcome that was
sufficiently successful to support another phase of shuttle diplomacy or to serve as the final foundation stone for Geneva. In this
regard, was the Sinai Accord of September 1975 a success? Egypt
and Israel did sign an agreement that was meant to assure that
there would be no resumption of hostilities in Sinai, at least for
three years. The trustee of peace thereupon concluded that shuttle
diplomacy might have run its course. The time had come, he said,
to move on to the negotiating structure offered by Geneva. But
was he proceeding within the context of final recourse or residual
issues? For the moment, the accord had embittered the Syrians and
the Palestinians, and there was some doubt that the atmosphere
would be conducive to negotiation if a conference were convened
at that point. In striving for an agreement on Sinai, Kissinger had
disregarded his own premise. In terms of Israeli security, too much
was accomplished in the accord. Many Arabs were left with the

sense that their choices were either to abandon negotiations or to proceed to Geneva as a final recourse and therefore only on their own terms—that is, with the Palestinians officially represented.

The Sinai Accord, in fact, did not provide a satisfactory foundation for convening Geneva. By Kissinger's logic additional shuttles should have occurred. But in Syrian and Palestinian eyes the accord was not sufficiently successful to support another phase of the shuttle. Only Syria could negotiate on Golan, and the Arabs had formally placed responsibility for the future of the West Bank in the hands of the PLO. If the shuttle was to continue, then it was up to Sadat to negotiate yet a third step on Sinai, and he had gone as far as he dared if he hoped to remain within the context of the Arab nation. After the Sinai Accord, Kissinger at times seemed near desperation over resuming the negotiations. During a visit of Prime Minister Rabin to Washington in February 1976, there was vain discussion of perhaps creating some room for maneuver by ignoring the Palestinians and accepting Hussein as a negotiating partner in a West Bank settlement. But Jordan's king was moving in the opposite direction—toward accommodation with the Syrians, who still felt rebuffed by the Sinai Accord. As long as Hussein remained on this tack he would not become part of such a scheme.

Kissinger also suggested an exploratory meeting of those who had already been involved in the disengagement agreements sanctified at Geneva. At such a gathering formal negotiating positions need not be assumed and all parties need not be represented. If some Arabs did not attend, the effort need not be considered a failure. By excluding the PLO temporarily, the necessity of compelling Israel to deal with the Palestinians need not be faced; and while probing for areas of negotiation, the United States need not commit itself on critical issues. The Soviets, however, refused to cooperate with Kissinger on this idea and the suggestion was set aside. Finally, Kissinger obtained authorization from Israel to approach Egypt, Jordan, and Syria on the possibility of negotiating for a limited objective—an end to the state of war. If the Arabs showed interest, bargaining could take place over how much territory Israel would relinquish for a condition somewhat short of a formally declared peace. It was a clear effort to return to shuttle diplomacy and to avoid Geneva until all parties could approach a general conference with the idea of resolving residual issues.

The problem that had overtaken Kissinger was that only the Egyptians and not the Arabs were a party to the Sinai Accord. In contrast, Assad had seen to it that the Golan disengagement was an Arab rather than just a Syrian understanding by having it sanctified in advance by other Arab leaders. Kissinger had preserved a certain elegance in the two disengagement agreements and in the Sinai Accord by mediating between Israel and one Arab state at a time. But in view of the configurations of the Arab nation, did not shuttle diplomacy have a structural flaw? Was it really possible to negotiate successfully with one Arab state or leader at a time? Most Arabs believed not. At each step of the shuttle, the Arabs nervously contemplated where and when the next move would take place. While negotiating in a bilateral format, they experienced the national compulsion of wanting to see all Arabs involved in the negotiations. In preparation for the negotiation of the Sinai Accord, even Sadat had called for simultaneous movement on Sinai, Golan, and the West Bank. For the trustee of peace, simultaneous negotiations could only amount to a mindboggling juggling act that would certainly exhaust even Kissinger. For the Israelis such a performance would generate close to unbearable pressure. Even within the Arab body politic, agitation could become so severe under conditions of simultaneous negotiations that any semblance of Arab unity would be shattered. Without preserving at least a minimum of Arab unity a subsequent general conference would be futile. Nevertheless, what Sadat and other Arabs were trying to say was that Geneva would indeed be a failure unless there was notable success in resolving issues through shuttle diplomacy, thereby giving the conference the aura of a gathering for dealing with residual matters.

Such is the travail of a statesman as he attempts to structure a negotiating situation. The task of convening a peace conference or establishing communications among governments is often dismissed as a formality that precedes the real work of negotiations. In the case of the Middle East, the formal and well-established approaches of international diplomacy to structuring negotiations have often proved inadequate. Without shuttle diplomacy the entire effort might have amounted to little more than the initial meeting at Geneva and a plethora of diplomatic messages among Washington, Cairo, Jerusalem, Damascus, and Riyadh. More than likely, the results would have been the compounding of frustration and a sense of futility for all who had been engaged for so long in the Middle East game. Kissinger's structure did have certain shortcomings, but through his unorthodox approach to negotiation he exposed the underlying currents present in diplomatic exchange in a way they had never been seen before. For the first time others could examine the edifice of negotiation and perhaps determine how any talks in the future might be organized to bring the efforts of statesmen yet another step closer to peace in the Middle East.

9

A Philosophy
of Negotiation

As long as the world must live with the Arab-Israeli standoff observers will probably have differences of opinion over what Kissinger really accomplished with his shuttle diplomacy. Viewed in and of themselves his achievements were meager—a disengagement of forces in Sinai and along the Golan Heights and the transfer of some inhospitable territory and a few low-yielding oil wells from Israel to Egypt. The issue of conflicting national legitimacies remained virtually unresolved. Neither side really agreed to allow the other to live in peace. But from another perspective, what would the years following the 1973 war have brought had there been neither troop disengagements nor the establishment of buffer zones policed by United Nations forces? It is fair to speculate about how long it would have been before the Arabs and the Israelis again slipped into open hostilities.

In the context of the larger historical picture, an observer might note that over the years a pattern had emerged in the Middle East —a theme that was played originally in 1948 and repeated again in 1956 and in 1967. In each instance a crisis was followed by the intercession of the United States working with a number of other governments identified as the United Nations. The purpose of the intercession was supposedly to ease tensions. In no case had anyone really expected a permanent peace. The UN-sponsored nego-

tiations that took place in Cyprus in 1949, the evacuation of Sinai
arranged by Eisenhower in 1956, and the Rogers Plan in 1969 all
had this element in common. On each occasion Arabs and Israelis
eventually became exasperated with conditions and another round
of fighting ensued. In view of this larger picture, could anything
different be expected in 1973? Had Kissinger actually influenced
the situation, or did it have an impetus beyond manipulation, reflecting existing power relationships and precluding him or anyone
else from breaking the pattern that had emerged on three previous
occasions since the founding of Israel?

Kissinger has been accused by some critics of only managing a
conflict and not really working toward a settlement. But even if his
efforts are discounted, it must be acknowledged that Kissinger
brought the Middle East closer to peace than previous mediators.
Now from time to time Arabs and Israelis actually talked in a
reasonable manner about peace. They negotiated over political
matters. For the first time since 1949 representatives met in full
public view. Israel's existence was acknowledged more broadly
than ever before by Arab leaders through Security Council resolutions and by the understanding several of them reached at the
Arab chiefs of state meeting at Rabat in November 1973. Sadat's
intention to negotiate with Israel rather than to fight was openly
accepted by other Arab leaders. The Israelis also took a significant
if tenuous step. In March 1976, for the first time, they sat at the
Security Council with Palestinian nationalists.

However limited these achievements, a feeling of hope developed from Kissinger's diplomatic maneuvering—an excitement
that heretofore had not been present in attempts to conclude an
Arab-Israeli settlement. By mid-1976 it could be said that the
Middle East had changed. The usual internecine bickering among
Arab leaders, the plots and counterplots, were all proceeding at the
usual high level; the killing of one Arab by another as Syrians,
Lebanese, and Palestinians worked out their destinies in the fighting at Beirut and the massacres at Tel Zaatar and Damhour
reached shocking proportions. But through it all, Sadat, Assad,
and Hussein, with the approval of the Saudi monarchy, remained
committed to some form of negotiated settlement with Israel. This
fact, side by side with traditional Arab rivalries and with formal

dedication to the so-called Arab cause of the Palestinians, generated much of the turmoil in which the Arabs found themselves. They were all involved in basic contradictions of an important transition, and they knew it. An incipient Arab commitment to a negotiated settlement no doubt existed prior to the advent of shuttle diplomacy. Henry Kissinger, however, had a major part in nurturing the new outlook, which could easily have been smothered under the stultifying practices of traditional diplomacy.

Changing Perceptions

If new attitudes were in fact emerging, it is necessary to go beyond an analysis of what Kissinger actually achieved and ask how he managed to accomplish it. Did he bring anything new to Middle East negotiations? Previous chapters have given attention to Kissinger's personalized approach to diplomacy that has been identified as his appealing to Arabs through the similarities of American populism and Arab-Muslim egalitarianism. The influence of American technology and an abiding desire of many Arabs to develop their societies according to the American technological bias have also been suggested as factors that helped move Arabs toward an accord with American thinking on the Middle East. But something more was at work. The ethos of populism and American technology may have provided the undergirdings of the American position, but how did Kissinger exploit the climate they afforded to shape the Arab-Israeli negotiations? Thus we confront the negotiating philosophy and technique of Henry A. Kissinger.

At the height of his Middle East success Kissinger visualized his approach to negotiation in the following way:

> The art of negotiation is to set goals that can be achieved at a given time and to reach them with determination. Each step forward modifies old perceptions and brings about a new situation that improves the chances of a comprehensive settlement. . . . [Progress can be thwarted] by asking too much as surely as by asking too little.[1]

As a mediator Kissinger saw himself as a force for change rather than a counselor who simply brought two sides together through techniques of compromise. Negotiation was essentially a cerebral process of changing perceptions to create new attitudes with which

the negotiants could see the value of further change. In order for
the process to function, it was necessary to operate solely within
the current time frame, avoiding hypothetical consideration of
what might arise in the future. Any projection of issues into the
future could only divert the two sides from differences that were
current and perhaps soluble. Negotiants need not address the future, because as new situations emerged many old problems would
disappear with discarded perceptions. The success of Kissinger's
diplomacy hinged on progress—movement—not on the achievement of some specified goal or the resolution of any particular
issue. Consequently, limited achievable objectives had to be the
substance of the exercise, lest one or another negotiant be confronted with a demand to sacrifice a position that included core
values of its body politic.

Kissinger's approach to mediation allowed for inventiveness,
flexibility, and a bold use of inducements—but only as long as the
steps to be taken were small. Each step would allow a further step.
Because the process itself was more important than any particular
objective, participants could never have a clear view of any agreement toward which they might be working. The ultimate objective
was an abstraction—a partial settlement comprised of anything the
Arabs and the Israelis would accept at a given time. Stated briefly,
Kissinger held an experiential and perhaps even a romantic notion
of negotiation. The substance of his process was derived from
conscious perceptions of reality managed by an adroit mediator.
It was totally attuned to the intellectual quality of the time in
which he worked.

The style of Kissinger's shuttle diplomacy does not appear to
have emerged completely until the Israeli-Syrian negotiations in
May 1974 over disengagement on the Golan Heights. Its elements,
however, were present from the outset. First he would seize the
high ground by establishing a firm context for negotiation with a
series of explanations and interpretations that in effect defined
conditions. He emphasized the history of the situation and interpreted what he alluded to as its larger realities. His usual practice
was to devote his initial sessions with his counterparts to developing the strategic implications of the negotiations ahead—the impact of a successful outcome on movement toward peace and the

horrors of the conflagration that would almost surely ensue if the negotiations were to fail. He identified for each side what they could reasonably expect from the negotiations. He attempted to create an awareness of the problems of the other negotiant and an understanding of the limitations that the decision to negotiate had imposed on the former enemy. These reviews were lengthy, encompassing what Kissinger considered to be every aspect of the situation.

In November 1973, when Kissinger negotiated the initial cease-fire agreement between Golda Meir and Ismail Fahmy, he directed his efforts toward convincing each side that the Middle East had before it the only chance of peace for perhaps the next generation. In the case of the Golan disengagement, he again stressed that failure could lead to an all-out war. He advised Arab and Israeli leaders alike that the Middle East had a history of lost opportunities and that in the end his efforts could prove as fruitless as those of secretaries of state before him unless each side gave weight to the larger considerations of peace.

Such exhortations served the short-term purpose of avoiding hostilities as well as the grandiose hope of achieving peace. They formed the basis, therefore, for taking small steps to reach limited goals. Kissinger instructed the negotiants that in the first instance they should devote attention only to actions that were required to reduce the possibility of renewed fighting. Other issues should temporarily be set aside. This theme was developed at the time of the Sinai disengagement; it was used again in the Golan negotiations; and when talks on the Sinai Accord were suspended in March 1975, Kissinger pointed out the mistake of the two sides in not being concerned over the possibility of imminent conflict. Gloomily he predicted that without some agreement there would surely be a resumption of hostilities by July.

With his threat of impending doom Kissinger no doubt hoped to discipline the Arab and Israeli leaders by giving negotiations a decisive quality. His purpose was to push each side into making the concessions that were required for some sort of agreement. For the Israelis, Kissinger had an additional element that shaped the context of negotiations. The United States hoped not only to avert a Middle East war but also to avoid oil embargoes. Thus Kissinger, as well as the Arabs and the Israelis, had compelling reasons to achieve an agreement. The choices were not those of the Middle East countries alone. American interests also required consideration, and this realization lay heavily on Israel because of its special relationship with the United States. If the United States was to do something for Israel—provide military, economic, and diplomatic support—then Israel must do something for the United States—make reasonable concessions.

Usually Kissinger succeeded in getting Arab and Israeli leaders to accept the context within which he set negotiations. At least neither Arab nor Israeli negotiants argued with him about it. The meaning he associated with negotiations consisted largely of truisms and generalized concepts with which anyone would have a difficult time quarreling. But the context was important. It provided reference points he could use to guide proceedings during sessions of hard bargaining. Who was prepared to say that a few kilometers of territory one way or the other was worth the resumption of open warfare? With his context established, Kissinger felt that he had some assurance of where reason would take the negotiants. One Israeli official described Kissinger's approach as often low-key and subtle. "There is no table pounding, no threats; just an appeal to what he would have you believe is sweet reason."[2] It was to be expected, therefore, that Kissinger would prevail only as long as he retained the power of definition and avoided scenes fraught with emotion. In fact, he lost control of the March 1975 negotiations after the Israelis challenged his definition of their security and resorted to emotional displays in countering his arguments. In this instance table-pounding did take place.

After setting the context for negotiations, Kissinger invariably asked each side to explore with him various ideas on how a limited agreement might be achieved. Essentially he was asking, "In the existing setting, what problems are within the bounds of negotiation?" Consistently he directed attention to matters that were open to rational consideration. With the exception of the final stages of the March 1975 negotiations on Sinai, when Kissinger's sweet reason did not prevail, he usually found some way of accepting the logic, if not always the content, of his counterparts' arguments. Kissinger probably knew the Israelis better than the Arabs, and at times considered his relationship with them "en famille" because of the special relationship. As a result, he was less patient with Golda Meir's or Rabin's stubbornness than with the constant shifting and probing of Assad. The relationship with Sadat was smoother; here Kissinger found someone who appreciated process as much as he did.

In many ways, Sadat's position was the key to Kissinger's success. Egypt was the strongest of the confrontation states, and it enjoyed the support of Saudi Arabia—the most powerful of the Oil Arabs. The coincidence of outlook between Sadat and Kissinger was fortuitous. Like Kissinger, Sadat took a broad strategic view of a situation. He had started a war, not to destroy Israel, but to break the impasse created by the 1967 hostilities and to set the scene for a negotiated settlement. He accepted American support for Israel as a fact of life. In Sadat, Kissinger had an advocate of a negotiated settlement who was not inclined to contest small issues to the point of bringing negotiations to a standstill. On many issues Sadat was prepared to "leave it to Henry." What he wanted was a peace that could be sustained within Arab politics and that took note of Egypt's national dignity. Few mediators have been so fortunate as to have a principal negotiant of this outlook.

Properly, Kissinger liked to work jointly with a negotiant to develop ideas that included indications of a willingness to make concessions and that therefore would be of interest to the opposing party as topics of discussion. The objective was to place the negotiants at opposite ends of a single continuum, thereby assuring that, if the two sides then made reasonable concessions, their positions would eventually meet. At the outset of the negotiations on the Egyptian-Israeli disengagement, Kissinger characterized the operation as moving toward "positions which both sides can accept because they reflect the just aspirations of both sides, and this is the role which the United States is attempting to perform."[3]

Actually the process was somewhat more complex than that. A meeting of the minds was not always possible, as Kissinger well knew. The trick was to rephrase old issues so that each side could emphasize different nuances of an agreement while fully accepting a minimum position that it would carefully observe. Kissinger had to show sufficient understanding of each side's position to induce it to make the concessions that were necessary for this process. While he was required to recite the arguments of both the Arabs and the Israelis, he could adopt the position of neither. It would have made him an advocate and ended his mediator's role. Yet he could not position himself too far from the views of either side if he hoped to encourage the changes in perceptions that would bring the two closer together. Thus, he was required to play a double game, avoiding a consistent position for all to see and representing himself somewhat differently to each side when it was advantageous to do so. Much of this was done with illusion, principally through his technique of offhand, casual, and at times uncomplimentary remarks about the personalities of one side while discussing matters with the other. He thereby created the impression that he was more sympathetic to the position of his conversant than to that of the adversary.

Having defined the situation and positioned himself in this way, Kissinger's task was essentially to close the gap between the Israeli and Arab negotiants. As he saw it, the preliminary steps devoted to establishing the context of his mediation permitted him to start negotiations "with a very large area of understanding of what objectives would be realized. So I think that while we presented some ideas of our own ... our positions have approached each other very substantially."[4] The imagery of a gap that required closing was evoked repeatedly throughout the various negotiations, and Kissinger's behavior was clearly guided by this conceptualization. As he presented ideas and elicited reactions, his purpose was described as whittling down the difference.

In his discussions with Arabs and Israelis, Kissinger characterized difficulties that arose as "conceptual hurdles," and in each case his attention was directed to either changing perceptions that permitted the negotiants to clear the obstacle or developing alternatives that allowed them to circumvent it. In dealing with the Egyptians at the time of the 1973 cease-fire he questioned the wisdom of their demand that Israel return immediately to the October 22 troop positions around Ismailia and Suez City west of the canal. Through negotiation, he argued, Egypt very possibly could acquire a disengagement line somewhat east of Suez. Why worry, therefore, about Israeli violation of the cease-fire when it was now possible to obtain so much more through American mediation?

Likewise in his efforts to persuade the Arab leaders to lift the oil embargo, he argued for a new perception. Economic pressure may have been legitimate, he said, before the American-sponsored negotiations between Israel and Egypt had started. But the Arabs had made their point, and to continue withholding the oil that was so vital to the American economy constituted an excessive act. His technique was productive. Initially, the Arabs had insisted that lifting the embargo be tied to an Israeli "commitment" to withdrawal from the occupied territories. Kissinger was able to change their position to an understanding that they would forgo the embargo when there was evidence of "some movement" by the Israelis on the Sinai and Syrian fronts, complemented by "good faith" on the part of the United States as a mediator.

Another case of changing perceptions occurred when the Syrians and Israelis reached an impasse over the location of the demarcation line in the Golan disengagement. As an alternative to the Syrian view, Kissinger proposed that Israel give up some of the land in dispute but be permitted to retain part of it with the understanding that its forces would not fortify that area heavily. Assad accepted the argument that it was more important to establish a pattern of Israeli concessions than to force a single pullback that could have the effect of stiffening Israel against further withdrawals. Thus Kissinger's efforts to negotiate various tradeoffs and substitutions were facilitated by changing the outlook of the negotiants.

A final instance of changing perceptions was Kissinger's success in persuading the Israelis in the negotiation of the Sinai Accord to give up their demand that the Egyptians pledge themselves to nonbelligerency. Instead, Israel settled for the idea of a relatively long-range commitment that Egypt would not be the first to resume hostilities. There was very little real difference between the outcome of nonbelligerency and the commitments Sadat ultimately accepted. The Israelis received a stronger assurance of peace than they had enjoyed prior to the agreement. At the same time, Sadat

avoided a step as irrevocable in appearance as declaring nonbelligerency and was thereby spared at least some of the criticism that
was to be expected from the Arabs who still rejected negotiations.

An important element in the Israeli acceptance of this modified
Egyptian commitment under the Sinai Accord was the assurance
of continued American aid and political support extended to Israel
by Kissinger. The substance of this American commitment was
considered in chapter 6, and the process by which Kissinger made
commitments will be the subject of chapter 11. Commitments
themselves, however, do not vitiate the importance of the *form* of
Kissinger's argumentation in getting the Israelis to accept something less than a pledge of nonbelligerency on the part of Sadat.
Even with promises of aid, Kissinger still had to convince the
Israelis that less binding language was worth the chances they
would take. Prescribing and gaining acceptance of a different conceptualization of nonbelligerency did represent success by Kissinger in changing an Israeli perception. Something less than nonbelligerency was worthwhile after all. Heretofore the Israelis had
maintained that they would withdraw beyond the Sinai passes for
nothing else.

Even after the exploration of ideas at length and the development of negotiable positions, bringing the negotiations to a successful conclusion embodied difficulty. Ideas were Kissinger's
stock-in-trade. But if either side presented a fully identifiable position, the other usually had difficulty accepting the suggestion for
fear that it would find itself negotiating on its adversary's terms.
At the outset of the first negotiations on Sinai, Moshe Dayan was
the source of many ideas regarding disengagement and the eventual pullback of Israeli forces to the Gidi and Mitla Passes. Accordingly, Sadat, in accepting these ideas, was plagued by an anxiety
that he might be playing into the enemy's hands.[5] Above all else,
Kissinger realized that he had to avoid a confrontation. He preferred, therefore, to work with ideas that were not tied too closely
to one side when he talked to the other. In transmitting preliminary views between negotiants, he would sometimes identify
as his own an idea that had originated with the antagonist. He
would contend that acceptance of this view was needed in order
to induce movement on the part of the other. In this way he moved

each side along step by step without its having to acknowledge that it was dealing directly with the proposals of the enemy.

This process occurred almost automatically in the first Sinai agreement. Arriving in the Middle East on January 11, 1974, Kissinger attempted to present ideas fairly and to give his best judgment on the items that a viable agreement could include. Trust in the mediator was high, as was the element of distrust between sides. Kissinger's interpretations and suggestions soon acquired the semblance of an "American plan," even though Kissinger avoided this term. In both the Sinai and Golan disengagement negotiations, when the pace lagged he would offer some ideas of his own for surmounting obstacles. At this point in the Golan talks he substituted a thinning out of Israeli forces for Israel's relinquishing territory. As Kissinger entered this phase of negotiations, the American contribution to the area of agreement was seldom in sharp focus. As an Israeli official put it, "He rarely represents it as his own plan but rather as a fatherless creation that he is willing to present to the other side if we will encourage him to do so."[6] Simultaneously, he would recite the progress that had already been made and the objectives each had achieved. He would also press the argument that success was far more valuable than the few remaining concessions that had to be made.

When Kissinger sensed that there was little possibility of achieving further changes in perceptions, or when he believed that the negotiants were close enough on a sufficient number of items for them to envisage an agreement, he would initiate an exhaustive search for draft passages that would be acceptable to both sides. It was within this context that an American plan could emerge insofar as he now became the originator of formulas suitable for an agreement rather than the stimulator and conveyor of ideas and the source of judgment on what the other side might accept. The American plan, however, never took the form of a comprehensive proposal for peace. It was always fashioned from the bits and pieces of draft language he had already persuaded the negotiants to accept. In such instances the proposal identified with Kissinger was much different from a full-blown plan announced unilaterally from Washington with all the characteristics of an imposed solution. The so-called plans developed through shuttle diplomacy were a device by which Kissinger put into words whatever he sensed the Arabs and Israelis were close to thinking anyway.

On only one occasion did Kissinger depart from his practice. It was the autumn of 1974; the PLO was moving toward its ascendency through Arafat's appearance at the United Nations. Talks on the possibility of beginning another round of negotiations on Sinai were foundering because of difficulties in developing common ground for negotiations between Israel and Egypt. At this point Hussein felt sufficiently encouraged after a visit to Washington to propose the withdrawal of Israeli forces from a strip of territory along the Jordan River. Kissinger countered with an alternative suggestion for Jordanian administrative control on the West Bank, but under Israeli military supervision. The idea was set forth in some detail, and while the American secretary of state presented the proposal as if it were his own, it was in fact a variation of an idea developed by Israeli Defense Minister Peres. Before using this proposal Kissinger had not taken the time to modify the Arabs' perceptions in a way that would have permitted them to be moved closer to the Israelis on this idea through the gap-closing procedure. The proposal represented an Israeli reality that was totally alien to the Arabs. It was not negotiable within their own sense of what was politic. Upon hearing of the proposal, Assad upbraided Kissinger for even considering a West Bank solution that excluded the Palestinians. "For a few kilometers on the West Bank," he said, "you are risking a major conflict with the Palestine Liberation Organization that could lead to an inter-Arab War."[7] It was a prophetic statement. Largely because of contradictory perceptions on the ultimate shape of a Palestinian entity, Assad himself within eighteen months was to fall into an inter-Arab war with the PLO in Lebanon.

Assad's was not the only objection; Hussein considered Kissinger's proposal an insult. It allowed him no opportunity to regain territory other than through a complete and direct refutation of PLO legitimacy. At the time the proposal was presented, acceptance would not have permitted the Jordanian monarch to remain within an Arab national context. The effect of Kissinger's suggestion was to compel the Arabs to choose between Hussein and the PLO. Hussein had no choice, therefore, but to capitulate to the Arab sentiment aroused by the incident and to acquiesce in the move of the Arab leaders at the summit conference in Rabat in November 1974 when they designated the PLO the sole representative of the Palestinian people. This experience instructed the mediator in the wisdom of the step-by-step process of first developing ideas, then advising each negotiant on what the other might accept, and finally closing the gap as he moved them toward a position that both could at least grudgingly tolerate. The announcement of preconceived plans assaulted sensitivities and hardened perceptions. It was not a good means of inducing change. In June 1979, following the Israeli-Egyptian Treaty, Ezer Weizman, Israel's defense minister, registered implied criticism of Begin's approach on this very point when he asked to be removed from his country's delegation to the negotiations with Egypt over the West Bank. Weizman saw the difficulties involved in Begin's insistence on holding to rigid plans for a West Bank settlement— it was an approach that gave no room for changing Egyptian perceptions.

Momentum

In his definition of the art of negotiation, Kissinger had said that modifications in perceptions bring new situations that improve the chances of a comprehensive settlement. In order to achieve this end, he felt the necessity of always moving on to new situations— any situation that was a step closer to a settlement, and by whatever means that were available. Kissinger and his aides, therefore, were preoccupied with momentum—meaning simply an inclination on the part of the negotiants to move on to new situations. If the trustee of peace could change a sufficient number of perceptions and change them fast enough, he hoped to create a frame of mind on the part of Arabs and Israelis that would permit them to accept even further changes. With rapid movement it was likely that the negotiants would get caught up in the essence of compromise. Movement would induce a broader view of what a settlement might mean, and each negotiant would be more inclined to make concessions with the confidence that the other was prepared to do the same. Essentially, Kissinger was telling the negotiants that if they listened to him, they would be propelled toward a comprehensive settlement. More was involved, therefore, than the quality of the change Kissinger hoped to effect in perceptions. The pace of change was also important. It was all part of his emphasis on process over content in negotiation. In Kissinger's style of diplomacy, momentum went hand in hand with changing perceptions.

When Kissinger negotiated the cease-fire agreement between Egypt and Israel, journalists who were present observed that he was intent on fostering the appearance of momentum by overwhelming both sides with ideas and suggestions for an agreement.[8] Another journalist who accompanied Kissinger during March 1975 for the first attempt to achieve the Sinai Accord said of Kissinger's approach, "He believes that any agreement, however lacking in specific political concessions, would in itself be a major political action insuring stability in the Middle East."[9]

It was not just outside observers who concluded that in Kissinger's view the process of reaching an agreement was more important than the agreement itself. The Israelis too saw in his mediation the importance of momentum as a means of assuring success. At the time of the breakdown of the Sinai talks in March 1975, Israeli officials made this point and said that they did not share his view. On another occasion Israeli Defense Minister Peres characterized Kissinger's approach, saying that it was "to move for the sake of moving."[10] In musing over his experience with Kissinger, Assad said, "He talked of the necessity of moving quickly without stopping over small matters. He did not seem to desire to dwell on trivia, but seemed to conceive of movement to peace in long strides forward."[11]

In the minds of Assad and others who dealt with him, Kissinger's rationale for movement in negotiations seemed to be twofold. For the short run it assured tranquillity and for the future it promised a broader base for additional agreements. But despite this look into the future, Kissinger himself was essentially oriented toward the present. He would do anything, suggest anything, offer anything that would produce momentum toward an early agreement. Following the Sinai disengagement in January 1974, he pointed out to newsmen who had accompanied his party on the first shuttle that, of the many items on which the United States had given assurances to one or both negotiants, only two or three had any further relevance. The others either had been rendered redundant by changes in viewpoints or had already been implemented within the negotiating process. The United States, for example, was already supporting Israel. The pledge to continue support, which Kissinger made during the negotiations, had little real meaning from the standpoint of modifying official American behavior. It was reassuring to the Israelis, however, and helped them make concessions that otherwise would not have been forthcoming.

Another example was Israeli concern over the Egyptian blockade of Israeli shipping at Bab el Mandeb. At the time the Sinai disengagement was concluded, the blockade had been lifted for two months. As long as momentum toward a settlement was maintained, it was not likely that the blockade would be reimposed, and assurances to Israel against the resumption of this impediment to its shipping need not influence U.S.-Arab relations. The same could also be said of the assurance given to Israel that the United Nations Emergency Force could be disbanded only by the Security Council. Such a pledge was normative and hardly operational. If giving this assurance contributed to a mood that permitted the Israelis to move toward an agreement, Kissinger was glad to do so. Everything possible was done to generate momentum.

In some cases Kissinger was also willing to permit the negotiants to define a future situation in exchange for a present concession. While urging the Israelis and the Syrians toward a disengagement agreement on Golan, he agreed that the United States would condone and politically support a military response by Israel if it were again attacked by Palestinian terrorists across Syrian lines. He seemed to have little concern that such an understanding could someday prove to be counterproductive to American relations with Syria. In Kissinger's estimation, the future would be more likely to take care of itself if an agreement could be reached now. Thus was the pace of negotiations maintained.

Shuttle diplomacy was ideal for a negotiator who relied on momentum insofar as the shuttle was the embodiment of movement. There was the trustee of peace, moving from country to country as if to whip the negotiants on to greater speed in the proceedings. The shuttle also had an unending quality about it. When

he was not actually in motion himself, Kissinger was meeting the
steady stream of Arab and Israeli visitors who came to Washington
for the preliminary and preparatory discussions that preceded a
shuttle. And when the shuttle began, the pace was extrahuman.
Could anyone imagine the preoccupied William Rogers, the discriminate Dean Rusk, the fidgety John Foster Dulles, or the
olympian Dean Acheson sitting for sixteen straight hours with
Hafez al Assad or locked in an all-night session with the Israeli
cabinet?

Such was the stuff of shuttle diplomacy. From the relatively
reasonable pace at the beginning of the first shuttle, when sessions
with Sadat were interspersed with visits to the High Dam at Aswan
and the pharaonic temples at Luxor, Kissinger moved quickly to
an accelerated tempo. In a single day he would hold talks first in
Israel, then in Egypt, and finally return to Israel to start afresh
the next morning. The usual sense of propriety associated with
diplomacy at the highest levels was set aside. Upon arriving in
Cairo at 10:00 P.M. or in Damascus at midnight he would go
directly to the office of the Egyptian or Syrian president. On one
such occasion, after being closeted with Assad until 4:00 A.M., he
returned at 9:30 the next morning for three more hours of discussion and then went off to Jerusalem to talk to the Israelis. The
Kissinger style created a sense of urgency that pressed the negotiant into movement. His intensity could not be other than
infectious.

If Kissinger was preoccupied with developing momentum, then
it was quite natural for all parties to the Middle East negotiations
to be concerned over whether at any point he was losing that
momentum or conversely whether he was developing a sufficient
amount of it to sweep them into positions they found uncomfortable. Momentum soon became a yardstick against which to measure the negotiations. At one point when the Egyptians held discussions with the Soviet Union over arms shipments, the Israelis
quickly concluded that Sadat was backsliding; he had turned away
from mediation. Kissinger's effort, the Israelis asserted, had lost
momentum. When Israeli concessions were not forthcoming
rapidly enough, the Arabs made the same observation.

The importance of the pace of negotiations could not be overestimated. One striking example occurred in June 1975, when Kissinger, after three months of cajoling, succeeded in prying from the Israelis some concessions they had not been prepared to offer before the negotiations were suspended in March 1975. Hope for a settlement had dimmed after the breakdown in the talks. Finally on June 24 the new Israeli position was conveyed to Sadat through the American ambassador in Cairo. The Egyptian leader's response was positive and instantaneous. The mood immediately changed. Things were moving. Hopes for a settlement soared. Had Sadat hesitated and complained about the Israeli position, this reaction would not have occurred, and Kissinger would have had little with which to work.

The issue of who would control the pace of negotiation created more difficulty for Kissinger in his relations with the Israelis than with the Arabs. Obsessed with their security and faced with a domestic constituency that focused on the highly emotional issues of protecting the Golan settlements and preserving the historic homeland embodied in the West Bank, the Israeli negotiators were determined not to be pressured into ill-advised moves which Kissinger referred to as taking risks for peace. They contested Kissinger's control of the pace of negotiations, principally because of their apprehension that the American secretary of state was moving without sufficient regard for their national sensitivities. They were single-minded in their belief that succumbing to American pressure would only invite additional pressure. Such was the Israeli view of momentum.

Most observers agreed that particularly after Rabin succeeded Golda Meir as prime minister, the Israeli government was too weak to take any action that would be vociferously criticized by its domestic opposition. A cabinet crisis was almost certain to follow an unpopular concession. Consequently, when Kissinger developed momentum through his technique of exploring ideas, the Israelis would attempt to slow the pace by asking for clarification on some point or another. In such cases Kissinger would be required to go to Cairo or Damascus, not with new ideas, but to recapitulate previous discussions. In these instances he was retracing his steps, and the pace of negotiations was thereby slowed. Certainly this problem was a major concern during the negotiation of the Golan disengagement. On some occasions when the Israelis asked for clarification, the Syrians raised new questions about matters that Kissinger thought had been settled. The placement and dimensions of the buffer zone between Syrian and Israeli forces were particularly difficult in this respect.

For the Arabs, momentum had a different meaning. As the pace quickened in any sequence of negotiations, attention was centered on regaining occupied territory, a concern that was identified less with the Arab nation than with the interests of some Arab state, whether it be Syria, Egypt, or tentatively Jordan. Kissinger, after all, was not negotiating over the national issue embodied in the Palestinians. Conversely, as momentum waned, Arab concerns turned from the occupied territories and centered on Palestinian rights. In November 1974, when the Arab chiefs of state met in Rabat and recognized the PLO as the sole legitimate representative of the Palestinian people, the move was justified partially in terms of the assertion that Kissinger's diplomacy had lost its momentum. In fact, Kissinger's detractors within the Arab camp delighted in pointing to any evidence of a decline in the pace of negotiations as a setback for the American mediator.

A similar situation occurred after the Sinai Accord in which Kissinger virtually accepted Israel's terms for any further negotiations in order to get Israeli assent to the agreement he was then negotiating. Assad and the Arabs of the so-called Rejection Front quickly saw in the accord the extension of Isarel's military potential as well as implications for separating Egypt from the Arab nation. In this atmosphere Kissinger could not generate momentum among Arabs. Thereafter, almost as a barometer of trouble ahead, the importance of territorial concessions by Israel to the Arab states declined and that of the national issue expressed through the Palestinians increased. Through Syrian efforts, PLO representatives were invited to participate in the formal Security Council debates regarding the civil disturbances among Palestinians on the occupied West Bank. At this time the Arabs—with even Sadat in support of the move—pushed the General Assembly into establishing an Ad Hoc Committee on the Exercise of the Inalienable Rights of the Palestinian People. Israel responded that such moves threatened efforts to achieve peace in the Middle East. What the Arabs were actually saying in these cases was that the slow pace of Israeli withdrawals and the improbability of an early meeting of the Geneva Conference vitiated any necessity to assume a negotiating stance or to convey signals of moderation to Israel. Momentum had gone by the board. Reaffirmation of the Arab national symbol had at least temporarily become more important.

Particularly in the second sequence of talks on the Sinai Accord, Kissinger showed special concern for preserving momentum by continuing the chain of bilateral negotiations. Through intense bargaining that centered on trading Israeli concessions for American commitments, he won Rabin's approval to initiate the next step—a modest accord on Golan. He knew that a second round of talks with Syria could not result in Israel's relinquishing more than a few square kilometers of occupied territory, but that was not the point. Kissinger was thinking of the process itself and of maintaining some semblance of momentum. Israel was not enthusiastic about the prospect of further talks on Golan, and when Kissinger arrived in Damascus on August 23, 1975, he found that Assad wasn't either. There wasn't enough in it for the Syrians. An additional step on Golan appeared, however, to be the only alternative that might be open to Kissinger for continuing negotiations. He could not hope to hustle Sadat into yet another agreement quite so soon. While the thought of a Jordanian-Israeli agreement on the West Bank was tantalizing, the Arabs had made it clear that in West Bank negotiations, the trustee of peace would encounter the PLO, and the Israelis were not ready for that. If Kissinger wanted further negotiations, they must be with Syria, but he could not bring Assad around to his point of view that even a token agreement covering a few feet of territory was better than no agreement at all. Kissinger had failed to recapture his cherished momentum.

Thereafter, Kissinger's initiative virtually died. The consensus of Western diplomats serving in the Middle East seemed to be that the momentum of American diplomacy had run its course. Little more was to be expected of Kissinger. Yet no observer could help noticing that all the participants remained in place. Neither the Arabs nor the Israelis had assumed such an antagonistic position, either toward the other or toward the United States, that a future initiative by Kissinger or perhaps his successor was impossible. Avenues of exploration were still open.

Despite the recriminations between Assad and Sadat when the latter accepted Kissinger's Sinai Accord, the Syrian president thereafter seemed to orient many of his moves toward the prospects of an American type settlement. Assad structured his intervention in the Lebanese civil war in 1976, as well as his new relations with King Hussein, to allow for an accommodation with Israel. He avoided actions that would be counterproductive to any resumption of negotiations. In this regard Assad assiduously abided by Israel's demand that Syrian troops not enter Lebanon's border region with Israel. No Syrian bravado this time. As Kissinger's successor, Cyrus Vance, was to discover during a visit to the Middle East in February 1977, the problems involved in moving toward a settlement were enormous. Yet, both sides were still interested in negotiations. No one had burnt any bridges. Within a day momentum could be revived by a dramatic announcement that negotiations were about to be resumed. Such was the legacy of Kissinger's diplomacy—cerebral and at times ephemeral, an endless pursuit of the elusive momentum.

Ultimately Sadat was to adopt Kissinger's preoccupation with momentum as his own guiding star. While the Carter administration was haggling with Arabs and Israelis alike over the conditions for resuming the Geneva Conference, Sadat in November 1977 seized the initiative with his daring visit to Jerusalem. The momentum of negotiations was immediately revived. It was to be lost again in the disputes that arose from the meeting of Sadat and Begin on Christmas Day 1977 in Ismailia. But in the meantime new perceptions had been developed that brought the two sides a few steps closer together. The same process was repeated in September 1978 when Sadat without a moment's hesitation accepted Carter's invitation to meet Begin at Camp David. After this meeting more wrangling ensued, but in the flush and exhilaration of the momentum generated by the remarkable spectacle of an American president, an Israeli prime minister, and an Arab leader spending thirteen days locked up in a Maryland mountain retreat, perceptions had again been changed, and we were finally to see an Israeli-Egyptian Treaty in March 1979. At this point problems developed. In pressing Sadat to make concessions, Carter acted in a way that precluded future momentum. Other Arabs were still not ready for the Israeli perception of Palestinian administration combined with Israeli security on the West Bank. In this tandem everyone knew where sovereignty would really lie. It was a perception over which Kisinger himself had stumbled when he agreed to present it to the Arabs in 1974. Now it was to alienate not just the Rejectionists, Assad, and Hussein but the Saudis as well. Sadat was driven into isolation while the United States was compelled to take on additional commitments in order to serve as the point of political egress that Egypt had heretofore maintained through its Arab friends. Such are the links that bind together the various concepts of Middle East politics.

The Psychological Factor

The style of Henry Kissinger was distinct from that of other statesmen who would guide America's foreign relations. His diplomacy of process was concerned with the state of mind of the negotiants. Changing perceptions hinged on the influence he could acquire over the thinking of others. The techniques by which he developed momentum were devoted to creating within Arabs and Israelis a desire for new conditions. He played on their hopes and fears, strengths and weaknesses as no previous secretary of state had done, and he was fully aware of what he was doing. During a private conversation with a long-time observer of the Middle East, Kissinger once likened his techniques to those of a psychological counselor. For long periods during his sessions with Sadat, Assad, and the Israelis, he permitted them to do the talking. It was enough for him to set the context of the discussion and to fashion it as a vehicle for developing ideas. Paramount to the psychological aspect of the process was a commitment by the participants to a negotiated settlement. Thereafter, Kissinger saw therapeutic value in permitting the negotiants themselves to work through as many of the problems of peace as they could with little more than a well-placed question here and there from the mediator. That Kissinger was imbued with a psychological outlook on negotiation was evident from his allusion to the Israelis' "Masada complex" and his characterization of Assad as a man of split attitudes—fascinated by the prospect of ending Syria's isolation from the West but troubled over being the first Syrian to deal with Israel.

The overt tensions of the mad rush Kissinger liked to generate in his quest for momentum did not necessarily characterize his relations with negotiating counterparts. Tensions might arise during lengthy sessions, but they were different from those that were evident in the public displays of unending motion that distinguished the shuttle. During the negotiating sessions much of the tension was internal—unexpressed—as each participant wrestled individually with the necessity to balance concessions, counter-moves, rational arguments, and national sensitivities. In his relations with the Arab leaders, Kissinger avoided situations in which they felt the necessity to argue with *him*; any dispute was with the Israelis whom Kissinger only half represented. In fact, Kissinger proved to be particularly adept in his personal relations with Arabs, and as his experience increased he developed considerable confidence in his ability to deal with them on their own terms. One of the more salutary practices he followed in meetings with Arab leaders was his willingness to spend long hours reviewing the business at hand. Someone unfamiliar with Arab customs and psychology might ask what Kissinger could possibly do in a sixteen-hour meeting with Assad. Perhaps his use of this approach was inadvertent at first, but as the Arabs responded he warmed to the technique, telling American colleagues on one occasion that he fully understood Arab mentality.

Indeed, it was his ability to grasp the Arab sense of propriety in business and social exchange that served Kissinger so well in shuttle diplomacy. Long meetings do not necessarily mean that the pace is slow or the discussion tortuous. Rather, they are a way of developing personal contact which has a value separate and distinct from the business being conducted during the session. Even in the most contemporary settings, and with individuals who are fully conversant with Western ways, remnants of traditional etiquette persist in Arab society. If an association is to be fruitful, it must be appreciated; and participants must give evidence of that appreciation. Nothing serves a Western negotiator better than to be able to deal in terms of broad philosophical generalities, to interject a bit of himself into the encounter, or to dabble in what can be called the lore of the land—its culture, history, family relationships, and even scandals. Arabs also share much of the American sense of humor. Throughout long sessions such matters are interjected into the discussion from time to time, perhaps for diversion from the standpoint of the American, but more in terms of enriching personal association for the Arab.

One striking instance of this Arab practice occurred during the negotiations over Golan. After long and tedious hours of discussing the location of the disengagement line, the group temporarily set aside its business for a midnight buffet. Some points of business continued to be discussed, but conversation also turned to lighter matters. As the session continued, it seemed altogether appropriate when General Mustafa Tlas, Syria's defense minister, recited some of his own poetry. However little Kissinger and his aides appreciated the finer points of Arabic rhyme and rhythm, this interlude demonstrated the type of relationship the trustee of peace was able to develop with the Arab leaders. The outsider who is able to insinuate himself into these aspects of Arab life soon realizes that the elaborate social formulas are not pointless. From the sharing of extended personal contact comes a sense of personal obligation and an impulse to accommodate. It is not that Arabs feel compelled to acquiesce in negotiations, but they do have a social need to be accommodating. From the aura of a shared experience, propriety requires an appreciation of the position of all participants.

Much of what Kissinger did followed this pattern. The academic context into which he set his negotiations served the purposes for which Arabs use dialogue. In the Middle East an academic and philosophical tone can be advantageous to someone who is inclined to visit. Kissinger instinctively seized on this point. He used humor liberally, and he had the intuition to employ time in the same manner. His technique of having the mediator and the negotiant search for ideas together hit a responsive chord in Arab practice. Most ideas may be disregarded, but such a pursuit is a greatly appreciated pastime. Here was the real meaning and the psychological quality of Kissinger's relations with the Arabs.

The psychological factor as applied to the Israelis did not always work to Kissinger's advantage. The curious thing about the Israeli's outlook was that, in spite of their record of undisputed victories over the Arabs in previous tests of strength, once the negotiations began, their stance was that of the weaker of the negotiants. Perhaps they appeared to be on the defensive because they were concerned with the territorial status quo while Kissinger and the Arabs were striving for change. Their obsession with security and their insistence on assuring that no concession weaken Israeli defenses also gave them a narrower, more rigid, and weaker-appearing position than the Arabs. The Israeli viewpoint was particularly striking when compared with Sadat's expansiveness, his lack of concern for details, and his trust in Kissinger's initiative.

Eventually the Arabs grasped and began to play with the defensive aspects of Israeli mentality. It was not uncommon for Arab spokesmen to contend that in the long run Israel could not maintain itself in the Middle East and that it had better treat now while the moderate Arabs were willing. An observer who neglected the psychological factor might wonder what everyone was talking about in this topsy-turvy conglomeration of positions, counter-positions, and modes of expression. In assessing the actual nature of conditions, it was necessary for Kissinger to avoid falling into these states of mind himself because they did not reflect the realities of Arab and Israeli power within the short time frame in which he chose to work.

The Israeli psychology greatly influenced the negotiating process itself, principally as it was manifest in the Israelis' distaste for taking positions. First they wanted to see what the Arabs were prepared to offer. One of Kissinger's principal problems, in fact, was to persuade the Israelis to take a position or express an idea that was open to modification. The Israelis' defensive outlook also influenced their negotiating objectives. Imbued with the idea that an Arab attack could never be launched without Egyptian involvement, they centered their attention on the necessity of neutralizing Egypt. About all they wanted from Kissinger were moves that would lead to this end. The Israeli outlook constituted a trap for Kissinger. To play on their terms would alienate the Arabs who feared nothing more than the split in their ranks that a separate Egyptian-Israeli peace would represent.

The Critique

The diplomacy of changing perceptions, building momentum, and attending to psychological factors did not, of course, escape criticism. Unlike most other secretaries of state since World War II, Kissinger did not frame his arguments in terms of legality; consequently, he did not focus on rights or morality. Perhaps his most vociferous and powerful critic in the United States was George W. Ball, undersecretary of state during the Kennedy and the Johnson administrations. Ball emerged as a major spokesman for a foreign policy viewpoint that was identified with the Democratic party. Himself a lawyer, Ball stressed cognition and legality in his criticism of Kissinger's approach to policy; and he showed little appreciation for Kissinger's emphasis on process or the consequent necessity for giving attention to the present rather than the future. For Ball, process must always have a clear objective. It could not stand alone as it did for Kissinger.

Ball concluded that Kissinger's "addiction to the tactical opportunity so often diverts him from his ultimate destination it is impossible to identify the stars from which he takes his bearings. His guiding purpose is . . . to maintain a shifting balance of power—an act which . . . becomes a tour de force with no meaning beyond the virtuosity of the achievement. . . . It is a policy strictly for the short term." Ball brushed aside "Kissinger's ritual chatter about maintaining the diplomatic momentum" and castigated the abstact nature of the outcome toward which Kissinger directed his efforts as being "niggardly in its objectives" insofar as its only declared purpose was to bring a "generation of peace." For those such as Ball, Kissinger's policy lacked content.

In contrast to Kissinger, Ball preferred clear policy guidelines that could be identified with legality—principles to be found in explicit and morally binding practices of the international community. "Diplomacy based merely on the manipulation of power without reference to an accepted body of rules or principles leaves no permanent monument," he said. "An enduring structure . . . must have solid foundations based on conformity to a set of standards widely regarded as equitable." This legal perspective led Ball directly to the consideration of right and morality, and he believed that U.S. policy under Kissinger was flawed by its indifference to higher values—liberty and the dignity of the individual. "What is missing . . . is a moral theme to give coherence to what we, as a nation, are trying to do."[12]

Ball was not the only one who spoke in terms of principles and moral themes. Both Arabs and Israelis did likewise. As each would have it, all the situation required was the establishment of principles. Thereafter, the work of the negotiants was simply to move toward the implementation of these moral prescriptions. But in considering principles, the Arabs and Israelis thought of different things. The Arabs sought an eventual acknowledgment by the Jewish state that it would withdraw from the sacred territory of the Arab nation captured in 1967 and accept the legitimacy of the Palestinians' claims. For their part, the Israelis still saw Arab reservations in any consideration of just how Israeli security would be assured as the Arab nation worked out its destiny on the basis of higher principles. But the Arabs could point to similar principled (and therefore one-sided) views on the part of the Israelis who insisted on glorifying (and keeping) the Golan settlements and sanctifying their claim to the historic homeland of the West Bank. While the Jewish nation reveled in this self-realization, the Arabs were supposed to accept a perfect peace, something akin to what existed among the Benelux countries.

If Ball wanted to base diplomacy on principles, here they were in perfect contradiction and with few rational means of bringing about modifications that would allow for meeting of minds. It would appear that under these circumstances Kissinger's negotiating style, which emphasized process over content had much to commend it. As an outlook for a nation approaching relations with those beyond its borders, Ball's pronouncements were praiseworthy; but as guidance for a trustee of peace operating between Arabs and Israelis, they could not always be expected to be useful. A framework similar to the morality and principled play recommended by Ball became a major theme in the early foreign policy of the Carter administration. It raised questions about whether Kissinger's successors would recognize and choose to apply any of the advantages embodied in shuttle diplomacy.

10

The Method of Kissinger's Diplomacy

Kissinger's diplomacy is often viewed as being distinctive because of its prominent style. This style was derived largely from his personal view that negotiations rested on the need to change perceptions and emphasize short-run objectives, to recognize the psychological factors at work in any situation, and to develop a momentum that culminates in an agreement that can sustain peace for a reasonable period of time. Going beyond personal style, it is also necessary to consider the components of the mediator's performance. Was there a sense of order that made his activities purposeful, or did he simply accept whatever situations confronted him and proceed intuitively? Here we examine the method of Henry Kissinger's Middle East diplomacy.

Careful Planning

As a mediator, Kissinger combined apparently disparate qualities. While he was quick to exploit ideas, perceptions, and chance developments as they appeared in the unfolding of discussions, his preparations for negotiation were meticulous. He left little to chance. What sometimes appeared to be a high element of uncertainty in his maneuvers was not uncertainty at all but simply a penchant for drama. Admittedly, Kissinger never tried to determine in advance exactly what might be included in any particular

session, but once the participants had assumed a negotiating posture, he worked with considerable precision to keep them in position and to move them along to some form of disengagement
agreement or accord. His attention was on the negotiants, not on
the document they were drafting. Consistent with his emphasis on
personal relationships, he used every channel and influence available to pressure the negotiants into making concessions. Herein lay
a force for predictability that many negotiators do not attempt to
incorporate into their work.

When Kissinger made his early visits to the Middle East and
returned with an agreement for a cease-fire along the Suez Canal,
and then when he negotiated disengagement agreements in Sinai
and on the Golan Heights, the public hailed this miracle-maker
who seemed to have some magic not possessed by those who had
previously attempted to mediate between Arabs and Israelis. Kissinger was viewed as a hero who had accosted a deadly monster
almost by chance, sufficiently unconcerned about what might be
in store for him that he took along nothing with which to defend
himself other than his wits. Actually, shuttle diplomacy was no
such battle against unknown dangers, and Kissinger was not as
casual as he appeared. The initial shuttle from which the Sinai disengagement was achieved did have a spontaneous quality about
it, but thereafter every effort was made to remove any element of
the unexpected.

Great care was taken to prepare the way for Kissinger's mediation. On one occasion he even talked King Hussein into a secret
meeting in the desert with Golda Meir and Moshe Dayan to search
for common ground that would support West Bank negotiations.
Usually, however, his schemes were less flamboyant. A favorite
approach to planning was proximity talks—a necessary device
because of the refusal of Arabs to confront Israelis directly in
negotiations. This vehicle had first been used in 1949 when Israeli
and Arab representatives sat in separate rooms at negotiations
held on Cyprus while United Nations mediators communicated
between them. Somewhat less dramatic than the shuttle itself,
proximity talks were a prelude from the same score as the shuttle
but with different overtones and without the finale. During proximity talks Kissinger acted as a mediator much as he did

during a shuttle. It was just that with this vehicle he was not usually dealing with chiefs of state, and all activity was taking place in Washington rather than between Middle East capitals.

In November 1973, following the October War, Kissinger had hit on this approach to negotiation when he had Golda Meir, Ismail Fahmy, and the Syrian deputy foreign minister, Muhammad Ismail, in Washington simultaneously to discuss a cease-fire. Again, prior to the Golan shuttle, proximity talks were used. The fact that they were considered secondary to shuttles provides some insight into the importance Kissinger attached to flair, notoriety, and drama in shuttle diplomacy compared to the actual content of discussions.

Kissinger's preliminary steps did not always have the structure of the proximity talks. He also relied on a steady stream of visitors coming to Washington as a favorite means for setting the scene for his final efforts. In this case he would undertake an intense round of direct exchanges over a relatively short span of time. In August 1974, when he was attempting to determine how he might best proceed after the Golan disengagement, he saw in rapid succession Israeli Foreign Minister Allon, Jordanian Prime Minister Rafai, Egyptian Foreign Minister Fahmy, Syrian Foreign Minister Khaddam, King Hussein, and Saudi Foreign Minister Saqqaf. In early September Israeli Prime Minister Rabin visited. During June and July 1975, a similar procession of Egyptian and Israeli officials came to Washington in preparation for the Sinai Accord. In addition, both President Ford and Kissinger met with President Sadat in Austria.

Another means used by Kissinger in preparing for a shuttle was the precursory visit to the Middle East. In all, he traveled to the area on twelve occasions—three times in 1973 when he established his mediating capacity, once with President Nixon in June 1974 on a largely ceremonial visit, the four occasions on which he actually undertook formal negotiations with a shuttle, and four times in which he identified his purpose as exploratory discussions in preparation for negotiations. When the purpose was simply to develop ideas in advance of a shuttle, explicit announcements were made in Washington prior to his departure that the secretary of state did not intend to conclude an agreement. Each tour was followed by a statement regarding the extent of the differences that remained between the two sides and a suggestion of when a shuttle might become plausible.

The plethora of trips, visits, and exchanges was not simply to set the mood or to explore possibilities. The participants actually made commitments and reached understandings regarding what they could agree on when formal negotiations were finally launched. The tedious nature of the Golan negotiations and the failure of the first attempt to conclude the Sinai Accord demonstrated that a lot still remained to be done when Kissinger finally took the field. One interpretation of Kissinger's technique is that the substance of agreement was developed in the preparatory steps. In the shuttle itself his purpose was to help the leaders over the psychological or conceptual hurdles involved in actually signing an agreement with the other side. For the Arabs, this problem was the recognition of the legitimacy of the Jewish state that was implicit in the conclusion of a formal understanding. For the Israelis the difficulty was the deep distrust that drove them to demand more in the way of security guarantees than could reasonably be expected from the agreements Kissinger was negotiating.

Looking for a moment at Kissinger's failure rather than at his successes, it might be said that the obstacles precluding an agreement in the shuttle of March 1975 occurred because the two sides were fully aware of his usual careful preparations and of his refusal to risk his reputation in a less than successful effort. No slap-dash for Kissinger, thought Sadat and Rabin. Thus they assumed that, when he agreed to undertake a shuttle, concessions on the part of the other were in the offing and an agreement that Kissinger himself could visualize was a virtual certainty. But this was not the case. In fact, Kissinger had been uneasy about the March shuttle because he was not satisfied with the extent of prior commitments. In this instance the Israelis had pressed for early negotiations with the idea that Kissinger would use them to win further concessions from Sadat. Making concessions themselves was not foremost in the Israelis' minds. Against his better judgment, Kissinger agreed. The subsequent rigidity of the Israeli position in the negotiations could only cause him to wonder how they viewed the process he was directing. In this instance, our mediator had no greater flexibility than either negotiant.

After the March 1975 failure, Kissinger was doubly cautious. In fact, in August 1975, the shuttle that culminated in the Sinai Accord was supposed to be little more than a formality with all the negotiating having been done in Washington. Immediately after his March failure, Kissinger had made it clear that he would not go to the Middle East again until he was confident that an agreement was at hand. Ford's meeting with Sadat determined that Egypt was still committed to an agreement at the highest level. The American ambassadors in Cairo and Tel Aviv were given a larger role in dealing with the respective leaders to whom they were accredited, and on this occasion Kissinger did not make his usual preliminary visit to the area. Before initiating his final shuttle Kissinger had the Egyptians and Israelis working from a single draft agreement that he had prepared in Washington from an assortment of phrases provided by each of the two sides and tentatively accepted by the other.

Some problems did develop, not so much over the facts of the situation or the obligations to be undertaken by either side, but with regard to the extent to which the various agreements would be made public. The Egyptians were at first hesitant, for example, to accept an open commitment to permit American technicians to be stationed in Sinai for the purpose of operating the early warning aircraft detection system. Sadat also preferred to avoid public undertakings that would permit Israeli vessels freedom of navigation in the Gulf of Suez and allow Israeli cargoes transit rights through the Suez Canal. The only substantive issue raised by Egypt at the time of the shuttle was a minor difference over the disposition of troops in areas adjacent to the buffer zone occupied by United Nations forces. Final agreement on the publicity to be afforded various matters was achieved early in the shuttle and an understanding was also reached on troop locations. With these problems resolved, one hurdle remained—the exact language to be used in extending American commitments to Israel on oil supply, economic and military aid, diplomatic support at the United Nations, and coordination of policy on the Palestinians, particularly as it pertained to their role at any future sessions of the Geneva Conference. Bargaining on these items continued throughout the shuttle. Finally, at 5:45 A.M. on September 1, 1975, after an all-night session with the Israelis, Kissinger had his agreement. George Ball, alluding to Kissinger's diplomacy as "theater," derided it as entertainment that could distract for only so long. The results of this final shuttle, he said, were "as fixed as a professional wrestling match," and he questioned whether Kissinger's direct intercession at this point was necessary.[1] Even though most of the work had been done at preparatory sessions in Washington, Kissinger believed that the final step required the vivid imagery of his presence and the human contact he brought to Arab-Israeli relations. Thus the concept of the shuttle and Kissinger's personal approach to diplomacy were sustained to the end.

Communication

Kissinger was the consummate diplomat insofar as he understood the importance of communication, not just in terms of the quality of his own arguments but also from the standpoint of the influence that the volume of advice from a wide variety of sources could have on the negotiants. While Kissinger conducted the negotiations himself, he knew that his was not the only voice that could speak in favor of agreement. He therefore solicited the assistance of anyone who had influence with a negotiating leader and who would urge making concessions and reaching an accommodation, at least with Kissinger if not with the other side. The attention he devoted to communication served to emphasize the importance he placed on process.

The effectiveness of massive communications operations in influencing Israel was limited because of the Israelis' feeling that most of the world had turned its back on them. Those who did not support Israel would not have influence with it. Most admonishments from abroad went unheeded. Moreover, Kissinger had no need to orchestrate voices from diverse sources to press the Israelis to accept a settlement. A less-than-sympathetic chorus of governments, joined even by the Europeans, was constantly harping that Israel should get on with it and settle the problem that could cost their own economies precious oil in the event of another Middle East war.

Kissinger did attempt to cultivate one channel of influence capable of moving Israel toward an agreement—the American Jewish community. Jewish leaders were kept apprised of developments during most negotiations. As Kissinger well knew, the Israelis pressured the Republican administration through the Jewish community and used the community's influence to develop support in Congress on particular matters. What had always been a conduit for Israeli pressure proceeding in a single direction, Kissinger hoped to make into a two-way street. He apparently reasoned that the administration could employ Jewish leaders who would point out to the Israelis that, more and more, Israel's success in getting its way with the United States government depended on an acceptance of some features of the official American point of view. There had to be a quid pro quo for American support. In effect Kissinger wanted Jewish leaders to make the Israelis aware of the facts of political life.

Before the final shuttle that preceded the Sinai Accord, Kissinger met with Jewish leaders explicitly for this purpose. When he returned to the United States with the accord in hand, Jewish leaders were invited to the White House. To an extent, his purpose was to win their support in getting congressional approval for stationing American technicians at the early warning electronic stations to be established in the Sinai under the terms of the agreement. But he was concerned about other matters as well. It was not so much that he was worried about the possibility of the Rabin government's disassociating itself from an agreement it had just concluded. Rather, he feared that, under pressure from Israeli hawks, Rabin might not be able to sustain his position and could be driven from office in a public uproar over the agreement. Because the general Israeli outlook troubled him, Kissinger made a direct appeal for his diplomacy in a speech to the Jewish American Congress. It was his first appearance before that body, and the message was his usual assertion that Israel must accept risks if peace was to be achieved. One of these risks was the sale of U.S. military equipment to moderate Arabs, a policy American Jews had always opposed. The official point of view was stressed by

Ford and Kissinger at sessions with Jewish leaders as well as in talks with the Israelis themselves. In all these cases, Kissinger was attempting to influence opinion not just in Israel but in the entire Jewish nation. Again, all exigencies were accounted for. Kissinger left little to chance.

The use of a variety of communications channels to move a negotiant toward accommodation had much more scope with the Arabs than with the Israelis. In his dealings with the Arabs, Kissinger recognized that substantial progress in any set of negotiations could be made only within a larger Arab consensus. Consequently, he did not spend his time simply talking to Sadat or Assad. He also worked quite carefully through other Arab leaders. By means of continuous contacts with a number of chiefs of state, he was able to allay the fears that arose from the image of his attempting to vitiate the influence of Arab nationalism by dealing with only one Arab state at a time. By keeping lines of communication open with all Arab leaders, he hoped to win their overt support for the sequence of negotiations in which he happened to be involved at the time. If that proved impossible, perhaps he could at least forestall open hostility to his efforts. Consequently, from the time of his first visit to the Middle East to negotiate a cease-fire between Egypt and Israel in November 1973, Kissinger established personal relationships with President Boumediene of Algeria, King Faisal and later King Khalid of Saudi Arabia, King Hussein of Jordan, and King Hassan of Morocco.

Particularly during the Golan negotiations Kissinger employed other Arabs to push Assad toward an agreement. Faisal and Sadat pressured Assad to provide the list of Israeli prisoners of war held by Syria, thereby establishing an atmosphere conducive to negotiations. Assad had originally hoped to use the list for bargaining purposes. At critical points in the talks Kissinger would dispatch one of his aides to see Hussein, Faisal, or Boumediene, urging that leader to recommend to Assad that he keep an open mind about disengagement. Sadat, of course, could always be counted on for this purpose. In fact, he inundated Assad with a barrage of messages and on one occasion sent the Egyptian defense minister and also his chief of staff to Damascus to argue in favor of disengagement.

In subsequent negotiating sequences, Kissinger continued to draw on Arab resources to further his mission. A particularly effective ploy was visiting Riyadh in order to acquire Faisal's or Khalid's blessing. The Saudi ruler was powerful. To many of the Arab people his approval exemplified legitimacy for those who received it. To the other Arab leaders he was someone to heed. It was not just the Saudis on whom Kissinger lavished attention. On one occasion the Egyptians were perplexed when Kissinger went to Kuwait to assure full Arab support for his negotiations. Some Egyptians were not quite sure what Kuwait had to do with an agreement. It was an indication of the caution with which Kissinger proceeded. As long as conditions permitted, he did not even hesitate to use the Russians to achieve his purpose. Thus he attempted to enlist Soviet support in persuading the Arabs to lift the oil embargo, and he benefited from the Soviets' urging of the Syrians to enter into the disengagement agreement with Israel.

Perhaps Kissinger's most unrewarding task in attempting to secure overwhelming Arab support for an agreement under negotiation was his effort in March and again in July and August 1975 to convince the Syrian leadership that an Egyptian-Israeli accord on Sinai was not contrary to Syrian or Arab interests. The long hours he spent with Assad and Foreign Minister Khaddam were of no avail. In the aftermath of the Sinai Accord, when the Syrians and Palestinians were particularly disturbed over being abandoned by Sadat, Kissinger met with Arab representatives at the United Nations in order to improve the diplomatic atmosphere and to emphasize his offer to negotiate a further agreement between Syria and Israel. Even at this juncture he was not prepared to abandon Arab sentiment to those in the Arab world who opposed his diplomacy. Perhaps sympathetic Arabs could still be influential in getting Assad to change his mind and negotiate a second agreement on Golan. In this instance, Kissinger did not succeed, but he was determined to use every channel available on the supposition that communications sent by an assortment of routes would contribute to his objectives.

Kissinger supplemented his official network of communications with effective use of the press. Over the years it had been the practice for journalists to be on hand for important negotiations.

Kissinger went a step further and permitted them to travel on the same plane with him. Moreover, they were taken along on each leg of the shuttle, flying sometimes twice in a day between Israel and either Syria or Egypt. In-flight press briefings, often by Kissinger himself, became the practice. The material he imparted was not just the usual background that was supposed to be "off the record," or at least not for attribution. Most of what Kissinger said was meant for public dissemination, often with the identity of the source being only partially concealed as a senior American official.

Kissinger was apparently concerned with more than having a well-informed public or being accommodating to the press. By conveying information through journalists he hoped to influence the mood of negotiations. The problem with the Arabs in this respect was perhaps the more difficult. A largely positive outlook from Rabat to Kuwait was of vital importance to Kissinger's efforts. Without it the negotiating leader—whether it be Sadat or Assad—could experience the feeling of national isolation. Neither Kissinger nor his aides could be in constant personal contact with leaders who were not directly involved in the negotiations. Yet only by immersing the negotiating process in open communications could Kissinger give all Arab leaders a sense of proximity to events and prevent them from feeling ignored, which could in turn engender hostility. The press was utilized as a secondary channel to preserve the positive mood. Kissinger is reported to have said to Israeli negotiators that the American journalists accompanying him acquired nothing through official U.S. channels except what he told them, and he only told them things that served the negotiations.[2]

One of Kissinger's favorite practices in working through the press was to exude optimism over his activities even when cold analysis of the situation was sufficient to plunge the most optimistic observer into the depths of despair. Sometimes he would assert that a general understanding existed and that only minor points remained to be clarified, when in fact the negotiants were at odds over fundamental issues. With such assertions he hoped to maintain an upbeat tone for his mediation. It was not unusual for Kissinger himself to express optimism in public, only to admit privately that he was virtually overwhelmed by the complexities of the situation he faced.

In pursuit of a favorable negotiating atmosphere, Kissinger sometimes went so far as to try to create the news. While negotiating the Golan disengagement, for instance, the Syrians, and perhaps the Israelis as well, attempted to apply pressure with artillery barrages across the cease-fire line. Whoever started the shooting, the other side always responded in kind. Despite his best efforts, Kissinger could not at first persuade either side to stop. For the sake of his mission, he did the next best thing and attempted to deemphasize the importance of the shelling by declaring that it was on the wane. When the Israelis flatly contradicted this contention, Kissinger stood his ground and maintained publicly that his assessment of the situation was accurate.

Kissinger also used the press to create a sense of drama and thereby seize the attention of the negotiants. One of his better moves was the flight to Damascus in February 1974 to receive a list of Israeli prisoners of war from Assad and to deliver it personally to Golda Meir. Actually Kissinger already had the list. When he received approval from Assad to provide the Israelis with the names, he could have sent it via a State Department telegram for delivery to Prime Minister Meir by the American ambassador in Tel Aviv. Instead, he opted for the dramatic gesture. Had it not been fully reported in the press, this incident would not have had the intended impact. The style of shuttle diplomacy was overt, incorporating action that suggested achievement. It was ideal for news coverage, and Kissinger made the most of it. With this kind of personal attention, who could deny that the trustee of peace was showing the good faith in mediation on which the Arabs insisted or concern for Israel's boys in a way that brought an emotional response from every Jew? The impact of Golda Meir's joyous tears on receiving the names was multiplied a million times by press coverage of an act that could have been performed with a routine message.

Then there was the sense of urgency that Kissinger fostered through press statements. When a shuttle began to lose momentum, he sometimes amplified the tensions of negotiation by acnouncing to the press that time was running out and that he was prepared to abandon his efforts and return to Washington if the negotiants could not achieve a breakthrough. As the negotiations on Sinai encountered difficulty in March 1975, he made a series of public statements expressing abject pessimism over the future of the Middle East and ultimately predicted open conflict within three months if something was not done to revitalize the negotiating atmosphere. Such a signal would have had less impact had it been conveyed only within the confines of the negotiating room; Kissinger was using the media to pressure the negotiants. As the March 1975 incident was to demonstrate, neither side wanted to bear the onus of responsibility for a breakdown in the talks, and Kissinger could easily create such an impression with his public statements. He did, in fact, point the finger at Israel in assessing blame for the suspension of his mediation. Although the Israelis complained vociferously, they returned to the negotiating table with the very concessions they had previously refused to make.

To a lesser extent, Kissinger also used the media to commit each side publicly to ideas its negotiators had previously been willing to express only in private. This tactic made it more difficult for either side to reverse itself. An example occurred at the beginning of the negotiations on Golan. Assad was still an enigma to Kissinger. He had privately indicated a willingness to negotiate, but suddenly, in a public statement, he called for the withdrawal of all Israeli forces from the Syrian territory occupied during the October War and an acknowledgment by the Israelis that they would eventually withdraw from the area occupied during the 1967 war as well. The Israelis were far from certain about the wisdom of attempting to negotiate with the Syrians in the first place, and had Assad's declaration been allowed to stand, it might have been sufficient cause for the Israelis to terminate future contacts. But before the Israelis could publicly reject Assad's position, Kissinger asserted in a public statement of his own that the Syrians did not insist on Israel's agreeing *in the first instance* to a complete withdrawal to the June 1967 lines. This, in fact, was Syria's position, and fortunately, Assad had nothing more to say.

There was little doubt that the medium through which Kissinger's message was sent was as important as the message itself.

Newsmen were openly advised by the secretary of state to listen to him rather than to the Arab and Israeli leaders whose statements he characterized as maximum positions and posturing for domestic consumption rather than an expression of their actual negotiating stance. Because of the role Kissinger was performing, his statements would be newsworthy both in Israel and in most Arab capitals even though he might contradict various Arab and Israeli leaders. Had his response to Assad's statement been made in private, the Israelis could still have rejected further contacts amidst the confusion created by the unexpected Syrian demand. At the very least, they would have felt compelled to respond to Assad, reaffirming their claim to the Golan Heights and thereby making negotiations unlikely. Thus by judicious use of the press did Kissinger create room for negotiation.

Another use of the press was to blunt counterforces that were sometimes working against the mediation effort. In this regard, by calling public attention to the attempts of the Soviet Union and the radical Arabs to frustrate one or another of his sequences of negotiations, Kissinger could belittle their efforts and strengthen the resolve of the Arabs who had accepted the route of a negotiated settlement. By standing center stage and commanding the attention of the world, he overwhelmed such opposition or at least kept it on the defensive. He was intent on preventing general anti-American expression from dominating the airwaves, the viewing screens, and the front pages—from determining the political mood that was so important to his style of diplomacy. The attempt of the PLO to create tension and throw negotiations into a turmoil by attacking an Israeli kibbutz just as Kissinger was preparing for the Golan shuttle was offset as much by public denunciation of this act as by Kissinger's private assurances to the Israelis that the attack was not inspired by Syria.

Kissinger was not universally successful in his efforts to use the press to create and maintain a salutary atmosphere for negotiations. Probably one of the greatest fiascos on the public side of his diplomacy occurred in October 1974, when he was attempting to set the scene for a new shuttle in which he intended to negotiate either a disengagement of forces along the Jordan River or possibly a second agreement on Sinai. The accumulation of events that followed was revealing from the standpoint of Kissinger's use of the media, because as troubles mounted, he pressed harder to facilitate matters through public channels. In the process his practices became more apparent.

The situation was delicate. Kissinger was confronted by the Israelis with a demand that the Arabs become more explicit about nonbelligerency. Otherwise, additional occupied territory could not be relinquished. It was a quid pro quo that the trustee of peace knew the Arabs would reject. In the Arab way of thinking, such a demand was so far from the realm of possibility that it was tantamount to the Israelis' purposely ending any further opportunity for negotiation. Kissinger's task, therefore, was to get each side to enter into the preliminary steps for a shuttle in the belief that negotiations would center on its own perception of a satisfactory agenda even though the other side considered such an approach unacceptable.

A visit to the Middle East was selected as the occasion for this difficult task; and at least at the outset, Kissinger chose to use a large element of public diplomacy in closing the rather extensive gap between the two sides. Of necessity, his maneuvers were intricate. First, during a stopover in Israel, he announced that he had reached an understanding with Israeli officials on the "procedures and principles" that might be followed in the next round of negotiations. The nature of these principles, however, was not revealed to the press. His statement was meant to create a sense of optimism. In response, Foreign Minister Allon reminded the newsmen that in fact no substantive agreement had been reached during Kissinger's visit. Considerable doubt was thereby raised in Arab minds. Were the Israelis still insisting on nonbelligerency, or weren't they? At this point Kissinger chose to let Allon's remarks pass, but he had lost ground in the exchange and would be compelled to start from scratch when he reached his first Arab capital.

While in flight to Riyadh, he told the journalists who were accompanying him that, although he did not endorse the concept of nonbelligerency, some kind of agreement that met Israel's security needs would be necessary. By denying the concept but in effect acknowledging the content of nonbelligerency, Kissinger probably hoped to appear sympathetic to both sides and also to find a formula that made the situation seem positive. Once again attempting to give bouyancy to his mission, he deemphasized the issue of nonbelligerency in talks with Saudi officials. After a meeting with King Faisal, he told the world from the airport prior to his departure that Saudi Arabia continued to support America's step-by-step approach to peace. Visits to Saudi Arabia were directed largely toward the public exposure they gave Kissinger's diplomacy. The airport statement from Riyadh was to become a favorite tool which he employed on several occasions to create a positive outlook toward his efforts.

The announcement of Faisal's support could have started some momentum, but again Kissinger was embarrassed when Sadat, in a joint press conference in Cairo, refused to subscribe to Kissinger's view that the future of the West Bank could best be negotiated between Israel and Jordan. The American secretary of state attempted to dispel the black mood that seemed to hang over his mission by claiming to see "indications that we are making progress toward peace in the area." Nothing Sadat offered the press on this occasion provided factual support for such optimism, but at least he did not say anything that was damaging to Kissinger's only option to Jordanian-Israeli negotiations—the negotiation of a second Sinai agreement. To this point the visit had been a horrifying failure, in both its confidential and its public aspects. The next stop was Damascus where Kissinger again tried to create the impression through the press that he and the Arab leadership—this time in the person of Assad—were essentially in agreement on another round of shuttle diplomacy. The response here was even worse. The Syrians resented Kissinger's optimism. They believed that he had misrepresented Assad as having been less tough in his attitude on the next step in military disengagement with Israel than had actually been the case. A spokesman responded angrily after Kissinger's departure that, contrary to the impression left by the American visitor, there had been sharp differences between Assad and the secretary.

Kissinger's purpose, of course, was to use the media to reinforce his mission by attempting to convey to each Arab and Israeli leader that collectively they had moved into positions that were no longer in total contradiction. Despite divergent interpretations of

320 THE LAST CRUSADE

how territory might be exchanged for some assurance on Israel's security, Kissinger was attempting to say that there was movement and that the negotiants were approaching a point at which talks would be possible. In this way he might gain acquiescence for the next round of negotiations; and following his tour, to begin preliminary talks in Washington. Actually the Arabs would not trade nonbelligerency for territory. It was an Israeli perception, and spadework still had to be done in private diplomacy before the press could be used productively in the way Kissinger had attempted. Even with the series of rebuffs he had experienced on this mission, he could not admit failure. At a stopover in Algeria on his return to the United States, he again asserted that he had developed an Arab-Israeli consensus that would permit the resumption of negotiations. But privately Kissinger reflected pessimism. He compared his experience to working his way through a minefield. He had never seen leaders so tense, he said, and the whole peace effort could easily blow up at any time.

Kissinger's sensitivity to communications provided an indication of the care with which he approached negotiation. The ability to communicate meant the ability to influence. Those having such potential could be used by the mediator. Thus all leaders of the Jewish and Arab nations were important to Kissinger; and when he did not have an opportunity to enlist their support directly, he tried to reach them through the media. His efforts were not futile. All were aware of his methods and attentive to his signals. Despite the criticism heaped on Kissinger for his excessive devotion to secrecy, no secretary of state had ever established contact with more foreign leaders in direct pursuit of a mission or relied more assiduously on the press in achieving his purpose. For those who wished to follow carefully the nuance and the implicit aspect of the public side of Kissinger's diplomacy, most of the story was on the record. Public knowledge was necessary if he was to change perceptions. Those who raised objections to Kissinger's supposed secrecy were actually taking exception to the personal and experiential form of his diplomacy. The public record that he left was not sufficiently authoritative for their taste. The issue of his lack of openness was, therefore, misplaced. He did enter into secret understandings, but probably no more so than any of his predecessors. In fact secrecy was not really the point of contention with critics; rather, it was his style as a statesman and mediator.

Incrementalism

In achieving the interaction between changing perceptions and momentum that led to limited agreements, Kissinger practiced a technique that might be considered incrementalism. It derived from his sense that the art of diplomacy was in part to set goals that could be achieved. He readily acknowledged that within his step-by-step diplomacy he factored problems "into individual and, therefore, manageable segments." Without this approach, he said, "the intractability of the issues would only be compounded by their being combined."[3] By adding one increment of understanding to another, as conditions allowed, he attempted to work toward a series of limited agreements that he hoped someday would amount to a comprehensive settlement.

Kissinger's style of diplomacy was a process in which there was growth and development. Nothing was obvious. There was no such thing as a hidden situation, rule, or solution that was already a reality and that only had to be brought into the open in order to become part of the negotiating environment. Kissinger shunned the approach of the legally inclined statesman who believes that only a settlement from a narrow range of options will fit the criteria of international principle. In a way, legality gives a predetermined quality to diplomacy.

Kissinger did not seem to appreciate the legalist's sense of discovery. Rather he exuded a strong spirit of creativity as he led Arabs, Israelis, and even himself into new perceptions that in turn would support new situations. A mediator using this approach could have few preconceived notions about a settlement and no conviction that a single good idea or moral principle could lead to an agreement. Just as fast as an idea developed, it could be made unacceptable by another idea or perception, or even by an old Arab or Israeli prejudice that Kissinger was unable in any given instance to overcome. As movement occurred in negotiations, Kissinger had to be prepared to fashion an agreement from whatever concepts were expressed, adding together those ideas that appeared workable and disregarding any that threatened to sour the mix.

In practicing incrementalism, Kissinger employed various devices. First, he liked to think in terms of the phases of a particular set of negotiations—an approach that amounted to little more than setting his concept of changing perceptions into a time frame. In initial phases, often before the shuttle began, he emphasized only limited objectives. These, he claimed, would allow the negotiants to be somewhat more flexible than when critical issues were introduced into the bargaining. By restricting the scope of early concessions, he apparently hoped to accustom the two sides to the negotiating process. He openly advised them not to attempt to accomplish too much. Agreement on a few items here and there was sufficient.

Inherent in Kissinger's incremental diplomacy was the building-block process—dealing with individual questions that, when not related to overall national objectives, could be agreed upon without too much difficulty. In the case of the Egyptian-Israeli disengagement in January 1974, there was general agreement from the outset that Israel would pull back about twenty miles, that a United Nations peacekeeping force would occupy a buffer zone between the Egyptian and Israeli armies, and that strict limitations would be placed on the number of troops and the amount of equipment that could be maintained by either side in the areas adjacent to the buffer zone. The Egyptians had also tentatively agreed before the negotiations started that the blockade at Bab el Mandeb would be lifted. These were the foundations, the building blocks, that could be put into place during the initial phase of negotiations to create a sense of achievement without subjecting the negotiants to the tensions associated with bargaining over critical issues.

Likewise on the Syrian disengagement, the Israelis were prepared to relinquish most of the territory gained in the October War and establish a buffer zone occupied by United Nations forces. The Syrians were willing to discuss these matters and agreed to an exchange of prisoners of war, although the timing of this act was at first uncertain. In both agreements the two sides accepted Security Council resolution 338 on which the October

1973 cease-fire was based. At the outset of the March 1975 negotiations on the Sinai Accord, the Israelis agreed to retreat to, but not beyond, Mitla and Gidi passes and to bargain over the return of the Abu Rudeis oil fields to Egyptian control—all in exchange for substantial political concessions. While it was unclear what these concessions might be, Sadat stated that some political gestures were in the offing. In all instances, Kissinger developed fully any positions over which there was only limited contention. Each item was identified as a starting point, but it was never discussed in the context of its relationship to some preconceived notion of a formal agreement that might be reached in the future.

Having identified the material with which he had to work and laid the foundations for his undertaking, Kissinger set about the business of building an agreement. In this second phase of any negotiating sequence, he again approached problems incrementally. From his efforts to put together the assortment of ideas, suggestions, and countersuggestions that he had collected from the two sides, the problems emerged. By this time he could define some of the limited objectives toward which all appeared to be moving. Usually these were formulated to fit the material that was available to him. Many of the more difficult issues were avoided. In the Sinai disengagement few serious problems developed. It was almost too easy. In the Golan disengagement tedious hours were devoted to locating the demarcation line around Quneitra, thinning out the forces on either side of the buffer zone, deciding on the size of the United Nations peace-keeping force, and disposing of the Israelis' demand that Syria give a written assurance that no Palestinian guerrilla operations would originate from Syrian territory. In the case of the abortive March 1975 negotiations on the Sinai Accord, difficulties centered on the insistence of the Israelis that Sadat formally declare non-belligerency, how much of the mountain passes Israel would surrender, and whether the Egyptian position at Abu Rudeis would be an enclave or a long finger of territory stretching down the Sinai side of the Gulf of Suez.

In the final phase of negotiations, after general understandings had been developed, the items to be included in the agreement had been identified, and the issues that remained had been addressed,

Kissinger would undertake the drafting of a text in full knowledge that all differences had not yet been resolved. Even at this point, he divided his material into manageable pieces. He would get agreement on whatever sentences and phrases he could, and literally place in brackets the portions that he or one of the two sides had suggested but on which there were still differences. These portions of the document then became the subject of concern, with various formulas being tried in order to determine what might satisfy both sides. Israeli humorists poked fun at the secretary, depicting him with odd notes and understandings falling from his pockets as he transcribed new partial sentences and potentially useful phrases on old candy wrappers, half-full cigarette packs, or anything else in sight while attempting to piece together an array of ideas that would permit him to arrive at some sort of contrived agreement.

When an impasse developed, Kissinger never cleaned the slate and started from the beginning. By factoring the material into its components, he found it possible to retain partial texts and to incorporate into the main body of an incomplete draft agreement new ideas that would eventually permit the two sides to agree on something. It was an important feature of his negotiating technique. Factoring and his incremental approach were totally compatible with his use of rational argument to change perceptions and build momentum.

Another way in which Kissinger factored material was to establish discrete areas of negotiation in order to avoid having tensions over one matter adversely influence discussion on another. Accordingly, he shied away from attempts at a comprehensive settlement to be achieved at a general peace conference. As he himself had said, he did not want the intractability of separate issues to be compounded by their being considered simultaneously. Two items on which such conflict and contradiction could have occurred were the major concerns of the United States in the Middle East—the security of Israel and an assured flow of Arab oil to the American economy. In this noteworthy example of keeping issues separate, Kissinger insisted that the oil embargo and the oil pricing controversy were in no way linked to the Arab-Israeli problem. On the question of oil he felt the necessity from time to time to be abrasive and not altogether friendly toward the Arabs. He charged that the embargo was blackmail, and he raised the possibility that the West might use force if oil supplies were ever again withheld. In a United Nations speech, he asserted that high oil prices could result in the breakdown of world order. His hard line was meant to lower prices, or at least forestall further price increases. Because the matter was a source of some tension between the United States and the Oil Arabs, its introduction into the Middle East negotiations could only have complicated Kissinger's efforts at mediation. After all, these same Oil Arabs were sometimes important as channels of communications for influencing Sadat or Assad.

Quite naturally Kissinger liked to keep the U.S. policy of arming Israel separate from his role as a mediator, and for a while he was remarkably successful. When the arms issue was raised by the Arabs, he avoided justifying the American position except to imply that the Arabs should understand the dynamics of that relationship. He gave such discussions a positive tone by alluding to what the United States was already doing for Jordan and Saudi Arabia in arms supply. Generally he never pursued the topic, and he was fortunate insofar as Sadat accepted American military support for Israel as being nonnegotiable and saw little value in calling attention to it.

On occasion Kissinger would belie his own contentions. After going to great lengths to keep U.S. arms policy separate from the negotiations, he expressed his displeasure with Israel in the wake of the breakdown of the Sinai talks in March 1975 by refusing to negotiate new arms supply arrangements with the Jewish state until after the United States had reviewed its Middle East policy. It was a dangerous precedent. If Kissinger could make this association, so could the Arabs. In future negotiations, when Israel was not forthcoming with concessions, the Arabs could suggest such recourse. If the United States did not respond to their suggestion, the Arabs might doubt American sincerity. Kissinger would have done better to let it appear that his hands were tied on this matter, because to a large extent they were.

In some respects Kissinger accentuated his error when he made American arms commitments to Israel such a large part of the

Sinai Accord. In effect the accord acknowledged where the United States would stand if it ever had to choose between the Arabs and Israel. It was not something the Arabs did not know, but it was poor diplomacy to remind them of the fact. Kissinger was not as careful as he might have been. He had taken a step that was incompatible with American mediation. Assad's bitterness with Sadat over the accord and the friction it engendered centered on these parts of the agreement. They made Sadat a party to an arrangement that emphasized distinctions between one Arab country and another insofar as the regaining of territory in Sinai seemed to strengthen the Israelis' ability to withstand Syrian pressures for territorial transfers in the Golan Heights. Assad's perception rendered further negotiations virtually impossible. In fairness to Kissinger, it should be noted that he was aware of the dangers involved in linking American arms aid to Israel with a Middle East settlement. He had intended for the memoranda covering U.S.-Israeli military relations to remain confidential. He understood Arab sensitivities, and it was not reasonable to wound them at a time when they were critical to further steps toward peace.

One of the most difficult types of situation Kissinger encountered as mediator occurred when one side or the other demanded that a certain concept be accepted "in principle" before negotiations proceed. The principles the Arabs tried hardest to establish were that Israel agree to eventually withdraw from all occupied territories and to recognize the rights of the Palestinians. The Israelis, in turn, sought Arab acceptance of the imminent necessity to enter into a condition of de facto and de jure peace with a Jewish neighbor. Kissinger always attempted to avoid such issues. Pronouncements on principle were essentially future-oriented. They reflected intentions that could be far removed from the situation over which he was attempting to negotiate. Their introduction into the discussion added an element of tension without contributing to the limited solution he hoped to achieve. His practice in these cases was to look beyond the demand embodied in the principle and determine what it really represented, then try to satisfy that desire partially by some other means. Usually he would dissect the claim into its components and strive for an understanding on some of these. Here again, Kissinger relied on his factoring technique as a prelude to the incremental building of an agreement.

The best example of this tactic was his handling of the Israeli demand that Egypt accept the status of nonbelligerency. He recognized the position for what it was—an effort by the Israelis to increase their sense of security. He had little chance at this stage in Middle East developments of extracting such a concession from any Arab leader. When the Israelis first made their claim, perhaps six months before the March 1975 negotiations in which it became an issue, Kissinger began to explore the possibility of Egypt or even Jordan taking steps privately that would incorporate the elements of nonbelligerency. We have already seen that on this occasion he told correspondents who accompanied his ill-fated tour of October 1974 that he did not mean to give an endorsement to nonbelligerency as proposed by the Israelis. Rather, he was seeking Arab concessions that would meet some Israeli security needs, but under another label.

As the preliminaries to the March 1975 shuttle continued, Kissinger redefined nonbelligerency as a pledge by Sadat that he would not be the first to start a war. He also saw the lengthening of the duration of any agreement that the Egyptians and the Israelis might conclude as implying nonbelligerency. The longer the agreement was to be in force, the greater would be Israel's sense of security. During the shuttle itself, Kissinger succeeded in getting the Israelis to rephrase their demand—Egypt must provide evidence of its intention to seek a political rather than a military solution to the Middle East conflict. Instead of nonbelligerency, they described the condition as a renunciation by both sides of the use and the threat of force. Israel also defined nonbelligerency in terms of various components—a muting of anti-Israeli propaganda, an end to the economic boycott, no further diplomatic harassment, the beginning of trade and commercial communications, and a reopening of the Suez Canal with Israel afforded use of the waterway. Once the concept was expressed in terms of its content, Kissinger had an operational situation. There was a possibility of getting an agreement on some of the items included in the definition.

Sadat was not willing to agree to all of these points, but he too was prepared to discuss a version of factored nonbelligerency. As the negotiations continued, and as a result of Kissinger's prodding, Sadat ultimately agreed to state that henceforth he would be prepared to resolve conflicts by diplomatic rather than military means. In another statement on the concept, he also accepted the idea of settling disputes by means of negotiation for the duration of any agreement. He would, in fact, honor the agreement until it was superseded by another one. He would exclude paramilitary as well as military activities against Israel from his territory, and he would renew the mandate of the United Nations peacekeeping forces on an annual basis rather than follow the existing practice of extending it every six months. The Egyptians were also prepared to make limited commitments with regard to the Arabs' economic boycott of Israel and to drop some of their more vociferous propaganda against the Jewish state. These features were eventually formalized in the Sinai Accord and its accompanying memoranda, but the word *nonbelligerency* was never used.

Dividing a concept into its various parts was therefore a viable approach for circumventing demands derived from principle. On occasions when Kissinger failed to utilize this tack, he encountered difficulty. In a moment of exasperation during the March 1975 negotiations on Sinai, he attempted to ease his burdens by asking the Israelis to indicate in a general sense whether they were prepared to relinquish the mountain passes and the Abu Rudeis oil fields under some conditions yet to be specified. The Israelis feigned surprise that Kissinger would ask for a statement of principle and responded that in this case Egypt should agree to negotiate principles as well and in some general or abstract way accept the idea of nonbelligerency. Kissinger's request was a mistake. In one exchange of views he had lost considerable ground. Like most declarations about principle, his suggestion would have achieved nothing unless the negotiants considered it a prelude to an action they were prepared to take. The chimera of progress can be present in statements of principle because a negotiant seems to have identified an end he is willing to accept. In the Middle East negotiations, such talk only hardens positions because neither side regards a statement of principle as an indication of its own obligations. Rather, each wants to use principle only as a way of dictating what the other should do. Principle has normative connotations and only emphasizes the differences that separate the negotiants. Kissinger's usual technique, which seemed preferable, was to seek out points that were not the center of contention and over which the two sides might agree. With luck, these items would not assume dimensions that permitted them to be elevated to a matter of principle.

Despite its obvious advantages, Kissinger's practice of dealing with segments of a problem rather than with the problem itself was the source of a basic tension between the United States and the Arabs. At the Rabat conference of Arab leaders in October 1974, the PLO representatives attacked Kissinger's step-by-step approach because it did not address the Arabs' national issue until the final stage of the negotiations. Kissinger saw virtue in approaching the more viable issues first, lest settlement on all issues be endangered by an impasse over some particularly difficult item that had not been treated in order of ascending complexity. The Palestinian issue, therefore, was to be tackled last in Kissinger's scenario, and the PLO feared that if substantial agreement were ever reached on territorial issues, Arab leaders might be prepared for all practical purposes to see the Palestinians' cause disregarded.

By the same token, as Egypt approached the negotiations on the Sinai Accord, the Syrians expressed suspicion that Kissinger's real intent was to improve Israel's security position by dividing the Arabs. Egypt would be satisfied on Sinai, Assad feared, while he would be left to face Israel alone with his claim on Golan yet to be realized. In order to allay Arab suspicions, Kissinger pressed the Israelis quite hard during the August 1975 negotiations to accept a "modest" agreement with Syria within a reasonable period after concluding the Sinai Accord. He hoped to preserve the advantage of his factoring technique, but at the same time, if he could embody in each agreement a commitment to undertake subsequent negotiations on another front, his approach would also appear sequential and the Arab fear of incremental negotiations as a device for dividing them might be dispelled.

Kissinger's penchant for factoring problems and building agreements incrementally created similar problems for his relations with Israel. On one hand, many Israelis saw their interests being served by a strategy of trading territory for peace as conditions permitted. Negotiating over limited issues was compatible with their tactics. As an alternative, there was the desire for a definitive peace, which drove some Israelis to favor a comprehensive settlement. But when they examined the idea carefully, they had reason for skepticism. Many Israelis feared that the real American purpose was essentially a resuscitation of the Rogers Plan with extensive Israeli withdrawals from the occupied territories as part of a comprehensive peace agreement. In all probability, during a general conference Israel would be pressured into making concessions that would bring that plan into being. Negotiating over small increments of territory in exchange for limited Arab political concessions had the advantage of satisfying the U.S. desire for progress without stepping into the snare that comprehensive negotiations could constitute.

Nevertheless, the Israelis were still uneasy with Kissinger's practice of factoring issues because they feared that piece by piece they would bargain away territory—and therefore security— while getting in return little more than useless Arab promises of partial peace that did not amount to peace at all. They even feared that such an outcome might be Kissinger's intent. Acting on this fear, the Israelis carried out during the Sinai negotiations what can only be considered a brilliant maneuver. First, they insisted that, once the accord was concluded, any future negotiations would take place only upon specific agreement by the United States and Israel. This stipulation applied to negotiations both on a comprehensive settlement and on limited agreements. In effect, it precluded Israel from being pushed into negotiations it did not favor. Further, with regard to Egypt and Jordan, the Israelis insisted that future negotiations were to be for an overall settlement, and it was clear that only bilateral negotiations would be satisfactory. In one stroke the Israelis turned aside what they considered to be the excesses of Kissinger's incremental diplomacy. Because of the understanding regarding Egypt and Jordan, they need not accept the incremental approach on Sinai or the West Bank. At the same time, they made any general peace conference contingent on their acceptance. To the extent that the United States honored this agreement, Israel was protected from American pressures to enter negotiations in which Kissinger might either pick away at their position or broach the Rogers Plan with its stipulation for a withdrawal from virtually all occupied territory.

Kissinger openly expressed his vexation over the negotiants' attitudes after his initial successes on Sinai and Golan. He recognized pressures favoring both incrementalism and a comprehensive approach, but his final judgment was that, if issues could no longer be handled one by one, negotiations would become so complex as to confound any mediator. Whenever he failed to factor a problem into its constituent parts, warning signals appeared. Both the Arabs and the Israelis were prepared to join comprehensive talks, but each wanted to do so under conditions that were unacceptable to the other. Thus Kissinger probably had little choice but to proceed as far as he could with his incremental diplomacy.

At times Kissinger himself felt that the Sinai Accord had brought his negotiations to a plateau that could be exceeded only by a comprehensive settlement. This view was expressed by his aides on numerous occasions. The refusal of the Syrians to negotiate over small pieces of Golan; the necessity of dealing with the Palestinians in any consideration of the West Bank; and the obsession of the Israelis first with their security, then with the historical homeland, and finally with the integrity of the Golan settlements left him with few options. Consequently, during the spring of 1976, Kissinger informed the concerned parties that, following the American presidential elections, if Ford remained in office, negotiations would be resumed, but this time on a comprehensive basis. Incremental diplomacy had run its course, and some of his colleagues claimed that Kissinger's assertion on comprehensive negotiations represented his true intentions. Yet aides conceded that the problem of the Palestinians at a general peace conference had not been resolved, and no one was absolutely sure how the negotiants would react when it was necessary to deal with a comprehensive settlement on Golan or the West Bank. At the time, the Americans were engaging in a certain amount of wishful thinking over the more difficult aspects of the Palestinian problem being resolved within the context of the Lebanese civil war. Assad could conceivably emerge as a relatively moderate spokesman for an Arab front consisting of Lebanon, Syria, Jordan, and a new group of Palestinian representatives. It could be hoped that he would remain committed to a negotiated settlement and lead this grouping into peace with Israel. Despite this musing over future possibilities, Kissinger's promise of comprehensive negotiations had all the earmarks of a holding operation that would keep the Syrians as well as the Egyptians and Israelis committed to a negotiated settlement until the United States, whether under continuing or new leadership, was again prepared to assert itself in the Middle East. Even with Kissinger's support for comprehensive negotiations, it could not be concluded that his incremental diplomacy would not resurface to prove useful in future efforts at a settlement.

The Place of Ambiguity

Incrementalism allowed Kissinger to use pieces of issues in a cumulative fashion to bring Arabs and Israelis into agreements that might never have been concluded if problems had been confronted in their entirety. But he also found that irreconcilable differences could arise over even the small points with which he concerned the negotiants. Thus he resorted to another technique— ambiguity. Because of the almost total absence of mutualities on which peaceful relations might be built, it was sometimes useful for Kissinger to permit the negotiants to have different interpretations of the same agreement if that was the only way to get them to agree in the first place. Contradictions in declared negotiating assumptions had to be permitted. Phraseology had to be such that each side could portray the results of negotiations in a way that was compatible with its national objectives. The only absolute requirement for assuring that an agreement endured was an understanding on the *minimum commitment* each side had accepted. For the Israelis this minimum was to withdraw from the territory stipulated in each agreement. For the Arabs it was to avoid, within some prescribed context, any action that pointed unequivocally to the use of force against Israel. Beyond these features, agreements included formulas that carried secondary commitments which were useful insofar as they broadened the Arab-Israeli relationship. Varying interpretations did not threaten peace, even though an outright difference over any such obligation would make the mediator's task more difficult as he attempted in subsequent negotiations to widen the area of understanding around it.

In his mediation, Kissinger was concerned with the potential of the immediate situation, not with the contingencies of the future. It was necessary to get an agreement before there was any need to worry about one of the signatories breaking it. The impact of agreement would shape the future conduct of negotiants. Problems need not arise even though formal agreement did not always mean complete understanding on all matters included within the text.

Kissinger utilized ambiguity in a number of ways. Often, in the process described in the previous chapter, he used it to protect one negotiant from the psychological hazard of affirming a suggestion coming from the other. To this end he would be purposely vague about the origin of an idea. Ambiguity was also present in the assurances given Israel regarding the future behavior of Egypt. Many of the assurances that Kissinger passed along to the Israelis while urging them to make concessions originated with Kissinger himself, not with Sadat. It was fair to ask, Whose were they? Certainly not Sadat's. But when Kissinger was pressed on this matter, he too disclaimed obligation, asserting that the United States had not engaged in a legally binding commitment as a result of these undertakings. Ambiguity of identity in such cases was used quite openly by Kissinger in moving the negotiants toward an agreement. The only question was how far he could carry the negotiations with this technique before either Sadat disavowed the assurances or the Israelis bridled at proceeding insofar as Sadat's position could not be precisely discerned. It was indeed a technique that had diminishing returns.

Shuttle diplomacy also masked the direction of negotiations. This ambiguity was the result of Kissinger's factoring issues into their constituent parts. The welter of small details over which he negotiated and his capacity for using whatever material was at hand to shape an agreement sometimes made it difficult to determine just where the negotiations might lead. Kissinger's task was to keep this sense of the ambiguous within a positive context by convincing each side that, despite the uncertainty, its position remained intact.

Finally there was ambiguity of meaning, an old and established game. Security Council resolutions 242 of 1967 and 338 of 1973 served as the foundation for the various agreements Kissinger negotiated. They affirmed the territorial inviolability and the political independence of all the states in the area. While these documents were accepted by the parties to the dispute, they were not interpreted in the same way by the two sides. The earlier resolution had affirmed the principle of Israeli withdrawal "from territories occupied in the recent conflict." But did this language mean all the territories or just some of them? The Arabs held one interpretation and the Israelis the other. At the time the resolution was drafted, the English text had been worded at the insistence of the United States to allow for this difference. Constant wrangling over the issue had led to Arab exasperation and ultimately contributed to the 1973 war. Herein lay the danger of unresolved ambiguity on minimum commitments. Words could be used, but what did they mean?

One early example of Kissinger's use of ambiguity of meaning was the provision in his original six-point cease-fire proposal that Egypt and Israel "settle the question of the return to the October 22 positions." As noted earlier, the Egyptians thought this agreement was intended to set into motion a sequence of events that would result in the Israelis' withdrawing to their October 22 battle positions. Sadat had agreed to the cease-fire in the belief that Kissinger understood and even shared this view. It was a case of what Sadat interpreted as a minimum Israeli commitment. Some consternation developed when Sadat's assumption proved to be mistaken. In accepting the cease-fire the Israelis had no intention of relaxing their stranglehold on Suez City or the Egyptian Third Army trapped east of the canal. It was only the conclusion of the Sinai disengagement agreement in January 1974 and the withdrawal of all Israeli forces well to the east of the canal that prevented this ambiguity from becoming the source of bitter recrimination involving the mediator as well as the negotiants. One minimum commitment had superseded another, and this time Israelis abided by it. Despite some difficulty, ambiguity had permitted Kissinger to begin the process of changing perceptions, and momentum precluded his running afoul of the contradictions that accompanied the use of less-than-precise language.

In the Golan disengagement agreement, similar ambiguities developed. First of all, Syria refused to accept any commitment that would preclude its use of "paramilitary" action, which supposedly left open the possibility of Palestinian attacks against Israeli settlements from Syrian-controlled territory. The very essence of the Syrian position in entering into negotiations thereby became ambiguous, but Kissinger was prepared to leave it that way as long as he could open a route to agreement.

The Golan agreement also allowed uncertainty over how far either side could go in maintaining or improving its military positions in front-line areas. In a dispute on this item Kissinger had resorted to highly ambiguous terminology to get an understanding. Israel, the two sides ultimately agreed, would not "heavily" fortify its side of the lines in the Quneitra area. No number of tanks, troops, or artillery was ever mentioned in conjunction with this stipulation, although precise formulas were specified for armament in the various zones of the Golan Heights and for other portions of Syria that the Israelis had temporarily occupied in 1973 and that were recovered by Assad. Similarly, Syrian latitude in arming Mount Hermon was left vague. Difficulty eventually arose when Syrian forces proceeded to improve roads in the area. The Israelis contended that this act amounted to the strengthening of their military positions. But the dispute was over a secondary commitment, and neither side allowed it to reach major proportions.

Another case in which ambiguity prevailed was the issue of the Mitla and Gidi passes. Sadat would not make concessions without control of the passes, and the Israelis contended that nothing Egypt was prepared to offer was worth relinquishing these vital positions. Each side was committed to its own public on the question. Kissinger finally succeeded in developing a formula that Egypt could construe as complete control and the Israelis could interpret as maintaining a foothold on the eastern slopes of Mitla and Gidi. Even with these problems, the disengagement agreements were relatively straightforward matters associated with troop withdrawals. Compliance could be demonstrated with observation by the United Nations peacekeeping forces. The difficulties that arose were not overpowering, and a few uncomplicated ambiguities could resolve them.

Kissinger's Middle East diplomacy demonstrated an important fact about ambiguity. It permitted negotiants to accept commitments while retaining a sense of having preserved their freedom of action. Everyone wanted the future unencumbered, and if Kissinger could allow for this desire, he could perhaps involve the negotiants in additional commitments. The compulsion for a sovereign state to sustain the appearance of having all options open was revealed in the extended negotiations on the Sinai Accord. Quite early in the discussions Sadat had indicated that he was prepared to accept an agreement of three years' duration. In the eyes of the Syrians he thereby provided the Israelis with a respite during which they would not have to negotiate seriously over Golan or Palestinian rights. It also offered them time to develop a military capability that insulated them from Arab threats of force and might even preclude the necessity of any future agreement. The relationship between a lack of ambiguity and the absence of constraints on Israeli behavior was made clear in the Syrians' contention that a three-year accord with Israel was more damaging to the Arab position than the same Egyptian assurance for an indefinite period. Without a specified duration, an Arab threat of force could always be implied.

In response to this Syrian criticism, the Egyptian leader cloaked his position in ambiguity. The assurance not to go to war, Sadat said, remained contingent on Israel's subsequent progress in concluding agreements on other fronts. Sadat's was a unilateral position that the Israelis could not accept. Was he prepared to live up to a three-year commitment, or wasn't he? But such matters were secondary. Kissinger's question to the Israelis was: Is Sadat prepared to sign an agreement whatever his current intentions? But the incident did require the trustee of peace to argue to the Israelis that, no matter what public explanation Sadat offered of his position, as long as he abided by the accord, Israel's position was unaffected. There was a good possibility that the agreement itself would serve to discipline Egyptian behavior, in which case, Israel was better off with it than without it.

In fact, the Egyptian attempt to interpret the Sinai Accord as a second troop separation rather than an agreement that incorporated significant political commitments was an effort at ambiguity, making it appear from the Arab perspective that little had been done and that options for military action and political maneuvering were not foreclosed. Somehow the simple act of disengaging military forces seemed to embody less of a commitment with regard to future Egyptian conduct than agreements on Israeli use of the Suez Canal, some easing in Egyptian application of the Arab boycott, and the proviso that Egypt would not participate so wholeheartedly in diplomatic attacks against Israel in the international arena.

Ambiguity was not only useful in moving Arabs and Israelis toward an agreement; it was also vital in preserving the position of the United States in the Middle East. A constant factor in Kissinger's mediation was his inability to contend that the United States was unaffected by Middle East disputes. He could not use the principal ambiguity of most mediators—namely, that his country had neither a direct commitment in the dispute nor an interest (other than humanitarian) in its outcome. In fact, the United States had an unqualified commitment to Israel's survival and security. At the same time, it had a strategic and economic interest in Arab oil. As the American commitment to Israel became manifest in various side agreements for military and economic aid and diplomatic support, Kissinger worked to retain sufficient ambiguity in his position to allow for a congenial relationship with important Arab governments.

But this effort, in turn, caused him difficulty with the Israelis. When President Ford, in a joint communique with King Hussein, agreed to continue consultation between the United States and Jordan with a view to addressing at an appropriately early date the issues of particular concern to Jordan, including a Jordanian-Israeli disengagement agreement, the Israelis thought they could detect ambiguities that signaled an American shift toward the Arab position. The Israelis felt the same way about American attitudes that allowed PLO participation in the Security Council proceedings. After all, the announced American position was to refuse to deal with the PLO until it acknowledged Israel's legitimacy and accepted United Nations resolutions promoting security for all states in the Middle East.

The American response to this dilemma revealed another use of ambiguity. It permitted the mediator to express an attitude without implying that he would act upon it. In its diplomatic stance the United States would assume a positive outlook on some possible future situation but without promising to work toward that end. In this regard, the United States maintained the ambiguity of its position with a series of seemingly explicit statements that only served to cloud the existing situation when considered in the light of the American relationship with Israel. Perhaps the most repeated formula was the assertion that the United States would not permit the Middle East situation to stagnate. Usually an equivocal position was the best Kissinger could hold out to the Arabs. It was the essence of the American approach to the Palestinian problem. While asserting that progress toward peace must be made, the United States was adding to Israel's military strength, thereby increasing the independence of the Jewish state by making it less susceptible to the pressures used by Kissinger to wring concessions from it. It was as if the United States had two policies. The Arabs had a choice. They could accept American statements, or they could consider the implications of American actions. From the standpoint of some Arabs, the position of the United States was not just ambiguous but purposely deceitful.

Perhaps Kissinger's most dedicated use of ambiguity was in preserving for the United States some freedom of action as he entered into commitments and gave assurances that encouraged the negotiants to make concessions. When negotiations progressed from troop disengagement to the realm of political questions, this process became more pronounced, and Kissinger devoted more attention to the matter of careful language. In the Sinai Accord this concern became his major preoccupation. The accord itself, with its annexes and the stipulation for the operation of an early warning system by American personnel, was relatively uncomplicated. Lines of territorial control were adjusted and armament was to be limited in the buffer zones—eight infantry battalions (eight thousand men), seventy-five tanks, and sixty artillery pieces with a range not to exceed twelve kilometers. In no case, however, could the agreement stand alone. The accompanying secret documents outlined the conditions that supported even the limited achievements of the accord, and here Kissinger worked for qualifying statements that the United States might use in avoiding future obligations.

Rather than agreeing to arm the Israelis, "the United States Government was to make every effort to be fully responsive, within the limits of its resources and Congressional authorization and appropriation," to Israel's military and defense requirements. On the question of military supply, the United States would enter into "a joint study [with Israel] of high technology and sophisticated items, including the Pershing ground-to-ground missile." In the event of a comprehensive peace conference the United States would "seek to concert" its position and strategy with Israel and "make every effort" to ensure that all substantive negotiations were on a bilateral basis. On oil supply, the United States would "give special attention" to Israel's import requirements, and on Bab el Mandeb the United States would "support Israel's right of free and unimpeded passage." In the event of a violation of the accord the United States would consult with Israel and Egypt on "possible remedial action."[4]

All these cases indeed included a commitment, but there was no statement of what it might be. What did Kissinger mean when he told Sadat that any Egyptian request for U.S. arms would be given "serious consideration"? When the accord was presented to Congress, senators and representatives wanted to know how to interpret the secret assurance to Israel to "consult on what support, diplomatic or otherwise, or assistance" the United States might provide Israel "in accordance with its constitutional practices." In conjunction with the words "diplomatic" (meaning political support) and "assistance" (meaning materiel), did the word "otherwise" refer to the eventuality of American military intercession on behalf of Israel?

And what was the meaning of the three pledges Sadat claimed Kissinger had given him? In a press conference, the Egyptian leader described them as being quite precise—the United States "guarantees that Israel will not attack Syria"; the United States will "do all it can to insure the participation of the Palestinians in any settlement"; and the United States "pledges to bring about a disengagement similar to the first disengagement agreement on the Syrian front after the conclusion of the second disengagement agreement on the Egyptian front."⁵ When the Israelis challenged the validity of any assurance Kissinger might have given Sadat with regard to their freedom of military action against Syria, a State Department spokesman responded that the key word Sadat had omitted was "unprovoked"—Israel would not make an *unprovoked* attack on Syria. On the question of the United States facilitating a second accord on Golan, the spokesman said, the missing words were "make a serious effort" to achieve this end.

For Kissinger these formulas were important. For one thing, he contended that the language was less binding than Israel and Egypt had sought. With regard to supplying Israel with Pershing missiles, he said, "All we've agreed to is to study the problem. We have not made a commitment."⁶ In that case, what was the meaning of the phrase, "with a view to making a positive decision," which the Israelis insisted on affixing to the sentence on Pershing missiles? Perhaps in the Sinai Accord, Kissinger was more specific than he had intended. The anger of the Palestinians and Assad over the accord could be said to have resulted from too few ambiguities being introduced into Kissinger's commitments to Israel.

The use of ambiguity was clearly within Kissinger's view of the art of negotiation. It was the means by which a mediator could achieve a change of perceptions without thwarting progress by asking too much of the negotiants. He used it skillfully to disguise the identity of negotiating proposals, the direction in which his mediation might be leading the negotiants, and even the very meaning of the agreements and side-agreements the Syrians, Egyptians, Israelis, and Americans concluded. Ambiguity was of value for at least four purposes:

It permitted two governments with contradictory negotiating assumptions to enter an agreement that they could interpret differently to their respective nations.

—It gave those negotiants who accepted a commitment a

sense of an unencumbered future and of preserving freedom of action.

—It was a way for the mediator to express an attitude sympathetic to a point of view held by one of the negotiants without indicating that in the future his actions would be guided by that perception.

—It allowed the mediator to state that he was undertaking a commitment without saying exactly what that commitment might be.

From this fabric of ambiguity, Kissinger's agreements emerged.

Despite what many considered to be a superficial approach to peace, Kissinger, by using ambiguities, recognized a salient feature of mediating in the Middle East. In view of the deep conflict of national purpose between Arabs and Israelis, any ironclad agreement would have placed all participants in a position of having to forgo the pursuit of national objectives. Such a change could not take place abruptly. It could be achieved only by stages and over an extended period of time. We were to see this perception quite clearly in subsequent negotiations in October and November 1978 when Begin was willing to accept an allusion to some form of autonomy for the Palestinians on the West Bank but would not accept the timetable Sadat wanted for when this act might occur. In Arab-Israeli negotiations ambiguities permitted each negotiant to set his own pace of explicit commitment independent of the trauma of signing a treaty comprised of heretofore noxious provisions. This feature was necessary if any agreement was to be achieved. It explains the pronounced opposition of Arab leaders to the Israeli-Egyptian Treaty. Sadat's commitments under this agreement did not contain any of the ambiguities that allowed him to retain his maneuverability within the context of Arab nationalism.

Kissinger's behavior reflected an understanding of this aspect of the mediator's mission. From time to time he was compelled to be explicit in order to get Israel to make a concession, and in these instances he preferred to confine such language to unpublished memoranda. The memoranda, in fact, were another element of ambiguity, and his activities proceeded fairly well until these were made public on the Sinai Accord. Thereafter, with much of the ambiguity stripped away and with the extent of the American commitment to Israel revealed, he could not persuade the Syrians to enter into new negotiations.

Perspective

As a means of placing Kissinger's negotiating philosophy and diplomatic method in perspective, it is useful to examine an alternative approach to negotiations that was sponsored by some of his critics. Essentially, the plan called for a comprehensive settlement to be attempted in the first instance at a multilateral conference— a reconvening at Geneva to focus attention on the major differences between the Arabs and the Israelis. This approach, which was mentioned in previous chapters, had been bruited about since the time of the first disengagement agreement. It was polished to its most coherent form under the auspices of the Brookings Institution in late 1975 by a group of experts that included both Zbigniew Brzezinski, who was to become Carter's national security advisor, and others who were to work for the new president.[7] The alternative approach of comprehensive settlement was the route chosen by the Carter administration in its early days.

Under the Brookings proposal the mediator would acknowledge at the outset certain claims of each of the two sides. Then he would press the other for acceptance. In addition to agreeing to a formal peace, the Arabs would be asked to allow open borders with Israel—that is, trade, communication links, cultural exchange, tourism, and eventually even diplomatic representation. A time-phased quid pro quo would be established between these items and some interpretation of the things the Arabs wanted— recognition of Palestinian rights and a return of the occupied territories. United Nations peacekeeping forces would continue to patrol Arab-Israeli borders. In addition, a means for achieving demilitarization and regional arms limitations was to be developed. The proponents of this model of negotiation would have the mediator first attempt to get an agreement in principle on proposed tradeoffs and then devote his efforts to establishing a schedule over a number of years under which one of the increments desired by the Israelis would be exchanged for one of those desired by the

Arabs. Unlike Kissinger's approach, which depended on changing the perceptions of the negotiants, the subject of negotiation was to be the actual content of the agreement for which all were striving.

The difficulty with the alternative approach was getting the two sides to agree that a segment of peace as defined by the Israelis could be equated with a segment of peace as defined by the Arabs. This technique of equating major concessions accentuated national purpose and therefore distinctions between Arabs and Israelis. It set the scene for unprecedented haggling. There was considerable doubt, for example, that the Israelis wanted *anything* so much that they would agree to the Arabs' definition of the Palestinian issue in order to acquire it. In the absence of an appropriate inducement, Kissinger's critics would find themselves willy-nilly in the business of attempting to change the Arab or the Israeli perception of the Palestinian issue before they could proceed with negotiations. They would ultimately be driven to following Kissinger's path but without having acknowledged the importance of perception to their negotiating plan.

A fundamental assumption remained unspoken. The premise of the Brookings plan was that each side must recognize that continued adherence to its long-held national views meant yet another war. Presumably both the Arabs and Israelis found peace such an imperative that they were prepared to abandon some of their national perceptions for it. Without this assumption, how could the proponents of the alternative course expect Arabs and Israelis to enter into talks structured on the comprehensive model? Kissinger did not have to take this position with his approach of accepting national perceptions for what they were and working to change them gradually as he moved step by step toward peace. Whereas Kissinger had seen changing perceptions as an outcome of negotiations, his critics assumed a change of perceptions as a starting point.

As complex as Kissinger's diplomacy might have been, complexities were also present in the Brookings report. It was clearly a reaction to Kissinger's diplomacy. In reviewing his activities it listed only what it considered their negative features. Its tone was that of drawing lessons from Kissinger's experience in terms of situations and practices to be avoided. No effort was made to investigate what might have been positive about his method and style. This outlook pointed the experts who wrote the report in a curious direction when they came to formulating their own recommendations. First, the report observed that the two sides had been left by the Sinai Accord with such a sense of sacrifice that, for a considerable period after the conclusion of the accord, they could contemplate neither future negotiations nor the concessions necessary for another agreement. Were the modest achievements of the accord, it asked, worth this price? Could diplomacy proceeding in this way go very far? Moreover, step-by-step diplomacy had led to divisions and recriminations among Arabs, while a high degree of Arab unity was considered necessary for a settlement. In addition, the Soviet Union was increasingly annoyed at being left on the sidelines, and the report assumed that the Soviets still had the capacity for perpetuating sufficient mischief to undercut any agreement sponsored solely by the United States. Finally, the Brookings study worried about Congress, which was described as being uneasy over the commitments assumed by the United States in step-by-step diplomacy. Congressional support for the American aid that would surely be part of any final settlement was critical to implementing an agreement. It might be advisable, the report implied, to follow a course with which Congress was more comfortable. Questions were also raised about where a partial solution could next be attempted with a reasonable prospect for success. After the Sinai Accord, the leaders of Syria and Israel had expressed skepticism over the feasibility of an agreement on Golan except within the framework of an overall settlement. A partial withdrawal of Israeli forces from the West Bank was not likely as long as the Arabs insisted that the PLO have a role in such negotiations. As yet, Israel and the Palestine Liberation Organization had each refused to recognize the other. What then, the Brookings study asked, could the future of step-by-step diplomacy be? Only time was to give us the answer. Due to a change in Sadat's perceptions, the world was to witness yet a third step on Sinai, combined with an attempt on the part of the Egyptian president to establish the basis for a subsequent step in which other Arabs might be brought into negotiations over the West Bank.

From the record, Kissinger's critics considered themselves justified in questioning his methods, but they failed to develop any positive methods of their own. They did not explain how a general conference and an attempt at a comprehensive settlement could avoid the difficulties Kissinger had encountered or why some of the warning signals, which always seem to be flying in the Middle East, could not still be handled within the context of shuttle diplomacy. Looking again at the difficulties the report associated with Kissinger's method, inter-Arab tensions (at least between Egypt and Syria) had abated little more than a year after the signing of the Sinai Accord. No one ever really abandoned the idea of a negotiated settlement, whatever the sense of sacrifice that the report saw the Arabs experiencing from the second Egyptian-Israeli agreement. Again in 1977 and 1978, most of the Arab leadership, led by Syria, expressed outrage over Sadat's visit to Jerusalem and the Camp David negotiations. But as long as Sadat did not step totally outside the Arab context might not the fury again ultimately abate? Some Arabs accused Sadat of moving beyond the limits of the Arab nation in signing the Israeli-Egyptian Treaty. But shortly thereafter the idea was floated that if the United States would establish direct and open contacts with he PLO, the Arab nationalists might modify their opposition to the treaty. Who could say how far changing perceptions might go?

As for the Israelis, by early 1977 they were once again intermittently indicating a preference for step-by-step negotiations over a comprehensive settlement. The negotiations that ultimately emerged from the Sadat initiative were certainly less than comprehensive. Concerning the report's other points of criticism, the Arab drift toward the West progressively limited the Soviets' ability to play a spoiler's role. Congress, on the other hand, is always unpredictable. Thus the reservations expressed in the Brookings report with regard to Kissinger's diplomacy did not lie at the core of the real problem associated with achieving a Middle East peace. If Kissinger was to be criticized, it should have been for tying the United States military arrangements with Israel so closely to the Sinai Accord.

The problems cited by the report were not really inherent in Kissinger's method, and the alternative approach sugguested by the Brookings paper had few answers itself. In its scenario the new plan still employed time phases, much as Kissinger had done. The issue of Jerusalem, for example, was to be resolved at a late stage in the negotiations. After an agreement had been reached, implementation was also to be phased. The plan saw implementation, in fact, in Kissinger-like increments. It even acknowledged that, as the process proceeded, interim steps might become feasible. What, then, were the differences from Kissinger's diplomacy?

The alternative approach did have a distinct feature. Its aim was to induce peace by establishing principles at a general conference; it tended toward George Ball's moral/legalistic approach. But as we have seen, this was a questionable way to negotiate in the Middle East. The Carter administration without noticeable success was to spend the better part of 1977 attempting to establish the underlying principles upon which comprehensive negotiations could proceed.

Indeed, a fundamental difference in negotiating philosophy separated the two approaches. With the power and influence of the United States, an American mediator might be able to bring the two sides to the conference table, but without changes in Israeli and Arab national perceptions, could he devise an agenda or induce movement toward a settlement? The deep undercurrents of conflicting national legitimacies had long prevented Arab and Israeli leaders from accepting a solution depicted in terms of compromise on state interests. For the Brookings report to suggest that this was no longer the case implied that a change had taken place, but here the advocates of the comprehensive solution were caught in another unstated assumption. They never determined when this change might have begun, how far it might have proceeded, or when it might be sufficient to support the type of peace they foresaw. They did not concern themselves with its nature or how it might influence negotiations. Their concept of the situation with which the United States was dealing seemed unusually static.

11

The Art
of Commitment

Kissinger's technique in working toward an agreement was characterized by the four practices discussed in the previous chapter: careful planning, the exploitation of all channels of communication that could influence the perceptions of the leaders involved, the factoring of major issues into their component parts in order to make them more manageable, and the use of ambiguities to allow each participant (including the mediator) his own interpretation of the limited agreements into which the two sides were being asked to enter. Kissinger's immediate objective in his mediation was to extract commitments from which agreements could be fashioned. In acquiring commitments he consistently relied on three means: he gave formal assurances in the name of the United States government, thereby providing the element of trust that was not to be found between the Arab and Israeli negotiants; he used inducements to strengthen the motivation for undertaking commitments; and when all else failed, he reduced the burden of commitment by sharing it with the negotiants.

Assurances

In mediating between the Arabs and the Israelis, Kissinger was confronted with an array of issues that did not lend themselves to compromise and commitment. The antagonists were not being asked in most cases to assume the same obligation. Rather, they were trading distinct commitments concerning matters that were perceived as being inherent to sovereignty, reserved for unilateral initiative, and not open to international agreement. At the outset of negotiations, for example, Sadat could not see himself openly agreeing to rebuild Ismailia, Suez, and Port Said, the cities in the Suez Canal zone. Yet Israel demanded just that. It was not a question of Sadat's being unprepared to rebuild the cities; he just could not accept this condition in a formal public document concluded with Israel. The same was true with regard to automatically renewing the mandate of the United Nations peace-keeping force. Nor could he agree to control the more vitriolic outbursts of the press and radio or to refrain from blockading Israeli shipping at Bab el Mandeb even while a state of belligerency existed between the two countries. For their part the Israelis could not agree to limit their freedom of retaliatory action against Egypt or Syria.

At the same time, the two sides had no difficulty telling Kissinger what they were prepared to do in the absence of a specific agreement embodying such obligations. This situation applied even to Sadat's adamant refusal to accept a state of nonbelligerency. He was willing to give assurances to Kissinger on steps he would take that amounted to the same thing, but he could not accept nonbelligerency itself. Rather than simply note these attitudes, Kissinger chose to use them to construct a framework of indirect understandings. It seemed appropriate for him to accept an informal statement from one of the two sides on some observance it was prepared to follow and then pass it along to the other as an assurance given in the name of the United States government. What another mediator would have used as only a starting point for discussions leading to a supposedly binding agreement, Kissinger employed more resourcefully. The importance of an agreement was neither its moral nor its legal quality, but its influence on the behavior of participants in the ongoing negotiations. With Kissinger's style of diplomacy, an initial understanding was just as important for having been conveyed through the mediator as for having been duly signed, sealed, and cataloged in the archives of legal memorabilia. Kissinger's indirect assurances had an effect other than providing the framework for agreement. In terms of the negotiating process, as opposed to the content of the ensuing agreement, the assurances were a facilitating factor. They constituted an element of ambiguity that permitted the negotiants to agree without experiencing a sense of restriction or irretrievable loss of freedom at the hands of an enemy.

Kissinger's indirect assurances took a variety of forms. The Egyptian commitment on the blockade of Bab el Mandeb was conveyed in a letter from Sadat to Nixon. Similar exchanges took place with Ford on the Sinai Accord. The Israeli assurance to enter a second round of negotiations on Golan was accepted by Kissinger orally. Whatever the form in which these understandings were transmitted to Kissinger, he generally conveyed them to the other side in memoranda of agreement on points of view the United States had accepted from a negotiant in the course of negotiations. Four such documents accompanied the Sinai Accord. Once again using Bab el Mandeb as an example, the United States in an attached memorandum affirmed the principle of freedom of navigation and unimpeded transit through the straits and stated that it would support Israel's right to free and innocent passage through such waters.

Kissinger's approach did have its dangers for a mediator. One interpretation of the breakdown of the March 1975 shuttle was that ultimately Israel refused to accept Sadat's informal assurances conveyed through Kissinger. From the Israeli standpoint, the process was as follows: Kissinger would get Sadat to say something the Israelis wanted to hear and then tell it to Golda Meir or to Rabin, Allon, and Peres as if it were an unqualified commitment. Kissinger was aware of the limitations on the validity of the American assurance. "The United States cannot substitute its efforts," he said on one occasion, "for the good will, for the willingness to cooperate, for the readiness to relate the immediate to the long-term interest of the parties involved. . . . Ultimately, progress depends on the willingness of all parties to be conciliatory and to make the moves that are necessary, and the United States' effort cannot substitute for the effort of the parties concerned."[1] As cogent as this statement might have been, persuading either side to enter into a formal agreement on a sensitive matter—and virtually everything became sensitive—constituted a lengthy process during which the mediator was compelled to trade heavily on the strength of indirect assurances regarding what each side was prepared to do in the absence of formal agreement. Kissinger's judgment on just how far either side would travel down this road was critical.

Kissinger continuously attempted to refine his practices, and ultimately he found a way of giving indirect assurances the substance that was necessary to placate the Israelis. Middle ground between the open agreement and an indirect unpublished assurance was an assurance that ultimately became public through undetermined channels. In the case of the Sinai Accord, the press boldly reported quite early in the negotiations that the formal agreement between Egypt and Israel would be accompanied by various secret Egyptian assurances conveyed to the Israelis through Kissinger. Media accounts of their nature were essentially correct, and the Egyptians did not seem to be disturbed over the appearance of such reports in what could have been considered a serious breach of confidence. The secret provisions were published *unofficially*. As a result Sadat believed that he was still in a position to refute the attacks of Arab radicals when they asserted that he had betrayed the national cause. He could scoff at press reports of assurances given by Kissinger somewhat more easily than at public agreements that he had signed.

At the same time, because the assurances were known, the Israelis felt more secure. As public knowledge, the assurances seemed to have greater power of commitment. Perhaps this form of understanding would not bind the Egyptians to any particular course of action. But the important point was the influence on Kissinger. As a published document an assurance could not be dismissed quite so easily simply as a stop along the way to a comprehensive settlement. The idea of a *public secret indirect assurance* was fraught with contradictions. It constituted a horrifying spectacle for the conventional diplomat. For Kissinger it seemed to be a means of moving the participants one more step toward an agreement, and its presence in the negotiations apparently caused him no mental anguish.

Inducements

As we have noted, Kissinger's style of diplomacy emphasized process over content. As part of the negotiating process, he had to reinforce any motivation the negotiants might have for changing the situation in the Middle East. He had to offer inducements —some influence on the judgment of the negotiants that would move them to react to his initiative in a way that was complementary to the achievement of limited agreements.

In diplomacy, inducements are often considered in negative terms. As a scholar, Kissinger himself had written, "Where no penalty for noncompliance exists—no *ultimo ratio*—there is no incentive to reach agreement."[2] As a statesman, and particularly as a mediator, Kissinger was to demonstrate that quite often an inducement could also be a negative formulation of an essentially positive factor. To the extent that he emphasized the negative, his diplomacy always rested on positive acts intended by the United States. The penalty, or negative feature, was the omission of these acts, and it was in this respect that Kissinger portrayed costs for those who would not proceed with him along the way of limited agreements. Whether it be the economic aid, materiel, and diplomatic support provided by the United States to Israel, or the economic assistance offered to Egypt and ultimately to Syria, Kissinger's argument was not how fortunate the recipient might be when the positive inducement was received, but rather how unfortunate it would be if the inducement were withheld. The argument had various degrees of persuasiveness with the individual negotiants.

Material and diplomatic largesse was not Kissinger's only inducement. His most compelling point was the value of preserving the negotiating process itself. He played on a curious combination of trust in him as a mediator, fear of the consequences of his failure, and hope in his ability to move the other side to make the concessions that each wanted from its adversary. Success rested on first developing an expectation of agreement and then suggesting that the expectation might not be realized. Statements by Kissinger and his aides expressing cautious optimism were combined with assertions that the situation was more difficult than they had anticipated. As the bargaining process proceeded, they nurtured a positive sense through repeated allusions to the value of preserving what the negotiants had already achieved. A feeling of contingent loss was created by expressing regret over the waste if all this effort were dissipated because of a stalemate that arose when one side or the other would not make a small concession still needed to keep the process active. Finally, Kissinger's promise to offer suggestions of his own if the two sides could only narrow the gap between them a little more constituted a positive pressure for achievement. This process aroused in the negotiants a combination of hope and apprehension that spurred them toward agreement.

Kissinger had one more ploy. Whenever the negotiants were not responsive, he would threaten to terminate the negotiations. Early in his Middle East initiative he used the threat deftly within the context of Arab national politics. By entering into a cease-fire agreement and then a disengagement of forces, Sadat had, in fact, committed himself to negotiation as opposed to confrontation, a position that he sustained with support from Saudi Arabia. If Kissinger suddenly withdrew, Sadat could find his judgment discredited. Thereupon he would be open to attacks from radical Arabs, isolated from his nation as the popular will swung against negotiations, and in dire political straits. Kissinger exploited the situation to its utmost when he threatened to discontinue his mission and not negotiate an agreement between the Syrians and the Israelis if the oil boycott was not terminated. Sadat and the Saudis were thereby motivated to persuade the other Arabs to lift the embargo. After six weeks of intense pressure, they achieved their objective. Arab oil was again flowing directly to the United States, and Kissinger had initiated the preliminary moves aimed at a Golan disengagement.

It seems likely that in March 1975—the one time Kissinger carried out his termination threat—he caught both sides by surprise. In the case of the Golan disengagement he had announced the intention of abandoning his efforts but had lingered long enough to permit the negotiants to respond. His precipitous decision in the case of the Sinai Accord made an important point. Israel's only alternative to war was American diplomacy. As for Sadat, he had based his entire policy not just on negotiations but on keeping the

United States engaged as a means of squeezing concessions from the Israelis. After the talks were suspended, reports emanating from Washington that step-by-step diplomacy was dead only heightened concerns that Kissinger might even ignore the clear signals from Egyptians and Israelis that they preferred the shuttle to the other options open to them. The incident demonstrated that Kissinger's efforts in and of themselves were a major inducement for the negotiants to continue.

Kissinger was dealing with subtle factors when he moved negotiations along by threatening to abandon his mediation efforts. On the side of the Arabs, he was exploiting whatever commitment they might have to the negotiating process. This sense of obligation existed on two levels—a general commitment to a negotiated settlement as opposed to a resolution of the Arab-Israeli problem through war, and a more short-run and specific commitment to one of the individual sequences of negotiations sponsored by Kissinger. At the first level, Sadat was committed to a strategy of negotiation, which clearly limited the options available to him in regional politics. In the case of the Sinai Accord, for example, the Egyptian leader saw the many problems the agreement embodied with regard to the wedge it could drive between Egypt and Syria and the military benefit it would give Israel. The Egyptians were quite uneasy about the conditions that had emerged from Kissinger's mediation, and at one point Sadat's foreign minister, the man who was identified with Egypt's policy swing toward the United States, even advised against signing the accord. But by mid-1975, when Sadat faced this situation, he would have been repudiating his own policy of two years' duration if he had rejected the accord and run the risk of having Kissinger again suspend his mediation. Where would Sadat go from there?

Assad's position was somewhat more qualified. Generally he was committed to a negotiated settlement, but he had never gone so far as to disavow the possibility of returning to the more traditional Arab posture of confrontation. He retained the option of claiming that negotiation had been little more than a tactic for maneuvering toward an outcome that would eventually be reached through the use of force.

Whatever Sadat's and Assad's initial degree of commitment to a comprehensive settlement, it was intensified once they agreed to the negotiation of a limited agreement. Kissinger's elaborate preparations made certain of that. As part of this second level of commitment, Kissinger's purpose was to lock the negotiants into so committing their own prestige to the negotiating process that they preferred some type of agreement to no agreement at all. At this point they felt a sense of loss when Kissinger threatened to terminate his mediation if concessions were not forthcoming. The Arabs could still reject the mediator's efforts and refuse to make some of the compromises he proposed, but the threat not to work for a limited agreement, once the Arabs were committed to it, was effective in moving them to make concessions.

The meaning of Kissinger's inducement for the Israelis was no less complex. The force of his threat rested on nothing more substantial than national anxieties. As a people, Israelis stood alone and isolated in an indifferent and sometimes hostile international community. Only the United States supported them. They were aware of the implicit influence of American Jewry on U.S. policy. Israelis might talk with bravado, but would any sane Israeli want to put to the ultimate test the proposition that Israel was free to do as it wished and still be assured of American support in the knowledge that a growing proportion of America's oil supply hung in the balance? Kissinger made the most of the affairs of the mind. Concessions might be painful, but the Israelis could not totally turn their backs on negotiations once the process was underway.

The manner in which Kissinger shaped inducements, at least before the March 1975 breakdown in negotiations, was a reflection of both his approach to diplomacy and his assessment of the American position in the Middle East. Neither was satisfactory to his critics. From time to time foreign policy experts ensconced in academia contended that Kissinger had more leverage with the negotiants than he was using. Such criticism was from proponents of *negative inducements*. There was some question whether they understood Kissinger's negative formulation of positive inducements. In an abstract sense it would seem that American power was such that Kissinger could have been more assertive in his demands on the negotiants and more comprehensive in the agreements he attempted to achieve. On occasion, he did edge toward the strident course suggested by his critics, but each time he veered back to his own approach of changing perceptions.

Kissinger's conduct of Middle East affairs raised a fundamental question: How much latitude did he really have in using negative inducements? With regard to the Arabs he had little indeed. As vice president, Ford had once mumbled something about the United States withhholding food shipments from the Arab countries if the oil embargo continued.[3] This proposition was so meaningless that it was virtually embarrassing. When Kissinger asserted that the West refused to suffer economic strangulation from the oil embargo and could eventually be driven to use military force in order to assure access to oil, the uproar was so great that he found himself attempting to ward off peace-minded commentators in the United States and Europe with all sorts of lame rationalizations about how the statement was meant only to strengthen moderate Arabs in their struggle with the radicals.

Some critics also suggested withholding American technology, particularly in conjunction with the Arab insistence that companies wishing contracts under Saudi, Kuwaiti, or Abu Dhabi development programs give assurances that they had no business relations with Israel. But would the American economy forgo billions of dollars in business and armament sales to implement such a negative inducement at the very time that the United States was paying billions more for Arab oil? After all, the contracts with Arab countries were a critical factor in preventing even larger deficits in the balance of payments than those that did occur.

The use of negative inducements against the Arabs, therefore, seemed unlikely, and the same could be said of the prospect for their use with Israel. When Kissinger, at a televised news conference, announced his reexamination of American policy in the aftermath of the suspension of the March 1975 negotiations, he was compelled to say that the study was "not designed to induce Israel to alter any particular policy." He also implied that, if the Israelis did not set forth positive ideas on how to close the gap with Egypt, the United States would be required to make suggestions of its own. Kissinger was quick to add, however, that under no circumstances would the United States attempt to impose a solu-

tion on Israel.[4] The qualifiers attached to these allusions to negative inducements may have appeared to some observers as clever
subtleties that were meant to reassure the American Jewish community. Whatever their intent, they demonstrated that the
pressure Kissinger could bring to bear on Israel rested more on
Israeli fears than on what the United States would actually do.
When the application of negative inducements within the context
of the special relationship was carefully examined, it became clear
that this option had its limitations. The frustrations for Kissinger
were only too apparent. If not negative inducements, what force
could cause the Israelis to modify their position? The United States
had been offering positive inducements for years, but these had
led to no appreciable change in the Israelis' thinking. Positive inducements were ineffective, and in the American political setting,
negative inducements were not totally credible. Kissinger therefore
resorted to the relatively mild approach of negative formulations
of positive inducements.

The Israelis and the Arabs both seemed aware of the tensions
involved in Kissinger's use of inducements. They took positions on
this issue that were similar and that complemented their respective
strengths. Curiously, each side chose a positive formulation of the
inducements that were available to it in bargaining with the United
States. Israeli spokesmen consistently expressed their belief in the
symbiotic nature of the mutually beneficial relationship between
the United States and Israel. Negative inducements were harmful
to both, they said. Israel could not respond to American negotiating suggestions unless the warm nature of the special relationship was constantly reaffirmed. This Israeli view was not just a
national feeling; it was a government policy that was explicitly
stated following suspension of negotiations on the Sinai Accord.
The Arab stance was no different. In lifting the oil embargo, the
Arab Organization of Petroleum Exporting Countries (AOPEC)
noted: "The Arab oil ministers are aware of the fact that oil is a
weapon which can be utilized in a positive manner in order to lead
to results, the effectiveness of which may surpass those if the oil
weapon was used in a negative manner."[5]

Superficially, the preference of Kissinger's domestic critics for
a more aggressive American approach to the Middle East had a

certain logic. But, for all that this preference might have offered in the way of negotiating philosophy, it lacked a great deal in terms of practical politics. Kissinger, in fact, had only one real inducement—his threat not to bring the two sides together. The Arabs and the Israelis both needed American mediation. Left to their own devices, they would surely slip into another war with all the horrors it held for the people of the Middle East. Each was fully aware of this prospect, and for many people on both sides it was unpalatable.

Commitment

A final factor in Kissinger's Middle East diplomacy that requires examination is the manner in which he utilized commitments by the United States to help achieve his objectives. In his mediation, Kissinger continually maintained that he had accepted no legal obligations in the name of the United States government. In a sense, such statements were accurate. Obligations of the sort to which he referred were made contingent on the American constitutional process—that is, they were subject to the approval of Congress. Most noteworthy among these were various undertakings to provide economic and military assistance to one or another of the negotiants and to participate in the supervision of the agreements Kissinger negotiated, even to the point of sending American civilian observers to operate some of the electronic surveillance equipment at Mitla and Gidi passes. In each case Congress had to provide the required funds.

When confronted with the necessity of approving the dispatch of 200 American technicians to Sinai, some congressmen feared that such an obligation could embroil the United States in any future Middle East war. Actually, it did not have to be any more of a commitment than that assumed by the countries that provided troops for the United Nations peacekeeping forces in Sinai and Golan. If the United States did not resist such involvement, it was only because of our insistence on having a major role in Middle East affairs.

Other commitments assumed by Kissinger were not unique to the mediator's role. The high-flying reconnaissance and observation missions the United States agreed to conduct over the disengagement areas were predicated on the United States's possessing a technology that was not available to the international peace-keeping forces. The flights precluded a great deal of on-the-ground observation that would have been difficult to arrange. Moreover, this commitment was little more than a legitimization of an existing U.S. operation.

The various commitments to extend economic and military aid could be viewed in much the same manner. Support for Israel was set firmly in the context of the longstanding special relationship. After the 1973 war, this aid would have been extended in large amounts even if the United States had not assumed the role of the Middle East mediator. Certainly, American diplomatic support of Israel at the United Nations was not contingent on direct U.S. involvement in the Middle East negotiations. Likewise, with regard to economic assistance to Egypt and Syria, it was part of an American attempt to wrench influence in the area away from the Soviet Union. U.S. assistance to the Arabs was little more than a step that served relatively straightforward national interests within the framework of Soviet-American competition. In all these cases Kissinger was, in fact, quite conservative with the obligations he assumed. When viewed in these broad descriptive terms, his commitments did not seem excessive. Certainly they were not unique from the standpoint of the type of obligation he had accepted or in terms of the rationale that could be put forth in their defense in association with U.S. foreign policy objectives. Moreover, Kissinger's commitments were useful in facilitating an agreement between Arabs and Israelis.

But beyond the fine line of legal obligation delineated by Henry Kissinger, the United States ultimately acquired commitments that were to set the limits on official American behavior in the Middle East. Kissinger himself conceded that the United States would become involved in any violation of the agreements that he had negotiated because in such a case "one or both of the parties is going to ask us for diplomatic support and in that sense it is of course true that our judgment as to who violated the agreement will affect the course that we will pursue."[6]

The principal obligation assumed by Kissinger in relation to his shuttle diplomacy, therefore, was the American commitment to pursue negotiations. This undertaking seemed unequivocal. The United States secretary of state devoted the better part of two years to planning and executing his mediation. Not only did he make numerous trips to the Middle East, but he and President Ford periodically asserted that the United States could never permit stagnation in the Arab-Israeli negotiations. They vowed to press continuously for further concessions until a comprehensive settlement was achieved. There was nothing passive, therefore, about the American posture. The purpose of Ford's meeting with Sadat in Austria two months after the failure of the March 1975 shuttle on Sinai was to determine whether Sadat was still committed to diplomatic steps under American auspices. But the meeting also provided powerful and positive confirmation that the United States itself remained committed to an active role in negotiating a settlement.

For the negotiants the American commitment had special meaning, one that exceeded a mere willingness to be an honest broker. Sadat repeatedly justified his negotiating stance by asserting that only the United States could extract concessions from the Israelis. United States officials responded to Sadat's dependence by developing an exceedingly cordial relationship with the Egyptian president. Sadat was clearly orienting Egypt's international position away from the Soviet Union and toward the United States. In exchange for this shift, indeed for his ingratiating attitude toward the United States, Sadat expected American pressure on Israel to relinquish the occupied territories. A major factor for the Syrians when they undertook the Golan disengagement negotiations was also a belief that Kissinger could win concessions from the Israelis. And Israel too believed in the American commitment. Throughout all negotiations, an important feature was the assurance by the United States that all its moves were directed toward the survival and security of the Jewish state.

These expectations of the negotiants went far beyond the limitations Kissinger set on the legal obligations of the United States government. Essentially they were open-ended. If stalemates required participants in the negotiations to make new concessions —that is, to reaffirm their commitment to peace—there was no reason why the two sides should not also look to an extension of the American commitment as an appropriate means for resolving an impasse. After the two disengagement agreements were concluded and planning for the second round of negotiations on Sinai was initiated, this feature of the negotiations began to emerge. First Sadat raised the possibility of a U.S. guarantee of regional peace for the duration of the negotiations. The plan was set aside, but it signaled a desire for an extension of the U.S. commitment. To Sadat, it was clearly meant as a substitute for an Egyptian declaration of nonbelligerency which the Israelis hoped to obtain in the forthcoming negotiations.

Shortly thereafter, Kissinger did begin to assume for the United States obligations that would otherwise have been expected to accrue to the negotiants. In exchange for Israel's surrendering the Abu Rudeis oil fields, he was prepared not only to guarantee petroleum deliveries from Iranian sources, but also to compensate Israel for making the concession by paying annually for these oil shipments. In effect, an American commitment would help carry the burden Israel would normally have sustained alone in relinquishing control of territory that was acquired by force in contravention of a basic principle of the United Nations. Kissinger was indeed trading heavily on the American commitment.

This new direction in the negotiations was abruptly ended by the suspension of the March 1975 shuttle, but when negotiations were resumed, it soon became apparent that no change had, in fact, occurred. Upon his arrival in Washington in June 1975, Israeli Prime Minister Rabin made it clear that in exchange for another agreement with the Arabs, he wanted not Egyptian but American political commitments. In entertaining Israeli proposals, Kissinger permitted the entire negotiating process to be altered. In earlier exchanges, he had first assured that the two sides were talking about the same thing, and then he had served as an intermediary, an impartial counselor, and an inspirer of ideas, helping to narrow the gap between them. In the final stages of the Egyptian and Syrian disengagement agreements, U.S.-backed assurances had proved necessary to cement an understanding, but in neither case had American obligations provided the foundations of an agreement. In the second attempt to negotiate a Sinai Accord, it was different. Before making concessions to Egypt, the Israelis wanted some rather firm indications of the nature of the quid pro quo to be offered by the United States.

With Rabin's new demands, Kissinger was faced with two distinct sets of negotiations. First, he must arrive at an understanding with the Israelis regarding a variety of arrangements between the United States and Israel. Then he must negotiate with Sadat, almost as if he were operating on Israel's behalf. As the negotiations proceeded—this time without an extended shuttle—Kissinger maintained that he was not endorsing the proposals of either side. It was a difficult position for him to hold.

For the Israelis, a Sinai Accord was almost secondary. What they wanted were clear and firm guarantees with regard to their security. Thus in a U.S.-Israeli economic agreement signed in May 1975, the United States included a joint statement of opposition to the boycott. Among the conditions Rabin brought to Washington the following month was a precise understanding on oil-sharing in the event of another embargo. He also asked for coordination of policy on Geneva and the West Bank as well as an American assurance not to bring undue pressure on Israel to negotiate a second agreement of consequence with Syria. Another Israeli proviso was that the PLO must be excluded from the sessions of any Geneva Conference. In addition, Rabin wanted a reaffirmation of the assurance that the United States would never permit a modification of the Security Council resolutions that had terminated hostilities in 1967 and 1973 and that were to Israel's liking because they were vague with regard to how much of the occupied territories was to be returned to the Arabs. Concerning the possibility of the Syrian or the Egyptian government's unilaterally ordering the withdrawal of the United Nations peacekeeping forces from Golan or Sinai, Kissinger even reviewed with Rabin the possibility of the United States's providing a "substitute force." The prospect of direct U.S. military intervention under certain conditions was discussed, but no commitment was ever made on this point.

In the Sinai Accord Kissinger had succeeded in getting his agreement, but in so doing he fundamentally changed his relationship with each side. American commitments had replaced Arab and Israeli concessions as the substance of negotiations. Kissinger had influence with the Arabs as long as they believed that only the United States could persuade Israel to make concessions and that it was prepared to do so. When the contents of the Sinai Accord and its accompanying memoranda were revealed, observers soon concluded that Kissinger had seriously compromised his ability to obtain additional concessions from Israel. Indeed, had Kissinger been so intent on achieving an agreement that he had bargained away his own negotiating tools? It appeared that he might have been operating in contradiction of one of his own premises. In identifying the art of negotiations he had said that progress could be thwarted "by asking for too much as surely as by asking too little." Perhaps the same could be said about *giving* too much.

What Kissinger had allowed the Israelis was a long stride toward a militarily invincible position in the Middle East and the prerogative of deciding unilaterally the conditions under which they would agree to additional negotiations. In an imperfect world, the Israelis had achieved everything for which they might have hoped. As a result, they were less motivated to bear the tensions and strains of negotiation.

How, an observer of Kissinger's diplomacy might ask, had Israel achieved such an advantageous position? First, they had used one of Kissinger's own tactics and factored critical issues into constituent parts. They had not talked about Israel's security in a broad sense, but only in terms of its components. One by one they had extracted from Kissinger American commitments that moved them toward the situation they wanted. No single American commitment associated with the Sinai Accord changed the security situation in the Middle East, but the composite of the commitments did alter it. The Israelis relinquished the Abu Rudeis oil fields and the territory west of Gidi and Mitla passes. Egypt accepted an assortment of commitments that pointed toward nonbelligerency. But the real meaning of the accord was the American commitments that complemented Israel's security.

In some respects George Ball's criticism of Kissinger's diplomacy was now justified. The emphasis given to the minds of the negotiants and to the influence that the act of reaching an agreement was to have on their perceptions had led to errors. Kissinger was so devoted to *process* compared to *content*, and so imbued with the importance of the present, that in order to get an immediate agreement, he had made commitments that in effect militated against future agreement. His personal commitment to the negotiating process had resulted in an outcome that in fact was contradictory to his objective. The Israelis had understood quite well the real nature of the American commitment to negotiation.

What Kissinger had done was to surrender his only functional inducement. He could no longer threaten the Israelis that he would refuse to mediate in their behalf with the Arabs. Henceforth, the Israelis need not care whether he was willing to mediate. The dynamics of shuttle diplomacy had rested on Kissinger's ability to preclude either the Arabs or the Israelis from achieving a paramount objective except through his intercession. The Israelis wanted a total and perhaps unrealistic sense of security. Kissinger's task was to stand astride the path to this goal while convincing the Israelis that they could approach it only through negotiations that he sponsored. It was not easy, because along the way he also had to convince them that they did not see their own security in proper terms. He was compelled to argue that Israeli security did not lie in the retention of the occupied territories or in the total denial of Palestinian legitimacy.

For the Arabs the broader implications of paramount national objectives rested on a sense of international acceptance and the recognition of Arab power. Again, Kissinger's task was to impede this purpose while gaining Arab acceptance of the proposition that only through his mediation could they approach their goal. The task was difficult because Israel had always been the main obstacle to the Arabs' collective purpose, and Kissinger had to persuade Arab leaders that in all probability they could not establish their power or gain international acceptance at the expense of Israel.

In the Sinai Accord, Kissinger gave the Israelis a heightened sense of security that was *not* linked to future negotiations. In order to reestablish the conditions on which his diplomacy depended, he would, therefore, have been required to create a degree of anxiety among the Israelis over their future security while offering to relieve the condition he had created by mediating once again between Israel and the Arabs—and all within the confines of the "special relationship." In the meantime, Israeli affinity for the historical homeland and the Golan settlements had only become more pronounced. The Sinai Accord had made Kissinger's task complex, and his willingness to share commitments with the negotiants contributed to this complexity. To an extent Carter was able to reestablish the mood necessary for negotiation by nurturing a healthy anxiety on the part of the Israelis with the assertion that the United States supported and would work for a Palestinian homeland.

Kissinger's approach to diplomacy had much to commend it. He structured negotiations purposefully; he established a firm context for dialogue; and he recognized the importance of changing men's minds. He was not working for a simple accommodation of interests. He planned the negotiating process carefully and brought into play virtually all relationships available to him as channels for pressuring the negotiants. He proved the value of negotiating incrementally as a means of leading long-standing enemies to acknowledge that agreement with the other side was not unreasonable. He demonstrated an unusual talent for interjecting into agreements ambiguities that permitted everyone to be satisfied with some feature of the results. He formalized the use of indirect assurances, an implement most diplomats ignore. He had the insight to understand that, even with recalcitrant negotiants, his willingness to mediate between them, and conversely his threat to terminate that mediation, could be a powerful inducement in getting them to make concessions.

But in Kissinger's strength there was also weakness. His dedication to the negotiating process led him to extend American commitments that ultimately brought the process to a standstill. Actually, the weakness may have been that his approach required mediation to be intense and personalized, while the stamina necessary for this undertaking exceeded the capacity of any single person. There was also the question of whether the Kissinger approach could be generalized and practiced by a statesman of another temperament, and under other conditions.

A critical examination of Kissinger's diplomacy does, therefore, reveal defects. But on balance, it pointed to new and productive techniques for dealing with an old problem. After the Sinai Accord, a year and a half was to pass before the Carter administration reactivated American mediation. Yet the negotiating structure developed by Kissinger remained intact. Sadat and (with a certain amount of circumspection) even Assad admitted that they were still committed to negotiation. They retained this position in the full knowledge that Kissinger's diplomacy had resulted in the relative strengthening of Israel's military capability, and without the Jewish state's having been compelled to relinquish the more vital portions of the occupied territories. Admittedly, even prior to the 1973 war, Sadat and Assad had accepted the wisdom of exploring a negotiated settlement. Kissinger had not created this predilection. He had only nurtured it and prevented its passing from the scene as a phenomenon of short duration. Under conditions that had existed prior to Kissinger's shuttle diplomacy, the realization that American mediation had helped the enemy would have been sufficient to send the Arabs into wild denunciation of the United States and to have them scurrying back to a close relationship with the Soviet Union. But this did not happen. Here was the new element that was the result of Kissinger's work and with which his successors could proceed. A fundamental change had occurred in the Arab attitude toward the United States.

Kissinger's style of diplomacy had proved suitable for mediating the Arab-Israeli problem. Even the 1975 Brookings Institution study tacitly acknowledged the necessity of following many of Kissinger's practices. The changing of perceptions as a means of moving toward a settlement could not be avoided. Therefore, why not center attention on this essentially experiential feature of negotiation? Surely Kissinger's techniques required only minor adjustments and slight redirections. Much work remained to be done, for example, in the United States itself. A change in American perceptions on the matter of equity in a Middle East settlement was a task left largely unattended by Kissinger and the presidents he served. In negotiations themselves, an excessive American commitment to either party to the dispute was a major danger against which Kissinger had not guarded sufficiently. Going back to the words of Kissinger himself, we find that this very advice was given: "The United States cannot substitute its efforts for the good will, for the willingness to cooperate, for the readiness to relate the immediate to the long-term interest of the parties involved. . . ."

12

The Inadequacies of a Nonsettlement

The purpose of this book has not been simply to review the diplomacy of Henry Kissinger; nor has it purported to suggest a foolproof plan for achieving an Arab-Israeli settlement. For some time, we have had information that should have permitted us to conclude that, before a settlement can be achieved, Arabs, Israelis, and any American administration attempting to mediate their dispute must adopt new ways of thinking about the Middle East. My discussions of the problems of Arab unity, the dynamics of isolation in Arab politics, the Arabs' feelings of weakness, the alien reality of negotiation for both Arabs and Israelis, their conflicting legitimacies, their competition for implicit influence over American opinion, Israel's drive for regional dominance, and the intangible assets of the United States in working with Arabs have all been directed toward providing new perspectives. The potential of Kissinger's style of diplomacy, which hinges on changing the perceptions of the Middle East antagonists, also points toward new ways of looking at the Arab-Israeli standoff.

We can better understand the necessity for new thinking about an old problem if we view the Middle East situation in a larger context. The most striking feature of the developments emanating from the October 1973 hostilities may have been their effect on our perceptions of power. Traditional power, which ultimately came from the barrel of a cannon or more recently from the war-head of a missile, must now share the world scene with a variety of power that we have long known but have identified only indirectly with political influence. What was formerly a natural resource to be had by man for the cost of taking it from the ground now permits its possessor to claim a place in world councils. No doubt it always did, but the influence to be realized from the resource was formerly enjoyed by the foreign exploiter rather than by the oil-producing nation itself.

Throughout the modern era industrialized countries have utilized their technology, their control of resources, and the economic power that these have provided to develop domestic environments conducive to the furtherance of their influence in the world. Now we face a situation in which others want to share that influence, not by developing a competing industrial-techological-military complex, but simply by controlling a single resource. The viewpoint of the oil-exporting countries seems stark to us because, at the outset at least, the possessors of oil are not satisfied to wait until they transform it into weapons, technology, and organization as we did with our resources before making claims to power. It is almost as if they are demanding that the nuances and subtleties of international practice be set aside and that we adopt a new brand of diplomacy that rests on a single consideration—raw materials. The most that can be said at this time about their chances of success is that the world power balances and the international moral climate are such that practices of the past, when states with the clear military advantage would have seized the resource or those having industrial strength could have squeezed any new contender for power out of the competition of international politics, do not seem applicable. Thus we are left with the question of whether we can do without the resource, or whether we must accommodate those who wish to practice the unidimensional diplomacy of raw materials.

The thesis advanced here is neither that of the pacifist who attempts to achieve world order by ignoring power nor that of the developmentalist who intends to guide the world toward homogeneity through transfers of resources and technology with the hope that relative success will make the naked use of power less likely.

Rather, my argument comes from the suggestion that economic, social, and technological progress in Western society has gradually placed us in a dependent position of which we have not been totally aware. Our dependence is now apparent. Power has acquired new dimensions because we have established our prosperity on a rate of resource consumption that we can no longer sustain from our own endowment of natural wealth. In fact, the entire world is having a difficult time satisfying our ravenous appetite for oil. As a result, we will probably have to readjust our thinking on matters pertaining to international relationships. If we are to continue our present ways, we have no choice but to accommodate the possessors of the new power.

Very few countries that have achieved independence since World War II have a true stake in the Western-conceived rules of international practice or in the transnational and international structures we have devised from them. During the past thirty-five years, new nations have tested our international predispositions, creating much of the chaos that we associate with Asia, Africa, and Latin America. Our way of thinking about problems and doing things is no longer accepted by the international community as always being the best way. Drastic revisions in world order are being demanded by the so-called Third World. The North-South dialogue during 1976 and 1977 over the distribution of national income among countries is only one vivid example of the changes that are being sought. Those peoples who stand between the industrialized West and the Soviet Union believe that they should have a voice in structuring, staffing, and operating the institutions that are designed to give some semblance of order to relations across political boundaries. We, of course, are convinced that, for purposes of political and economic stability—that is, for the prosperity of all concerned—the relative newcomers to world politics should be content to work within existing structures and present practices.

Some changes in our thinking are occurring. Certain eminent economists have long since concluded that their discipline, as taught and practiced in the United States, is not based on flawless theory, nor does it represent a natural condition. The concept of the free market is beginning to be regarded as a construct that serves the purpose of those who hold economic power. It should not be surprising that conventional thinking of political scientists about world order probably gives this same advantage to those who hold political power. The world's oil exporters, including the Arabs, are fully aware of this situation. They now sense their own power, and they know that, as long as they are willing to operate through what are essentially *our* structures, using *our* rules, they will not be able to employ this power to achieve *their* ends. At a minimum they want the composition and policies of international institutions to change in a way that will reinforce their own attributes. The oil exporters are asking for a greater voice in determining how their claim to the world's total resources is to affect the world's well-being. Why American leaders should be startled or outraged by this demand remains a mystery to anyone who has worked for very long on international problems. At best the umbrage expressed by some Americans and Israelis may be viewed as insincere—a ploy in the continuing game of international politics. At worst it conveys a sense of cultural superiority. In either case it is shortsighted. Certainly, all previous new arrivals on the world scene who had the power to sustain a claim to shaping international relationships seized a role in world politics. So it is with the Oil Arabs.

Within this context Israel becomes relatively insignificant, and if it is to have a secure future, its interests are probably to be found in Western acceptance of Arab legitimacy rather than in the minor territorial acquisitions made in the 1967 war. In any Middle East settlement, an open invitation for the Arabs to join the purveyors of power may mitigate Arab feelings of inferiority and vindictiveness. This is not to suggest that Israel's integrity must be sacrificed in order to achieve peace. But if the Israelis want to fit peacefully into the Middle East environment as they contend, they must act accordingly. There will no longer be a place for sustaining the Jewish state simply on the basis of constant infusions of psychic exuberance derived from Israel's defying every Arab perception. In the long run, Israel too must make some accommodation to the new dimensions of power.

Any outside state that takes an active role in the drama of the Arab-Israeli struggle has two broad areas of policy in which to operate. It can attempt to manipulate the hostile and unstable conditions in the Middle East in some way that gives short-run protection to its minimal interests. Or it can attempt to change the existing situation to one less characterized by tension and therefore less threatening to its long-term interests. For the past thirty years the United States has followed the former course and only intermittently directed its energies toward the latter. Whether we admit it or not, our policy has been based on a calculated nonsettlement.

But a manipulatory approach linked to a policy of calculated nonsettlement rests on the curious supposition that the Arabs will never be able to exercise the power that the economics of oil has given them—that is, that they cannot inflict an unacceptable level of hurt and injury on the United States and Israel. Not only is this assumption questionable, but it has been buttressed by an even more dubious proposition. It has become popular to question the legitimacy of the Arabs' mounting financial accruals by arguing that the staggering amount of goods and services represented by the Saudi, Kuwaiti, and Libyan foreign exchange earnings cannot possibly be used by these countries. Something "unnatural" is taking place. The upshot of the Arabs' good fortune, some have concluded, is that our international financial structure is being thrown into chaos, and if we are all not to face ruination, we had better do something about it. But where does this type of thinking lead? Is it not more honest to recognize that the underlying assertion of such arguments is the old tune that Arabs cannot be trusted and that we should therefore resist their twofold effort at assuming a world role commensurate with their new power and working for certain ends that they consider worthy?

In our consideration of possibilities for negotiations in the Middle East, it has already been demonstrated that the chance of success in using negative inducements (threats or force) to achieve peace is indeed remote. Anyone dedicated to the resolution of Arab-Israeli difficulties has little choice but to approach the Arabs with positive inducements. But in a larger sense, are we developing a frame of mind conducive to the use of positive inducements when we premise action on resentment of Arab power? For their part, the more prominent Arab players in the game of oil politics have indicated repeatedly that they are prepared to limit themselves to

positive inducements if we will do the same. Thus the refusal of
Saudi Arabia and the United Arab Emirates in January 1977 to
follow the other members of OPEC in opting for a 10 percent
rather than a 5 percent increase in the price of oil. Largely due to
Saudi influence, world oil prices remained stable from January
1977 until January 1979, despite the erosion of oil earnings due
to American inflation. Had the Saudis not thought in terms of
positive inducements in urging the United States to help find a
solution to the Arab-Israeli problem, they might have been more
inclined toward larger price increases.

In May 1977, at the time of Saudi Crown Prince Fahd's visit to
the United States, the Saudis were sending mixed signals over how
they intended to behave in the future. Authoritative reports
emanating from Riyadh just prior to the visit affirmed the possibility of the Saudis' using the oil weapon if no progress occurred in
working toward an Arab-Israeli settlement. These were followed,
however, by Fahd's assurance in Washington that oil would not be
used in this way. Here was the difference between the potential for
negative inducements and the Arab hope that more could still be
achieved with a positive approach. The juxaposition of the two
Saudi statements was meant as little more than a reminder that, in
the long run, oil could not be separated from the Middle East
situation. The question under discussion at that time was not a
new embargo or a quantum jump in oil prices but whether Saudi
Arabia would agree to pump oil at a rate that would permit the
United States to continue its existing patterns of consumption and
at the same time establish a six-month petroleum reserve. Only
with increased purchases from Saudi Arabia could both be accomplished. We were, in fact, asking the Saudis for the wherewithal to withstand the pressures of the oil weapon!

Again in 1978 the Saudis sent mixed signals. While expressing
an interest in the continuation of a price freeze on oil that would
be to the United States's advantage, they were critical of President
Carter's peace initiative with Egypt and Israel. Toward this end
they established closer working relationships with the Arab leaders
who opposed Sadat's efforts to conclude a peace with Israel. But
still the Saudis were not prepared to kick over the traces with
negative inducements. Perhaps it was as Secretary of Treasury

Blumenthal said: "We've learned a lot since 1973–74. We've learned about the limits of power that they [OPEC] have as a group and about the direct impact of their price decisions on what they buy. They are beginning to understand that there is no free lunch for anyone, not even for them."[1] The same statement would also have been applicable, of course, had it been made by a Saudi official about the United States. The fact that OPEC in December 1978 stunned the industrialized world with a 14.5 percent price increase to be spread over the subsequent year probably had something to do with the Saudis' dissatisfaction with our policies on the Middle East, Iran, and the Horn of Africa and their desire to show us something about the limits of power and the end of the free lunch. Nevertheless, in June 1979, when OPEC instituted another price increase, the Saudis were again a force for moderation despite their disillusionment over the Israeli-Egyptian Treaty.

Thus positive and negative inducements have nuances that go far beyond the relatively unsophisticated issue of an oil embargo. Rather than simply to withhold the oil needed for the reserve or to elevate the level of American contingency by increasing prices, the Saudis expressed sympathy for the American position with the expectation that the United States would reciprocate on an issue of importance to the Arabs. In this way a special relationship can be forged and sustained. At the heart of such exchanges is an overpowering interdependence. The United States's growing dependence on Arab oil is complemented by the Arabs' commitment to Western and largely American technology. Both forces help keep the two sides within the bounds of positive inducements. A successful relationship does not depend solely on our providing the technology and the Arab's selling the oil. The Arabs have also begun to accept Israel's existence, and they are at least talking less about walking to El Aqsa Mosque at the Dome of the Rock in Jerusalem on Arab-controlled soil. For our part, we have accepted and expressed the necessity for providing the Palestinians with a homeland as well as for the Israelis to relinquish virtually all of the occupied territories. Such is the interplay of positive inducements.

Only Israel and the radical Arabs feel it necessary to view the situation in terms of negative inducements. With Arab unity still imperfect, Iraq and Libya, which lack a sufficient resource base to exert the Saudis' critical influence on the petroleum market, do not yet have the confidence to deal with the United States and Israel with positive inducements. Although some leaders of the PLO are trying mightily to change their perceptions, they still see in any settlement a prospect for the sacrifice of even pared-down Palestinian aspirations. As a result, they too have difficulty accepting positive constructs of negotiations.

The Israelis' problem is different. To the extent that the world adopts the new convention of power—that is, a diplomacy of raw materials—Israel is left powerless. Its dependence on the United States and the pressure to accept American dictates are accentuated. On the other hand, power measured by the old conventions of military strength makes Israel more than a match for all its Arab neighbors combined. The dispute between the Israelis and the Carter administration in the spring of 1977 over the proper components of a settlement to be discussed at any reconvening of the Geneva Conference arose because of the American drift toward the new conventions of power while Israel held avidly to the old. A measure of this difference was evident in the Israeli conviction that, even as a country of 3 million people with a faltering economy, they could still design and manufacture jet fighters and tanks, albeit with many American components. At the time, American policy makers were thinking so differently about what was important to Middle East stability that they did not even put Israel on a list of preferred customers for U.S. manufactured weapons that was being devised as a step toward limiting arms sales abroad. Israel's friends in Congress were quick to call this oversight to the attention of the president, who rectified his error.

In acknowledging the necessity of operating within the limits of positive inducements, the United States and ultimately Israel face the issue of accepting Arab reliability. Unless the Arabs are assumed to be reliable, there is little basis for the Israelis' making the concessions that will be necessary for an accommodation. At some juncture the United States and Israel must change their perceptions of the Arabs. This course is neither easy nor apparent for Israelis. Even the United States commitment to positive inducements and its protestations of accepting Arab reliability are not yet firm. The simultaneous equations that emerge from my argument are:

Accepting Arab reliability	+	Acknowledging the new conventions of power	= Working for fundamental change in the Middle East.
Denying Arab reliability, exploiting Arab weakness, assuming Arab inability to use the new power	+	Holding to old conventions of power	= Opting for nonsettlement by continuing to manipulate existing conditions.

These relationships are not proposed as hypothetical alternatives; rather, given the ambivalence of American policy, it seems that solutions are being sought simultaneously by both routes. Dedication to the second equation is particularly strong in Israel, and whenever American policy bends to comply with Israeli perceptions, it too assumes these characteristics. A case in point has been the United States's refusal to enter into even informal discussions with the PLO.

There has remained the lingering hope that the United States can free itself from the necessity to treat with the Arabs. Almost with glee, oil experts during 1978 continued to point to the excess capacity of the OPEC producers, implying that pressures for income would eventually drive them into price competition with one another for sales in the industrialized West. The erosion of OPEC unity, and therefore Arab power, was foreseen in the failure of worldwide oil consumption to increase as fast as it had been projected, and pride was taken in new discoveries of non-OPEC oil in Alaska, the North Sea, along China's coast, and especially in Mexico where extractible oil was estimated at 83 percent of that held by the Saudis. All were displayed as evidence that in the long run the United States would not be dependent on Arab oil and could escape playing the game of positive inducements in the Middle East. But this elation faded in the oil crunch of 1979. Careful assessment showed that being less dependent on Arab oil did not mean being independent of it. It would still be many years before we could disregard Arab perceptions.

It is always dangerous to predicate the actions of a government or leadership group, including that of Saudi Arabia, on economic considerations when these run counter to longstanding national aspirations. It is true that the Saudis' perceptions are changing, but do their plans for their own technological and economic transformation outweigh any inclination toward redressing national grievances against the Arabs' old enemy? Are the Saudis so enmeshed in positive inducements that they will no longer use the oil weapon? It is within this range of considerations that American policy has to be formulated.

There is a flaw in supposing that the Saudis will not use the power they possess while the Israelis continue to use the power that is not even theirs. Certainly at the time of Kissinger's diplomacy, it took more than Jewish self-reliance to make the Israelis a match for their neighbors. The added ingredient that continued to tilt the balance in favor of the Israelis was the massive economic and military assistance they received from abroad—American power. By the time the Carter administration came to office the real issue was not so much between Israeli and Palestinian rights as between Arab and American power. Arab leaders said as much when they asserted repeatedly that only the United States could bring peace to the Middle East. It seemed, therefore, that a solution depended on the Oil Arabs' bringing pressure on the United States and nudging it into action while retaining an essentially friendly relationship with us. But did the Saudis have this much diplomatic skill? To assume that they could manage their new power so adroitly would perhaps be the ultimate expression of our acceptance of Arab reliability.

And what was required of the United States while the Arabs were so engaged? In the Arab-Israeli conflict we have constantly faced the problem of changing minds, not enunciating some ingenious scheme for peace. Because minds change slowly, step-by-step diplomacy has perhaps been the only sensible course. The test for the mediator is to have sufficient discipline to be constantly aware of his purpose and to persevere in attempting to achieve it. The situation has called for the United States to pressure the Israelis, not so much in terms of specific concessions, but from the standpoint of changing their minds about how they could achieve peace and prosperity. Some observers of the Middle East scene may dismiss as little more than semantics the difference between forcing the Israelis to make concessions and persuading them to change their perceptions. But in diplomacy, the definition of purpose can be important, particularly for a mediator occupying the American position. It can determine the nature of dialogue, the questions addressed in negotiations, the answers that are given, and ultimately how the United States uses the political resources at its disposal to pressure Israel and the Arabs into an accommodation.

Privately Israeli leaders in both the Rabin and Begin governments indicated that they had done some thinking about contingency plans in case differences over a settlement brought about what seemed to them a final confrontation with the United States. Generally they conceded that, in the face of American determination, Israel might have to change its position. From time to time tensions did develop between the two countries while Kissinger was actively pursuing step-by-step diplomacy. Subsequently the Carter administration also adopted a policy that included some unpalatables for Israel—a homeland for Palestinians and the surrender of virtually all of the occupied territories.

But the Israelis did not intend to capitulate easily. In a stance that was replete with contradictions, Prime Minister Begin responded to American proposals by forcefully asserting that he would negotiate over (but never surrender) the West Bank. In his formulation, Palestinians without the PLO and within an Israeli security network could have home rule in those parts of the West Bank not assigned to Jewish settlements. The Camp David agreements and the Israeli-Egyptian Treaty permitted Israel to pursue its security objective of separating Egypt from the other Arabs by negotiating over peace (and Sinai) exclusively with Sadat. The thought of somehow retaining the West Bank while negotiating with King Hussein rather than the PLO remained foremost in Israeli minds. During this interlude American officials believed some progress was being made toward peace. But they could not totally ignore the conditions under which this movement was taking place. It was at the expense of American influence with Syria, Jordan, and even Saudi Arabia, and without these countries were the chances for peace really being enhanced or was the

United States following the policy of a calculated nonsettlement?

These observations and tentative suggestions would be incomplete without some acknowledgment that, in changing Arab minds, the United States has had a handicap no less weighty than that involved in changing Israeli minds. It is remarkable, in fact, that after years of so much talk and so little action we could still enjoy the relations that we did with the Arabs. Herein lay a warning. American support for bilateral Israeli-Egyptian negotiations could be justified in terms of their being another step toward peace. The Arab outlook on this matter (and I continue to believe that an Arab outlook exists) will ultimately depend on our ability to convey in words and deeds a type of sincerity that convinces the Arabs that none of our discrete initiatives contributes to a policy of calculated nonsettlement. It is indeed very esoteric business when a single act can be interpreted either as part of a calculated nonsettlement or as a genuine step toward peace, depending on how our intentions are assessed. But the Arab perception is something that we cannot easily shrug off. From the outset of Kissinger's negotiations Sadat labored hard to make the United States more than a mediator. We were to become a "partner" in the Middle East negotiations. The Camp David agreements confirmed this role. Sometimes even American officials behave as if they do not understand what Sadat meant. Essentially his strategy is to put us in a position in which Arab capabilities will preclude us from ever falling back on the calculated nonsettlement. To do so would be viewed as our resorting to negative inducements, and these are beyond the purview of negotiations in the continuing game of Middle East diplomacy. While oil may not be a weapon, it is an effective political and economic lever, and it can assure that our acts are indeed limited to positive steps toward arriving at a Middle East accommodation.

Notes

Chapter 1

1. Ibrahim Juma', "The Ideology of Arab Nationalism," in *Political and Social Thought in the Contemporary Middle East,* ed. Kamal N. Karpat (New York: Praeger, 1968), p. 5.
2. Abd al Rahman al Bazzaz, "A Summary of the Characteristics of Arab Nationalism," in *Political and Social Thought,* ed. Karpat, pp. 52–53.
3. *New York Times,* January 5, 1975, p. 17.
4. Michel 'Aflaq, "The Socialist Ideology of the Ba'th," in *Political and Social Thought,* ed. Karpat, p. 196; Muta Safadi, "Philosophy of the Unified Arab State," in *Political and Social Thought,* ed. Karpat, p. 222.
5. Elie Salem, "Problems of Arab Political Behavior," in *Tensions in the Middle East,* ed. Philip W. Thayer (Baltimore: Johns Hopkins University Press, 1958), p. 70.
6. 'Aflaq, "Socialist Ideology," pp. 190–91.
7. Safadi, "Philosophy of the Unified Arab State," p. 224.
8. Ibid., p. 221.
9. Abbas Mahmud al Aqqad, *Democracy in Islam,* 1952; *see* Nadav Safran, *Egypt in Search of Political Community* (Cambridge, Mass.: Harvard University Press, 1961), pp. 215–18.
10. Muhammad al Ghazzali, *Our Beginning in Wisdom* (Cairo: Dar al-Kitab al-'Arabi, 1951).
11. Khalid Muhammad Khalid, *From Here We Start* (Cairo: Dar al-Nil 'al Tala'at, 1950).
12. United Arab Republic, *The Charter* (Cairo: Information Department, 1962). The draft of the national charter was presented by President Gamal Abdal Nasser at the inaugural session of the National Congress of Popular Powers on May 21, 1962.
13. Gamal Abdal Nasser, *The Philosophy of the Revolution* (Cairo: Dar Al-Maaruf, 1955), pp. 66–67.
14. *Suez Ten Years After* (London: British Broadcasting Company, 1967), p. 46.

15. Charles D. Cremeans, *The Arabs and the World* (New York: Praeger, 1963), p. 38.
16. Jean and Simonne Lacouture, *Egyptian Transition* (London: Methuen, 1958), p. 478.
17. "The Manifesto of the United Arab Republic," in *The Israel Arab Reader,* ed. Walter Laqueur, 2d ed. (New York: Bantam, 1971), p. 129. This document was signed by the presidents of Egypt, Iraq, and Syria at the time they were attempting to revive the UAR in April 1963. The preamble contains a statement of Arab principles reflected in most other documents formalizing the relationships in Arab politics. In part the preamble states:

"The delegations in all their discussions were inspired by faith that Arab unity was an inevitable aim deriving its principles from the oneness of language bearing culture and thought, common history-making sentiment and conscience, common national struggle deciding and defining destiny, common spiritual values stemming from Devine [*sic*] messages and common social and economic understanding based on liberty and socialism."

Chapter 2

1. Anouar Abdel-Malek, *Egypt: Military Society,* trans. Charles Lam Markmann, (New York: Random House, Vintage Books, 1968), p. 273.
2. Gamal Abdal Nasser, *The Philosophy of the Revolution* (Cairo: Dar Al-Maaruf, 1955), p. 56.
3. Malcolm H. Kerr, *The Arab Cold War,* 3d ed. (London: Oxford University Press, 1971), pp. 17–22, 90–91.
4. Ibid., pp. 28–30, 69.
5. *New York Times,* November 20, 1973, p. 5.
6. *New York Times,* November 29, 1973, p. 16.
7. *New York Times,* January 6, 1974, p. 10.
8. *Associated Press*—Kuwait, December 26, 1973.
9. *New York Times,* March 28, 1974, p. 1.
10. *New York Times,* May 2, 1974, p. 7.
11. *New York Times,* February 27, 1975, p. 6; March 9, 1975, p. 3.

Chapter 3

1. Robert A. Goldwin, ed., *Readings in Russian Foreign Policy* (London: Oxford University Press, 1959); Adam Ulam, *Expansion and Co-existence,* 2d ed. (New York: Praeger, 1974); Hendrick Smith, *The Russians* (New York: Quadrangle/New York Times Book Co., 1976).
2. Robert J. Lifton, *Revolutionary Immortality: Mao Tse-tung and the Chinese Cultural Revolution* (New York: Random House,

1968); Stanley Karnow, *Mao and China* (New York: Viking Press, 1972).

3. Morroe Berger, *The Arab World Today,* (Garden City, N.Y.: Doubleday, Anchor, 1964); Sania Hamady, *Temperament and Character of the Arabs* (New York: Twayne, 1960); Raphael Patai, *The Arab Mind* (New York: Scribner's, 1973).

4. *New York Times,* February 20, 1974, p. 11.

5. *New York Times,* January 16, 1975, p. 41.

6. *New York Times,* October 6, 1974, p. 6.

7. *New York Times,* November 4, 1974, p. 12.

8. *New York Times,* November 29, 1973, p. 16.

9. *New York Times,* March 18, 1974, p. 3.

10. *New York Times,* January 7, 1975, p. 2.

11. *New York Times,* January 3, 1975, p. 2; January 20, 1975, p. 12. Kissinger's comments appeared in *Business Week* (January 13, 1975).

12. *New York Times,* December 30, 1974, p. 23; Washington Post Service—Beirut, December 29, 1974; Robert W. Tucker, "Oil: The Issue of American Intervention," *Commentary,* January 1975, pp. 21–31; Miles Ignotus, "Seizing Arab Oil, A Blueprint for Fast and Effective Action," *Harper's,* March 1975, pp. 45–62.

13. *New York Times,* January 20, 1975, p. 12.

14. *New York Times,* April 20, 1975, p. E-2.

15. Henry Kissinger, *The Troubled Partnership,* (Garden City, N.Y.: Doubleday, Anchor, 1966), p. 18.

16. *New York Times,* January 10, 1975, p. 3.

17. *New York Times,* March 20, 1975, p. 3.

18. *New York Times,* November 21, 1973, p. 16.

19. *New York Times,* February 25, 1974, p. 1.

20. United Press International—Washington, January 11, 1974.

21. *New York Times,* November 15, 1974, p. 1.

22. *New York Times,* September 24, 1974, p. 1.

23. *New York Times,* October 9, 1974, p. 9.

24. Speech to Egyptian army officers by Gamal Abdal Nasser on March 28, 1955. Text appeared in *Al Ahram* on the following day.

25. *New York Times,* January 23, 1974, p. 1.

26. *New York Times,* December 9, 1973, p. F-4.

27. *New York Times,* October 5, 1974, p. 3.

Chapter 4

1. Theodor Herzl, "The Jewish State," in *The Israel-Arab Reader,* ed. Walter Laqueur, 2d ed. (New York: Bantam, 1971), pp. 6–7. Originally published in 1896.

2. Ibid., p. 9.

3. "The Manifesto of the Bilu," in *Israel-Arab Reader,* ed. Laquer, p. 4. From a statement issued by Russian Jews at Constantinople in 1882.
4. Herzl, "Jewish State," p. 9.
5. "The Manifesto of the Bilu," p. 4.
6. *New York Times,* November 14, 1974, pp. 22–23.
7. *New York Times,* March 27, 1975, p. 31.
8. "The Basle Declaration," in *Israel-Arab Reader,* ed. Laquer, p. 12. Issued by the First Zionist Congress in August 1897.
9. *New York Times,* July 9, 1975, p. 1.
10. Herzl, "Jewish State," p. 9.
11. *New York Times,* December 28, 1974, p. 23. The Jewish author, Elie Wiesel, expressed this sentiment in a feature article.
12. *New York Times,* February 5, 1975, p. 21. Statement of United Jewish Appeal and Federation of Jewish Philanthropies.
13. *New York Times,* March 6, 1975, p. 9. Statement by Prof. Yaakov Katz of Hebrew University.
14. *New York Times,* February 4, 1975, p. 2.
15. *New York Times,* March 6, 1975, p. 9.
16. Herzl, "Jewish State," p. 11.
17. Morris Fine and Milton Himmelfarb, eds., *American Jewish Year Book,* vol. 74 (New York: American Jewish Committee and Jewish Publication Society of America, 1973), pp. 523–29.
18. Harold D. Lasswell and Abraham Kaplan, *Power and Society* (New Haven: Yale University Press, 1950), pp. 116–17.
19. Malcolm H. Kerr, *The Arab Cold War,* 3d ed. (New York: Oxford University Press, 1971), p. 133.
20. William B. Quandt, Fuad Jabber, and Ann Mosley Lesch, *The Politics of Palestinian Nationalism* (Berkley: University of California Press, 1973), p. 50.
21. *New York Times,* October 15, 1974, p. 1.
22. *Ibid.*
23. *New York Times,* November 19, 1974, p. 1.
24. *New York Times,* October 29, 1974, p. 1.
25. *New York Times,* January 6, 1974, p. 1.
26. *New York Times,* July 15, 1975, p. 1.

Chapter 5

1. *New York Times,* July 29, 1975, p. 3.
2. *New York Times,* September 25, 1975, p. 6.
3. *New York Times,* August 26, 1975, p. 1.
4. *New York Times,* September 11, 1975, p. 5.
5. *New York Times,* September 2, 1975, p. 1.

6. *New York Times,* September 10, 1975, p. 20.
7. *New York Times,* September 2, 1975, p. 17.
8. *New York Times,* December 9, 1973, p. 5.
9. *New York Times,* May 1, 1975, p. 2.
10. United Nations Security Council Resolution 242, November 22, 1967.
11. *New York Times,* November 3, 1975, p. 37.
12. *New York Times,* September 5, 1975, pp. 1, 4.
13. *New York Times,* September 29, 1975, p. 9.
14. *New York Times,* September 28, 1975, p. 15.
15. *New York Times,* August 8, 1975, p. 2.
16. *New York Times,* October 21, 1975, p. 5.
17. *New York Times,* October 6, 1975, p. 20.
18. *New York Times,* April 10, 1975, p. 18.
19. Seymour Martin Lipset and Everett Carll Ladd, Jr., "Jewish Academics in the United States: Their Achievements, Culture and Politics," vol. 72, *The American Jewish Yearbook,* ed. Morris Fine and Milton Himmelfarb (New York: American Jewish Committee; Philadelphia: Jewish Publication Society of America, 1971), pp. 89–128.
20. Everett Carll Ladd, Jr., and Seymour Martin Lipset, "War-Shy Professors Divided over Middle East," *The Chronicle of Higher Education,* December 1, 1975, p. 10.
21. Seymour Martin Lipset, *Revolution and Counter-Revolution,* rev. ed. (Garden City, N. Y.: Doubleday, Anchor, 1970), pp. 383–89, 398–99.
22. *New York Times,* August 8, 1975, p. 2.
23. Ibid.
24. *New York Times,* January 29, 1975, p. 3; February 14, 1975, p. 1; May 22, 1975, p. 1.
25. *New York Times,* March 6, 1975, p. 6.
26. *New York Times,* November 3, 1975, p. 37.
27. *New York Times,* November 7, 1975, p. 4.
28. *New York Times,* May 27, 1975, p. 5; September 11, 1975, p. 1.
29. *New York Times,* January 10, 1975, p. 51.
30. *New York Times,* February 19, 1974, p. 36.
31. *New York Times,* May 27, 1975, p. 1.

Chapter 6

1. *New York Times,* November 29, 1973, p. 14.
2. *New York Times,* August 31, 1975, p. 8.
3. *New York Times,* March 27, 1975, p. 31.
4. *New York Times,* November 1, 1974, p. 9.

384 NOTES

5. Stanley Hoffman, "A New Policy for Israel," *Foreign Affairs* (April 1975), pp. 405–31; Nadav Safran, "Engagement in the Middle East," *Foreign Affairs* (October 1974), pp. 45–63.
6. *New York Times,* January 13, 1974, p. E-1.
7. *New York Times,* September 13, 1974, p. 8.
8. *New York Times,* October 15, 1974, p. 3.
9. *New York Times,* March 24, 1975, p. 1.
10. *New York Times,* September 28, 1975, p. 17.
11. *New York Times,* February 21, 1975, p. 4.
12. *New York Times,* August 18, 1974, p. E-4.
13. For the text of the accord and its annexes and the attached memoranda see *New York Times,* September 2, 1975, p. 16; September 17, 1975, p. 16; September 18, 1975, p. 4. Additional secret provisions were cited in *The New York Times,* October 1, 1975, p. 14.
14. *New York Times,* October 1, 1975, p. 5.

Chapter 7

1. *New York Times,* December 10, 1974, p. 7.
2. U.S., Department of State, "Department Gives Position on Palestine Issue," Harold E. Saunders, deputy assistant secretary of state for Near Eastern and South Asian affairs, before the Special Subcommittee on Investigations of the House Committee on International Relations, in *The Department of State Bulletin* 73 no. 1901 (December 1, 1975): 797–800.
3. *New York Times,* April 22, 1974, p. 1.
4. *New York Times,* January 8, 1976, p. 3.
5. Taha Hussein, *The Future of Culture in Egypt,* trans. Sidney Glazer (Washington, D.C.: American Council of Learned Societies, 1954), pp. 2, 3, 17–18, 20.
6. George McKenna, ed., *American Populism* (New York: Putnam, 1975).
7. Maxime Rodinson, *Islam and Capitalism,* trans. Brian Pearce (New York: Random House, 1973), pp. 22–23, 27, 116, 182.
8. Ibid., p. 164.
9. *New York Times,* November 13, 1973, p. 16.
10. International Monetary Fund, Statistics Bureau, *Direction of Trade,* annual no. 12 (1976) (Washington, D.C.: International Monetary Fund and International Bank for Reconstruction and Development). Although Somalia and Mauritania are members of the Arab League, they are excluded from these calculations.
11. "The Manifesto of the United Arab Republic" in *The Israeli-Arab Reader,* ed. Walter Laqueur, 2d ed. (New York: Bantam, 1971), p. 130.
12. Estimates provided by American Friends of the Middle East,

Washington, D.C., and Office of Near Eastern Affairs, Division of Cultural Affairs, Department of State.
13. *New York Times,* September 9, 1974, p. 2; *The Chronicle of Higher Education,* February 3, 1975, p. 21.
14. United Press International—Beirut, November 11, 1973.
15. *New York Times,* November 29, 1973, p. 49; June 30, 1975, p. 1; November 6, 1975, p. 2.

Chapter 8

1. *New York Times,* January 16, 1975, p. 41.
2. Marvin Kalb and Bernard Kalb, *Kissinger* (Boston: Little, Brown, 1974), pp. 495, 499; *New York Times,* October 26, 1973, p. 1.
3. Kalb and Kalb, *Kissinger,* p. 487; *New York Times,* October 25, 1973, p. 18.
4. United Press International—Washington, November 10, 1973; *New York Times,* December 13, 1973.
5. Associated Press—Washington, January 10, 1974.
6. *New York Times,* January 16, 1974, p. 1.
7. *New York Times,* March 9, 1976, p. 8.

Chapter 9

1. *New York Times,* September 24, 1974, p. 1.
2. *New York Times,* March 19, 1975, p. 4.
3. *New York Times,* January 6, 1974, p. 1.
4. *New York Times,* February 14, 1975, p. 3.
5. Edward R. F. Sheehan, *The Arabs, the Israelis, and Kissinger* (New York: Reader's Digest Press, 1976), p. 108; *New York Times,* January 18, 1974, p. 1.
6. *New York Times,* March 19, 1975, p. 1.
7. *New York Times,* October 31, 1974, p. 3.
8. Robert C. Toth, special feature, *Los Angeles Times,* November 10, 1973.
9. *New York Times,* April 7, 1975 p. 12.
10. *New York Times,* December 18, 1975, p. 17.
11. *New York Times,* September 28, 1975, p. 17.
12. George W. Ball, *Diplomacy for a Crowded World* (Boston: Little, Brown, 1976), pp. 306–7, 309–10, 312.

Chapter 10

1. George W. Ball, *Diplomacy for a Crowded World,* (Boston: Little, Brown, 1976), p. 311.
2. Matti Golan, *The Secret Conversations of Henry Kissinger,* (New York: Quadrangle/New York Times, Bantam, 1976), p. 175.

3. *New York Times,* September 21, 1975, p. E-2.
4. *New York Times,* September 17, 1975, p. 16; September 18, 1975, pp. 1, 16; October 1, 1975, p. 14.
5. *New York Times,* March 3, 1976, p. 1.
6. *New York Times,* September 18, 1975, p. 1.
7. *Toward Peace in the Middle East, Report of a Study Group* (Washington, D.C.: Brookings Institution, 1975).

Chapter 11

1. *New York Times,* July 17, 1975, p. 1.
2. Henry Kissinger, *The Troubled Partnership* (Garden City, N. Y.: Doubleday, Anchor, 1966), p. 18.
3. Associated Press—San Clemente, January 9, 1974.
4. *New York Times,* March 27, 1975, p. 1.
5. *New York Times,* March 19, 1974, p. 20.
6. *New York Times,* January 23, 1974, p. 1.

Chapter 12

1. *New York Times,* November 24, 1978, p. 1.

Index